To the Next Generation

Melissa, Daniel, Benjamin, and Elliot
Alexander, Anna Sophia, Nicholas, and Peter

Distributed to the Trade by National Book Network, 15200 NBN Way, Blue Ridge Summit, PA 17214. To order call toll free 1-800-462-6420 or 1-717-794-3800. For all other inquiries please contact the AEI Press, 1150 Seventeenth Street, N.W., Washington, D.C. 20036 or call 1-800-862-5801.

Library of Congress Cataloging-in-Publication Data

Federal preemption : states' powers, national interests / editors,
  Richard Epstein, Michael Greve.
      p. cm.
    Includes index.
    ISBN-13: 978-0-8447-4254-0
    ISBN-10: 0-8447-4254-6
    1. Exclusive and concurrent legislative powers—United States. 2. Federal
government—United States. 3. State governments—United States.
I. Epstein, Richard Allen, 1943- II. Greve, Michael.

      KF4600.F42 2007
      342.73'042—dc22

                                                              2007014801

11 10 09 08 07   1 2 3 4 5

Federal Preemption

Federal Preemption

States' Powers, National Interests

Editors

Richard A. Epstein and
Michael S. Greve

The AEI Press

Publisher for the American Enterprise Institute
WASHINGTON, D.C.

Contents

Preface

Kenneth W. Starr

A few years ago, a senior government official from Mexico said to me, only half jokingly: "You have a problem. Your country does not have a name; 'United States' is not, truly, a proper name." I thought then—and think now—that this dinner-time observation, while odd (especially coming from someone whose country is officially called "Estados Unidos Mexicanos"), is revealing. The truth is that our name, the United States of America, quite aptly captures and precisely conveys what we are: A unitary constellation of diverse units called states, spread across a vast North American continent, defined since the mid twentieth-century inclusion of Hawaii as extending into the middle of the Pacific Ocean. What is it that makes the appropriateness of our name obvious to us, but obscure to others?

We Americans know who we are. We are those North Americans who chose to separate violently—through revolution—from the British mother country. Other North Americans, our good friends and close neighbors in Canada, also separated from that same mother country, but through evolutionary, not revolutionary, means that took two centuries, not seven years, to complete. Unlike our own separation, the Canadian experience has produced, at least thus far, no seminal reflections on the theory or practice of politics and government. We, then, are North America's pioneers; not merely, or even principally, in the geographic sense of exploring and traversing a continent but in the historical and political sense. In modern times it is only the United States of America that has successfully conducted a political revolution that ended neither in devastation nor tyranny but in the self-conscious creation of secular arrangements, fundamentally new to the world, for promoting, preserving, and inculcating liberty.

We recognize that our name does convey some inherent tension, not to say contradiction.[1] A paramount principle of our constitutional arrangement is that the deal of 1787 is irrevocable. A diamond among nations, the United States of America is forever. Texas may have gained independence from Mexico through revolution, but once having joined the United States, it forever lost that independence. Having joined up in 1845, Texas could not go back on its commitment in 1861, as President Abraham Lincoln and the Union Army forcibly reminded it.[2] Today, every American unthinkingly assumes that both the United States and the individual states that comprise it will last into the indefinable future—and therein lies the conundrum of "United States." On the one hand, "state" connotes perpetual sovereignty and perpetual sovereignty connotes perpetual independence. On the other hand, "united" connotes unity and perpetual unity connotes an increasing and mutual interdependence. The "United States," considered as a plural noun, are fifty individual entities that are both independent and interdependent. The "United States," considered as a singular noun (as it has been since shortly after the Civil War), is and must be a singular, individual nation—one unified entity. We pledge allegiance to the one flag of the United States. We describe it as "one nation under God." We pray in song that God will continue to "bless America," as He has so abundantly in the past; that He guide "her," not "them." As Mr. Lincoln recognized at Gettysburg, "our fathers brought forth on this continent a new nation," not simply a new conglomeration, like the North American Treaty Organization.

This volume explores some of the fascinating and fundamental issues presented by the enduring paradox of one perpetual sovereign consisting of other perpetual sovereigns, an arrangement that political theorists down through the ages have deemed self-contradictory. Americans instinctively believe in the practicality of simultaneously preserving difference and maintaining unity, both among sovereign states and between sovereign states and a single, sovereign nation. This volume helps to show that this peculiarly American belief—our nation's aspiration to create perpetually independent, interdependent, and unified sovereign entities—is no contradiction and no impossibility. We recognize, intuitively as much as consciously, the paradoxical duality of our nation. On the one hand, the greatest figures who prevailed in our most heated constitutional struggles—Lincoln, Marshall, Madison, and Hamilton—all stood squarely for union and for the center as against the periphery. On the other hand, the Anti-Federalists—those who opposed from the start the centralization of power in our Constitution—surely were onto something as well.[3] We continue to sense intuitively the potential evils of centralized power. Lord Acton's dictum is not lightly dismissed. And quite apart from outright corruption, oppression, or abuse, we intuitively recoil from the idea of "one size fits all," the proposition that our hopes for happiness and fulfillment somehow lie in beneficent national measures reaching into our smallest communities and neighborhoods. Taxes to the national government may be the cost of civilization, but we worry about regulation that sweeps too broadly, say Sarbanes-Oxley, or even the homogenizing requirements of the nobly intentioned No Child Left Behind law.[4]

We also worry about the power of centralized monopolies to stifle innovation. A fundamental insight of the Sherman Act, sensibly interpreted, is that marketplace power can be wielded improperly.[5] If the commercial innovator of yesteryear, seeking to live off aging intellectual capital, turns its attention to devising anticompetitive measures for snuffing out further innovations by others, the Sherman Act is and should be deployed as a bar. But if our law recognizes this danger in the private marketplace, surely analogous dangers of centralized governmental arrangements are all the more clear and threatening.

Great ideas may be born in fertile creative minds enjoying what some have called the leisure of the theory class,[6] but they are often proved in the laboratories of local and state government. Consider James Q. Wilson, formerly at Harvard and now, at the pinnacle of his career, at Pepperdine, where he is the Ronald Reagan Professor of Public Policy. Wilson and George Kelling fashioned, famously, the "Broken Windows" theory.[7] It was a faithful application of this new theory in New York City, beginning on the subway system in the early 1990s, that spurred the wave of crime eradication that contributed mightily to the restoration of that great American city.[8] Or consider Milton Friedman, whose "cry from the heart" in *Free to Choose*[9] was picked up by, among others, Michael Joyce and the Bradley Foundation, thus seeding the birth of school choice programs in Milwaukee, Cleveland, Washington, D.C., and elsewhere.[10]

Or consider welfare reform and the innovative work of a great, inspiring governor, Tommy Thompson. His "Wisconsin Works" program, known as

W-2, replaced the degrading and debilitating (for its clients) Aid To Families With Dependent Children program.[11] As then governor Thompson put it with Midwestern simplicity, "It is an employment program rather than a welfare program." Because of the W-2 program and others like it, the old order of welfare, with its powerful political support from the apparatus of the welfare state, including powerful allies in the cultural elite, was eventually forced into retreat in the face of powerful ideas and irrefutable facts—so much so that a Democratic president accepted Tommy Thompson style welfare reform at the national level.[12] Born in think tanks, universities, and the best minds our nation has to offer, all of the above ideas, and countless others, were proved in the laboratories of state and local government.

Perhaps, quite naturally, we want to have our cake and eat it too. We will be anti-Federalist one moment and nationalist the next. Perhaps Justice Sandra Day O'Connor was right, after all, in warning (in a decidedly different context) against even trying to fashion or adopt a "Grand Unified Theory" of constitutional law.[13] At the risk of engaging in an exercise in futility, I cannot resist offering the following, potentially unifying, principle: Take federalism seriously, including honoring the traditions of what has long been called the police power, but take equal care to combat economic parochialism and protect the national marketplace.

Under this unifying principle, judges and justices would vigorously protect states' abilities to experiment in their core areas of responsibility. Crime eradication, poverty relief, family governance, morals regulation, together with primary and secondary education, have in the past formed the core responsibilities of state and local government, and they should continue to do so today. All three branches of the federal government should be wary of interfering with state experimentation in these fields, whether by judicial ukase, as in *Roe v. Wade*, or by Congressional enactment, as in the No Child Left Behind law, or by giving in to temptations to indulge in strained executive branch implementations of federal statutes, as in the recent Oregon assisted suicide case.[14] Equally important, all three federal branches of government also should recognize and respect states' sovereign right to direct their own officers and refrain from pressing those officers into real or metaphorical federal uniforms—except perhaps where the most severe exigencies so demand. The Supreme Court was quite right in deciding *New York v. United States* and the Brady Act cases as it did.[15]

At the same time, the Commerce Clause should be taken equally seriously, as should the never-ending demands of our national economic union. The underlying concerns leading to the gathering in 1787 in Philadelphia were largely economic in nature: the need to create a structure of government that would safeguard the world's largest economic union.[16] Then, as now, economic protectionists and other forces of parochialism were ceaselessly working in state legislatures, state executive offices, and state courthouses to undermine that economic union and divide the spoils of the dissolution.

The nature of the problem of state extraterritoriality, protectionist barriers, and parochialism has changed dramatically during my own legal career and has become increasingly acute. The recent litigation explosion and resulting tort crisis[17] and the concomitant rise of state officials eager to employ state-sponsored litigation to undermine the federal policies they oppose[18] are new ailments that plague the modern-day civil litigation system.[19] In this new era, courts must be increasingly vigilant to guard against state parochial protectionist statutes in disguise;[20] the ever-expanding problem of opportunistic trial lawyers; and the abuses of aggressive state attorneys general.[21] The same concerns that prompted James Madison to insist on empowering the national government to regulate interstate commerce (the *only* substantive power not included in the Articles of Confederation[22]) counsel in favor of displacing state common law, statutes, and regulatory standards that intrude on federal prerogatives or discriminate against out-of-state commerce. When Congress does address the national marketplace, its work should be interpreted like the Constitution itself—generously, not grudgingly, or burdened with an anti-Federalist thumb on the scales, such as the "presumption against preemption."[23]

We need judges and justices who intuitively understand the importance of protecting our vast commercial republic and who are willing to use the historic role of the federal judiciary to that end. Fear of past misuse of judicial power, especially those that formerly occurred in the name of the Due Process Clause, should not cause justices to shrink from the legitimate use of their Article III power to strike down parochial and protectionist state laws, regulations, and judicial decisions. It will not do as a practical matter to say, "Let Congress police the states." Today, Congress is much too busy appropriating funds for bridges to nowhere, railing against oil companies, and determining whether its authorization to use military force against

Islamic extremists allows the president to use the National Security Agency as a tool to protect Americans from Islamic extremists. But even when it emerges from its current low ebb, as surely it will, Congress will find that it cannot possibly police and redress every improper incursion on federal authority by the legislative, executive, and judicial branches of all 50 state governments. If that job is to be done at all, it must be the federal judiciary that does it.[24]

The Supreme Court has become rightly focused in recent decades on cabining the use of its own power and eliminating the Court's own, most antidemocratic excesses. But this paramount concern has caused the Court, in some cases, to shrink from exercising the historic and proper role of the federal judiciary in protecting the unified economy that brought this nation to global greatness. Too often, the Court has exhibited an anticonstitutional fear of judicial power, even when it is employed to vindicate principles deeply rooted in the very structure of the Constitution itself. Mr. Lincoln, in his day, did not shrink from violently vindicating the proposition that, even though the Constitution's text is silent as to its duration, our union of states is perpetual. In our own day, judges and justices should not shrink from invoking that same constitutional structure, as they must, to ensure that our national marketplace, our ever-fruitful economic union, is preserved and passed on to future generations. The great Justice Benjamin Cardozo said rightly that our union means we must sink or swim together in the waters of commerce.[25] Today those waters are beginning to teem with ravenous sharks bearing the beguiling markings of the several states. Judges and justices should stand ready to harpoon these sharks as soon as they surface.

Notes

1. See *Hooven & Allison Co. v. Evatt*, 324 U.S. 652, 671-72 (1945) (discussing the different meanings of the term "United States").

2. See *Texas v. White*, 74 U.S. 700 (1868).

3. See Michael W. McConnell, *Active Liberty: A Progressive Alternative to Textualism and Originalism?*, 119 Harv. L. Rev. 2387, 2394–95 (2006) (reviewing Stephen G. Breyer, *Active Liberty: Interpreting Our Democratic Constitution* (New York: Knopf, 2005)).

4. Sarbanes-Oxley Act of 2002, Pub. L. No. 107-204, 116 Stat. 745; No Child Left Behind Act of 2001, Pub. L. No. 107-110, 115 Stat. 1425 (2002).

5. See, *e.g.*, *United States v. Aluminum Co. of Am.*, 148 F.2d 416, 443 (2d Cir. 1945) (L. Hand, J.).

6. See, *e.g.*, Samuel Estreicher, *In Defense of Theory*, 10 Green Bag 2d 49, 51 (2006); see also Robert H. Bork, *Coercing Virtue: The Worldwide Rule of Judges* (Washington, D.C.: AEI Press, 2003) 1–14.

7. James Q. Wilson and George L. Kelling, "Broken Windows: The Police and Neighborhood Safety," *Atlantic Monthly*, March 1982.

8. See George L. Kelling & William J. Bratton, *Declining Crime Rates: Insiders' Views of the New York City Story*, 88 J. Crim. L. & Criminology 1217 (1998).

9. Milton Friedman & Rose Friedman, *Free to Choose: A Personal Statement* 150–88 (New York: Harcourt, Inc., 1980).

10. See, *e.g.*, *Zelman v. Simmons-Harris*, 536 U.S. 639 (2002).

11. See, *e.g.*, 1996 Welfare Overhaul, congressional testimony of Tommy G. Thompson (July 19, 2006), available at 2006 WLNR 12432362; Tommy G. Thompson, *Welfare Reformed: A Heritage of Success, A Legacy of Hope*, 16 Notre Dame J. L. Ethics & Pub. Policy 367 (2002).

12. Personal Responsibility and Work Opportunity Reconciliation Act, Pub. L. No. 104-193, 110 Stat. 2105 (1996).

13. See *Rosenberger v. Rector and Visitors of Univ. of Va.*, 515 U.S. 819, 852 (1995) (O'Connor, J., concurring) (noting lack of a single "Grand Unified Theory" for Establishment Clause); see also H. Jefferson Powell, *The Oldest Question of Constitutional Law*, 79 Va. L. Rev. 633 (1993).

14. *Gonzales v. Oregon*, 126 S. Ct. 904 (2006).

15. *New York v. U.S.*, 505 U.S. 144 (1992); *Printz v. U.S.*, 521 U.S. 898 (1997).

16. See, *e.g.*, *Or. Waste Sys., Inc. v. Dep't of Envtl. Quality*, 511 U.S. 93, 98 (1994) ("The Framers granted Congress plenary authority over interstate commerce in 'the conviction that in order to succeed, the new Union would have to avoid the tendencies toward economic Balkanization that had plagued relations among the Colonies and later among the States under the Articles of Confederation," quoting *Hughes v. Oklahoma*, 441 U.S. 322, 325–36 (1979)).

17. See, *e.g.*, Peter Huber, *Liability: The Legal Revolution and its Consequence* 1–18 (New York: Basic Books, 1990) 1-18.

18. See, *e.g.*, William H. Pryor, Jr., Remarks, *Regulation by Litigation: The New Wave of Government-Sponsored Litigation*, Manhattan Institute Conference 5-6, June 22, 1999. http://www.manhattan-institute.org/html/mics_1_a.htm (last accessed February 5, 2007); Richard A. Posner, Federalism and the Enforcement of Antitrust Laws by State Attorneys General in *Competition Laws in Conflict: Antitrust Jurisdiction in the Global Economy* 252, 255, 258–60 (Richard A. Epstein & Michael S. Greve eds., 2004); John C. Coffee, *Competitive Federalism: The Rise of the State Attorney General*, N.Y. L.J., Sept. 19, 2003, at 5.

19. See Michael S. Greve, *Federalism As A Trial Lawyer's Bill of Rights*, 29 Fall Human Rights 12 (2002) (discussing recent litigation campaigns by state attorneys general and trial lawyers); see also Robert R. Gasaway, *The Problem of Federal Preemption: Reformulating the Black Letter Rules*, 33 Pepp. L. Rev. 25 (2005).

20. See, *e.g.*, *Granholm v. Heald*, 544 U.S. 460 (2005); *Healy v. Beer Inst.*, 491 U.S. 324 (1989); *Bacchus Imps. Ltd. v. Dias*, 468 U.S. 263 (1984).

21. See, *e.g.*, Lester Brickman, *Lawyers' Ethics and Fiduciary Obligation in the Brave New World of Aggregative Litigation*, 26 Wm. & Mary Envtl. L. & Policy Rev. 243, 245 (2001); Hal Stratton, "Attorneys General in State of Collusion," *Wall Street Journal*, June 10, 1988.

22. See James Madison, *The Federalist* 45, 242 (George W. Carey and James McClellan eds., 2001) ("The regulation of commerce . . . is a new [national] power"); *Gibbons v. Ogden*, 22 U.S. 1, 9 Wheat. 1, 224, 6 L.Ed. 23 (1824) (opinion of Johnson, J.).

23. See generally Viet D. Dinh, *Reassessing the Law of Preemption*, 88 Geo. L.J. 2085 (2000) (arguing that, in contrast to existing belief, "federalism does not admit to a general presumption against federal preemption of state law").

24. See William N. Eskridge, Jr. & John Ferejohn, *Super-Statutes*, 50 Duke L.J. 1215, 1221 (2001); Robert R. Gasaway, *The Problem of Federal Preemption: Reformulating the Black Letter Rules*, 33 Pepp. L. Rev. 25, 27–31 (2005).

25. *Baldwin v. G.A.F. Seelig*, 294 U.S. 511, 523 (1935).

1

Introduction
Preemption in Context

Richard A. Epstein and Michael S. Greve[*]

"Preemption" has many different meanings and connotations, depending on the context. Literally, preemption means the right to buy before someone else—"pre" as in before, and "emption" as in purchase. In war, it refers to an attack—a "preemptive strike"—to get the upper hand over a rival. In bridge, preemption denotes high bids by players with weak hands and long suits who seek to block communication between their opponents by reducing the number of levels that they have available to bid. In its modern legal usage, preemption means the federal government's ability to trump, supersede, or displace state and local law—to "preempt" it.

The trusty Funk & Wagnalls dictionary does not include the legal definition among its recognized usages.[1] But today, more than ever, it ought to: once-esoteric questions involving federal preemption have become the subject of a prominent and often polemic public debate. Consumer advocates, plaintiffs' attorneys, and state officials argue that broad federal preemption claims—often made by federal regulatory agencies, without a clear congressional mandate—interfere with the states' historic police power to protect their citizens against corporate misconduct. Corporations and federal agencies respond that preemption is a much-needed safeguard against unwarranted and inconsistent state interferences with the national economy and against aggressive trial lawyers and attorneys general who upset carefully crafted regulatory compromises. Fierce struggles along these lines have become a focal point of political debate, judicial decisions, and legal commentary in a wide range of regulatory arenas, from financial regulation to automobile safety; from clean air laws to the regulation of telecommunications, energy, and other network industries; from securities law to consumer products standards; from pharmaceutical drugs to pesticides to outboard motors to mattresses.

In all these areas, billions of dollars hang on regulatory nuances and arcane points of legal interpretation, which explains much of the acrimony that now engulfs this once-placid domain. But the preemption debate is being waged in the shadow of broader, sometimes constitutional arguments concerning the role and utility of federalism and "states' rights" in a modern, highly mobile, and integrated economy. Legal scholars are sharply divided over both the substance of those arguments and the extent to which they should dominate economic considerations or statutory language in what has evolved through legislative compromise and judicial intervention into an enormous universe of heterogeneous and highly particular, industry- or area-specific preemption arrangements. Those disputes, however, proceed from two shared premises. First, no one is very happy with the Supreme Court's muddled doctrine and meandering decisions in this field. Second, it has come to be widely acknowledged—not universally, but to a far greater extent than only a decade ago—that preemption questions cannot be reduced to the judicial exegesis of (often ambiguous) federal statutes. While statutory interpretation is a large part of the preemption picture, preemption doctrine is also, and centrally, a question of institutional design and constitutional understanding.

What the preemption debate needs, to our minds, is an examination that reflects the delicate interplay between broad institutional considerations and regulatory detail. We need to get a picture of the forest without getting lost in the trees, while still recognizing that the trees constitute much of the ecology of preemption. To that end, we assembled legal theorists and practicing lawyers, liberals and conservatives, nationalists and states' righters, specialists and generalists—authors who have little more in common than stellar and well-deserved reputations in their respective fields and an awareness that the preemption question connects their professional interests to a very salient public debate.

In Part I, Viet Dinh and Stephen Gardbaum trace the antecedents of modern preemption law—respectively, the nineteenth-century understanding, and the transition from the *Lochner* Court to the New Deal. The New Deal largely settled the constitutional disputes of the earlier eras, but the essays demonstrate (to our minds at least) why the preemption debate would benefit from a better understanding of *why* those disputes were settled and on what terms. The contributions in Part II examine extant preemption law in a wide range of policy arenas, from drug regulation (Daniel Troy) to telecommunications (Thomas Hazlett) to banking, insurance, and corporate law (Hal Scott) to environmental policy (Thomas Merrill) to products liability (Samuel Issacharoff and Catherine Sharkey). Jointly and severally, the essays provide both an in-depth, nuanced examination of preemption "at work" and a good sense of the awesome range of legal and economic questions that fall under the heading of "preemption." Part III returns to the broader questions. Robert Gasaway and Ashley Parrish explore the internal logic of preemption doctrine; Ernest Young, its federalism dimension. Anne van Aaken's essay contrasts the American understanding of preemption with that of the European Union.

We shall not be shy in the Conclusion in articulating our own views on the contributors' perspectives and, in particular, on the many novel proposals for a revamped preemption doctrine. We are less certain on what to say by way of an Introduction to a set of essays that, to our minds, presents a gratifyingly well-rounded and multifaceted picture. We have chosen to emphasize function—that is, the role preemption law has served under shifting constitutional presumptions and economic and political conditions, on the intuition that the varying form of preemption follows its uncertain function. Our Bauhaus theory of preemption starts with the constitutional foundations.

Preemption, Supremacy, and the Alternatives

The vast judicial edifice of federal preemption is perched atop a single constitutional provision, the Supremacy Clause of art. VI, sec. 2 of the Constitution:

> This Constitution, and the Laws of the United States which shall be made in Pursuance thereof; and all Treaties made, or which shall be made, under the Authority of the United States, shall be the supreme Law of the Land: and the Judges in every State shall be bound thereby, any Thing in the Constitution or Law of any State to the contrary notwithstanding.

The familiarity of this arrangement tends to blind us to its striking features—first and foremost, its ostentatious legalism. "Supremacy" is attributed to federal *law*, not the federal government and its officials. Similarly, political officials disappear stateside: while the first portion of the clause should probably be treated as self-executing (so that no state legislator or executive officer should be free to openly disregard the dominant position of federal law), the only officials who are specifically addressed are "the Judges in every State." And the "notwithstanding" clause is quite different in character from a "subsidiarity principle" or other assignment criteria that structure modern federal constitutions elsewhere. It rather reads like a choice-of-law provision of the sort that one could find, and at the time of the founding did find, in an ordinary statute. Caleb Nelson has shown that the colonial legislatures included nearly identical *non obstante* clauses when they wanted courts to give full force and effect to a newly enacted statute—as opposed to harmonizing it, according to established judicial canons of construction, with earlier statutes governing the same subject matter. The Supremacy Clause, Nelson argues, is a *non obstante* clause that operates "vertically": in cases of conflict between federal and state law, dear judge, choose the federal law. Don't try to harmonize the two.[2] That seems correct as far as it goes, but from a functional perspective at least, it does not go far enough. Unlike a state-internal *non obstante* clause, the Supremacy Clause seeks to ensure cohesion among rival government authorities. The "mild influence of the magistracy," *The Federalist* explained, is the alternative to a singularly unattractive means of arresting the states' centrifugal tendencies— the enforcement of their common obligations by force of arms.[3]

There are other ways of ensuring the gains of multistate cooperation under a central umbrella. For a dramatic example, the Constitution for Iraq provides that in conflicts between nonexclusive national and *regional* law, regional law shall prevail within the region.[4] Whatever is supposed to ensure political stability and cohesion in that system (perhaps, a "government of national unity"), it cannot be law. Another option is to ensure cooperation by means of bargains, rather than choice of law: so long as the central government has access to adequate revenues, it can *pay* subordinate governments to enforce central directives. Many federal systems (such as those of Germany and India) operate on that principle.[5] The European Union also operates on a principle of member-state cooperation, except that reputational losses and gains, rather than monetary exchanges, are expected to ensure member-states' compliance. As Anne van Aaken's essay in this volume shows, such a system will generate a preemption regime very different from our own. To the founders, however, legal supremacy was the *only* alternative to the force of arms. This helps to explain why legalistic disputes over the precise scope of preemption occupy such a central place in the contemporary federalism debate: in a very real sense, that is how the system is supposed to operate.

The second striking feature of the Supremacy Clause is its extreme nationalism. As modern philosophers are fond of saying, its ordering is strictly lexical: the lowliest federal law trumps the loftiest state law. That logic, without more, leaves nothing to or of the states, at least as a formal matter. As Madison put it in *Federalist* 39, the union is entirely "national" in the operation of federal powers, by which he meant that those powers are supreme and, moreover, can be exercised without the assistance or intermediation of the states. To the extent that the system is federal, that is so because national powers are limited in their scope or "extent." They are, as Madison famously remarked, "few and defined."[6]

From the get-go, the debate over federalism, supremacy, and preemption has moved between those two poles—the ruthless logic of the Supremacy Clause, and the logic of limited and enumerated national powers. At one end, the Anti-Federalists and their disciples through the ages have worried that the "few and defined" federal powers are, upon inspection, neither few nor particularly well-defined. Their "federal" character has proven contestable in a way in which the "national" operation has not. Hitched to the Supremacy Clause, the expansion of substantive federal powers has turned into an engine of consolidation, just as the Anti-Federalists feared. At the other end lies the worry that the Supremacy Clause may fail to live up to its billing. If supremacy is to hold, somebody has to assert it with a modicum of regularity. That would be the courts or Congress. Both, however, may lack the will or the capacity, or both, to discharge the supremacy function. "Courts," to the founders, meant principally *state* courts, whose allegiance to the federal Constitution was questionable. Putting aside that historical concern (and the later creation of lower federal courts by Congress), judicial power operates through cases and controversies, at the instigation of private litigants. The enforcement of federal supremacy—a public good—rests on *private* litigation incentives, and that is not a comforting scenario. Congress, for its part, is fickle, slow, and populated by representatives whose parochial orientation may easily lead them to undervalue vital federal interests. The institutional calculus, moreover, depends not only on one's estimation of the institutional capacity and inclinations at the federal level but also on one's expectations about the states' conduct. Granting that the supremacy-enforcing institutions are sufficiently strong and motivated to redress occasional state infractions, are they strong enough to beat back a constant barrage of hostile state legislation?

One clue that concerns of this sort in fact troubled the founders is the structure of the Constitution. In contrast to all modern federal constitutions, the U.S. Constitution contains no catalogue of protected state functions or powers. What it does contain is a catalogue of state *disabilities*, listed in art. I, sec. 10. Some things, states may not do at all. These absolute prohibitions cover treaties with foreign nations and letters of marque and reprisal; the coinage of money, bills of credit, and debtor relief laws; ex post facto laws, bills of attainder, and laws impairing the obligation of contracts; and the granting of titles of nobility. Other state measures—duties on imports and exports, tonnage duties, state compacts and agreements with other states or with foreign nations, and the maintenance of standing armies—require the approval of Congress. At the end of the day, the provisions of art. I, sec. 10, too, require judicial enforcement and in that sense depend on the Supremacy Clause. But they are inconsistent with a cheerful confidence in the Supremacy Clause, standing alone.

A compelling way of understanding the constitutionally specified state disabilities—from a functional perspective—is to view them as a backhanded compliment to James Madison and his deep misgivings about the Constitution's Supremacy Clause. Both in his preconvention writings and at the Constitutional Convention, Madison vehemently argued for the far more draconian option of a national "Negative"—that is, a requirement of federal preapproval of state legislation—"in all cases whatsoever." Madison did not hedge this proposal with an enumerated powers proviso; he emphatically maintained that no state law of any kind should be allowed to take effect without prior approval by the Congress.[7] Madison did not treat his Negative as some bauble. It was the linchpin of his agenda at the Convention, and he insisted on it with a tenacity that bordered on fanaticism, before—and even after—it was rejected by a seven-to-three vote in committee.

What propelled Madison to propose so striking a limitation on state power was his fear of faction, forcefully articulated in *Federalist* 10. In his view, state autonomy over separate spheres was the villain of the peace. Strong states, he believed, spell political instability both for the union, where parochial tendencies and mutual aggression among states persistently threaten the potential gains of collective organization, and within the states, where a flood of ill-shaped legislation demoralizes citizens. The Articles of Confederation had amply illustrated both pathologies, and Madison traced them to one and the same source: the unrestrained operation of factional politics in the states. In that view, political stability and citizens' rights cannot be secured by means of an enforceable "peace pact" that blocks state aggression, while leaving the states' purely internal affairs untouched. Rather, the Constitution has to reach and redress the factional sources of instability within the states, which only Congress's national Negative could do.

Madison formulated his proposal before the federal institutions took shape at the Convention, and he was never very clear about how the Negative would actually work. It was killed sufficiently early in the Convention that we do not know, for example, whether it would have been subject to a presidential veto. Accordingly, a straightforward institutional comparison between the Negative and the Supremacy Clause is bound to be misleading. That said, the Convention very clearly understood those options as alternatives, and it weighed the respective institutional risks.

The genius of Madison's Negative is to make federal legislative transaction costs work for the preservation of the union. Under a federal legislative process that is encumbered by multiple obstacles to legislation—de facto supermajoritarian requirements[8]—a federal approval requirement will stop much state legislation in its tracks and thereby ease the pressure on both Congress and the judiciary. Congress no longer needs to mobilize a majority to arrest harmful state legislation; sheer inertia will do the job. For analogous reasons, the judiciary would not have to play so central a role in preserving the union. In fact, once Congress has approved state legislation, it is difficult (though perhaps not impossible) to think that a system of judicial review would allow the Court to strike down legislation that has received congressional blessing. The problem of commandeering recalcitrant state judges into enforcing federal law, which played such a prominent role in *Martin v. Hunter's Lessee* and *Cohens v. Virginia*,[9] would arise (if at all) in a much more attenuated form.

Those gains, however, would come at a price. One concern, prominent on the Philadelphia delegates' minds, was that the Negative would block much salutary (or at least harmless) state regulation, along with the bad laws. So long as the Negative contains no mandatory up-or-down provision, nothing stops multiple rounds of negotiation between a divided Congress and a hapless state, or indeed well-crafted coalitions among states, over the configuration of particular legislation. As political majorities are in constant flux at both levels, the national veto could easily leave a state, or any group of states, helpless to deal with matters that by any stretch of the imagination could concern only the internal affairs of each, at no conceivable risk to the union or sister states.

The case against the Negative is still stronger when one recalls that Madison's case for a powerful national government and the extended republic rested not only on higher transaction costs, relative to the costs of procuring majorities in state legislatures, but also on a filtration effect: large electoral districts, he hoped, would attract better, more public-spirited public servants than the hacks and petty demagogues in state legislatures. In his own lifetime, however (in fact, as early as 1789), Madison learned that one way or the other, the disreputable folks who inhabit state legislatures could manage to get themselves elected to Congress—and keep their original instincts.[10] That recognition makes the Negative look a lot less attractive. It does not even appear to be bound by the simple injunction that like cases have to be treated alike, so that the identical statute could be allowed in New York but blocked in Virginia. Even if these blatant forms of favoritism could be controlled, perhaps by the adroit use of state coalitions, remedies would be still harder to find with regard to other forms of abuse. Just setting the agenda as to which bills come forward in what order could influence substantially their prospects of passage, and the possibilities of log-rolling and coalition building are mind-boggling.

In the end, the choice between the Negative and the Supremacy Clause boils down to the question of which default provision produces the fewest unwholesome results. Think of states as factional cesspools and of the federal legislature as a comparatively public-spirited institution, and the

Negative becomes your first choice. Alternatively, think of state legislation as primarily state-internal and as only occasionally menacing to the union and of federal legislators and the judiciary as sufficiently energetic and trustworthy: the Supremacy Clause will do just fine.

The conflicted nature of this calculus did not escape the founders. For the general run of cases, the Convention rejected the Negative. As even Madison's usual allies said, the instrument would "disgust all the states." Why resort to that drastic means when, under the Supremacy Clause, a state law that ought to be "negatived" could always be set aside by judicial or congressional intervention?[11] However, the convention in fact adopted the Negative, or the even stronger medicine of an absolute prohibition, for certain classes of state laws—those that are listed in art. I, sec. 10 of the Constitution. Why some of the prohibitions are absolute and others conditional upon congressional approval is not entirely clear. Broadly speaking, however, the line between the sec. 10 prohibitions and the ordinary operation of the Supremacy Clause runs between external and internal affairs. Overwhelmingly, the (conditionally) prohibited state actions pose manifest external threats to sister states, whereas purely internal depredations are left to the operation of the Supremacy Clause to the extent that the federal government's enumerated powers reach those affairs and, beyond that scope, are left entirely unremedied under federal law.[12] At bottom, the pattern is Madisonian. The factional exploitation of in-state constituencies is costly for an enacting coalition—politically, because the losers can fight back at the ballot box, and economically, because the losers can "vote with their feet." Thus, stable factions will prefer to "export" the costs of their schemes to other states. The "external" prohibitions of art. I, sec. 10 curb factionalism on this margin, where it is bound to be most virulent.

Madison himself had little confidence in the Convention's compromise solution. Faction-ridden states, he lamented in a long postconvention letter to Thomas Jefferson, would evade all but the most comprehensive federal strictures. The suppression of factionalism on one margin—for instance, laws impairing the obligation of contracts—would only produce exploitation on a different margin, by different means. "The partial provision made" in the Constitution, Madison wrote, "supposes the disposition which will evade it."[13] And Madison held little hope that this logic would stop at the state borders. The internal-external distinction—common intellectual currency at the time, because it was a legacy of the debates over the Stamp Act—was sensible, so far as it went. But even an intuitive and theoretically plausible distinction cannot hold up in practice unless it is fortified by adequate institutional means. The Supremacy Clause, even when coupled with the Negative or an absolute prohibition over a specified range of state laws, would not answer to the task.

Madison's misgivings now strike us as exaggerated and the extreme nationalism of his Negative as misguided. In part, that sense derives from historical experience: the sober and belated recognition that factionalism can be as rampant at the federal as at the state level scrambles Madison's clear-cut preference for the national Negative. Also in part, improved economic theories help to account for our different intuitions. In his desperate effort to suppress state exploitation across the board, Madison failed to recognize that exploitation on the last margin is never as efficient as exploitation on the first (otherwise, the last would have been first). Too, we now know that the threat of exit of mobile production factors, which Madison never considered, may discipline state governments.[14] Writing as he did almost a full century before Marshall and Jevons and another eight decades before Charles Tiebout, however, Madison may be forgiven those oversights. And neither the marginalist revolution of the late nineteenth century nor the snazzy twentieth-century equilibrium models of competitive federalism can fully dispel the force of Madison's concerns. They echo in the case law of the nineteenth century—and to this day.

From Supremacy to Preemption

Viet Dinh's and Stephen Gardbaum's essays in this volume trace the trajectory of what we now call "preemption" through the nineteenth century and the *Lochner* era to the emergence of the modern, post–New Deal preemption regime. The crucial shift is from exclusive state and federal powers to concurrent powers and congressional intent.

For much of the nineteenth and early twentieth centuries, the Supreme Court thought of state and federal regulation as separate and mutually exclusive spheres—"interstate commerce" on one side, the states' "internal commerce" or "police powers" on the other. At the limit, that conceptual universe permits no truly concurrent state and federal powers and hence obviates any need for a doctrine of federal preemption. Defining the contours of federal and state powers (we would now say) is a question of jurisdiction, not preemption.[15] For that reason, "preemption" retained its literal meaning as the right to buy before someone else: it applied in connection with the rights conferred upon the occupiers of public lands to have the first right to acquire the property in question. In its now-canonical legal usage, "preemption" made its first appearance only in 1917.[16] At that time, Gardbaum explains, the *Lochner* Court supplemented the exclusive Commerce Clause, in the limited area where that construct left room for concurrent state power, with a preemption doctrine of "latent exclusivity": as soon as Congress exercised its enumerated powers, its intervention displaced state regulation in the entire field—regardless of whether state law conflicted with the federal law, and regardless of whether Congress had intended wholesale preemption.

When the enumerated powers doctrine was effectively abandoned in the New Deal and the congressional power to regulate commerce "among the several states" came to embrace the power to regulate commerce *within* the states and all forms of manufacture, agriculture, and mining that have some effect on commerce among the several states (including, notoriously, feeding one's own wheat to one's own cows),[17] the old doctrine of (latent) exclusivity would have implied a wholesale collapse into the center. To preserve a federalism balance, Gardbaum shows, the Supreme Court softened the dormant Commerce Clause and adopted a more attenuated, state-protective doctrine of federal preemption. The New Deal Court effectively abandoned the dormant Commerce Clause as a substantive limitation on state regulation of interstate commerce; henceforth, only *discriminatory* state regulations would be found unconstitutional. Coupled with the expansion of the federal commerce power, this entailed that state and federal powers run concurrent over practically the entire range of government regulatory and taxing affairs. The touchstone of whether and to what extent state regulation is preempted in the sea of concurrent powers now becomes a matter of congressional intent. State power is displaced only when Congress has intended that result either expressly or by clear implication. For the purposes of this Introduction, we emphasize two Madisonian themes that are central to understanding this transition: the fiendish difficulties of sorting federal and state functions along an external/internal dimension, and the operation of faction. As it turns out, and as Madison recognized, those themes are closely related.

A good place to start—seemingly far afield only at first impression—is one of the Madisonian Negatives in the Constitution, the Import-Export Clause of art. I, sec. 10:

> No State shall, without the Consent of the Congress, lay any Imposts or Duties on Imports or Exports, except what may be absolutely necessary for executing its inspection Laws: and the net Produce of all Duties and Imposts, laid by any State on Imports or Exports, shall be for the Use of the Treasury of the United States; and all such Laws shall be subject to the Revision and Controul of the Congress.

State duties are an imposition on external, interstate commerce, which Congress could mow down under even the most restrictive interpretation of the Commerce Clause.[18] Evidently, however, the founders considered such duties sufficiently likely, and sufficiently destructive, to erect special safeguards: a requirement of congressional approval and a requirement that excess funds to be paid over to the United States Treasury, which is a good reason for the states not to bother to collect them at all. The clause then exempts state inspection laws on the intuition, which would maintain its hold throughout the nineteenth century, that such laws are the embodiment of an "internal" state health and safety measure.[19] Perhaps reflecting a fear that states might abuse the exemption as a subterfuge for protectionist measures, the clause (so to speak) shifts mental gears again and insists that duties imposed for purposes of administering inspection laws must be *absolutely* necessary. In all these respects, the clause reflects the founders' clarity of thought: ensure open borders inside the United States, sustain state control over internal affairs, and protect that arrangement against factional pressures. Still, the nineteenth-century cases discussed by Viet Dinh betray the tenuousness of the conceptual distinctions.

In *Brown v. Maryland* (1827), Maryland sought to thwart interstate commerce by imposing a tax on importers instead of on imports. The two taxes differ in their incidence in that a tax on importers is not sensitive to the volume of goods sold, while the direct tax on imports is. But the need to prevent the circumvention of the constitutional prohibition against taxes on imports led Chief Justice John Marshall to strike down the tax on importers as a noxious variation of a tax on imports.[20] Like Madison, Marshall understood that "the partial provision made" in the Constitution would prompt efforts to evade it. The same structural issue surfaces in cases dealing with state laws regarding passengers. Passengers are not goods, and so the aim of preserving the national market had to be resolved by looking to the Commerce Clause rather than the Import-Export Clause. *City of New York v. Miln* (1837) upheld a state law that required all incoming boats into New York to first provide passenger rosters, and then to post bond against their becoming charges for the city of New York—a good way to make the boat operators more selective in choosing whom to transport. Crucially, this provision did not generate any extra funds that could be diverted for other purposes.

All inspection laws, however, are not cut from that cloth. In the *Passenger Cases* (1849), one of the defendant states (New York) dedicated the proceeds it received from a de facto head tax on immigration to maintaining a marine hospital, with "the surplus to be paid to the treasurer of the Society for the Reformation of Juvenile Delinquents in the city of New York." The state defended this arrangement as a classic police power exercise to protect public health, safety, and morals. Yet the point looks dubious: the use of the surplus for local needs makes it look as though the state has proposed a protective tariff in order to fund its own local operations, wholly apart from any health or safety risk arising from the movement of persons across state lines. Structurally, the planned diversion of funds poses the same risk as the diversion to local purposes of funds raised from the inspection of imports or exports. Justice John McLean was right to invalidate this tax on the ground that no state should be allowed to finance its entire operations through impositions on interstate commerce.[21] But in a lesson that holds true for the law of federal preemption today, the devil is often in the details. The size of the exaction and the direction of the payment count for a great deal in the analysis.

Cooley v. Board of Wardens of Port of Philadelphia (1851) confirms the point. At issue there was a Pennsylvania ordinance that required incoming vessels from out of state to employ local pilots—unless they chose to use their own pilots and to contribute sums equal to one-half the required fee to a pension fund for "the relief of distressed and decayed pilots, their widows and children."[22] Once again, the distribution of surplus funds was not caught by the Import-Export clause, but the protectionist elements that loomed in the *Passenger Cases* were also at work here. The Court sustained the regulation as relating to matters of peculiar local importance, which surely strikes a responsive chord. But when (as in *Cooley*) the local regulation is limited to ships from foreign nations and other states, it is appropriate to probe more deeply into the ordinance—an inquiry that, in *Cooley*, should have led to its invalidation.

Conceptually, the categorical distinction between the states' police power and the federal government's power to regulate interstate commerce founders on the awkward fact that countless state laws fit *both* descriptions. Even state inspection laws, it turned out, were by no means exclusively "internal." Once that recognition sets in, the logic of mutually exclusive state and federal jurisdictions begins to crumble. Even the earliest Commerce Clause cases contain laments to the effect that the problem of sorting federal enumerated powers from residual state powers, external from internal affairs, probably defies a clean solution. In practice the situation remained bearable so long as judicial sorting could remain sporadic. Starting in the late nineteenth century, however, cases testing these boundaries became the daily diet of the law, and the judge-made distinctions—enumerated federal powers versus state police powers—came under enormous pressure. Viewed collectively, the cases of that era contain the seeds for modern preemption doctrine. Some spoke of the need to be cautious before striking down state laws on the ground that they conflicted with federal precedents; others fretted about state laws that "frustrate the purposes of national legislation."[23]

The pressures increased with the growth of an industrialized corporate economy. One challenge came from the regulation of interstate externalities, spillovers, and hold-outs in the management of network industries (railroads at first, then telecommunications and power transmission). Here, the Supreme Court opted for wholesale federal management long before the New Deal revolution.[24] Another challenge—in many ways, the core of the New Deal transformation—was the recognition that the effective administration of national cartels (especially in labor and agriculture) necessitated controls over in-state conduct. (Concede the premise, and *Wickard v. Filburn* becomes an easy case.) In the decades leading up to these changes, judicial attempts to shore up the internal-external distinction with further epicycles—such as the distinction between "commerce" and "production," and the distinction between "direct" and "indirect" effects on interstate commerce—proved as contestable as the constitutional boundaries themselves. The situation grew worse when the functional justifications for the distinctions were subject to constant sniping from a generation of scholars who thought that national problems necessarily required national solutions. But if the Supreme Court is not slave to the election returns, it is surely vulnerable to public and academic criticism, especially when it all seems to run one way. Soon enough, the Supreme Court's conceptual edifice invited legal-realist ridicule.[25] Eventually, the enumerated powers doctrine collapsed. The Court moved from exclusive to concurrent powers, from jurisdiction to preemption, from constitutional logic to congressional intent.

One ought to resist an all-too-facile functionalism here. One of us (Epstein) has argued, unrepentantly, that the pre–New Deal Court got the cases roughly right and that economic theory provides a powerful tool to shore up the conceptual distinctions.[26] In substance, the older view sought to prevent states from disrupting network industries, while making it hard for them to cartelize competitive ones. Irrespective of that normative commitment, moreover, the variegation of modern regulatory regimes tends to belie that notion that an industrialized, complex economy *invariably* demands centralized solutions. Corporate governance, for a conspicuous example, is obviously of vital importance to the economy. Still, it has remained largely subject to decentralized, competitive, state-by-state regulation, albeit for political and institutional rather than constitutional reasons. As advertised earlier, we believe that those nuances matter in understanding the broader picture.

Still, there is no gainsaying that the older constitutional learning broke down. We suggest that it did so in large measure for a reason that Madison anticipated—the lack of an *institutional* mechanism to stabilize the enumerated powers regime either at the federal or at the state level. What would sustain that regime, Madison hoped, was filtration: public-spirited national legislators would tend to the great affairs of war and national commerce, leaving the states safely to the administration of their quotidian affairs.[27] But as noted earlier, the system never produced that type of legislator, and when the concomitants of industrialization—mass parties, improved communications—reduced the slack between local constituents and their national agents, the increased demand for federal intervention was bound to increase its supply.[28]

Nor were states likely to put up much resistance to those tendencies. In a sense, the case for central regulation seems weaker, not stronger, after industrialization, which greatly increased mobility of capital and labor: from a Madisonian perspective, Tiebout competition for producers and consumers should reduce the need for federal intervention. The losers' ability to vote with their feet disciplines the states' internal politics and provides partial protection against factional mischief and exploitation. (One could say that the exit threat does part of the job that Madison's unenacted Negative was supposed to do.) States, however, will experience competition as a loss of autonomy, and they will often clamor for federal intervention in the form of minimum standards—even at the price of federal interference in their "internal" affairs, such as labor regulation—to block "destructive" competition among the states. It was left to corporations, Justice Robert Jackson wrote in the wake of the New Deal, to carry "the states' rights plea against the states themselves."[29] That defense of the old order failed, of course, and federalism and preemption took a different form.

Preemption in the Post–New Deal Era

The prevailing theme that runs through the post–New Deal case law, we noted earlier (with reference to Gardbaum's article), is a concern over federal excess and a loss of state autonomy. The vast expansion of the commerce power, the argument runs, forbids the latent field preemption of the pre–New Deal era, lest the system collapse into the center. To preserve the federal "balance," exclusive jurisdictional force of federal regulation was watered down into implied preemption and further checked by a presumption against preemption. The canonical exposition is still Justice William O. Douglas's opinion in *Rice v. Santa Fe Elevator* (1947):

> [W]e start with the assumption that the historic police powers of the States were not to be superseded by the Federal Act unless that was the clear and manifest purpose of Congress. Such a purpose may be evidenced in several ways. The scheme of federal regulation may be so pervasive as to make reasonable the inference that Congress left no room for the States to supplement it. Or the Act

of Congress may touch a field in which the federal interest is so dominant that the federal system will be assumed to preclude enforcement of state laws on the same subject. Likewise, the object sought to be obtained by the federal law and the character of obligations imposed by it may reveal the same purpose. Or the state policy may produce a result inconsistent with the objective of the federal statute.[30]

A decade after the New Deal revolution and after the end of World War II, the time had come to settle on doctrines that would accommodate and give some regularity to the realities and compromises of the New Deal. The modern dormant Commerce Clause (closely related to preemption) took shape in that latter half of the 1940s.[31] Relative to the pre–New Deal doctrine, as noted, the new one was quite limited in scope, and indeed, the New Deal revolution entailed that the controversies and compromises over the governmental architecture—prominently including federalism—would play out in subconstitutional fields.[32] Many, perhaps most, of the compromises of that era have stuck, so that the evolution of the post–New Deal period comes in the increased sophistication of the statutory compromises made against this background, not in profound doctrinal shifts. For a prominent example, the demise of federal common law in *Erie Railroad* 1938—by its architects' estimation, the proudest and most central element of the New Deal order—had already become orthodoxy by the time of *Rice*, and a challenge to *Erie* remains heresy to this day. The Administrative Procedures Act was enacted in 1946, a year before *Rice*; soon, Justice Jackson would famously describe it as a "formula upon which opposing social and political forces have come to rest."[33] That, though, is conspicuously not true—or at least is no longer true—of *Rice* and preemption.

To be sure, one should not exaggerate the difference. *Erie Railroad* soon had to accommodate a "new" federal common law, and Jackson's characterization of the APA has proven excessively optimistic. (Administrative law underwent a tumultuous reexamination in the 1970s, and some of its aspects—prominently, relating to judicial review—remain contested.) Still, an informal "market test" suggests that practicing lawyers, and very few legal scholars, are clamoring for a reexamination of *Erie* or even for increased Supreme Court intervention in administrative law cases. On preemption, in contrast, just about everyone is begging for clarity, reformation, and Supreme Court guidance. Perhaps the most common complaint is that the Supreme Court perennially failed to apply the analytic categories of *Rice* in a consistent fashion. Consistent inconsistency, however, is often a sign of deeper problems.

The first sentence of the canonical *Rice* passage states the "presumption against preemption." The use of the words "clear and manifest" suggest that overcoming that presumption will be an uphill battle. Yet, the sentences that immediately follow announce and organize the rules of "implied" (rather than express) field, obstacle, and conflict preemption, each illustrated with statutory and case examples. Obviously, the canons pull in different directions—the presumption against preemption, toward the states; implied preemption, toward federal power. For good reason, Justice Felix Frankfurter suggested in his dissent in *Rice* that the notion of a "clear and manifest" intent that is nonetheless implied rather than expressed is inherently contradictory.[34] The *Rice* majority itself appeared to recognize the difficulty, for the just-quoted passage trails off into an expression of confoundment:

> It is often a perplexing question whether Congress has precluded
> state action or by the choice of selective regulatory measures has
> left the police power of the States undisturbed except as the state
> and federal regulations collide.[35]

Perplexing, indeed. One need not be a legal realist to suspect that conflicting canons will eventually unravel. One camp will insist that the Supreme Court should dispense with artificial canons altogether and do with preemption statutes what it does, or ought to do, with all other statutes—read the statute for what it says and enforce it accordingly, without any presumption one way or the other. That position, pressed most energetically by Justice Antonin Scalia,[36] can draw support both from a traditional understanding of the Supremacy Clause and from the fact that the canons appear to operate at cross-purposes. A second and third camp will insist that the Supreme Court should resolve the tension by adhering to one presumption while discarding the other. The contributions by Young and by Gasaway and Parrish, though far more sophisticated than our simple taxonomy here, can be read in this context. A fourth camp will suggest that perhaps, the confused presumption game illustrates the wisdom and cogency, if not necessarily the sustainability, of the earlier pre–New Deal view. (Our Conclusion sketches the contours of an argument along these lines.) Each camp starts with the observation that the canons are manipulable, manipulated, and in tension. But the difficulties in identifying a sustainable preemption formula go deeper.

The preemption edifice rests on the same notion that sustains post–New Deal administrative law and much constitutional law: the will of the Congress shall prevail. The congressional intent baseline raises the specter that preemption law can only be as coherent as the statutory universe on which it operates. That limitation poses no serious problem so long as one has confidence in the regulatory model that informed *Rice*—the regulation or, less charitably, the cartelization of the economy one industry at a time. So long as insurance remains a distinct business line and banking another, it may make no great difference—at least from the vantage of legal economy and coherence—that they operate under radically different preemption regimes. Likewise, the inherent tensions of preemption law remain manageable so long as state and federal regulators pull in the same direction—for example, when the U.S. Department of Agriculture manages national cartels for some commodities, while leaving states free to administer local or regional cartels (as for raisins or milk) under general federal supervision.[37]

These arrangements, however, and the consensus understanding on which they rested, broke down beginning in the 1960s, on account of economic as well as political and ideological factors. Hal Scott's article on financial industries presents a version of the economic forces: a congressional-intent-based preemption regime that segments industries—banking today, insurance tomorrow, securities offerings the next—will come under pressure as new technologies and business models emerge and private actors start arbitraging the regulatory boundaries. The telecommunications industry, the subject of Thomas Hazlett's essay here, illustrates the same phenomenon.

The political and ideological forces, to our minds, likewise have to do with the loss of confidence (first on the Left and then on the Right) in the New Deal regulatory model, especially the performance of "captured" agencies charged with superintending individual industries (such as the Federal Aviation Administration, the Food and Drug Administration, or the Federal

Communications Commission). With respect to preemption, two aspects of the demise of the New Deal regulatory consensus carry special weight: the greatly increased heterogeneity and detail of federal preemption regimes, and the increased salience of interest group conflict both at the central level and in a vertical, state-to-federal dimension.

By way of illustrating the heterogeneity problem, consider employer-provided health insurance, where the Employee Retirement Income Security Act (ERISA), a federal deregulatory statute, provides large employers with comprehensive preemptive protection against state regulation: states may not impose any requirements "relating to" ERISA-covered plans. As Justice Scalia observed in one ERISA case, though, "every curbstone philosopher" knows that everything is related to everything else, so the language cannot mean what it says.[38] Literally dozens of ERISA preemption decisions have attempted to expound what it does mean, in high stakes contexts in which, for example, potential tort liability of medical care organizations for medical decisions was on the line.[39] The pressures on the doctrine are enormous, both because states—shades of a Madisonian theme—have proven creative and energetic in their attempts to regulate around ERISA and because the adjacent fields are nonpreempted (and, in the case of insurance, reversely preempted in favor of the states). A still more important variation of this theme is products liability, where preemption could serve as a defense against tort suits under state law. The outcomes often hang on exquisite points of legal detail, such as the meaning of the word "requirement" or "standard" from one federal statute to the next, or the question of whether the federal enactment preempts "state law" or "a state law."[40] The common structural questions of products liability clash with minute differences among federal statutes, many of them enacted before the emergence of the modern products liability regime.

The political and ideological difficulties arise from the fact that interest groups that get beat at one level of government will seek to fight again at another level. In that environment, preemption becomes a battle over the extent to which the federal "losers" may still occupy local veto points. The politics, it bears mention, have cut both ways. Throughout the post–New Deal era and well into the 1970s, wholesale preemption was the agenda of the labor movement, which believed that no good would come from allowing employer interests to escape from the National Labor Relations Board into the states. In the wake of the deregulatory initiatives of the 1980s, the fronts reversed. Proregulatory constituencies discovered state liability law and state attorneys general as access points for their agendas, and corporate interests came to rely on federal preemption as an increasingly vital line of defense. Daniel M. Troy presents a spirited take on federal preemption in the context of prescription drugs and medical devices, where the fight over tort preemption has been fought with particular ferocity on all sides. But as Samuel Issacharoff and Catherine Sharkey's essay shows, the constellation of forces has been much the same in other regulatory areas.

Many of our contributors offer innovative proposals to revamp preemption regimes and doctrines in this contested field. Hal Scott urges an exclusive federal charter for insurance and a withering away of state bank charters. Dan Troy pleads for more aggressive federal agency preemption of state-based liability claims. Thomas Merrill proposes judicial preemption "default rules," derived from preexisting legal materials. Ernest Young advocates a more explicit—and generous—recognition of federalism interests in preemption cases. Robert Gasaway and Ashley Parrish advance a specific proposal to streamline the conceptual apparatus of preemption law. As already threatened, our Conclusion will present our own take on those proposals and the broader controversy, but we end our Introduction on the functionalist note on which we began. The Madisonian problems—to sort federal and state functions in some coherent fashion and to reduce the potential for factional abuse—are still with us. After the New Deal, the traditional, constitutional doctrines did no longer, and perhaps could no longer, organize this set of problems. Preemption and its corollaries must now serve as substitutes—a presumption against preemption *in lieu* of enumerated powers constraints, implied preemption *in lieu* of exclusive federal jurisdiction. One suspects that something gets lost in the translation and that the function of preemption to substitute for a good chunk of the old constitutional architecture puts an awful lot of weight on the doctrine— perhaps, more weight than it will bear in any form or shape. Again, we shall withhold our judgment for the Conclusion. But the central status of preemption doctrine amply warrants the broad-ranging and in-depth examination in the following essays.

Notes

*This chapter has benefited from spirited comments at a work-in-progress session at the University of Chicago and a legal history workshop at New York University Law School. Our thanks to Corina Wilder, University of Chicago Law School, class of 2008, for her excellent research assistance.

1. See Funk & Wagnalls *New Comprehensive International Dictionary of the English Language*, 9994 (1982).

2. Caleb Nelson, *Preemption*, 86 Va. L. Rev. 225 (2000).

3. Alexander Hamilton, *The Federalist* 15 (Indianapolis: Liberty Fund, George Carey and James McClellan, ed. 2001) 71.

4. Iraqi Const., art. 117, cl. 2 (United Nations translation, available at http://portal.unesco.org/ci/en/files/20704/11332732681iraqi_constitution_en.pdf/iraqi_constitution_en.pdf).

5. Cooperative fiscal arrangements have also come to govern large areas of regulation and administration in the United States. State and local government must not only not violate but affirmatively enforce federal mandates on education, environmental policy, etc. But those areas are governed by principles of contract and unconstitutional conditions—precisely not by supremacy. See, *e.g.*, *Pennhurst State Sch. and Hosp. v. Halderman*, 451 U.S. 1, 17 (1981) (conditional funding arrangements are "in the nature of a contract"). See also David E. Engdahl, *The Spending Power*, 44 Duke L.J. 1 (1994).

6. James Madison, *The Federalist* 39, 199; James Madison, *The Federalist* 45, 241.

7. It is not entirely clear whether Madison really envisioned a requirement of congressional *preapproval*. His Negative was modeled largely on earlier colonial practice, whereby the privy council could set aside colonial laws for any reason. The privy council regime held laws to be in force until negated and respected the validity of all acts taken subsequent to passage and prior to negation. Under that system the default is set in favor of the validity of state action, so that it becomes ever harder to invalidate a law the longer it has been in effect. Most convention delegates, however, appear to have understood Madison as insisting on congressional preapproval; for example, they wondered aloud about the fate of state laws left in limbo while Congress was not in session. Madison himself mused that the Negative might require an "emanation" of the federal government in the states (most likely, a kind of federal proconsul), and he tried to meet the delegates' practical objections by suggesting that the Negative could allow for exceptions in cases of emergencies. These discussions make sense only on the "prior approval" interpretation. For good discussions of the Madisonian Negative and its fate at the convention, see Charles F. Hobson, *The Negative on State Laws: James Madison, the Constitution, and the Crisis of Republican Government*, 36 Wm. & Mary Qtr'y 215 (1979); Larry D. Kramer, *Madison's Audience*, 112 Harv. L. Rev. 611 (1999). For a somewhat longer exposition of our discussion in these pages, see Michael S. Greve, *Compacts, Cartels, and Congressional Consent*, 68 Mo. L. Rev. 285, 310–19 (2003).

8. See generally Saul Levmore, *Bicameralism: When Are Two Decisions Better Than One?* 12 Int'l Rev. L. & Econ. 145 (1992); John McGinnis & Michael Rapaport, *Our Supermajoritarian Constitution*, 80 Tex. L. Rev. 703 (2002).

9. *Martin v. Hunter's Lessee*, 14 U.S. 304 (1816); *Cohens v. Virginia*, 19 U.S. 264 (1821).

10. Richard A. Epstein, *The Federalist Papers: From Practical Politics to High Principle*, 16 Harv. J. Law & Pub. Policy 13 (1993).

11. Max Farrand, ed., "Madison's Notes, July 17, 1787," 2 *The Records of the Federal Convention of 1787* (New Haven: Yale University Press, rev. ed. 1937) 28.

12. Admittedly, this correspondence to an internal-external distinction is imperfect. The prohibition against *ex post facto* laws, for example, would appear to protect most-ly in-staters. The Contracts Clause is ambiguous: it can be viewed as a somewhat overbroad protection against state aggression against out-of-state debtors (Hamilton's take on the clause in *The Federalist* 7, 31) or as a protection of private rights against state governments (Madison's account in *The Federalist* 44, 232). See Michael McConnell, *Contract Rights and Property Rights: A Case Study in the Relationship Between Individual Liberties and Constitutional Structure*, 76 Cal. L. Rev. 267, 283–93 (1988). Still, the general pattern is clear.

13. Jack N. Rakove, ed., "Letter from James Madison to Thomas Jefferson (Oct. 24, 1787)," *James Madison: Writings* (New York: Library of America, 1999) 146.

14. See Charles Tiebout, *A Pure Theory of Local Expenditures*, 64 J. Pol. Econ. 416 (1956). On the constitutional role of exit rights, see Richard A. Epstein, *Exit Rights Under Federalism*, 55 Law & Contemp. Prob. 147 (Winter, 1992).

15. The distinction survives to this day in some contexts, but only as a matter of statutory law rather than constitutional taxonomy. See, *e.g.*, *FERC v. Mississippi*, 456 U.S. 742 (1982); *New York v. FERC*, 535 U.S. 1 (2002) (FERC regulations pursuant to the Federal Power Act exclude concurrent state authority).

16. *N.Y. Cent. R.R. v. Winfield*, 244 U.S. 147, 169 (1917).

17. See *Wickard v. Filburn*, 317 U.S. 111 (1942).

18. In *Woodruff v. Parham*, 75 U.S. 123 (1868), the Supreme Court held that the clause applies only to foreign commerce, not interstate commerce. It is certainly true that the Import-Export Clause was in part intended to protect the federal monopoly over foreign tariffs, but the contention that the clause applies exclusively to foreign commerce is almost certainly wrong. *Camps Newfound/Owatonna v. Harrison*, 520 U.S. 564, 624-37 (1997) (Thomas, J., dissenting).

19. See, *e.g.*, *Gibbons v. Ogden*, 22 U.S. 1 at 203 (1824).

20. *Brown v. Maryland*, 25 U.S. 419 (1827).

21. *Smith v. Turner (The Passenger Cases)*, 48 U.S. (7 How.) 283, 403 (1849).

22. *Cooley v. Bd. of Wardens*, 53 U.S. (12 How.) 299, 311–14 (1851).

23. *Sinnot v. Davenport*, 63 U.S. 227, 243 (1859); *Davis v. Elmira Sav. Bank*, 161 U.S. 275, 283 (1896).

24. The *Shreveport Rate Cases* 234 U.S. 342 (1914) made it clear that any Congress could regulate local lines that were in competition with national ones. Later, in

Wis. R.R. Comm'n v. Chicago Burlington & Quincy R.R., 257 U.S. 563 (1922), the Court allowed federal rate regulation of all intrastate lines whether or not in competition with the interstate routes.

25. See, *e.g.*, Thomas Reed Powell, *State Income Taxes and the Commerce Clause*, 31 Yale L.J. 799 (1922).

26. Richard A. Epstein, *The Proper Scope of the Commerce Power*, 73 Va. L. Rev. 1387 (1987); Richard A. Epstein, *The Cartelization of Commerce*, 22 Harv. J. Law & Pub. Policy 209 (1998); Richard A. Epstein, *How Progressives Rewrote the Constitution* (Washington: Cato, 2006) 19–35.

27. James Madison, *The Federalist* 10, 47.

28. See Frank Easterbrook, *The State of Madison's Vision of the State*, 107 Harv. L. Rev. 1328 (1994).

29. Robert Jackson, *The Struggle for Judicial Supremacy: A Study of a Crisis in American Power Politics* (New York: Alfred A. Knopf, 1941) 160.

30. *Rice v. Santa Fe Elevator*, 331 U.S. 218, 230 (1947) (citations omitted).

31. See, *e.g.*, *H.P. Hood v. DuMond*, 336 U.S. 525 (1949).

32. Henry Melvin Hart and Herbert Wechsler, "Preface to the First Edition," *The Federal Courts and the Federal System* (New York: Foundation Press, 2003) (1953) ix.

33. *Wong Yang Sung v. McGrath*, 339 U.S. 33, 40 (1950).

34. *Rice*, 331 U.S. at 242–45.

35. Ibid. at 230–31.

36. See Justice Scalia's opinions in *Cipollone v. Liggett Group*, 505 U.S. 504, 544–56 (1992); *AT&T Corp. v. Iowa Utils. Bd.*, 525 U.S. 366, 379 (1999).

37. See *Parker v. Brown*, 317 U.S. 341 (1943).

38. *Calif. Div. of Labor Stds. Enfc't v. Dillingham Constr.*, 519 U.S. 316, 335 (Scalia, J., concurring).

39. *Aetna Health v. Davila*, 542 U.S. 200 (2004); and *Pegram v. Herdrich*, 530 U.S. 211 (2000).

40. *Geier v. Am. Honda Motor Co.*, 529 U.S. 861, 867–68 (2000); *Sprietsma v. Mercury Me.*, 537 U.S. 51, 962–64 (2002).

PART I

Constitutional Context

1

Federal Displacement of State Law: The Nineteenth-Century View

Viet D. Dinh

The word "preempt" only entered the constitutional lexicon when Justice Louis Brandeis used it in a dissenting opinion in 1917.[1] Borrowing from a long-standing aspect of property law that favored the first developers of unoccupied land,[2] he turned it into a metaphor for the relationship of overlapping state and federal law. Thus, throughout the nineteenth century, the Court did not speak to "preemption doctrine" as such, but rather framed the question more broadly, as part of the constitutional division of authority between the federal and state governments.

In examining the federal-state constitutional structure and, more specifically, the circumstances under which federal law supersedes state law, the Court dealt with three separate strands of analysis. First, the Court aimed to discern the scope of constitutional authority possessed by the federal government. The Court spoke of federal legislation "superseding" state law (harkening back to the language of repeals)[3] because constitutionally authorized acts of Congress were "paramount" over contrary state action through the Supremacy Clause.[4] Second, the Court wrestled with whether Congress had been granted "exclusive" authority over a given topic. Finally, the Court sought to protect the states' reserved police power by deciding whether an actual conflict between federal and state law existed that warranted superseding the state law.

This terminology signifies more than simply a semantic difference with modern preemption doctrine. Displacement analysis in the nineteenth century focused on the Supremacy Clause and constitutional structure rather than congressional intent. The landmark case of *Gibbons v. Ogden* (1824), the

Supreme Court's first major foray into the world of preemption, explores these three major doctrinal strands with which the Court—and the nation— was struggling. Over time these three separate inquiries became closely intertwined. It is unhelpful to impose anachronistically the current spectrum of specific categories of state law displacement upon the early doctrinal developments in this field.[5] However, as these three doctrinal strands are explored, first in *Gibbons*, and then in the subsequent nineteenth-century cases, the precursors to modern preemption doctrine emerge.

Stripped of the modern judicial gloss, the constitutional structure demarcating the division of federal and state legislative authority is straightforward: Article I, Section 8 enumerates the powers of Congress; Article I, Section 9 limits the powers of Congress; Article I, Section 10 limits the powers of the states; and the Tenth Amendment reserves to the states the legislative powers not delegated to Congress and prohibited to the states. Since this structure did not divide every power neatly between federal and state legislatures, Article VI established that "the Laws of the United States which shall be made in Pursuance [to the Constitution] . . . shall be the supreme Law of the Land . . . any Thing in the Constitution or Laws of any state to the Contrary notwithstanding." The Supremacy Clause, as this provision is known, requires courts to favor federal law over state law if there should be a conflict. The Court's decisions in the nineteenth century manifest its attempt to understand and delineate the function and application of this constitutional structure.

A review of the constitutional structure is instructive because it serves as a reminder that Congress was given no express power to void state laws. This is all the more significant because such a power was proposed and rejected at the Constitutional Convention.[6] Governor Edmund Randolph's proposal on May 29, 1787, which became known as the Virginia Plan, listed among the powers to be given to Congress the authority "to negative all laws passed by the several States, contravening in the opinion of the National Legislature the articles of Union."[7] The resolution containing this power was adopted without debate or dissent after minor changes and exceptions on May 31, 1787, by the committee of the whole House.[8] On June 15, 1787, William Patterson introduced an alternative set of resolutions which became known as the New Jersey Plan. No authority to negate state law was included in the resolution granting affirmative powers to

Congress.[9] Instead, a separate resolution, following the resolution concerning the judiciary, offered a concept very similar to what became the Supremacy Clause.[10]

The competing proposals were directly discussed when the convention debated the report of the committee of the whole House. Madison warned against the "propensity of the States to pursue their particular interests in opposition to the general interest" and advocated "the negative on the laws of the States as essential to the efficacy & security of the Genl. Govt."[11] Governor Robert Morris of Pennsylvania objected to a congressional negative power because "[a] law that ought to be negatived will be set aside in the Judiciary departmt. and if that security should fail; may be repealed by a Nationl. Law."[12] In consequence, Randolph's proposal for a legislative power to negative state laws was defeated by a vote of three to seven.[13] By unanimous consent the convention immediately adopted an alternative proposal by Luther Martin, similar in substance to Patterson's sixth resolution and almost identical in form to the Supremacy Clause.[14] Subtle modifications in the Committee of Detail and the Committee on Style and Alteration gave us the clause as we know it.[15]

The Supremacy Clause thus does nothing to indicate an additional grant of authority to Congress; instead it sets forth the hierarchy between federal and state laws, serving as a constitutional rule to resolve conflicts between those laws. For state law to be displaced, either the Constitution must have excluded state action by granting the power to Congress alone, or congressional action pursuant to an affirmative grant of power under article I, section 8 must conflict with the state law. In either case, the Constitution requires the Court to disregard the state law.

Federal Authority and Supremacy

The supremacy strain of state law displacement received its most significant foundation with *Gibbons v. Ogden* (1824). New York had granted a monopoly on the use of steamboats in the state's rivers. Thomas Gibbons, a citizen of New Jersey who had a coasting license under Congress' Federal Navigation Act of 1793, was held by state courts to have violated the monopoly. He appealed to the Supreme Court, arguing that the federal law conflicted with and trumped the state monopoly. The issues presented in *Gibbons* were several fold: first, did Congress have the requisite authority, under the Commerce Clause, to pass the Navigation Act? Assuming that Congress has such authority, may it pass the Act in contravention of the state's monopoly grant of police power?

John Marshall's opinion for the Court decided the case as a conflict between the federal licensing law and the state monopoly. The important question, he declared, was "whether the laws of New-York . . . come into collision with an act of Congress."[16] If they did, "the act of Congress . . . is supreme; and the law of the State, though enacted in the exercise of powers not controverted [by the Constitution], must yield to it."[17] To determine whether the federal act did indeed conflict, Marshall turned to statutory construction—deciding whether "license" meant permission and entitlement to trade or merely, as Ogden argued, conferred an American identity. The Court held that Congress had the power to pass the Navigation Act (and thus to issue the license to Ogden) under the Commerce Clause; that is, Congress had acted within its scope of power over commerce, an area under which federal law, by way of the Supremacy Clause, displaces state law—at least so far as the two conflict. Here, it would be impossible to comply with both the state and federal law.

Modern familiarity with both the case and the concept of supremacy make it difficult to appreciate the full weight of this decision. The five-day oral argument by the finest advocates of that day is a reminder of how unsettled this principle was at the time.[18] A concurring opinion suggests that there was no need to find a conflict between the laws at all.[19] Nevertheless, both the authority of Congress to regulate interstate commerce and the authority of the Court to employ the Supremacy Clause against states were confirmed. However, no other state laws were struck down during Marshall's time on the Court.[20]

One of the first cases to come before Marshall's successor, Roger Taney, received much different treatment. In *City of New York v. Miln* (1837), the Court went out of its way to avoid a "collision" analysis.[21] At issue was a state law which required all ships arriving at the New York City harbor to provide a list of passengers and to post a bond against those passengers becoming public charges. The Court rejected a Commerce Clause challenge to the law on the "impregnable" ground that the state law was a proper exercise of the state's "police power," not a commercial regulation.[22] Refusing to base its decision on the Supremacy Clause, the Court nevertheless distinguished *Gibbons* on the ground that, "in this [case], no such collision exists."[23] Petitioner had argued that two federal laws created a conflict—one of which required a list of passengers and cargo for revenue purposes and another of which required documentation of identifying information about passengers to be submitted to the secretary of state for record-keeping. The Court opined that there was no conflict between these provisions: first, for the rather formalistic reason that the federal laws operated on the voyage, but the state law operated once the passengers disembarked; second, because the purposes of the state and federal laws were different. Justice Joseph Story dissented on the ground that the commerce power was exclusively granted to Congress and claimed that Marshall would have joined him had he lived.[24]

Confusion about federal exclusivity of the commerce power led to extraordinarily splintered decisions in the *License Cases* (1847)[25] and the *Passenger Cases* (1849),[26] temporarily distracting from Supremacy Clause analysis. If the commerce power meant that only Congress could act on any subject within that field, then no conflicts would arise under the Supremacy Clause because all state laws would be displaced by the Constitution itself.

However, in 1851, *Cooley v. Board of Wardens* brought coherence to Commerce Clause doctrine and ensured a significant role for conflict analysis for the future.[27] At issue was a state regulation requiring all ships entering the port of Philadelphia to take on a local pilot or pay a fee. Justice Benjamin Robbins Curtis concluded that there was no conflict with any federal laws because Congress' "legislation manifests an intention, with a single exception, not to regulate this subject, but to leave its regulation to the several states."[28]

After *Cooley*, conflict analysis under the Supremacy Clause became actively used to strike down state law. In *Sinnot v. Davenport* (1859),[29] the same federal licensing statute that was important in *Gibbons* became an issue again. Alabama required vessels in its waters to file a statement identifying each vessel and its owners. Suit was brought claiming the state law conflicted with the similar requirements of the federal statute. The Court struck down the state law, declaring, "it can require no argument to show a direct conflict between this act of the State and the act of Congress regulating this trade."[30] Despite the bold assertion, there is a subtle shift in reasoning. Unlike the situation in *Gibbons*, an individual could have complied with both laws. With *Davenport*, redundancy became a ground for conflict. Seeking to lay to rest the idea still flowing from *Miln*, that exercises of state police power should be given special status even when they conflicted with federal law, the Court asserted that the Supremacy Clause applied without regard to the source of the state power.[31] However, in what appears to be conciliatory dicta—that would later be used to create a "presumption against preemption"—the Court declared:

> We agree, that in the application of this principle of supremacy of an act of Congress in a case where the State law is but the exercise of a reserved power, the repugnance or conflict should be direct and positive, so that the two acts could not be reconciled or consistently stand together. . . . [32]

Nevertheless, the presumption against preemption would take significant time to develop.

The foregoing discussion should not lead one to believe that the only power relevant in supremacy cases was the commerce power. The Court had very early ruled several other of the Constitution's affirmative grants to Congress to be nonexclusive. For example, the power to establish a uniform bankruptcy system was held not to bar state action discharging the payment of debts in *Ogden v. Saunders* (1827), over Marshall's dissent. Congress episodically passed bankruptcy statutes that displaced state law, but even while the federal laws were in force the Court was unsympathetic to parties who sought to construe the Bankruptcy Act so broadly as to require striking down only tangentially related state laws.[33] Even after the Bankruptcy Act of 1898 established the continuous presence of federal law on the topic, it was still noted that "state laws are thus suspended only to the extent of actual conflict with the system provided by the Bankruptcy Act of Congress."[34]

The level of conflict necessary to strike down a state law became somewhat ambiguous. In 1847, Justice Levi Woodbury suggested in his separate opinion in the *License Cases* that conflicts should only be found in the clearest circumstances, an "actual collision."[35] Similar language is repeated as late as 1912.[36] Yet, the Court simultaneously seemed eager to construe conflicts. In *Pensacola Telegraph Co. v. Western Union Telegraph Co.* (1877),[37] the Court interpreted a federal law permitting companies to use the "public domain" along post roads and across navigable waterways for telegraph lines extraordinarily broadly. Florida had granted a monopoly to one company in the state, which the Court struck down, declaring that the federal statute "substantially declares . . . that the erection of telegraph lines shall, so far as State interference is concerned, be free to all who will submit to the conditions imposed by Congress."[38]

By the end of the century, even broader language began to creep into opinions. In *Davis v. Elmira Savings Bank* (1896),[39] while comparing state and federal laws concerning insolvent banks, the Court described an express conflict as that which "either frustrates the purpose of the national legislation or impairs the efficiency of these agencies of the federal government to discharge the duties for the performance of which they were created."[40] This seems like needless dicta because the statutes covered virtually the same ground and thus could have been found to conflict regardless, but it demonstrates how much more capacious a concept conflict supremacy had become. This broader concept of conflict, as explored later in this chapter, led haltingly toward what is now known as obstacle preemption.

Exclusivity

Throughout the nineteenth century, the Court faced the difficulty of identifying which topics were granted exclusively to the federal legislature, first in broad strokes and later in finer detail. Directly facing the question for the first time in *Sturges v. Crowninshield* (1819),[41] the Court distinguished between concurrent and exclusive powers of Congress. A creditor challenged a New York insolvency statute, claiming the constitutional provision that Congress could "establish . . . uniform Laws on the subject of Bankruptcies throughout the United States" should bar states from setting up their own systems.[42] While the law was ultimately struck down as a violation of the Contracts Clause, Justice Marshall concluded that there was no conflict under the Bankruptcy Clause because Congress had not yet chosen to act on its authority: "It is not the mere existence of the power, but its exercise, which is incompatible with the exercise of the same power by the states. It is not the right to establish these uniform laws, but their actual establishment, which is inconsistent with the partial acts of the states."[43] In doing so, he confirmed the idea that the states retained concurrent power with Congress over some topics, at least until Congress acted.[44]

In *Gibbons v. Ogden*, Marshall expanded on both the conflict analysis under the Supremacy Clause and the exclusiveness of the commerce power which would become so significant later. He observed that Congress's power over commerce "is complete in itself, may be exercised to its utmost extent, and acknowledges no limitations, other than are prescribed in the Constitution."[45] He stopped short of deciding "whether this power is still in the States . . . whether it is surrendered by the mere grant to Congress, or is retained until Congress shall exercise the power"[46] because Congress had, in fact, acted. Even without a specific holding on the issue, however, *Gibbons* is considered the foundation of the "dormant Commerce Clause." In the very brief decision in *Willson v. Black Bird Creek Marsh Co.* (1829), Marshall again referenced without ruling on the idea that a state law could be "considered as repugnant to the power to regulate commerce in its dormant state."[47] Twenty years later, when the majority in *City of New York v. Miln* grounded their decision on the special status of police powers, Justice Story wrote a vigorous dissent that sought to establish Marshall's dicta in *Gibbons*.[48] He would have held that the commerce power was exclusive and that states had no authority to regulate it regardless of Congress' action.

The confusion over Commerce Clause exclusivity lasted for some time. Part of the difficulty was that the language of the clause does not indicate exclusivity.[49] In the *License Cases* (1847), a splintered set of opinions upholding state restrictions on alcohol sales, at least four judges asserted that the commercial power was concurrent and limited only by conflict with federal law.[50] Two years later in the *Passenger Cases*, the Court, still splintered, struck down the laws of two states that charged a fee for every passenger brought to the state by ship. This time, three justices argued that the commerce power was exclusive, and three justices expressly rejected that view in favor of concurrent power.[51]

In 1851, the Court resolved the question of exclusivity in *Cooley v. Board of Wardens*: "Whatever subjects of this power are in their nature national, or admit only of one uniform system, or plan of regulation, may justly be said to be of such a nature as to require exclusive legislation by Congress."[52] Thus, wherever uniform regulation is desirable—specifically in areas where competition would impede economic efficiency and interstate commerce—the federal government has exclusive jurisdiction. (In these situations, the cost of a lack of uniform regulation outweighs the localized benefits that come with state regulation.) There remain, however, areas where state authority and policy experimentation would lead to beneficial differentiation and competition. These subjects, those that are local and where legislative discretion is appropriate—such as the pilot statute at issue in the case—are governed by conflict under the Supremacy Clause rather than exclusivity.[53]

This discussion augured what is now known as the dormant Commerce Clause. The *Cooley* Court construed the Constitution, apart from any action of Congress, to prohibit state intervention into a portion of the interstate commerce category. Yet, it also permitted concurrent power over similar state actions if the "nature" of the subject did not require national uniformity. This attempt to balance the sort of state laws displaced by the Constitution and federal law continued the pattern already begun. The police power distinction from *Miln* had comparable uses, although it was designed to protect the states from excessive action by Congress. And the later distinction between "direct" and "indirect" effects of state regulation of interstate commerce, while more oriented toward impact, still recognized that most state actions should not be voidable under the Commerce Clause.[54]

A common refrain in conflict analysis became that the statutes "cover the same ground."[55] Perhaps because exclusivity and conflict analysis under the Supremacy Clause had long been related inquiries, the Court also began to conflate them into what some scholars have called "latent exclusivity."[56] This exclusion is not triggered by the national nature of the action, but by the mere fact that Congress has acted. Whether this is best viewed as an expansive view of "conflict" or whether it is a species of exclusivity is frequently muddled by the language. In *Waite v. Dowley* (1876), for example, the Court upheld a state statute requiring a yearly list of the shareholders in a bank that had been challenged because a federal law required a similar list.[57] Addressing whether the two statutes "covered the same ground," the Court concluded they did not because the purposes were different—taxation versus public knowledge. The Court justified its conclusion by pointing out the necessity of nuance: "[T]he line which divides what is occupied exclusively by any legislation of Congress from what is left open to the action of the States is not always well defined, and is often distinguished by such nice shades of difference on each side as to require the closest scrutiny when the principle is invoked, as it is in this case."[58]

Constitutional exclusion and the broad form of exclusion based on congressional action seem linked in the perspective of the Court, particularly in the context of minimalist economic regulation. This is most evident during the period from 1912 to 1933.[59] For example, in *Leisy v. Hardin* (1890), the Court asserted that "inasmuch as interstate commerce . . . is national in its character, and must be governed by a uniform system, so long as Congress does not pass any law to regulate it, or allowing the States so to do, it thereby indicates its will that such commerce be free and untrammeled."[60]

Conflict: Actual and Implied

The third strand of *Gibbons* deals with the collisions that inevitably arise between federal and state law in areas where the two have concurrent jurisdiction. The nature of the conflict necessary for state law to be displaced has received various answers. Two cases very early in the Court's history suggest a greater breadth than was generally employed. In 1819, the Court decided *McCulloch v. Maryland*, striking down a state attempt to tax the Bank of the United States on the ground that: "States have no power . . . to retard, impede, burden, or in any manner control, the operations of the constitutional laws enacted by Congress."[61] The underlying theory seems to be that federal common law reveals an inherent prohibition on state taxation of federal objects.

An 1820 case by a divided court, *Houston v. Moore*, hints at future developments. A state law imposed a penalty on any militiaman who did not appear when ordered by the president, and a man who was prosecuted under the law argued that only federal law should apply. Justice Bushrod Washington wrote for the Court, upholding the law on the ground that Congress had not yet granted exclusive jurisdiction over military matters to federal courts martial (since they were not covered by the Judiciary Act of 1789), so states retained concurrent jurisdiction until Congress chose to act. However, he rejected "the novel and unconstitutional doctrine, that in cases where the State governments have a concurrent power of legislation with the national government, the states may legislate upon any subject on which Congress has acted, provided the two laws are not in terms, or in their operation, contradictory and repugnant to each other."[62] Washington's view would have dramatically enlarged Court responsibility for reviewing state laws.[63] It is unclear on what he based his view or how he thought the Court could distinguish between state and federal authority. Two justices concurred to make clear that they disagreed with the idea that concurrent power ended once Congress had acted on the issue. Justice William Johnson wrote against:

> . . . the exploded doctrine, that within the scope in which Congress may legislate, the States shall not legislate. That they cannot, when legislating within that ceded region of power, run counter to the laws of Congress, is denied by no one; but . . . to reason against the exercise of this power from the possible abuse of it, is not for a court of justice. When instances of this opposition occur, it will be time enough to meet them.[64]

Justice Story also remonstrated against the idea "that mere grant of such powers in affirmative terms to Congress, does, per se, transfer an exclusive sovereignty on such subjects to the latter."[65]

There is no hint of Washington's perspective again until Justice Story, flipping sides, affirms it in dicta for the majority in *Prigg v. Pennsylvania* (1842). In a case very much the product of the tensions that would lead up to the Civil War, the Court struck down a state law that criminalized seizing a fugitive slave on the ground that "the power of legislation upon this subject is exclusive in the national government."[66] Opponents of the law had advanced two other reasons to strike the law down: 1) the fact that Congress passed a statute on the subject of fugitives "suspended" any concurrent power of the states; 2) a direct collision exists between the state law and act of Congress. Justice Story, although basing the decision on exclusivity, wrote approvingly of the suspension argument:

> This doctrine was fully recognized by this court, in the case of *Houston v. Moore*; where it was expressly held, that where congress have exercised a power over a particular subject given by

the constitution, it is not competent for state legislation to add
to the provisions of congress upon that subject.[67]

Justice Roger B. Taney and two other justices would have grounded the
decision in the conflict with actual federal laws, while writing in favor of state
concurrent power "provided the state law is not in conflict with the remedy
provided by congress."[68] Justice McLean concurred on the exclusivity argument, rejecting any notion of concurrent power.[69] His opinion suggests that
he would have tried to avoid any use of the Supremacy Clause to resolve conflicts between state and federal law.[70] The multiplicity of opinions on this case
indicates the overlap and blurring of the supremacy and exclusivity analyses.

A decade later, in *Cooley*, this intertwining of analyses persisted. Justice
Curtis wrote the majority opinion that structured Commerce Clause
jurisprudence for the remainder of the century. In doing so, he expressly
reserved several questions that had been hotly debated, including the core
idea of field preemption, declaring that "[this opinion] does not extend to
the . . . general question how far any regulation of a subject by Congress,
may be deemed to operate as an exclusion of all legislation by the states
upon the same subject."[71] Thereafter, occasional cases would hint at the
possibility that congressional action covered a wider field than the express
terms of the law,[72] but none grounded their decision upon it. Sometimes
the Court would claim that only supremacy applied.[73] The Court even
seemed to express both perspectives at once:

> It should never be held that Congress intends to supersede or by
> its legislation suspend the exercise of the police powers of the
> States, even when it may do so, unless its purpose to effect that
> result is clearly manifested. This Court has said—and the prin-
> ciple has been often reaffirmed—that "in the application of this
> principle of supremacy of an act of Congress in a case where the
> State law is but the exercise of a reserved power, the repugnance
> or conflict should be direct and positive, so that the two acts
> could not be reconciled or consistently stand together."[74]

The Court's decision in *Sinnot v. Davenport* added yet another dimension
to the displacement analysis: redundancy. Again, as in *Gibbons*, the federal

licensing statute's applicability was challenged by the imposition of an Alabama state law with a similar purpose. Although compliance with both statutes was not an impossibility, the Alabama law was superseded because of the redundancy that application of both statutes would entail. *Davenport* thus expanded the scope of a direct conflict between federal and state law.[75]

Davenport marks the formative beginnings of the concept of latent exclusivity. According to this doctrine, in those domains in which federal law is not exclusive, when a congressional act covers the same ground as a state law, the state law yields and is superseded by federal law. Thus, the mere exercise of power by Congress is sufficient to displace state law on certain matters.

Finally, in *Southern Railway Co. v. Reid* (1912), the Court directly employed the field preemption idea when striking down a state statute regarding railroad rates after creation of the Interstate Commerce Commission:

> There is no contention that the Commission has acted, so we must look to the act. Does it, as contended by plaintiff in error, take control of the subject-matter and impose affirmative duties upon the carriers which the state cannot even supplement? In other words, has Congress taken possession of the field?[76]

Note the absence of recourse to congressional intent throughout the majority of the nineteenth century. Not until the 1930s did the Court begin explicitly to rely on purpose rather than structural analysis, but *Davenport* and *Reid* indicate the Court's progression toward congressional intent as the basis for analysis. The Court is prompted to examine areas where Congress has acted to "[take] possession of the field,"[77] thus begging the questions: What is the scope of federal law? What is the ground that the federal law seeks to cover? Thus, the Court must look to Congress's intent to answer those questions. This became necessary to allow interlocking layers of regulation.

Conclusion

The Court's nineteenth-century decisions attempted to understand and delineate the constitutional structure of powers delegated to federal and state governments. This structural analysis defined the Court's nineteenth-century approach to federal displacement of state law. The Court had three major tasks in this realm, each preliminarily explored in *Gibbons v. Ogden* and further developed throughout the century. First, the Court attempted to discern what level of constitutional authority the federal government holds— to define in which spheres the federal law remains "supreme" over state law. Where federal law and state law conflict, the Supremacy Clause mandates that the federal law displaces or preempts that of the state. Next, the Court demarcated those areas of law over which the federal government holds exclusive control. Based upon the powers explicitly delegated to Congress, it was clear that the federal government retains sole authority over certain areas of law, such as interstate commerce, but the Court was compelled to define the boundaries of these areas of law. Lastly, the Court was tasked with protecting the states' pervasive police power, particularly when it conflicted with federal law. This forced the Court to examine whether the laws actually conflicted, or whether it was possible for them to coexist. By the end of the century, as the Court continued to develop these three strands, with each federal law the Court was prompted to ask: What is the scope that this law is intended to cover? Did Congress intend that this law replace state law on the subject matter? May the two laws coexist? Thus, the end of the century suggests the emergence of modern preemption doctrine, which focuses more on an examination of congressional intent and less on inherent constitutional structure and authority.

Notes

1. See *New York Central R.R. v. Winfeld*, 244 U.S. 147, 169 (1917) (Brandeis, J., dissenting). See also Stephen Gardbaum's essay in this volume.

2. Congress had, from the earliest times, established laws regarding private acquisition of public land that favored those who first settled on and developed the land. See, *e.g., Sweeney's Lessee v. Toner*, 2 U.S. (2 Dall.) 129, 130 (1791); *Buford v. Houtz*, 133 U.S. 320, 327 (1890) ("Congress, by a system of laws called the 'Pre-emption Laws,' . . . confer[red] a priority of the right of purchase on the persons who settled upon and cultivated any part of this public domain.").

3. See Caleb Nelson, *Preemption*, 86 Va. L. Rev. 225, 241 (2000) (describing supersession of state law in relation to repeals doctrine).

4. See, *e.g., Chicago & Nw. R.R. v. Fuller*, 84 U.S. 560, 570 (1873) ("regulations of such a character as to be valid until superseded by the paramount action of Congress"); *Smith*, 48 U.S. at 497–98 ("[T]he very language of the Constitution may be appealed to for the recognition of powers to be exercised by the States, until they shall be superseded by a paramount authority vested in the Federal government.") (Daniel, J., dissenting); *Houston v. Moore*, 18 U.S. 1, 49–50 (1820) ("[I]n cases of concurrent authority, where the laws of the States and of the Union are in direct and manifest collision on the same subject, those of the Union being 'the supreme law of the land,' are of paramount authority, and the State laws, so far, and so far only, as such incompatibility exists, must necessarily yield.") (Story, J., dissenting). See also Stephen Gardbaum, *The Nature of Preemption*, 79 Cornell L. Rev. 767, 789 (1994) ("Both before [1917] and up until the 1940s, the term 'superseded' was generally used to describe the phenomenon."); ibid. at 802 ("Time and again, the Court stated that its preemption doctrine resulted from the "paramount" power that the Supremacy Clause grants to Congress over interstate commerce.").

5. For a critical analysis of the current state of that spectrum, see Viet D. Dinh, *Reassessing the Law of Preemption*, 88 Geo. L. J. 2085, 2100–13 (2000) (describing "preemption" under the categories of express preemption, conflict preemption, obstacle preemption, field preemption, federal common law, and the dormant Commerce Clause).

6. For a more extensive review of the development of the Supremacy Clause at the Constitutional Convention, see S. Candice Hoke, *Transcending Conventional Supremacy: A Reconstruction of the Supremacy Clause*, 24 Conn. L. Rev. 829, 858–72 (1992); see also Christopher R. Drahozal, *The Supremacy Clause: A Reference Guide to the United States Constitution* (Westport, Conn.: Praeger, 2004) 68–70 (providing a detailed timeline and comparison of the evolution of the clause during the convention).

7. M. Farrand, ed., I *The Records of the Federal Convention of 1787* (New Haven: Yale University Press, rev. ed. 1937) 21. The relevant resolution read in its entirety as follows:

> 6. Resolved that each branch ought to possess the right of originating Acts; that the National Legislature ought to be impowered to enjoy the

Legislative Rights vested in Congress by the Confederation & moreover to legislate in all cases to which the separate States are incompetent, or in which the harmony of the United States may be interrupted by the exercise of individual Legislation; to negative all laws passed by the several States, contravening in the opinion of the National Legislature the articles of Union; and to call forth the force of the Union agst. any member of the Union failing to fulfill its duty under the articles thereof.

8. The vote was nine to zero, with Connecticut divided. Benjamin Franklin successfully proposed to permit Congress to negative all laws inconsistent with treaties of the Union, and the committee postponed consideration of the last clause of the sixth resolution, which is not relevant here. See ibid. at 47.

9. See ibid. at 243.

10. Ibid. at 245. The complete text of the resolution is as follows:

6. Resd. that all Acts of the U. States in Congs. Made by virtue & in pursuance of the powers hereby & by the articles of confederation vested in them, and all Treaties made & ratified under the authority of the U. States shall be the supreme law of the respective States so far forth as those Acts or Treaties shall relate to the said States or their Citizens, and that the Judiciary of the several States shall be bound thereby in their decisions, any thing in the respective laws of the Individual States to the contrary notwithstanding; and that if any State, or any body of men in any State shall oppose or prevent ye. carrying into execution such acts or treaties, the federal Executive shall be authorized to call forth ye power of the Confederated States, or so much thereof as may be necessary to enforce and compel an obedience to such Acts, or an Observance of such Treaties.

11. Farrand, *supra* note 7 at 27. This, of course, was a central Madisonian theme. See ibid. at 169 (June 8, 1787); ibid. at 317 (June 19, 1787).

12. Ibid. at 28.

13. See ibid.

14. Ibid. at 28–29. Luther Martin proposed:

that the Legislative acts of the U.S. made by virtue & in pursuance of the articles of the Union, and all treaties made & ratified under the authority of the U.S. shall be the supreme law of the respective States, as far as those acts or treaties shall relate to the said States, or their Citizens and inhabitants—& that the Judiciaries of the several States shall be bound thereby in their decisions, any thing in the respective laws of the individual States to the contrary notwithstanding.

15. See Hoke, *supra* note 6, at 871-72.

16. *Gibbons*, 22 U.S. at 210.

17. Ibid. at 211. This entailed a rejection of the idea that, "[I]f a law passed by a State, in the exercise of its acknowledged sovereignty, comes into conflict with a law passed by Congress in pursuance of the constitution, they affect the subject, and each other, like equal opposing powers." Ibid. at 210. Even further, "Should this collision exist, it will be immaterial whether those laws were passed . . . in virtue of a power to regulate their domestic trade and police."

18. See Norman R. Williams, *Gibbons*, 79 N.Y.U. L. Rev. 1398, 1411 (2004).

19. See ibid. at 1419 (noting that Johnson's concurring opinion rejected the idea that the Federal Navigation Act had anything to do with the case).

20. See *Willson v. Black Bird Creek Marsh Co.*, 27 U.S. 245 (1829) (upholding a state dam across a navigable waterway even though it could have been construed as contrary to general federal provisions for navigation); ibid. at 252 (Marshall declared perfunctorily, "We do not think the act . . . can, under all the circumstances of the case, be considered as repugnant to the power to regulate commerce in its dormant state, or as being in conflict with any law passed on the subject.").

21. 36 U.S. 102 (1837).

22. See ibid. at 132; ibid. at 139 ("[W]e are of opinion, that the act is not a regulation of commerce, but of police; and that being thus considered, it was passed in the exercise of a power which rightfully belonged to the states."); ibid. at 137 (This is the strongest expression of state authority to act in overlapping ways: "[W]hilst a state is acting within the legitimate scope of its power, as to the end to be attained, it may use whatsoever means, being appropriate to that end, it may think fit; although they may be the same, or so nearly the same, as scarcely to be distinguishable from those adopted by congress, acting under a different power; subject, only, say the court, to this limitation, that in the event of collision, the law of the state must yield to the law of congress.").

23. Ibid. at 136.

24. See ibid. at 161.

25. 46 U.S. (5 How.) 504 (1847).

26. 48 U.S. (7 How.) 283 (1849).

27. See E. Parmalee Prentice and John G. Egan, *The Commerce Clause of the Federal Constitution* (Chicago: Callaghan and Co., 1898) 35 ("Since the decision of *Cooley v. Port Wardens*, the rule therein laid down has, with one important exception [*Smith v. Alabama*, 124 U.S. 465 (1888)], been followed in every case in the Supreme Court upon this subject.").

28. Ibid. at 320. This mid-nineteenth-century decision manifests a step toward the Court's ultimate use of congressional intent as the basis for federal displacement of state law that dominates the Court's twentieth-century opinions.

29. 63 U.S. (22 How.) 227 (1859).

30. Ibid. at 242.

31. Ibid. at 243, 244.

32. *Sinnot*, 63 U.S. at 243. *Mo., Kan. & Tex. Ry. Co. v. Haber,* 169 U.S. 613 (1898) would cite this passage as indication of a "settled rule" that "a statute enacted in execution of a reserved power of the state is not to be regarded as inconsistent with an act of Congress" unless the conflict is so direct they cannot be reconciled. Ibid. at 623. While this seems like a doubtful conclusion in light of the facts of *Davenport*, this interpretation was reaffirmed in *Reid v. Colorado*, 187 U.S. 137, 148 (1902) ("It should never be held that Congress intends to supersede or by its legislation suspend the exercise of the police powers of the states, even when it may do so, unless its purpose to affect that result is clearly manifest."), and all three cases were cited to undergird the assertion in *Savage v. Jones*, 225 U.S. 501 (1912) (upholding a state law that allegedly conflicted with the Food and Drugs Act) that:

> the intent to supersede the exercise by the state of its police power as to matters not covered by the Federal legislation is not to be inferred from the mere fact the Congress has seen fit to circumscribe its regulation and to occupy a limited field. In other words, such intent is not to be implied unless the act of Congress, fairly interpreted, is in actual conflict with the law of the state.

33. See David A. Skeel, Jr., *Bankruptcy Lawyers and the Shape of American Bankruptcy Law*, 67 Fordham L. Rev. 497, 497 (1998); see also *Mayer v. Hellman*, 91 U.S. 496, 502 (1875) (rejecting an invitation to strike down a state law about assignment of a trust to a creditor on the ground that "the statute of Ohio is not an insolvent law in any proper sense of the word," thus the Bankruptcy Act does not "suspend [its] operation").

34. *Stellwagen v. Clum*, 245 U.S. 605, 613 (1918); see, *e.g.*, *In re Watts*, 190 U.S. 1, 27 (1903) (indicating the supremacy of the federal bankruptcy law, yet leaving the door open to some state legislation).

35. *Thurlow v. Massachusetts*, 46 U.S. 504, 618–19 (1847) ("It is not enough to fancy some remote or indirect repugnance to acts of Congress, a 'potential inconvenience,' in order to annul the laws of sovereign States. . . . There must be an actual collision, a direct inconsistency, and that deprecated case of clashing sovereignties, in order to demand the judicial interference of this court to reconcile them.").

36. See *Savage*, 225 U.S. at 533.

37. 96 U.S. (6 Otto) 1 (1878).

38. Ibid. at 12.

39. 161 U.S. 275 (1896).

40. Ibid. at 283.

41. 17 U.S. (4 Wheat) 122, 193 (1819)

42. U.S. Const. art. 1, sec. 8. The alternative basis was the art. I, sec. 10 clause forbidding states to pass a "Law impairing the Obligation of Contracts." The court divided over which ground to use.

43. See 17 U.S. at 195–96 ("[U]ntil the power to pass uniform laws on the subject of bankruptcies be exercised by congress, the states are not forbidden to pass a bankruptcy law.").

44. See ibid. at 193. However, Marshall also noted that there were certain subjects where, even absent congressional action, state power did not exist. "[I]t has never been supposed, that this concurrent power of legislation extended to every possible case in which its exercise by the states has not been expressly prohibited. . . . Whenever the terms in which a power is granted to congress, or the nature of the power, require that it should be exercised exclusively by congress, the subject is as completely taken from the state legislatures, as if they had been expressly forbidden to act on it."

45. *Gibbons*, 22 U.S. at 196.

46. Ibid. at 200.

47. 27 U.S. at 252.

48. 36 U.S. 102, 153-61 (1837) (Story, J., dissenting).

49. See Dinh, *supra* note 5 at 2109.

50. See David P. Currie, *The Constitution in the Supreme Court: Contracts and Commerce, 1836–1864*, 1983 Duke L.J. 471, 500 (1983).

51. Ibid. at 502–3.

52. 53 U.S. 299, 319 (1851).

53. Ibid. at 321.

54. See, *e.g.*, *Wabash, St. Louis & Pacific Ry. Co. v. Illinois*, 118 U.S. 557 (1886) (establishing the direct-indirect distinction); *Leloup v. Mobile*, 127 U.S 640, 648 (1888) ("[R]egulations . . . directly affecting interstate commerce . . . would be an unauthorized interference with the power given to Congress.").

55. See, *e.g.*, *Reid*, 187 U.S. at 150 ("Our conclusion is that the statute of Colorado as here involved does not cover the same ground as the act of Congress, and therefore is not inconsistent with that act."); *N.Y., New Haven & Hartford R.R. Co. v. New York*, 165 U.S. 628, 633 (1897) ("[S]o long as congress deems it wise not to establish regulations on the subject that would displace any inconsistent regulations of the states covering the same ground."); *New York v. Compagnie Generale Transatlantique*, 107 U.S. 59, 63 (1883) ("This legislation covers the same ground as the New York statute, and they cannot coexist.").

56. See David E. Engdahl, *Preemptive Capability of Federal Power*, 45 U. Colo. L. Rev. 51, 53 (1973); Gardbaum's essay in this volume.

57. 94 U.S. (4 Otto) 527 (1876).

58. Ibid. at 533.

59. See Stephen Gardbaum, *Congress's Power to Preempt the States*, 33 Pepp. L. Rev. 39, 47–48 (2005).

60. *Leisy v. Hardin*, 135 U.S. 100, 109 (1890). See also *In re Rahrer*, 140 U.S. 545 (1891). See also, *e.g.*, *Covington & Covington Bridge Co. v. Kentucky*, 154 U.S. 204, 212 (1894) ("[W]herever such laws . . . are national in their character, the nonaction of congress indicates its will that such commerce shall be free and untrammeled.");

Parkersburg & Ohio River Transp. Co. v. Parkersburg, 107 U.S. 691, 702 (1883) (upholding reasonable fee for wharves but noting that in issues of national character, "the non-action or silence of congress will be deemed to be an indication of its will that no exaction or restraint be imposed"); Noel T. Dowling, *Interstate Commerce and State Power*, 27 Va. L. Rev. 1, 6 (1940) (commented that this is more revolutionary than it sounds because, unlike *Cooley*, "if the subject were held 'national,' a congressional negative would be presumed rather than a constitutional prohibition applied").

61. *McCulloch v. Maryland*, 17 U.S. 316, 436 (1819). In *U.S. Term Limits, Inc. v. Thornton*, 514 U.S. 779, 854 (1995) (Thomas, J., dissenting), Justice Clarence Thomas described the later case of *Osborn v. Bank of U.S.*, 22 U.S. (9 Wheat.) 783, 859–68 (1824), as a reaffirmation of "McCulloch's conclusion that by operation of the Supremacy Clause, the federal statute incorporating the bank impliedly pre-empted state laws attempting to tax the bank's operations."

62. *Houston*, 18 U.S. at 24. The case has long been identified as the first source of field preemption doctrine. See, *e.g.*, George Roumell and Peter Schlesinger, *The Preemption Dilemma and Labor Relations*, 18 U. Det. L.J. 17, 19 (1954) ("[T]he language of the majority opinion . . . contains the seeds of, if not the full exposition of, what is today the theory of total preemption.").

63. See Henry L. Bowden, Jr., *Comment, A Conceptual Refinement of the Doctrine of Federal Preemption*, 22 J. Pub. L. 391, 396 (1973).

64. *Houston*, 18 U.S. at 45.

65. Ibid. at 48–49. Story also wrote: "On the contrary . . . the powers so granted are never exclusive of similar powers existing in the States, unless where the constitution has expressly in terms given an exclusive power to Congress, or the exercise of a like power is prohibited to the states, or there is a direct repugnancy or incompatibility in the exercise of it by the States." He would later change his mind in *Miln and Prigg v. Pennsylvania*, 41 U.S. 539 (1842).

66. *Prigg*, 41 U.S. at 622.

67. Ibid. at 618. Story elaborated: "[I]f congress have a constitutional power to regulate a particular subject, and they do actually regulate it in a given manner, and in a certain form, it cannot be, that the state legislatures have a right to interfere, and as it were, by way of compliment to the legislation of congress, to prescribe additional regulations, and what they may deem auxiliary provisions for the same purpose."

68. Ibid. at 633.

69. See ibid. at 663 ("It is said that a power may be vested in the federal government which remains dormant, and that in such a case a state may legislate on the subject. . . . [This] is illogical and unconstitutional.").

70. See ibid. ("It would be as dangerous, as humiliating, to the rights of a state, to hold, that its legislative powers were exercised, to any extent and under any circumstances, subject to the paramount action of congress; such a doctrine would lead to serious and dangerous conflicts of power.").

71. *Cooley*, 53 U.S. at 320.

72. See, *e.g.*, *Sherlock v. Alling*, 93 U.S. 99, 104 (1876) (upholding state common law about liability of owner for damage by vessel) ("[U]ntil Congress, therefore, makes some regulation touching the liability of parties for marine torts resulting in the death of the persons injured, we are of the opinion that the statute of Indiana applies . . . and that . . . it constitutes no encroachment upon the commercial power of Congress."); *Morgan's Steamship Co. v. La. Bd. of Health*, 118 U.S. 455 (1886) ("But it may be conceded that whenever Congress shall undertake to provide . . . a general system of quarantine . . . all State laws on the subject will be abrogated, at least so far as the two are inconsistent. But, until this is done, the laws of the State on the subject are valid."); *Nashville, Chattanooga & St. Louis Ry. v. Alabama*, 128 U.S. 96, 99–100 (1888) ("It is conceded that the power of Congress to regulate interstate commerce is plenary; that, as incident to it, Congress may legislate as to the qualifications, duties, and liabilities of employees and others on railway trains engaged in that commerce; and that such legislation will supersede any state action on the subject. But until such legislation is had, it is clearly within the competency of the States to provide against accidents on trains whilst within their limits.").

73. *Smith*, 124 U.S. at 480 ("[The regulations] are parts of that body of the local laws which . . . properly governs the relation between carriers of passengers and merchandise and the public who employ them, which are not displaced until they come in conflict with express enactments of Congress in the exercise of its power over commerce."); *Mo., Kan., & Tex. Ry.*, 169 U.S. at 623 ("[Constitutionality] must of course be determined with reference to the settled rule that a statute enacted in execution of a reserved power of the State is not to be regarded as inconsistent with an act of Congress passed in the execution of a clear power under the Constitution, unless the repugnance or conflict is so direct and positive that the two acts cannot be reconciled or stand together.").

74. *Reid*, 187 U.S. at 148.

75. 63 U.S. at 242.

76. *Southern Ry. Co. v. Reid*, 222 U.S. 424, 437 (1912). Contrast this with *Mo. Pacific Ry. Co. v. Larabee Flour Mills Co.*, 211 U. S. 612, 623 (1909), a case from only three years prior:

> [T]he mere grant by Congress to the Commission of certain national powers in respect to interstate commerce does not of itself, and in the absence of action by the Commission, interfere with the authority of the state to make those regulations conducive to the welfare and convenience of its citizens. . . . Until specific action by Congress or the Commission, the control of the state over those incidental matters remains undisturbed.

77. *Southern Ry. Co.*, 222 U.S. at 424.

2

The Breadth vs. the Depth of Congress's Commerce Power: The Curious History of Preemption during the *Lochner* Era

*Stephen Gardbaum**

The *Lochner* era that lasted from roughly 1887 to 1937 is widely known for two related constitutional doctrines. First, the Supreme Court constitutionalized the free market and expressed a general hostility to government regulation of the economy.[1] Second, the Court enforced limits on the scope of national power in the name of the reserved powers of the states.[2]

The history of preemption during this period, however, casts serious doubt on the representational accuracy of a portrait of the *Lochner* Court painted only with these two broad brushes. For it reveals that, in relevant contexts, the Court favored not simply the market in the abstract but the *national* market. In essentially constitutionalizing the free movement of goods across state lines for the first time, the *Lochner* Court wielded the two doctrines of federal preemption and the dormant Commerce Clause more aggressively against the states than any other Court, before or since. In other words, its belief in a single national market trumped both its laissez faire and federalism commitments, for when the Court considered that economic union was at stake, it looked with favor on regulation at the national level and was keen to find that federal laws displaced state authority in situations where other Courts would not. In this sense, the *Lochner* Court was decidedly a proponent of economic nationalism. "It may be said," Justice Joseph Philo Bradley proclaimed as early as 1887, "that, in the matter of interstate commerce, the United States are but one country, and are and must be subject to one system of regulations, and not to a multitude of systems. The doctrine of the freedom of that commerce, except as regulated by congress, is so firmly established that it is unnecessary to enlarge further upon the subject."[3]

In embracing the vision of the United States as a single national market, the *Lochner* Court limited the states' regulatory powers in two complementary ways. First, it employed the dormant Commerce Clause to expand the scope of Congress's exclusive power over interstate commerce and so to reduce the possibility of state interference. Second, even where concurrent state authority was found to exist, the Court's preemption doctrine meant that it often failed to survive the exercise of federal power. This doctrine began with the clear establishment of the general constitutional principle of preemption for the first time. State laws that conflict with federal laws had always been viewed as void under the traditional principle of supremacy. Preemption, in contrast, entails that even state laws that do *not* conflict—and entire areas of concurrent state authority—may also be displaced when Congress exercises its enumerated powers. This distinct principle of preemption was previously controversial and never clearly established or applied.

Not only did the *Lochner* Court clearly establish and vigorously apply the principle of preemption for the first time, but in two crucial respects the specific doctrine employed was significantly more restrictive of state power than its modern counterpart. First, the Court conceptualized preemption not as a discretionary exercise of congressional authority but as an automatic consequence of federal regulation in a given field. State regulatory authority in that same field was "permissive" only and was necessarily terminated once Congress acted. For the *Lochner* Court, Congress's Commerce Clause authority was latently exclusive, there was no genuinely concurrent state power. Accordingly, congressional intent and its interpretation played little role in the analysis. In contrast, modern preemption doctrine, premised on genuinely concurrent state power, turns on the centrality of congressional intent and the categories through which that intent is interpreted. Second, and in consequence, the *Lochner* Court had no equivalent of the modern presumption against preemption. To the contrary, the latent exclusivity of federal power created either an irrebuttable or strong presumption *for* preemption.

Undoubtedly, the *Lochner* Court held a limited view of the *breadth* of Congress's Commerce Clause power, a posture that contributed considerably to its laissez faire and pro-state reputation. However, the Court combined that construction with a relatively unlimited view of the *depth* of the commerce power—the impact on state authority of a valid exercise of this power. These twin positions were exactly reversed during the New Deal. Although the New Deal Court expanded the breadth of national powers under the Commerce Clause, it also reduced the depth of that power by moving from latent exclusivity to genuine concurrency, and from well-nigh automatic preemption to a presumption against preemption.

The Intellectual and Constitutional Frameworks

The first two-thirds of the *Lochner* Court during which its national market philosophy was established—roughly 1887 to 1920—coincided initially with the Granger and Progressive movements at the state level and then increasingly (but not unconnectedly) with the first coordinated and systematic attempts by Congress to regulate interstate commerce. The Interstate Commerce Act of 1887, the Sherman Antitrust Act of 1890, the Revenue Act of 1894, the Lottery Act of 1895, the Pure Food and Drugs Act of 1906, the two Federal Employer Liability Acts of 1906 and 1908, the Hepburn Act of 1906 (which substantially expanded the ratemaking and other regulatory powers of the Interstate Commerce Commission), and the White-Slave Traffic Act (the Mann Act) of 1910 all predated Woodrow Wilson's presidency as the major legislative fruits of, or reactions to, the Granger and Progressive movements at the national level.

The federalism implications of this first great burst of national legislation under the Commerce Clause were a major issue on the minds of contemporary politicians, lawyers, journalists, and academics. The arguments on both sides foreshadowed those to be made twenty-five years later in the wake of the Great Depression, although they were more evenly balanced the first time around. On the one side, a growing body of opinion, including most but not all Progressive thought, favored increased national control of society and the economy. This school of thought culminated in the remarkable success of Herbert Croly's *Promise of American Life*, published in 1909, which played a major role in Theodore Roosevelt's break with the Republican Party and his New Nationalism program of 1912.

On the other side were states' righters of various stripes, including Jeffersonian Democrats. Illustrative of this school and its deep suspicion of the newly dynamic federal government are two articles published in the *North American Review* in 1908, pleading for resistance to these growing trends: one by Woodrow Wilson, then still president of Princeton, the other by Henry Wade Rogers, dean of the Yale Law School. Dean Rogers expressed general concerns about constitutional centralization:

> We are threatened with a revival of Federalism—a Federalism that is more extreme and radical than the leaders of the old Federal party ever countenanced. The argument proceeds on the assumption that the States have failed to perform their duty properly, so that great evils have grown up which the States cannot or will not remedy, and from which we should have been free if only the Federal Government had possessed the authority and not the States.[4]

Wilson's concerns were more focused:

> Uniform regulation of the economic conditions of a vast territory and a various people like the United States would be mischievous, if not impossible. . . . [T]he balance of powers between the States and the Federal Government now trembles at an unstable equilibrium and we hesitate into which scale to throw the weight of our purpose and preference with regard to the legislation by which we shall attempt to thread the maze of our present economic needs and perplexities. It may turn out that what our State governments need is not to be sapped of their powers and subordinated to Congress, but to be reorganized along simpler lines which will make them real organs of popular opinion.[5]

Wilson was, of course, successfully to oppose Roosevelt's New Nationalism with his own, somewhat vaguer but decidedly more pro-states' "New Freedom" platform in the 1912 election. Amidst these intellectual crosscurrents, the *Lochner* Court's preemption jurisprudence took shape.

At the outset of the *Lochner* era, the constitutional framework for federalism issues consisted of the following two prongs. First, the Court would ask whether federal power (over interstate commerce or anything else) was exclusive or concurrent with that of the states. Second, to the extent federal power was *not* exclusive, concurrent federal and state powers were regulated only by the principle of the supremacy of federal law. Concurrent state power would be trumped under the Supremacy Clause only if, and only to the extent that, state law actually conflicted with federal law. Due to the relative dearth of congressional exercises of the commerce power during much of the nineteenth century, the contours between national and state power over commerce were hammered out primarily in the context of the scope of state power in the absence of federal regulation— in constitutional parlance, the parameters of the dormant Commerce Clause. This was to end when the *Lochner* Court was squarely faced with the issue of the implications for continuing state authority of the new exercises of federal power.

The question of whether Congress's power to regulate commerce among the several states was exclusive or concurrent with the states had been a deeply contested one since *Gibbons v. Ogden* (1824), if not before. The Court avoided a definitive answer until 1851 when, in *Cooley v. Board of Wardens*, it settled on what is commonly referred to as "selective exclusivity": Congress's commerce power is in part exclusive and in part concurrent. The dividing line ran between subjects that are "in their nature national, or admit only of one uniform system, or plan of regulation"[6] (which "require exclusive legislation by Congress") and those that are not. In settling on this formula, *Cooley* also answered a broader underlying question that confronts all federal systems: should the conflict between the general economic benefits of a single uniform market and the sovereignty interests of the states in exercising traditional regulatory powers be resolved in favor of a constitutional norm of free, unrestricted movement of goods across state borders or in favor of sustained state authority? The *Cooley* Court compromised between the two conflicting values by affirming a limited constitutional norm of free movement that applied to some, but not all, of the subjects of interstate commerce.

By the time of the *Lochner* Court, the general principle of selective exclusivity had survived but the distinction between "inherently national" and "local" had been replaced by a distinction between "direct" and "indirect burdens" on interstate commerce. States have no concurrent power to regulate interstate commerce directly (which thus falls within the scope of Congress's exclusive power and so the dormant Commerce Clause), but where an exercise of their police powers has only indirect or incidental effects on interstate commerce, it is within their reserved powers and is at least concurrent with Congress.

The second prong of the pre-*Lochner* framework applied to such concurrent state powers. It had always been understood that the Supremacy Clause of Article VI operates to displace or trump state laws that conflict with valid federal laws.[7] What was open to doubt and not resolved until midway through the *Lochner* era was the question of whether state laws that do *not* conflict with valid federal law, and indeed all concurrent state authority, could also be displaced by Congress.

Throughout the nineteenth century up until the *Lochner* era, this issue—the issue of preemption—was understood to be distinct from supremacy. It was also subject to differing opinions and left unresolved. Early in the century, for example, Justice Washington had been a forthright proponent of preemption; Justice Story was an equally forthright opponent in favor of supremacy alone.[8] Later, the issue was left open in *Cooley*, when the Court expressly declined to resolve "the general question how far any regulation of a subject by Congress, may be deemed to operate as an exclusion of all legislation by the States upon the same subjects."[9] Indeed, in establishing the criterion for exclusive federal power as subjects requiring uniform national regulation, *Cooley* indirectly but strongly suggested that Congress lacked the power to preempt the states. After all, preemption is an alternative to exclusive federal power as a way of creating national uniformity: Congress can simply preempt all concurrent state power. The fact that the *Cooley* Court made uniformity the rationale and criterion for exclusivity strongly suggests that it did not believe this alternative means of ensuring uniformity existed.

Beginning in the mid-1880s, however, both parts of the *Cooley* compromise—on the scope of exclusive federal power and silence regarding preemption—underwent a profound shift.

The Early *Lochner* Court: 1887–1912

The *Lochner* Court quickly rejected the *Cooley* balance and decisively broadened the constitutional norm of free interstate movement of goods, thereby limiting the regulatory powers of the states in the name of economic nationalism. It did so in cases involving the most salient political issues of the day in which the competing claims of free movement of goods and state authority clashed: railroads and alcohol. State railroad regulation, a particular focus of the Granger movement, came first. In *Wabash, St. Louis and Pacific Railway v. Illinois* (1886), the Court extended the exclusive power of Congress over interstate commerce by holding that states lack the power to regulate the rate of even the purely intrastate leg of a railway trip extending beyond its borders. According to the Court, such state authority would directly interfere with interstate commerce. State regulation of intoxicating liquors was next and, if anything, more contentious. The *Lochner* Court's firm opposition to such laws as impediments to the nation's commerce ultimately brought it into conflict not only with the states but also with the express intent of a Congress that, under prohibitionist pressure, twice acted to overturn the Court's decisions and to bolster state power.[10]

In *Bowman v. Chicago & Northwestern Railway Co.* (1888), the Court held that states cannot ban imports of liquor, for such laws not only burden interstate commerce but also discriminate against it. Following this decision, Iowa enacted a statute prohibiting sale within the state of all intoxicating liquors, domestically produced as well as imported from other states. In *Leisy v. Hardin* (1890), the Court invalidated this statute under the dormant Commerce Clause. (In order to do so, it had to overrule a venerable Taney-era decision that had upheld an essentially identical, nondiscriminatory state regulation.)[11] Chief Justice Melville Fuller explained that Congress's exclusive power extends to all interstate movement of goods, including liquor. Moreover, in drawing the boundary between a valid exercise of the states' police power over purely intrastate affairs and a prohibited regulation of interstate commerce, Fuller stated that "the law of [a] State amounts essentially to a regulation of commerce . . . among the several states . . . when it inhibits, *directly or indirectly*, the receipt of an imported commodity. . . ."[12] The notion that a nondiscriminatory state law aimed not at the protection of domestic industry but at the health, welfare, or morals of its citizens is constitutionally objectionable simply because it may or does restrict the flow of imports compared to the *ex ante* situation comes as close to a one-sided constitutionalization of the free movement of goods as is possible within a federal system. It is a concept that was, as we shall see, rejected during the New Deal—and, more recently, called into question by the

European Court of Justice as the appropriate balance for the newly completed single market in the European Union.[13]

In the narrow window left open by the dormant Commerce Clause for state regulatory authority, the Court's preemption doctrine further augmented the push for uniformity. During the first decade of the *Lochner* Court until his retirement in 1897, the (somewhat unlikely) champion of federal preemption was Justice Stephen J. Field.[14] In a series of opinions starting in the mid-1870s, Field stated his own answer to the "general question" of preemption consciously left open in *Cooley*. Thus, in an 1888 opinion for the Court, Field declared:

> It is conceded that the power of Congress to regulate interstate commerce is plenary; that, as incident to it, Congress may legislate as to the qualifications, duties, and liabilities of employees and others on railway trains engaged in that commerce; *and that such legislation will supersede any state action on the subject.* But until such legislation is had, it is clearly within the competency of the States to provide against accidents on trains whilst within their limits.[15]

The difference between preemption and the ordinary operation of the Supremacy Clause is precisely that "any" state action on the subject will be superseded, not just conflicting state action. In this and in all other cases, however, Field's answer was dicta. Prior to 1912, a majority of the Court had no occasion to decide the preemption question directly either because (as here) there was no such federal legislation in place or, where there was, state law conflicted with it. It was to be nearly another quarter century before Field's position on preemption attained a general consensus on the Court and became official doctrine.

Rather than either entirely avoiding the issue or engaging in the sort of explicit and principled disagreements that sometimes occurred in the pre-*Cooley* era, however, the period before 1912 is generally characterized by confusion and ambivalence about supremacy versus preemption. For example, the Court declared "that whenever Congress shall undertake to provide . . . a general system of quarantine . . . all State laws on the subject will be abrogated, *at least as far as the two are inconsistent.* But, until this is done, the laws of the State on the subject are valid."[16] The same ambivalence characterizes Justice John Marshall Harlan's opinion in *Reid v. Colorado* (1902), an important case discussed below: it appears to assert both positions in the space of two pages. "When the entire subject of the transportation of live stock from one state to another is taken under direct national supervision," Harlan avers, "*all* local or State regulations in respect of such matters and covering the same ground will cease to have any force."[17] Soon, though, Harlan migrates from preemption to supremacy: "This Court has said—and the principle has been often reaffirmed—that 'in the application of this principle of supremacy of an act of Congress in a case where the State law is but the exercise of a reserved power, the repugnance or conflict should be direct and positive, so that the two acts could not be reconciled or consistently stand together.'"[18]

Only when the first sustained federal regulatory regimes such as the Interstate Commerce Act confronted the Court squarely and unavoidably with the issue of preemption did the justices finally, unequivocally, and unanimously hold that federal law could in principle displace all concurrent state regulatory power over an area, regardless of any conflicts between the two sets of regulations. Not surprisingly, this newly established principle also resulted in the first invalidations of state laws specifically on preemption grounds. In a series of railroad cases starting with *Southern Railway v. Reid* (1912), the Court invalidated numerous state laws even though the two sets of regulations, state and federal, did not conflict with each other. It did so because Congress had simply excluded *all* concurrent state authority, period.

Although the principle of preemption was thus universally established by the Court for the first time, two distinct conceptions of preemption—a stronger one and a weaker one—existed side by side, with individual justices generally adhering to one or the other. The first conception, dominant between 1912 and 1933, viewed preemption as an automatic, necessary, and inherent consequence of federal action because of the nature of Congress's authority over interstate commerce as latently exclusive.[19] Concurrent state authority over a subject matter exists only until Congress exercises its "plenary" or "paramount" authority over that field, at which point it is automatically and entirely preempted (except in the rare case of an express nonpreemption clause). Latent exclusivity is a distinct jurisdictional category, lying in between exclusivity *ab initio* (which rules out state

authority regardless of congressional action or inaction) and genuinely concurrent power (which asserts the possibility of two continuing sets of non-
conflicting regulations).[20] Accordingly, under this dominant conception,
Congress's commerce power is deep if not necessarily broad. While the
Court enforced limits on the scope of this power in the name of the states,
whatever falls within these limits was latently exclusive of state authority.

The second conception understood preemption as a discretionary
power of Congress to end the otherwise genuinely concurrent power of the
states. Exercise of this power required a manifestation of congressional
intent, express or implied, in the particular federal law. This second conception was a distinctly minority position until 1933 but then quickly
achieved what the automatic conception never had: a total monopoly.
Henceforth, the centrality of congressional intent, bolstered by a new presumption against preemption, was deemed necessary in the face of the
greatly enhanced scope and exercise of federal power.

The Dominant View

Southern Railway v. Reid and its companion case, decided in 1912, were the
landmark decisions. In combination, the cases (1) clearly established the
principle of preemption for the first time; (2) invalidated particular state laws
specifically on preemption grounds for the first time; and (3) set out the distinctive and dominant conception of preemption that characterizes this entire
period and distinguishes it from the period after 1933.

Both cases arose over a North Carolina statute requiring railroads to
receive freight for transportation whenever tendered and to forward it by a
route selected by the owner, with a $50-a-day fine plus damages for viola-
tions. The Supreme Court unanimously invalidated the North Carolina
statute on the basis that "Congress has taken control of the subject of rate
making and charging," so that the state no longer had concurrent power to
regulate the subject. "It is well settled," Justice Joseph McKenna wrote, "that
if the State and Congress have a concurrent power, that of the State is superseded when the power of Congress is exercised."[21]

In fact, this principle was far from "well settled." McKenna's opinion for
the Court introduced much of what would become the standard terminology

of preemption analysis, a terminology quite different from that employed under traditional supremacy analysis. Rather than the standard invocation of *Gibbons* or *Sinnot* and their language of conflicts, he spoke of "a Federal exertion of authority which takes from a State the power to regulate the duties of interstate carriers," and of Congress imposing "affirmative duties upon the carriers which the State cannot even supplement."[22] The facts prove what the language strongly suggests—a notion of preemption that extends far beyond supremacy. In *Reid* itself, the issue was clouded by the fact that there was an actual conflict between state and federal law. The railroad agent had refused to receive the freight because no schedule of rates for the shipment had been filed and published with the Interstate Commerce Commission, as required under the federal Interstate Commerce Act of 1887. As the Court observed, what the federal regulations forbade the carrier to do, the state statute required him to do.[23] In *Reid*'s companion case, however, no such conflict existed, because the required rates had already been filed. The only reason the railroad agent refused shipment, and so violated the state law, was that he negligently claimed not to know the destination.[24] The irrelevance of conflict under the new principle of preemption was expressed in his inimitable style by Justice Oliver Wendell Holmes in a case decided three years later: "[T]hat [the alleged absence of conflict] is immaterial. When Congress has taken the particular subject-matter in hand, coincidence is as ineffective as opposition, and a state law is not to be declared a help because it attempts to go farther than Congress has seen fit to go."[25]

The Court in *Southern Railway* also strongly suggested that it viewed preemption as an automatic consequence of federal action in a given field rather than a matter of discretionary congressional power and intent to preempt. It clearly embraced the concept of the "latent exclusivity" of federal commerce power over commerce that essentially negates a role for either congressional intent or any genuinely concurrent state power:

> [T]he power of the state over the general subject of commerce has been divided into three classes: "First, those in which the power of the state is exclusive; second, those in which the states may act in the absence of legislation by Congress; third, those in which the action of Congress is exclusive and the state cannot act at all."[26]

Strikingly, this classification rules out any genuinely concurrent state power. Unless within an area of exclusive power, states can only ever act before the federal government enters the field. As soon as Congress does so in any capacity, the states are ejected from the entire area of regulation, regardless of whether that is what Congress intended.

Among the most influential preemption cases of the era is *Chicago, Rock Island & Pacific Railway Co. v. Hardwick Farmers Elevator Co.* (1913). Citing *Southern Railway* as the sole precedent for the governing principles of law, the Court in *Hardwick* overturned a Minnesota statute regulating the delivery of interstate cars as superseded by the Hepburn Act of 1906. Chief Justice Edward Douglas White again stated the principle of automatic preemption as follows:

> As legislation concerning the delivery of cars for the carriage of interstate traffic was clearly a matter of interstate commerce regulation, even if such subject was embraced within that class of powers concerning which the state had a right to exert its authority in the absence of legislation by Congress, it must follow in consequence of [the Hepburn Act] that the power of the State over the subject-matter ceased to exist from the moment that Congress exerted its paramount and all embracing authority over the subject. We say this because the elementary and long settled doctrine is that there can be no divided authority over interstate commerce and that the regulations of Congress on that subject are supreme. It results, therefore, that in a case where, from the particular nature of certain subjects, the state may exert authority until Congress acts, under the assumption that Congress, by inaction, has tacitly authorized it to do so, action by Congress destroys the possibility of such assumption, since such action, when exerted, covers the whole field, and renders the state impotent to deal with a subject over which it had no inherent, but only permissive, power [citing *Southern Railway*].[27]

Congressional action automatically and necessarily "covers the whole field" and terminates state authority which is not "inherent but only permissive." In another railroad case decided that same year, Chief Justice White made the point even more dramatically:

> The conception of the operation at one and the same time of both the power of Congress and the power of the states over a matter of interstate commerce is *inconceivable*, since the exertion of the greater power necessarily takes possession of the field, and leaves nothing upon which the lesser power may operate. To concede that the right of a state to regulate interstate ferriage exists 'only in the absence of Federal legislation,' and at the same time to assert that the state and Federal power over such subject is concurrent, is a contradiction in terms.[28]

Exercise of Congress's commerce power necessarily terminates that of the states. Far from being a matter of congressional intent that could go one way or the other, much less carry a presumption against preemption, continuing concurrent state power regulated only by the Supremacy Clause in case of conflicts is declared "inconceivable."

Particularly instructive of the *Lochner* Court's preemption doctrine is a series of cases dealing with the Federal Employer Liability Act (FELA), under which the federal government attempted to regulate the liability of private railroads for employment accidents. In 1908, by a five-four vote the Court struck down FELA's first version because although it regulated liability for employees engaged in interstate commerce, it also purported to regulate liability for employees engaged in purely intrastate commerce.[29] Congress responded by reenacting the statute without the latter provisions. In 1912, a week after *Southern Railway*, the Court upheld this second statute in *Mondou v. New York* and, moreover, held that the revised FELA preempted state laws on the same subject: "[N]ow that Congress has acted, the laws of the states, in so far as they cover the same field, are superseded, for necessarily that which is not supreme must yield to that which is."[30] Although employer liability was a field traditionally occupied by the states, congressional action in this field was deemed sufficient for preemption. There was no discussion of congressional intent, much less any suggestion of a presumption against preemption.

Five years later, in the important case of *New York Central v. Winfield* (1917), the Court held FELA also preempted state laws that did not require proof of negligence for liability. While the statute was (like the others already considered) completely silent on whether its scheme was exclusive, Justice Van Devanter opined:

> It is settled that under the commerce clause of the Constitution Congress may regulate the obligation of common carriers and the rights of their employees arising out of injuries sustained by the latter where both are engaged in interstate commerce; and it is also settled that when Congress acts upon the subject all state laws covering the same field are *necessarily* superseded by reason of the supremacy of the national authority.[31]

Once again, the "necessarily" negates any notion that preemption is a matter of discretionary congressional intent. *Winfield* drew a long, strong dissent from Justice Brandeis, discussed below. The majority opinion, however, was of a piece with a now-established preemption doctrine that would continue to hold sway until 1933. Taken together, the Court's treatment of the two versions of FELA provides a good example of the proposition that although the *Lochner* Court enforced limits on the breadth of Congress's commerce power (striking down the first version), it held an expansive view of that power's depth: what is inside the limits is "plenary" and latently exclusive of state authority.

As late as 1925, Justice Pierce Butler, who eight years later was to write the landmark opinion in *Mintz* that ended its dominance, continued to embrace this conception: "It is elementary and well settled that there can be no divided authority over interstate commerce, and that the acts of Congress on that subject are supreme *and exclusive*."[32] Of course, "supreme" and "exclusive" are quite different qualities of federal law: while the former regulates conflicts with state law, the latter renders conflicts redundant by removing all state authority.

The notion of the latent exclusivity underlying automatic preemption was understood to reflect the particular nature of Congress's power over interstate commerce, described variously as "plenary," "paramount," "primary," or "all embracing." As the earlier quotes from *Mondou*, *Hardwick*, and *Winfield* show, however, the Court also suggested that latent exclusivity was a necessary consequence of the general supremacy of federal law. This is quite false. "The supremacy of the national authority" means only that where there is a conflict between state and federal laws on the same subject, the federal trumps. It does *not* mean that all state law in the same area is displaced. Moreover, even where there is express or implied congressional intent to displace all state law in an area, which would also conflict with and so similarly trump continuing state authority, this does *not* mean that such trumping is an automatic or necessary consequence of any federal regulation in a given area. It would take nearly another decade, however, before the Supreme Court, and Justice Butler in particular, would arrive at that insight.

The Minority View

A coherent alternative to the dominant conception of preemption as automatic and as reflecting the latent exclusivity of federal authority evolved only gradually. Developed by justices who were more conscious of preserving the states' police powers, it began as a series of seemingly ad hoc reasons for not finding preemption and tended to employ three different techniques: (1) acceptance of the automatic conception of preemption but denial of its application in a particular case, on the ground that state and federal laws did not cover the same field; (2) reliance on the principle of supremacy alone; and (3) moving congressional intent to center stage. At first, all three techniques were employed in essentially gunshot style to resist preemption findings. Only gradually did a coherent alternative conception emerge based on the third technique—that is, the notion that preemption is a discretionary congressional power, exercise of which requires manifesting an intent to end the otherwise genuinely concurrent power of the states.

Just as the dominant conception typically relied on and cited a mere handful of recent precedents—primarily *Southern Railway* and *Hardwick*—so, too, proponents of the competing conception relied almost exclusively on two cases: *Reid v. Colorado* (1902) and *Savage v. Jones* (1912). The major proponents of this alternative, less propreemption position were Charles Evans Hughes and Louis Brandeis.

Reid v. Colorado, the original case routinely cited by proponents of the alternative conception, upheld an 1885 Colorado statute preventing the importation into the state of cattle or horses with an infectious or contagious disease against a challenge based on Congress's Animal Industry Act of the previous year. The Court's conclusion was "that the statute of Colorado as here involved does not cover the same ground as the act of Congress, and therefore is not inconsistent with that act."[33] Although seemingly a decision based on supremacy and conflict principles, it is the following statement, unsupported by authorities, for which *Reid* was subsequently cited as the original source: "It should never be held that Congress intends to supersede, or by its legislation suspend, the exercise of the police powers of the states, even when it may do so, unless its purpose to effect that result is clearly manifested."[34] This statement (a) acknowledges the principle of preemption (as distinct from supremacy), (b) implies that preemption is a discretionary power of Congress rather than an automatic consequence of its action ("even when it may do so"), and (c) conditions exercise of this power on a clear manifestation of congressional intent. As noted earlier, however, Justice Harlan's opinion for the Court was still marred by traces of the confusion between preemption and supremacy that is the hallmark of the pre-1912 position. Despite this confusion and the unsupported status of the statement about intent, *Reid* was to have a long and illustrious career, first as the minority position and, after 1933, as the sole position.

Savage v. Jones was the other major antipreemption authority to coexist with *Southern Railway* and *Hardwick* throughout the *Lochner* era. Also like *Reid*, it was still cited after *Southern Railway* and its progeny were completely airbrushed out of the preemption picture when the Court in the 1930s and 1940s decisively switched from one conception to the other. *Savage* concerned the federal Pure Food and Drugs Act of 1906, one of the major national legislative achievements of the Progressive movement.[35] Specifically, it involved the impact of the federal law on an Indiana statute requiring a label disclosing the ingredients of commercial animal food. The opinion, written by Justice Charles Evans Hughes, employed all three antipreemptive tools without developing a clear and coherent alternative to the automatic conception. After rejecting a dormant Commerce Clause challenge to the state statute, Hughes initially framed the preemption issue in traditional supremacy terms:

> The question remains whether the statute of Indiana is in conflict with the act of Congress known as the food and drugs acts

of June 30, 1906. For the former, so far as it affects interstate commerce even indirectly and incidentally, can have no validity if repugnant to the Federal regulation.[36]

The Court then implicitly rejected a finding of automatic preemption by noting that Congress had not covered "the entire ground."[37] While the federal statute prohibited false or misleading statements concerning the ingredients of an article, it did not address failure to disclose the ingredients in the first place—which was what the state statute covered. The Court then proceeded to ask whether Congress had, nonetheless, exercised its power of preemption. Finding that it had not done so expressly, the Court turned to the possibility of implied preemption:

> The *intent to supersede* the exercise by the state of its police power as to *matters not covered* by the Federal legislation is not to be inferred from the mere fact that Congress has seen fit to circumscribe its regulation and to occupy a limited field. In other words, such intent is not to be implied unless the act of Congress, fairly interpreted, is in *actual conflict* with the law of the state.[38]

Here, the opinion touches all three antipreemption bases: "intent to supersede," "matters not covered by the Federal legislation," and the need for "actual conflict." A few sentences later, Hughes quotes the "clear manifestation of intent" statement from *Reid v. Colorado*. Finally, switching back to the supremacy focus with which it began, the Court concludes:

> No ground appears to exist for denying validity to the statute of Indiana. . . . [Its] requirements are not in any way in conflict with the provisions of the Federal act. They may be sustained without impairing in the slightest degree its operation and effect. There is no question here of conflicting standards, or of opposition of state to Federal authority.[39]

The only significant dissent in any of the foundational preemption cases between 1912 and 1920 came in *Winfield*, the case holding that FELA preempted state laws imposing strict liability for injuries on employers. Indeed, *Winfield* is the single major case in which the two competing conceptions of preemption were employed in opposition to each other and applied to the same law and facts. The dissent was written by Justice Brandeis—along with Hughes, the main opponent of automatic preemption. At nearly twice the length of Justice Willis Van Devanter's opinion for the Court, Brandeis's dissent presented a more focused and coherent alternative conception than either *Reid* or *Savage*.

As noted, Justice Van Devanter's opinion declared it settled that once Congress had acted upon the subject of employers' liability for employees' injury, all state laws covering the same field were necessarily superseded. By contrast, Brandeis framed the preemption issue as whether Congress has exercised a discretionary power:

> The majority of the Court now holds that [by enacting FELA] Congress manifested its will to cover the whole field of compensation for relief for injuries suffered by railroad employees engaged in interstate commerce; . . . and that it thereby withdrew the subject wholly from the domain of state action. . . . That Congress *could* have done this is clear. The question presented is: Has Congress done so? Has Congress so willed?[40]

Brandeis then claimed to restate the "definitely formulated . . . rules" for federal preemption of states' police power. According to him, these rules are: (1) under the dormant Commerce Clause, states can exercise their police powers even though this might indirectly affect interstate commerce; (2) "But the intent to supersede the exercise by the state of its police power . . . is not to be implied unless the act of Congress, fairly interpreted, is in actual conflict with the law of the state" (quoting from *Savage*); and (3) a state statute "is not to be regarded as inconsistent with an act of Congress . . . unless the repugnance or conflict is so direct and positive that the two acts cannot be reconciled or stand together."[41] This is obviously a highly selective restatement, ignoring the entire line of recent automatic preemption cases.

Brandeis continued: "Guided by these rules . . . we endeavor to determine whether Congress, in enacting the Employers' Liability Act, intended to prevent states from entering the specific field of compensation for injuries to employees arising without fault on the railroad's part, for which Congress made no provision."[42] The rest of his opinion was a lengthy examination of congressional will as manifested in (a) express legislative words (none to cover liability for all accidents), (b) whether Congress's specific action "necessarily excludes" the state law, and (c) the origin, purpose, and scope of FELA as disclosed in its legislative history. Brandeis concluded that the will of Congress to leave room for state action was far less clear in several other cases where state power had been upheld than it was in *Winfield*, and he insisted that "[t]he field covered by Congress was a limited field of the carrier's liability for negligence, not the whole field of the carrier's obligation arising from accidents."[43] Notwithstanding some passing references to conflict as the only basis for preemption, at least when Congress has not expressly covered the relevant field, and also to the only automatic preemption issue of what is the field covered by Congress's regulation and so subject to latent exclusivity, Brandeis's preemption analysis focused overwhelmingly on congressional intent.

The paucity of dissents and of direct confrontations between the two conceptions of preemption is a little surprising on a Court notable for its divisions in other areas, such as the breadth of the Commerce Clause and substantive due process. Possibly, prior to Justice Brandeis's nomination to the Court the year before *Winfield*, many justices did not consider preemption cases important enough or otherwise appropriate occasions for dissents. Typically, the opinions are brief. Alternatively, it may have had to do with subject matter. All the foundational cases for the stronger, latent exclusivity doctrine of preemption involved railroad regulation. In contrast, *Reid v. Colorado* and *Savage v. Jones*, which would become the foundation of the modern, more restrained preemption doctrine, involved health and safety matters. It is possible that, for certain justices, the regulatory context made a difference. Although there is no overt suggestion of this in the cases, some justices may implicitly have employed the stronger conception in areas more purely about interstate commerce and the weaker one in areas of more traditional state concern. On the whole, however, the Court's habit of deriving the dominant conception from very general statements about the nature of the commerce power belies the notion that this conception was developed as a special case, limited to railroad or network regulation cases.

More likely, perhaps, given the contemporary political and economic importance of the railroads and the frequency with which Congress exercised its commerce power in this area, is that the Court developed a general theory of preemption based on this model of regulation.

The New Preemption Paradigm

The strongly nationalist conception of the dormant Commerce Clause as mandating a single market was, like so many other constitutional restrictions on the states,[44] rejected by the New Deal Court. Initially, starting with *Barnwell* in 1938, the Court scaled back dormant Commerce Clause review to invalidate only discrimination against out-of-state goods, a substantial enhancement of state power that does not prevent diversity of even-handed regulatory regimes.[45] Then, in 1945, it retreated a little toward the *Lochner* era view by adding second prong to its analysis: the modern balancing test. The fairly strong presumption of constitutionality that it carries, however, as well as the explicit recognition of legitimate state interests even at the cost of free movement, make clear that there is now more constitutional space for state regulatory activity under the dormant Commerce Clause than during the *Lochner* era.

Likewise, the dominant conception of automatic preemption was abandoned. Beginning with *Mintz v. Baldwin* (1933),[46] the standard preemption test was, in essence, the principle originating in *Reid v. Colorado*: states would be preempted if and only if Congress clearly and affirmatively manifested its intent to do so. The *Southern Railway/Hardwick* strand premising preemption analysis on the latent exclusivity of federal authority over interstate commerce disappeared entirely from view.

Although *Savage* is the case primarily cited as authority for the change between 1933 and 1937, in reality it was the broader antipreemption implications of *Reid* that established the foundation of the modern framework. *Savage* stated that the focus on intent applied only once it had been determined that Congress had not covered a particular field (in that case, the required disclosure of ingredients). The more general statement in *Reid* (at least if taken in isolation) suggested that the search for congressional intent and the presumption against preemption was to apply even if Congress had regulated the relevant field. The modern test for preemption forged between

1933 and 1947 adopted that position, thus allowing genuinely concurrent and diverse regulations of *precisely the same subject* to continue in operation, as long as Congress has not manifested an intent to end state authority.[47] Indeed, from 1933 onward, the Court bolstered the antipreemptive implications of *Reid/Savage* by expressly acknowledging a presumption against preemption in areas of traditional state regulation for the first time.[48]

The reason for the replacement of conceptions was twofold. First, Hughes and Brandeis, the major proponents of intent analysis during the *Lochner* era, survived that era to continue arguing for it into the next. (Hughes retired to pursue his political ambitions in 1916 but returned as chief justice from 1930 to 1941. Brandeis served continuously from 1916 to 1939.) Second, by this later time, they were arguing in a far more propitious context because of the fundamental changes taking place in federal-state relations. Given the increased scope and exercise of federal power over interstate commerce, latent exclusivity threatened to eviscerate large areas of traditional state authority. Thus, the Court reached a new federalism balance: although the scope or breadth of the federal commerce power would increase, its depth would be diminished by holding that Congress's power is not latently exclusive but genuinely concurrent with the states.

Between 1933 and 1937, the final years of the *Lochner* Court, all major Supreme Court cases involving preemption upheld state authority. Several of the opinions in these cases were written by Brandeis and Hughes. In 1933, in one of his final preemption opinions for the Court, Brandeis applied his consistent framework to Congress's Grain Futures Act of 1922, which declared that "contracts for the future delivery of grain shall be unlawful unless the prescribed [federal] conditions are complied with."[49] A 1929 Missouri statute made all futures contracts in grain unlawful as illegal gambling. Even though both statutes regulated the same subject (grain futures), Brandeis held that Congress "evinced no intention to authorize all future trading if its regulations were complied with."[50] Since there was no actual conflict between the two, the state law was valid. Brandeis ended his opinion by citing *Savage* alone.

Chief Justice Hughes authored two significant preemption opinions in 1937 and another in April 1941, shortly before his retirement.[51] In each case, Hughes restated, cited, and applied his *Savage* framework to uphold state authority: where Congress chooses to cover or regulate only a limited field, intent to preempt state police power outside that field should not be implied unless, fairly interpreted, the federal law is in actual conflict with the state law. The essential redundancy of this final proviso is recognized in Hughes's final formulation of the test, which drops it: "According to familiar principles, Congress having occupied but a limited field, the authority of the states to protect its interest by additional or supplementary legislation otherwise valid is not impaired."[52]

Somewhat ironically, the opinion that inaugurated this line of cases was written not by Brandeis or Hughes but by Justice Butler. *Mintz v. Baldwin* (1933) posed the question of whether Congress's 1903 Cattle Contagious Diseases Act preempted a state's authority to apply its own inspection laws. Notably departing from his 1925 statement of the "elementary and well settled" principles of automatic preemption, Butler succinctly framed the preemption inquiry: "The purpose of Congress to supersede or exclude state action against the ravages of the disease is not lightly to be inferred. The intention to do so must definitely and clearly appear."[53] Although Butler cited *Savage* as authority for this proposition, he should more accurately have cited *Reid*. His analysis of the statutory text led him to conclude that the federal statute "disclose[s] the intention of Congress that, subject to the limitations defined, state measures may be enforced."[54] *Mintz* ushered in a new era of preemption law, the essentials of which remain in place to this day. First, states have genuinely concurrent authority over subjects that Congress may regulate under its commerce power. Second, terminating this concurrent authority is a discretionary power of Congress, not an automatic consequence of federal action. Third, Congress is presumed not to have exercised this power. Fourth, rebutting this presumption requires clear and definite manifestation of congressional intent to preempt.

Although *Mintz* established the principle *that* Congress must clearly manifest its intent to preempt, the full details of this new approach were not filled in until the Court explained *how* Congress can do so in *Rice v. Santa Fe Elevator Corp.* (1947). On that crucial issue, the Court took a middle-of-the-road approach. Having rejected the *Lochner* Court's conception of preemption, it declined to endorse an even stronger antipreemption position proposed by two staunch New Dealers: Harlan Fiske Stone (who succeeded Hughes as Chief Justice in 1941) and Felix Frankfurter. Stone and Frankfurter both argued that the necessary manifestation of congressional intent to preempt should never be implied by the courts: express preemption or an actual conflict between state and federal law are the only methods of displacing concurrent state authority.[55] In establishing the modern doctrinal categories of implied preemption—field preemption and obstacle preemption—*Rice* rejected that view.[56]

The most interesting case along the way is *Hines v. Davidowitz* (1941),[57] for three reasons. First, it is a rare case during the establishment of the new paradigm finding that state authority is preempted by a federal statute. Second, the special nature of the federal authority at issue in the case, which, for the majority, justifies the finding is deeply illuminating of this new paradigm. Third, Justice Stone's opinion, albeit a dissent, explicitly acknowledges the deep connection and interplay in the justices' minds between the need for expanding Congress's commerce power and reducing its preemption power.

Hines invalidated Pennsylvania's 1939 Alien Registration Act as preempted by Congress's 1940 statute of the same title, also known as the Smith Act.[58] The state statute required aliens to register once each year and to carry an alien identification card, and it fined them for failure to do so. By contrast, the federal statute provided for a single, one-time registration of aliens, did not require them to carry a card, and criminalized only willful failures to register. As the two statutes were not in irreconcilable conflict, the issue was whether all state authority over the subject-matter was nonetheless displaced. Having noted that "[t]he basic subject of the state and federal laws is identical—registration of aliens as a distinct group," the Court averred that the answer to the preemption issue "depends upon an analysis of the respective powers of state and national governments in the regulation of aliens as such, and a determination of whether Congress has, by its action, foreclosed enforcement of Pennsylvania's registration law."[59] It concluded that the nature of Congress's power over immigration and the need for broad national authority in this area meant that even if Congress's power is not exclusive it is not merely concurrent either:

> Any concurrent state power that may exist is restricted to the narrowest of limits; the state's power here is not bottomed on the same broad base as its power to tax. . . . The power to restrict, limit, regulate, and register aliens as a distinct group is not an equal and continuously existing concurrent power of state and

nation, but that whatever power a state may have is subordinate to supreme national law.[60]

In other words, federal power is "plenary" or "paramount." Substitute "interstate commerce power" for power over aliens here, and you have precisely the same conception of federal power that underlay automatic preemption during the *Lochner* era. After 1933, this conception of the nature of Congress's power over interstate commerce was untenable in a way that it was not during the *Lochner* era—and was still not over immigration.

Equally illuminating is Justice Stone's dissent—not so much because he effectively argues that the new preemption paradigm should apply equally to Congress's power over immigration as well as its power over interstate commerce but because his *explanation* of the new paradigm made explicit that the contours of the commerce and preemption powers are and should be linked:

> At a time when the exercise of the federal power is being rapidly expanded through Congressional action, it is difficult to overstate the importance of safeguarding against such diminution of state power by vague inferences as to what Congress might have intended if it had considered the matter or by reference to our own conceptions of a policy which Congress has not expressed and which is not plainly to be inferred from the legislation which it has enacted.[61]

This constitutional linkage is exactly the reverse of the old one. In place of the relatively constrained scope of federal powers combined with the automatic preemption of the states when these powers were validly exercised, the Court combined the enlargement of the permissible scope of congressional power with a presumption that state authority survives the exercise of these powers unless clearly ended by Congress.

This theme was similarly invoked the following year by Justice Frankfurter. In an opinion for the Court (albeit in a case not involving preemption), he observed of the Commerce Clause:

> Perhaps in no domain of public law are general propositions less helpful and indeed more mischievous than where boundaries

must be drawn under a federal enactment between what it has taken over for administration by the central Government and what it has left to the States. To a considerable extent the task is one of accommodation as between assertions of new federal authority and historic functions of the individual states. The expansion of our industrial economy has inevitably been reflected in the extension of federal authority over economic enterprise and its absorption of authority previously possessed by the States. Federal legislation of this character cannot therefore be construed without regard to the implications of our dual system of government.[62]

A few years later, in dissent, Frankfurter elaborated on this "accommodation" in the area of preemption:

Since Congress can, if it chooses, entirely displace the States to the full extent of the far-reaching Commerce Clause, Congress needs no help from generous judicial implications to achieve the supersession of State authority. To construe federal legislation so as not needlessly to forbid pre-existing State authority is to respect our federal system. Any indulgence in construction should be in favor of the States, because Congress can speak with drastic clarity whenever it chooses to assure full federal authority, completely displacing the States.[63]

And finally, on the losing side of the debate that culminated in *Rice*, he was provoked to spell out the specifics:

Due regard for our federalism, in its practical operation, favors survival of the reserved authority of a State over matters that are the intimate concern of the State unless Congress has clearly swept the boards of all State authority, or the State's claim is in unmistakable conflict with what Congress has ordered . . . So long as full scope can be given to [federal] legislation without undermining non-conflicting State laws, nothing but the clearest expression should persuade us that the federal Act wiped out

State fixation of rates and other State requirements deeply rooted in their laws.[64]

Although Stone and Frankfurter lost the argument about how Congress can manifest its intent, all members of the New Deal Court were on the same side in the broader goal of recalibrating preemption in the face of the expanded scope of the federal commerce power.

Conclusion

Given the change from automatic to discretionary preemption that I have charted, one would expect to find either no, or far fewer, express preemption provisions in *Lochner*-era statutes in comparison with statutes enacted under modern preemption principles. If preemption is not about congressional intent and its manifestation but only about the boundaries and substantive content of congressional regulation, express statements of intent would be redundant. By contrast, when the Court is engaged in the task of discerning Congress's intent for surviving state authority, Congress has an incentive to make its intent clear, one way or the other.

By and large, that is what we find. I have not conducted a comprehensive survey, but I examined the language of sixteen major federal statutes from the Sherman Act of 1890 to the Fair Labor Standards Act of 1938.[65] Not a single statute contains an express provision clearly preempting the states. Only one pre–New Deal statute, the Clayton Antitrust Act of 1914, contains explicit preemption language, and this is an explicit nonpreemption provision.[66] Although in seeming tension with latent exclusivity, such a provision, like Congress's power to consent to state discrimination against interstate commerce, would rather have been seen as an exercise of its "plenary" or "paramount" Commerce Clause power. Under that power, Congress can expressly elect to limit or circumscribe the covered field.

By contrast, at least four major pieces of New Deal legislation contain express nonpreemption provisions of various types. The Securities Act of 1933 and the Securities Exchange Act of the following year each contain reasonably straightforward nonpreemption clauses. Thus the latter states: "Nothing in this title shall be construed to prevent any exchange from adopting and enforcing any rule not inconsistent with this title and the rules and regulations thereunder and the applicable laws of the State in which it is located."[67] The Social Security Act of 1935 is perhaps the first modern statute to reject preemption in favor of "cooperative federalism"— exercising the power of the purse rather than of regulation—as virtually all of its substantive provisions contain federal standards that the states must meet if they wish to receive federal grant money. In each separate policy area, the Act lays out the terms for interaction on the issue between state and federal authorities. Finally, the Fair Labor Standards Act of 1938 contains express language permitting the states to legislate higher standards (of minimum wage, maximum hours, and child labor). In these four cases, Congress is arguably responding to the new preemption principles and attempting to make its intent clear.

Finally, my analysis suggests that federal statutes were more likely to be held by the courts to preempt state law during the *Lochner* era than during the New Deal era. In very general terms, this too is borne out by the facts, although, of course, the presence of antipreemption provisions in many of the later statutes means that Congress was at least as responsible for this finding as the courts. Thus, apart from the Clayton Act with its unusual antipreemption provision, only the Food and Drugs Act was held by the Court not to preempt *all* relevant state regulations, although those within the area covered by Congress were indeed preempted.[68] By contrast, no major pieces of New Deal legislation were held to preempt all state authority in the relevant area. The Securities Act, the Securities Exchange Act, the National Labor Relations Act, the Social Security Act, and the Fair Labor Standards Act were all held to preserve some concurrent state authority within the field regulated by Congress. Clearly, the climate was more hospitable for continuing state concurrent authority following a valid exercise of Congress's commerce power after 1933 than before. If this seems curious, the subtitle of this chapter is justified.

Notes

*Many thanks to Richard Epstein, Michael Greve, fellow panelists, and conference participants for extremely helpful comments on a previous draft, and to Scott Dewey at UCLA for superb research assistance. This article builds on and substantially develops arguments originally made in Part III, *The Constitutional History of Preemption*, of my 1994 article, *The Nature of Preemption*, 79 Cornell L. Rev. 769 (1994).

1. See Justice Oliver Wendell Holmes's famous statement in his *Lochner* dissent that "[t]he Fourteenth Amendment does not enact Mr. Herbert Spencer's *Social Statics*," *Lochner v. New York*, 198 U.S. 45, 75 (1905) (Holmes, J., dissenting). See also Stephen A. Siegel, *Understanding the Lochner Era: Lessons from the Controversy over Railroad and Utility Rate Regulation*, 70 Virginia L. Rev. 187 (1984) (arguing that the *Lochner* Court constitutionalized the free market and its outcomes by creating a constitutional right to the protection of property's free-market value).

2. Most famously in a series of Commerce Clause cases: *U.S. v. E.C. Knight*, 156 U.S. 1 (1895) (in its early years); *Hammer v. Dagenhart*, 247 U.S. 251 (1918) (in its middle period); *A.L.A. Schechter Poultry v. U.S.*, 295 U.S. 495 (1935), and *Carter v. Carter Coal Co.*, 298 U.S. 238 (1936) (in its final period).

3. *Robbins v. Shelby Cty. Taxing Dist.*, 120 U.S. 489, 494 (1887) (invalidating state tax on the basis that interstate commerce cannot be taxed at all by a state, even though tax does not discriminate against it). Of course, the reference to *Lochner* in characterizing the era should underscore the fact that the Court nationalized contract and property rights that were previously (and subsequently) a matter of state authority. That is, in adopting the position of the *Slaughter-House* dissenters (*The Slaughter-House Cases*, 83 U.S. 36 (1873)), the *Lochner* Court brought about the radical transformation in federal-state relations that the *Slaughter-House* opinion said had not been intended by those who framed and ratified the Fourteenth Amendment.

4. Henry Wade Rogers, *The Constitution and the New Federalism*, 188 N. Amer. Rev. 321, 323–24 (1908).

5. Woodrow Wilson, *The States and the Federal Government*, 187 N. Amer. Rev. 684, 688, 697 (1908).

6. *Cooley*, 53 U.S. 299, at 319.

7. For example, in *Gibbons v. Ogden*, 22 U.S. 1 (1824), Chief Justice Marshall held that the New York statute granting Fulton and Livingston the exclusive right to operate steamships between New York and New Jersey was in conflict with, and trumped by, Congress's 1793 navigation statute. Similarly, in *Sinnot v. Davenport*, 63 U.S. (22 How.) 227 (1859), the Court held that an Alabama statute requiring owners of steamboats navigating the state's waters to register under the penalty of a $500 fine was in conflict with an act of Congress providing for the enrollment and licensing of vessels engaged in the coastal trade and, therefore, inoperative.

8. See their conflicting opinions on this issue in *Houston v. Moore* and my discussion of it in Gardbaum, *supra* note 69 at 788–91.

9. *Cooley*, 53 U.S. at 320.

10. These federal statutes were the Wilson Act, 26 Stat. 313 (1890) and the Webb-Kenyon Act, 37 Stat. 699 (1913).

11. *The License Cases*, 46 U.S. 504 (1847).

12. *Leisy v. Hardin*, 135 U.S. 100, 123 (1890) (emphasis added).

13. See Joined Cases C-267 & 268/91, *Keck* and *Mithouard*, [1995] 1 CMLR 101, 124-25 (ECJ 1993). In *Keck*, the ECJ reconsidered and scaled back its definition of which member-state laws constitute "measures having equivalent effect" to quantitative restrictions in violation of Article 30 of the Treaty of Rome. This definition, strikingly similar to the one in *Leisy*, was that "all trading rules enacted by Member States which are capable of hindering, directly or indirectly, actually or potentially, intra-Community trade are to be considered as measures having an effect equivalent to quantitative restrictions." *Procureur du Roi v. Dassonville*, [1974] E.C.R. 837, 852. The *Keck* redefinition was that member-state laws restricting or prohibiting "certain selling arrangements" only violate the Treaty of Rome if they have a discriminatory effect on the marketing of imported goods.

14. "Somewhat unlikely" because during the Reconstruction era, Field had generally been a defender of states' rights, although he was also a very early proponent of substantive due process limits on the states as one of the two dissenters in *The Slaughter-House Cases*.

15. *Nashville, Chattanooga & St. Louis R'wy v. Alabama*, 128 U.S. 96, 99–100 (1888) (emphasis added).

16. *Morgan's Steamship Co. v. Louisiana Board of Health*, 118 U.S. 455, 464 (1886) (emphasis added).

17. 187 U.S. 137, 146–47.

18. Ibid. at 148 (quoting *Sinnot*, 63 U.S. at 243).

19. See David E. Engdahl, *Preemptive Capability of Federal Power*, 45 U. Colo. L. Rev. 51, 53 (1973).

20. Latent exclusivity of federal power, together with the automatic preemption of state law that it entails, is an entirely plausible federalism option and is formally employed today in the Federal Republic of Germany under Article 72(1) of its Basic Law: "In matters within the concurrent legislative power [of the Federation], the states shall have power to legislate so long as and to the extent that the Federation does not exercise its right to legislate."

21. 222 U.S. 424, 435.

22. Ibid. at 435–37.

23. Ibid. at 443.

24. See Alexander M. Bickel and Benno C. Schmidt, Jr., *The Judiciary and Responsible Government, 1910-1921* (New York: Macmillan, 1984) 273–74.

25. *Charleston & W. Carolina Ry. v. Varnville*, 237 U.S. 597, 604 (1915). See also *Southern Ry. Co. v. R.R. Comm'n of Ind.*, 236 U.S. 439, 448 (1915) (Lamar, J.): "The test,

however, is not whether the state regulation is in conflict with the details of the Federal law or supplement it, but whether the state had any jurisdiction of a subject over which Congress had exerted its exclusive control."

26. *Southern Ry.*, 222 U.S. at 435.

27. *Chicago, Rock Island & Pacific Ry. Co. v. Hardwick Farmers Elevator Co.*, 226 U.S. 426, 435 (1913).

28. *N.Y. Cent. & Hudson River R.R. Co. v. Bd. of Chosen Freeholders of the Cty. of Hudson*, 227 U.S. 248, 264 (1913).

29. *Howard v. Ill. Cent. Ry. Co.*, 207 U.S. 463 (1908).

30. *Mondou v. N.Y., New Haven, & Hartford R.R. Co.*, 223 U.S. 1, 55 (1912).

31. *N.Y. Cent. R.R.*, 244 U.S. at 148 (emphasis added).

32. *Mo. Pacific R.R. Co. v. Stroud*, 267 U.S. 404, 408 (1925) (emphasis added).

33. *Reid*, 187 U.S. at 150.

34. Ibid. at 148.

35. The constitutionality of the act itself under the Commerce Clause had been narrowly upheld the year before in *Hipolite Egg Co. v. U.S.*, 220 U.S. 45 (1911).

36. *Savage v. Jones* 225 U.S. 501, at 529 (1912).

37. Ibid. at 532.

38. Ibid. at 533 (emphases added).

39. Ibid. at 539.

40. *N.Y. Cent. R.R.*, 244 U.S. at 154 (Brandeis, J., dissenting).

41. Ibid. at 155 (quoting *Mo., Kan., & Tex. Ry. Co.*, 169 U.S. at 623).

42. Ibid. at 155–56 (emphasis deleted).

43. Ibid. at 169.

44. On the full range of preexisting constitutional limitations on the states that were lifted or reduced by the New Deal Court, see Stephen Gardbaum, *New Deal Constitutionalism and the Unshackling of the States*, 64 U. Chi. L. Rev. 483 (1997).

45. *S.C. Highway Dep't v. Barnwell Brothers, Inc.*, 303 U.S. 177 (1938).

46. 289 U.S. 346 (1933).

47. Hughes and Brandeis may have held this position during the *Lochner* era, but their respective opinions in *Savage* and *Winfield* do not compel this reading.

48. The canonical statement appears in the later case of *Rice v. Santa Fe Elevator Corp.*, 331 U.S. 218, 230 (1947) ("[W]e start with the assumption that the historic police powers of the States were not to be superseded by the Federal Act unless that was the clear and manifest purpose of Congress.").

49. *Dickson v. Uhlmann Grain Co.*, 288 U.S. 188, 198 (1933).

50. Ibid. at 199.

51. *Townsend v. Yeomans*, 301 U.S. 441 (1937); *Kelly v. Washington ex rel. Foss Co.*, 302 U.S. 1 (1937); *Skiriotes v. Florida*, 313 U.S. 69 (1941).

52. *Skiriotes*, 313 U.S. at 75

53. *Mintz v. Baldwin*, 289 U.S. 346, 350 (1933).

54. Ibid. at 352.

55. For my own defense of this view, see Stephen Gardbaum, *Congress's Power to Preempt the States*, 33 Pepperdine L. Rev. 39 (2005).

56. *In haec verba*: "Such a [clear and manifest] purpose may be evidenced in several ways. The scheme of federal regulation may be so pervasive as to make reasonable the inference that Congress left no room for the States to supplement it. . . . Or the Act of Congress may touch a field in which the federal interest is so dominant that the federal system will be assumed to preclude enforcement of state laws on the same subject [citing *Hines*, see note 189]. Likewise, the object sought to be obtained by the federal law and the character of obligations imposed by it may reveal the same purpose. Or the state policy may produce a result inconsistent with the objective of the federal statute." *Rice*, 331 U.S. at 230.

57. *Hines v. Davidowitz*, 312 U.S. 52 (1941).

58. 18 U.S.C. §2385.

59. Ibid. at 61–62.

60. Ibid. at 68.

61. Ibid. at 75 (Stone, J., dissenting).

62. *Kirschbaum v. Walling*, 316 U.S. 517, 520 (1942).

63. *Bethlehem Steel Co. v. N.Y. State Labor Rel. Bd.*, 330 U.S. 767, 780 (1947) (Frankfurter, J. dissenting).

64. *Rice*, 331 U.S. at 241, 245 (Frankfurter, J., dissenting).

65. 15 U.S.C. §12–27; 29 U.S.C. ch 8.

66. "[N]othing in this section shall be held to take away or impair the jurisdiction of the courts of the several States under the laws thereof; and a judgment of conviction or acquittal on the merits under the laws of any State shall be a bar to any prosecution hereunder for the same act or acts." Clayton Antitrust Act of 1914, sec. 9. In addition, the Volstead Act of 1920, the federal statute implementing prohibition, followed the text of the XIX Amendment in expressly finding room for state authority.

67. Securities Exchange Act of 1934, title I, sec. 6 (c), as originally enacted on June 6, 1934.

68. There appear to be no *Lochner* era precedents on the preemptive effects of the Sherman Act. The first case I was able to find was a 1937 case holding that the Sherman Act did not preempt Puerto Rico's relevant laws. *Puerto Rico v. Shell Co.*, 302 U.S. 253 (1937).

PART II

Applications

3

The Case for FDA Preemption

Daniel E. Troy

The mission of the U.S. Food and Drug Administration (FDA) includes both "protecting the public health by assuring the safety, efficacy, and security of human and veterinary drugs" and "advancing the public health by helping to speed innovations that make medicines . . . more effective, safer, and more affordable."[1] The FDA and its predecessors have worked to protect the public health for 100 years, since the Bureau of Chemistry first obtained regulatory authority with the passage of the Federal Food and Drug Act of 1906.[2] The FDA's administrative structure and expertise have evolved over the past century and continue to evolve to speed safe medicines to market. In its risk-benefit determinations, the FDA attempts to approve drugs, uses, and labels that optimize both safety and effectiveness, based on the best available scientific evidence.

In recent decades, the FDA's ability to fulfill its mission has been threatened by state courts and juries carrying out their own risk-benefit determinations without the benefit of the FDA's experience and expertise. In response to that threat and as part of its institutional evolution, the FDA has increasingly intervened in state court suits. It has also issued an explicit statement that its labeling requirements preempt claims under state tort law for failure to warn. This so-called "Physician Labeling Rule" has been the subject of considerable debate.[3]

I served as the FDA's chief counsel from August 2001 through December 2004. During this time, the FDA chose to assert its preemptive authority in a number of products liability cases, and I was involved in the initial briefing on this issue. My tenure also included much of the development of the Physician Labeling Rule. Obviously, I am not a wholly disinterested observer.[4] Still, the final rule was not issued until January 2006. The FDA's involvement in product liability cases has continued since my departure. My comments here represent my personal views, not the agency's.

My central point is that the FDA's increasingly explicit assertion that the Federal Food, Drug, and Cosmetic Act (FDCA) and its accompanying regulations preempt state law cannot be viewed as a unilateral change of direction. Rather, it is best viewed as a response to protect the FDA's mission and objectives, as defined by Congress, against independent threats emanating from state tort law, especially failure-to-warn suits. As these suits have grown in frequency and ambition, the threats they pose to public health concerns and to the FDA's mission have increased correspondingly. Both the FDA's increased intervention in litigation and its decision to include an explicit preemption statement in the Physician Labeling Rule reflect a recognition of that reality.

FDA Regulation: Drug Approval and Labeling

Prescription drugs are regulated more heavily than almost any other consumer product.[5] The process of developing and obtaining approval to market a new drug is long and expensive, taking close to fifteen years. By 2003, it was estimated to cost an average of $897 million per drug.[6] The last phase of this process is regulatory approval. Under federal law, new drugs must obtain premarket approval from the FDA to ensure that they are unadulterated and not misbranded. FDA approval is withheld until there is sufficient evidence for the FDA to find that the drug is safe and effective for its intended use. Manufacturers submit evidence to the FDA in the "New Drug Application" (NDA), which includes reports on investigations for safety and efficacy, as well as "adequate tests . . . to show whether or not [the] drug is safe for use under the conditions prescribed, recommended, or suggested in the proposed labeling."[7]

The FDA's determination of whether to approve a drug is based on a comprehensive scientific evaluation of the product's risks and benefits under the conditions of use prescribed. The determination balances risks and benefits, and safety versus effectiveness. In part, this balance is based on the proposed use, because higher doses may be more effective but carry greater risks. The spectrum from safe to unsafe and from effective to ineffective intersects at a point that optimizes both safety and effectiveness. The FDA's statutory mandate to serve the goals of safety and effectiveness requires it to try to balance those goals and reach that optimal standard.

In evaluating each drug, the FDA considers both "complex clinical issues related to the use of the product in study populations" and "practical public health issues pertaining to the use of the product in day-to-day clinical practice."[8] Practical public health issues include "the nature of the disease or condition for which the product will be indicated, and the need for risk management measures to help assure in clinical practice that the product maintains its favorable benefit-risk balance."[9] All of these factors help the FDA predict what drugs, uses, and labels will optimize safety and effectiveness.

It would be impossible to implement a drug approval process that sought to prevent all adverse reactions and costly beyond measure to do so. The FDA categorizes an adverse reaction as "rare" if it occurs in 1 in 1,000 cases. Yet even studies comprising 3,000 patients are unable to identify "uncommon side effects, delayed effects, or consequences of long-term drug administration."[10] Indeed, "to detect the difference between an adverse reaction incidence rate of 1/5,000 and 1/10,000, approximately 306,000 patients would have to be observed, which is far more than any study could achieve."[11] And to insist upon *no* adverse reactions would cause immeasurable harm to public health. As the American Medical Association (AMA) observed, "[t]o take the drastic step of forbidding marketing of a drug until all long-term consequences and interactions are identified through formal research would impose unacceptable costs in the form of untreated or inadequately treated illness."[12] In fact, many critics have argued that the approval process is already so strict and involved that it unnecessarily delays drugs and poses threats to public health.[13]

FDA approval of a drug is thus a determination that the benefits of having the drug available may outweigh the risks for certain patients, not that the drug is risk-free. Congress and the courts have made clear that public health is best served by bringing reasonably safe drugs to market and allowing physicians to make informed and autonomous prescribing decisions.[14] Physicians lack the time and resources to discover all research related to the risks and benefits of each drug on their own. To account for that, Congress created a system to distill and communicate relevant and reliable facts. That system depends on detailed, uniform, and scientifically grounded labels for all prescription medications.

Because of this effort to optimize both safety and effectiveness, the FDA's mission and its decisions to approve new drugs are qualitatively different from the missions and decisions made by many other consumer-protection agencies. For example, when the Consumer Product Safety Commission sets minimum standards for lawnmowers or children's toys, manufacturers are generally permitted to exceed these minimum standards. They may do so either to produce ultra-safe products for consumers willing to pay for that additional safety or out of a business-driven desire to reduce the likelihood that the manufacturer could ultimately be held liable for product-related injuries. Manufacturers of FDA-approved drugs do not have the same leeway. When the FDA approves a new drug, it does not set a minimum safety standard; rather, it balances the risks associated with the drug against the competing risks associated with not having the drug available and sets what it sees as an *optimal* standard.[15] Manufacturers can fail to meet that optimal standard by including less or more than the FDA requires.

This difference in regulatory approaches reflects a fundamental distinction between pharmaceuticals and many other manufactured products. The adverse effects associated with a given drug are generally the result of the drug's composition and are inseparable from the drug's beneficial effects. Accordingly, FDA approval of a drug does not require a determination that the drug is safe in all circumstances. Indeed, such a requirement would prohibit the approval of the vast majority of drugs. Instead, FDA approval constitutes a determination that, as a matter of public health policy and based on the available evidence, the drug is sufficiently beneficial to justify its widespread availability to prescribers, despite a risk of harm to certain patients.

This fundamental difference between drugs and other products remains relevant after FDA approval, throughout the life of a drug. Physicians and patients recognize that pharmaceuticals carry risks and evaluate treatment options with that in mind. There are two levels of risk-benefit balancing between the drug manufacturer and the patient. First, the FDA balances the societywide benefits and the risks of having the drug available. Second, a physician, often in consultation with the patient, balances the individual benefits and risks of taking the drug. The FDA's role in this second level of risk-benefit analysis is to ensure through regulation of labeling that physicians are appropriately informed of the known benefits and risks of a drug.

The labeling requirement is central to the FDA's mission. As the FDA has stated, "the primary purpose of prescription drug labeling is to provide practitioners with the essential information they need to prescribe the drug safely and effectively for the care of patients."[16] False or misleading labeling renders the product misbranded. Misbranding, along with adulteration, is one of the two dangers specifically targeted by the Federal Food, Drug, and Cosmetic Act. Misbranding is subject to a variety of penalties. It can even be cause for withdrawal of the drug's approval, showing that an FDA risk-benefit balancing that favors having the drug on the market depends on the labeling of the drug, and can be overridden by labeling defects.

An applicant seeking approval of a new drug must submit a proposed physician package insert to accompany the product. The FDA's regulations establish many and specific requirements for this labeling, including requirements for the content and format of information on the drug's risks. This information must be scientifically substantiated and may not be false or misleading. The applicant may not lawfully disseminate any package insert that substantively deviates from the FDA-approved version without first receiving agency approval.[17] As the FDA has explained, strict regulation is required because "labeling is FDA's principal tool for educating health care practitioners about the risks and benefits of the approved product to help ensure safe and effective use."[18] That judgment is then conveyed to physicians through labeling. Without full control of the content of drug labeling, the FDA could not effectively convey its risk-benefit information to prescribers.

The Effects of Liability Litigation

Regardless of its origin (induced by state tort law or elsewhere), a change in labeling can alter the balance struck by the FDA by either overemphasizing the risk or underemphasizing the benefit. In both situations, the change moves away from what the FDA has determined to be the optimal standard. Such shifts have been sought, and sometimes won, by product-liability plaintiffs, generally as a collateral effect of those plaintiffs' individual efforts to obtain compensation. Pharmaceutical torts based on claims of failure to warn and defective design have become economically significant, providing incentives for pharmaceutical companies to take actions that the FDA may neither intend nor desire.

Litigation against drug companies has long been recognized as a growth industry. Over one thirteen-year period, approximately 11,000 such cases were brought in federal court alone.[19] That trend appears to have continued unabated. Merck withdrew its painkiller Vioxx from the market in 2004. As of February 2005, seventy putative class actions had already been filed, in addition to hundreds of individual suits. Similarly, Wyeth (formerly American Home Products) has paid billions of dollars to litigate and settle claims stemming from voluntary withdrawal of the diet drug combination Fen-Phen—yet, as of 2004, it still faced lawsuits from more than 60,000 claimants who opted out of the class-action settlement.[20]

Many of these cases claim negligent failure to warn, that is, liability based on the failure to include possible adverse events in the drug label. Judges and juries are asked to determine what information should have been included in a prescription drug label, even though FDA has already made precisely that determination. However, as the First Circuit observed more than thirty years ago, "courts are not best equipped . . . to judge the merits of the scientific studies and objections to them. Specialized agencies like the FDA are created to serve that function."[21]

At least four effects of these suits vividly illustrate how the current liability environment is harming public health. First, the litigation environment stifles innovation in the pharmaceutical industry. Second, tort liability has reduced the availability of drugs. Fewer drugs are being researched and created, and existing beneficial drugs have been removed from the market because of crippling litigation. Third, the current liability environment plays a role in higher drug prices. Fourth, the current system creates incentives for drug manufacturers to seek FDA approval of labeling that includes indiscriminate and prolix lists of risks, threatening the ability of prescribers to evaluate accurately the risk-benefit profile of a drug for a specific patient. Physicians may reasonably react to such labeling by simply declining to prescribe a drug that is, in fact, appropriate. Or, physicians may underestimate risks because of the manner in which they are presented and therefore prescribe a drug with risks that actually outweigh its benefits.

Investment in Research. The negative impacts of the tort system on development of new technologies have been recognized for some time now. In 1988, the AMA already had warned that "[i]nnovative new products are not being developed or are being withheld from the market because of liability concerns or inability to obtain adequate insurance."[22] The decision to research a new drug and to try to bring it to market involves a calculation of expected benefits and expected costs. Massive tort verdicts can dramatically skew the cost side of that equation. Expenditures on research and development increase when liability costs decrease.[23] And, where the level of risk is high, the risk of liability is inversely proportional to investment in research and development activity.[24] As Justice O'Connor recognized nearly two decades ago, "[t]he threat of . . . enormous awards has a detrimental effect on the research and development of new products. Some manufacturers of prescription drugs . . . have decided that it is better to avoid uncertain liability than to introduce a new pill or vaccine into the market."[25] Courts deciding individual failure-to-warn suits have neither the institutional resources nor the mandate to account for these industrywide effects.

At one end, the liability regime may induce manufacturers to overinvest in the research, development, and marketing of drugs that carry low liability risks but a hope of gargantuan profits. At the other end, however, pharmaceutical manufacturers may take overly risk-averse positions with respect to drugs that, despite their unquestioned benefits, do not have the potential to produce large revenue streams.

The liability regime creates a particularly strong disincentive in areas where great strides in health protection and promotion can be achieved through preventive care, with vaccinations administered to healthy patients. In those settings, the risk-benefit analysis conducted by the FDA is at its greatest distance from the risk-benefit analysis that would be carried out by a manufacturer. For the FDA, the benefits of a vaccine are generally sufficiently high to justify rare (even if relatively certain) instances of adverse events. By contrast, for manufacturers, even extremely rare adverse events create a serious risk of astronomical jury awards. Vaccines are administered to healthy people early in life, so that any future disease or disability for which there is no clear cause can potentially serve as grounds for a lawsuit against a drug manufacturer.[26] Moreover, because the tort system awards damages based on a valuation of life, rewards for adverse reactions affecting people with greater earning potential—younger and healthier people—will be higher. Thus, administering any drug to healthy or young people carries a greater liability risk than administering a drug to elderly or sick people. Healthy patients who fall into demographic groups likely to be viewed as sympathetic plaintiffs—such as young children and pregnant women—serve as an even stronger disincentive.

The effect is amplified for vaccines because "[p]roducts with less market potential are more vulnerable to a given degree of liability potential."[27] Where vaccines are concerned, "[t]he profit per dose is low, and yet the perceived liability per dose is high."[28] Thus, the Institute of Medicine has recognized that "apprehensions [about tort liability] act as a deterrent to vaccine production and thereby threaten the public's health."[29] Indeed, "[r]ising liability costs during the 1980s reduced the number of firms producing vaccines for five serious childhood diseases from thirteen in 1981 to three by the end of the decade."[30] Concerns about liability have slowed the progress of particular identifiable vaccines, including an AIDS vaccine.[31] The development of contraceptives has similarly been slowed by liability concerns. Experiences like the forced withdrawal of Bendectin as the result of baseless tort suits, discussed below, have discouraged manufacturers from developing new products indicated for or associated with contraception and pregnancy.

Decreased Availability of Investigational or Approved Drugs. The liability regime adversely affects patient access to beneficial pharmaceuticals by causing the discontinuation of clinical trials and by forcing already-approved drugs and willing manufacturers from the marketplace.[32] The signal example of market withdrawal is Bendectin, a drug approved by the FDA for preventing nausea during pregnancy. Beginning in 1969, assertions that Bendectin could produce birth defects began to appear in scientific literature. Yet no sound scientific study ever demonstrated a causal relationship between the drug and birth defects, and the FDA continued to affirm its safety. Nevertheless, nearly 1,700 lawsuits were brought against the manufacturer. Although the company won most cases, in 1983 it withdrew the drug in the United States because its $18 million in annual legal and insurance costs had nearly overtaken its $20 million in annual sales.[33] This result harmed pregnant women suffering from nausea because no similarly effective treatment is available. It also served no public health goal because, as FDA reaffirmed in 1999, Bendectin was not withdrawn for safety reasons.[34] For the manufacturer of Bendectin, the costs and risks of litigation outweighed any remaining profit potential, even though the benefits to society, as determined by FDA, outweighed the risks.

Given the particular vulnerability of vaccines to liability effects, it is no surprise that tort liability has drastically diminished the availability of this category of FDA-regulated products. Nearly all manufacturers of the diphtheria, pertussis, and tetanus (DPT) vaccine withdrew from the U.S. market due to lawsuits alleging harmful side effects filed in the 1980s.[35] In 1987, the Centers for Disease Control and Prevention (CDC) announced that the sole manufacturer of a vaccine to prevent Japanese encephalitis would no longer supply the product in the United States because of product liability concerns.[36] And commentators discussing the shortage and then surplus of flu vaccine in the winter of 2004 have noted that there remain only two manufacturers licensed to sell the flu vaccine in the United States.[37] These vaccines have been approved because their benefits were judged to outweigh their risks by the expert agency assigned that task, and yet public access to those benefits has been curtailed because of liability concerns.

Increased Drug Prices. The current liability environment makes available drugs cost more than they otherwise would.[38] The revenue a pharmaceutical manufacturer generates by selling a drug must be sufficient to cover not only the costs of research, development, and production, but also the future litigation expenses the manufacturer can reasonably expect to incur. The higher these anticipated future expenses, the higher the price the manufacturer will charge to avoid losing money by selling the drug in question. Efforts to generate a profit—a goal that managers of publicly held companies have a fiduciary duty to pursue—require still-higher prices. Vaccines again provide a powerful example of this industrywide trend. Between 1980 and 1989, the wholesale price of most vaccines doubled or tripled— an increase of just less than twice the rate of inflation.[39] However, two vaccines with a higher perceived liability potential increased in price at a much higher rate. The oral polio vaccine, which can in some cases cause polio, increased in price "by a factor of almost seven" during the same period.[40] The DPT vaccine price increased even more dramatically, by a factor of more than forty, as "the pertussis component of this vaccine has long been suspected of carrying a small risk of very serious side effects."[41] In contrast, the price of the diphtheria and tetanus (DT) vaccine, which is similar to the DPT vaccine but does not contain the pertussis component, increased by a factor of just over two during the same period.[42] In short, empirical evidence shows a correlation between vaccine price increases and perceived liability potential. Obviously, higher prices for drugs lead to decreased access to those drugs, curtailing the public health benefit of those drugs.

Interference with Rational Prescribing. The liability system interferes with the basic objective underlying Congress's delegation to the FDA of the power to regulate prescription drug labeling—providing physicians with the information necessary to make rational prescribing decisions. The decision to prescribe a drug is rational when, on the basis of all scientifically credible information and a patient's medical history, the benefits associated with the use of the drug outweigh, for that particular patient, the risks associated with the use of the drug. In other words, a prescribing decision is not rational unless it is: (1) based on an accurate understanding of the risks and benefits of the drug at issue, considered in relation to other treatment possibilities; and (2) tailored to the unique circumstance of the individual patient. Congress created the statutory structure governing drug labeling to entrust responsibility for accurately informing physicians about the risks and benefits of individual drugs with the agency equipped to analyze and evaluate scientific research related to drugs. FDA approval of a label constitutes a judgment, by that expert agency, about what content and format will most effectively promote rational prescribing.

The current pharmaceutical-liability regime targets that expert judgment and invites judges and juries to substitute their own *ex post* view. A tort suit alleging a failure to warn is an explicit allegation that a manufacturer had a duty to supply a warning beyond that which the FDA found appropriate. The FDA judgment is of appropriateness, and not adequacy, because the goal is an optimally effective label. The effectiveness of a warning must be considered in the context of basic limitations on human ability to consider and process information. Particularly in a modern managed-care environment, practicing physicians are faced with numerous demands on their time and attention. They have limited time to devote to reading labeling and will only do so if they think the information included is reliable and worth reviewing. Therefore, on a systemwide level, rational prescribing depends on preserving the system's credibility through strict policing of the information included in labeling. On an individual-drug level, rational prescribing depends on the accurate presentation of the most important and relevant risk-benefit information.

Moreover, the liability regime encourages inaccurate representation of risks and benefits in two ways. First, by creating an incentive for drug manufacturers to include warnings relating to all possible risks, even those that are trivial, extremely rare, or unproven, it results in the provision of excessive and scientifically unsubstantiated risk information. This may discourage physicians from prescribing drugs in situations where a decision to prescribe would clearly be rational.[43] Second, by creating an incentive for manufacturers to seek to emphasize all risks equally, so as to avoid being penalized for impliedly deemphasizing any single risk, it results in the provision of *insufficient* or *misleading* risk information. This may encourage physicians to prescribe a drug in situations where a decision to prescribe is not rational. A label with excessive or misleading risk information will lead to nonrational prescribing decisions.

The Physician Labeling Rule provides a powerful illustration of the basic trade-off. The FDA perceived a need to call attention to the most critical risks and, hence, mandated disclosure of those risks—but only those risks—in a "highlights" section of the drug labeling. Paradoxically, that effort to assist prescribers in distinguishing risk levels would have increased manufacturers' exposure to litigation risks: ex post, plaintiff lawyers will always be able to argue that the risk to their clients, no matter how freakish or rare, should have been included in the "highlights." Preemption of state failure-to-warn suits was absolutely necessary to implement the central purpose of the Physician Labeling Rule—to improve the accuracy and information flow to prescribing physicians.[44]

Failure-to-Warn Suits: The Growing Threat and FDA's Response

As already noted, failure-to-warn suits under state law are not a recent invention. However, this once-exotic plant has grown like kudzu. The FDA's interventions in such lawsuits and its publication of the Physician Labeling Rule are best understood as overdue responses to the risk that these suits will overwhelm FDA's regulatory authority.

Declomycin. In the early 1960s, tetracyclines were hailed as "wonder drugs" because of their effectiveness against a wide range of bacterial threats. One of these antibiotics was Declomycin, which had greater potency that its predecessors and could thus be prescribed at lower doses. Gradually, evidence began to mount that tetracyclines, when administered to children during tooth development could cause permanent discoloration of the teeth. Evidence could only be gathered once children who had received the drug developed adult teeth. For that reason, and because Declomycin was developed later, when the FDA acted on the evidence and approved a label for most tetracyclines warning of tooth discoloration, it specifically excluded Declomycin. Lederle Laboratories (Lederle), the manufacturer of Declomycin, corresponded extensively with the FDA in 1962 and 1963 about the possibility of adding a warning to the Declomycin label. It was told that such a warning was premature.[45]

Carol Ann Feldman was administered Declomycin as an infant several times a year between 1960 and 1963 and suffered permanent tooth discoloration. She and her father, the prescribing physician, brought suit for failure to warn of the risk of tooth discoloration. They alleged that Lederle should have provided exactly the warning that the FDA had declared premature. The New Jersey Supreme Court examined Lederle's decision to continue marketing Declomycin, and forms of it intended for pediatric use, despite its belief that a connection with tooth discolorization existed and would affect physician prescribing decisions. The choices available to Lederle in 1962 and 1963, according to the majority opinion, were to suspend production of Declomycin until the FDA felt there was sufficient evidence for a warning, to remove the pediatric forms of the drug from the market, or to raise the cost of the drug across the board to raise funds to pay for legal settlements.[46] The majority found all of those options feasible and preferable to producing the drug without a warning and held Lederle liable.

That is precisely the opposite of the finding that the FDA made. Faced with the scientific evidence of the risks from other tetracyclines and the risk of removing a broad spectrum pediatric antibiotic from the market, at a time when the other "wonder drugs" were being restricted, the FDA determined that the health of the American public was better served by unrestricted availability of Declomycin. Although Lederle believed the similarities between Declomycin and other tetracyclines were significant enough to suggest that evidence of tooth discoloration would materialize, the FDA acted on the possibility that the different dosage for Declomycin would mitigate the effect. Lederle's conduct, which the court treated as unconscionable, was exactly the behavior that the FDA had determined would best serve the public health. The benefits from Declomycin in the time that it was available pending demonstration of a risk are shown by the fact that Feldman was administered the drug nine or ten times in that period, apparently to bacterial infections.[47] The FDA's determination was based on the best available evidence, which turned out, after the fact, to have been a losing gamble.

The reason for the difference between the New Jersey Supreme Court's view of appropriate behavior and the FDA's view is the court's limited view of the FDA's mission. The court declared that "Congress' overriding purpose in enacting the FDCA was to protect consumers from dangerous drugs and antibiotics" and found "no basis for concluding that Lederle was required to continue marketing Declomycin in forms and packaging intended for use by those it believed to be at risk—or indeed to continue marketing at all. Such a requirement would conflict with the predominant, express purpose for which the FDA was created."[48] By focusing exclusively on the risk-protection aspect, the court effectively imposed a precautionary principle on the FDA and the pharmaceutical industry that, if enforced, would have intolerable costs on the industry and public health.

Most importantly, the FDA *required* Lederle to behave as it did. Lederle rightly (but unsuccessfully) argued before the court that it was bound by a requirement for FDA approval of labeling changes. This is in keeping with the understanding within the pharmaceutical industry, and within the FDA, that changes to labeling cannot be made without FDA approval.[49] Thus, Lederle followed the FDA labeling requirements—and was held liable for violating conflicting state requirements. In effect, the manufacturer was held responsible for an expert determination made by the FDA with which the court disagreed.[50]

A similar decision was recently reached by the Vermont Supreme Court, in a case entitled *Levine v. Wyeth*.[51] Even though Wyeth had proposed a label change, which the FDA had rejected—specifically telling the company to "retain current verbiage"—the Vermont Supreme Court held the company liable. The essence of the plaintiff's claim was that Wyeth had acted tortiously by keeping the product on the market with the route of administration approved by the FDA. The court refused to find that the claim was preempted unless Wyeth could prove that the FDA had expressly barred Wyeth from changing the label with respect to the mode of administration of the product. Yet the FDA had manifested its clear belief, one that continues to be reflected in the current label, that the approved route of administration, despite its associated risks, was the medically appropriate. Tort liability in these and similar circumstances is an existential threat to the FDA. The determination of how much risk is tolerable for what benefit is a public policy determination requiring consideration of the costs and benefits to parties not before the court.[52] It is accordingly not resolvable with judicial standards and should be reserved for the political branches of government.

Proposition 65. California's Safe Drinking Water and Toxic Enforcement Act (Proposition 65) empowers citizens to bring suit against manufacturers for failures to include risk warnings, with the incentive of a share in the monetary penalty. Passed as a ballot in 1986, Proposition 65 requires a warning on any product containing a chemical known to the state to be a carcinogen or reproductive toxin. In 1987, FDA Commissioner Frank E. Young sent a letter to the governor of California asking that he recognize that FDA-approved products pose no significant risk and are exempt from the warning requirements. Commissioner Young explained the request:

> We are concerned that the creation of such special labels could cause a serious logistical problem that also might create serious public health problems. For example, the consumer may be confused when confronted by warning labels on large numbers of products and may be less likely to heed those warnings that have been carefully designed by FDA, Congress, and your State to protect against more significant and possibly more immediate harm.[53]

The FDA's letter clearly reflects the concerns over rational prescribing: a proliferation of warnings without emphasis on more significant risks causes confusion and decreases the utility of warnings. The California governor did not heed the request, and Proposition 65 was applied to FDA-approved products. This recalcitrance prompted continued FDA protests—and, eventually, lawsuits and acrimonious controversy over conflicts between Proposition 65 requirements and FDA regulation, which continue to this day.[54]

Nicotine replacement products, sold over the counter to aid in smoking cessation, work by replacing some of the nicotine found in cigarettes to ease cravings. Not surprisingly, they contain some nicotine. Nicotine was designated by the state of California as a developmental and reproductive toxicant in 1990. In 1997, the FDA responded to McNeil PPC, Inc., a manufacturer of over-the-counter nicotine replacement products, denying its request for permission to add a Proposition 65 warning to the label. In March 2001, the FDA confirmed in a letter to other manufacturers that using additional warning language to satisfy Proposition 65 could render their products misbranded under FDCA.

The FDA was motivated in that instance by a desire to promote rational use of the nicotine replacement products. When the products switched from prescription to over-the-counter in 1996, they bore labels that were the product of careful consideration by the FDA's Nonprescription Drug Advisory Committee, designed to promote rational use. As the chairman of that committee explained,

> This is one of the few instances where we have a product . . . that I would like lots of people to use, that I think we are underusing. . . . So we want to make sure that we are not introducing barriers that would prevent people from using them, and what is worse, somebody continuing to smoke.[55]

Because the risks of not using nicotine replacement therapy are far greater than the risks from the therapy (because smoking introduces higher levels of nicotine as well as other harmful chemicals), the FDA did not want to approve a label that would treat the two risks equally. Such a label would undermine rational use, diminishing the public health benefit from a product that the FDA had determined to be safe and effective.

However, in 1999, Paul Dowhal filed a citizen suit under Proposition 65 against manufacturers, distributors, and retailers of over-the-counter nicotine replacement products. The suit sought to force those entities to do exactly what the FDA sought to prevent—include a standard Proposition 65 warning that would have presented the risk from nicotine replacement in the same terms as the risks from smoking. The suit was brought against McNeil, the same manufacturer that had specifically been denied permission in 1997 to include a Proposition 65 warning.

McNeil and another defendant, SmithKline Beecham Consumer Healthcare, LP, both wrote to the FDA on several occasions requesting permission to include the Proposition 65 warning and seeking clarification of the labeling requirements. This attempt at defensive labeling, which would have negatively influenced use of the drug, consumed significant resources within the industry and within the FDA. For manufacturers, the costs associated with producing nicotine replacement products increased. Also, in addition to considering and responding to requests from the defendants in the suit, the FDA had to become directly involved in the legal proceedings to protect its mission and enforce its requirements. At the first stage of appeal, the FDA submitted an *amicus curiae* brief supporting the defendants. When review at that level failed, the FDA submitted a letter brief in support of the petition for review by the Supreme Court of California. In a 2004 decision, the Court squarely addressed whether the requirements of Proposition 65 frustrated the purpose of FDA's labeling determinations:

> [T]he FDA warning serves a nuanced goal—to inform pregnant women of the risks of NRT [nicotine replacement therapy] products, but in a way that will not lead some women, overly concerned about those risks, to continue smoking. This creates a conflict with the state's more single-minded goal of informing the consumer of the risks. That policy conflict justifies federal preemption here.[56]

The decision reflects a sound understanding of the balancing and expertise required by the FDA mandate. However, a great deal of time and expense went to protect the FDA's ability to perform its essential function.

Antidepressants. The FDA currently requires relatively strong suicide-related warnings in the labeling of certain antidepressants. However, two recent federally funded studies support concerns that these warnings may be causing a failure to prescribe antidepressants to depressed individuals that, in turn, leads to an even greater risk of suicide.[57] In particular, one of the studies found that for patients treated with newer antidepressant drugs (those included in a March 2004 FDA Public Health Advisory),[58] risk of suicide attempts was highest in the month before starting treatment and lower in each of the six months following initiation of treatment than in the month prior to initiation.[59] In other words, excessive warnings about suicide-related risks may have the paradoxical effect of increasing suicides by preventing appropriate prescription of antidepressants. Although these studies did not control for any placebo effect, they at least suggest a need for careful balancing of the risks and benefits of a drug versus the risks and benefits of any label warnings. Additionally, the example illustrates the intense pressure placed on manufacturers by the threat of tort liability, especially when the risk in question is a risk both of forgoing and undergoing treatment.

On three occasions, the FDA specifically considered and rejected claims that selective seratonin reuptake inhibitors, or SSRIs (a collection of drugs including Prozac, Zoloft, and Paxil), cause suicide. In 1990 and 1991, the FDA received two citizen petitions alleging a link between the SSRI Prozac (fluoxetene) and suicide. One petition sought market withdrawal; the other asked the FDA to require a "black box warning" in Prozac's labeling concerning a putative link between the drug and suicide. The FDA examined the data concerning the risk of suicide and other violent behavior and SSRIs and rejected both petitions. In 1997, the FDA declined to grant a third citizen petition requesting additional suicide warning language in the labeling for Prozac.

In evaluating the proposed labeling changes, the FDA sought out specialized expert advice. In 1991, the FDA requested that the Psycho-pharmacological Drugs Advisory Committee (PDAC) review the scientific evidence relating to the risk of suicide and the pharmacological treatment of depression. The PDAC determined unanimously that the evidence did not indicate that use of any particular drug or class of drugs to treat depression heightens the risk of suicide. The advisory committee also heard remarks from the then-director of the FDA's Division of Neuropharmacological Drug Products concerning the risk that modifying the labeling could misleadingly overstate the risk of suicide and cause a reduction in the use of pharmacotherapy to treat depression.

In 2002, the FDA conducted yet another internal review of scientific evidence regarding SSRIs and suicide. The review revealed no difference in the risk of suicide between patients using SSRIs and patients on placebo. However, after reviewing further studies the agency refined its position in late 2004 and early 2005. The FDA now warns that antidepressants, including Zoloft, "may increase suicidal thoughts and actions in about 1 out of 50 people 18 years or younger," and that "[s]everal recent publications report the possibility of an increased risk for suicidal behavior in adults who are treated with antidepressant medications."[60] As the federally funded studies discussed above indicate, though, applying that warning appears likely to have at least some of the negative consequences that caused the FDA to originally reject the change.

Sadly, the change in FDA policy reflected more than a shift in the weight of scientific evidence on both sides—it also reflected legal pressures. State tort actions led manufacturers to request defensive labeling, and the FDA expended considerable resources investigating those requests and defending its ability to function effectively. There has also been litigation related to the advertising of antidepressants, and the FDA has had to intervene in that realm as well in order to protect its functions.

In re Paxil Litigation. Paxil, an SSRI produced by GlaxoSmithKline (GSK), was approved in 1992 for the treatment of depression. In reviewing the NDA for Paxil, the FDA found no clinical evidence of drug-seeking behavior associated with use of the drug. The FDA concluded that Paxil is not habit forming and did not require language in the approved labeling stating that Paxil is associated with this risk. The approved labeling does, however, recommend that physicians gradually reduce dosages rather than abruptly halting use and that physicians monitor patients discontinuing the drug for syndrome symptoms.

On five separate occasions in 2001 and 2002 the Division of Drug Marketing, Advertising, and Communications (DDMAC) reviewed advertisements for Paxil claiming that the product was "non-habit-forming." DDMAC concluded that this statement was not false or misleading because, as the FDA previously had found in the NDA review, Paxil does not induce drug-seeking behavior. DDMAC suggested that GSK adjust the wording of one advertisement to state clearly that a doctor should be consulted before discontinuing Paxil. DDMAC determined that this additional statement ensured that the advertisement adequately communicated to patients the appropriate information about discontinuation.

Notwithstanding DDMAC's review of—and lack of objection to—these precise advertisements, a federal district court judge applying California law in August 2002 granted plaintiffs' motion to enjoin GSK from running advertisements for Paxil that included the "non-habit-forming" language. The court suggested that whether a drug advertisement was false or misleading could be a different issue under state tort law than under the FDCA. The FDA decided to participate in the case to preserve the agency's role in regulating prescription drug advertising. With the court's agreement, the FDA filed a brief contending that the court should have deferred to the FDA's determination that the advertisements were not false or misleading. On GSK's motion for reconsideration, the court reversed its original decision and declined to enjoin the advertising on the ground that information submitted by the FDA concerning DDMAC's review made the plaintiff less likely to succeed on the merits.[61]

Motus v. Pfizer, Inc. In November 1998, a candidate for city council and failing businessman named Victor Motus visited his doctor, appearing depressed and frustrated. His physician diagnosed moderate depression and prescribed Zoloft at 25 mg for seven days, followed by 50 mg of Zoloft for fourteen days. Six days after visiting his doctor, Motus committed suicide by shooting himself. His wife sued Pfizer, claiming that, under California law, the company had acted negligently by failing to warn adequately in the package insert and marketing materials that Zoloft could cause suicide. A U.S. District Court held that federal law did not preempt the plaintiff's state tort law claims. In making this finding, the court relied on cases finding that the FDA's regulation of labeling did not preempt all tort actions.[62] It did not carefully analyze whether requiring the additional warning language sought by the plaintiff would conflict with the FDA's conclusion that SSRIs do not heighten the risk of suicide.

On appeal, the FDA filed an *amicus* brief contending that the plaintiff's state-law claims could not stand. The FDA-approved labeling for Zoloft at the time discussed the risk of suicide that accompanies depression but did not identify Zoloft as a potential cause of suicide. The labeling thus reflected the FDA's specific finding of no causal relationship between Zoloft and suicide, contrary to the language that would have been included in the labeling had the plaintiff prevailed. In affirming the judgment of the district court, the Ninth Circuit Court of Appeals explicitly declined to reach the district court's preemption holding and instead rested its conclusion on the prescribing doctor's failure to read Pfizer's warnings or rely on information provided by Pfizer's representatives in making his decision to prescribe Zoloft.[63] As the doctor would not have been aware of any warning Pfizer issued, Motus could not prevail on a claim that the inadequacy of Pfizer's warnings caused her husband's death. Thus, the court did not reach the step of directly contradicting the FDA determination, or of analyzing whether requiring the specifically rejected label would have conflicted with FDA policy.

Kallas v. Pfizer, Inc. In *Kallas v. Pfizer, Inc.*, the parents of a fifteen-year-old girl who committed suicide while taking Zoloft sued Pfizer, alleging in part that Pfizer should have warned of an association between Zoloft and suicide, even if Pfizer was not required to state that Zoloft caused suicide. Pursuant to the U.S. District Court's request, the FDA filed a brief explaining its position on the case. It emphasized that at the time the young girl took Zoloft, Pfizer would not have been permitted to warn of an association between Zoloft and suicide. The FDA further noted that the agency's "accomplishment of its responsibilities would be disrupted and undermined if, driven in part by concerns about later state law tort liability, drug manufacturers were to engage in their own labeling determinations by adding warnings that, in FDA's judgment, were not based on reasonable scientific evidence of association or causation."[64] The court did not have the opportunity to rule on Pfizer's motion, as the parties settled the case shortly after the FDA filed its brief.

The FDA has continued to participate in these kinds of cases. That mode of protecting the agency's mission, however, is quite costly. One advantage of the explicit preemption statement in the Physician Labeling Rule is that it may reduce the need for FDA to submit *amicus* briefs in the myriad of cases around the country.

The Case for Preemption

Public policy concerns provide a potent rationale for FDA preemption, and Supreme Court precedents provide ample support for FDA's decision to exercise its preemptive authority. Three crucial cases—*Hillsborough County, Florida v. Automated Medical Laboratories, Inc.* (1985),[65] *Medtronic, Inc. v. Lohr* (1996),[66] and *Buckman Co. v. Plaintiffs' Legal Committee* (2001)[67]—directly concerned FDA requirements. The fourth central case is *Geier v. American Honda Motor Co.* (2000),[68] discussed in several contributions to this volume.

In *Hillsborough*, a Florida county passed two ordinances relating to blood plasma centers. The first imposed a license fee and required the centers to provide reasonable access and relevant information to the county health department. The second imposed testing and record-keeping requirements. This second ordinance incorporated FDA blood plasma regulations by reference but also imposed additional requirements beyond those set forth by the FDA. An operator of blood plasma centers challenged the ordinances in federal court, asserting in part that they were preempted by the FDA regulations.

The U.S. Supreme Court held that county ordinances were not preempted. In reaching its decision, however, the court put significant weight on "the clear indication of FDA's intention *not to pre-empt*" when it promulgated the original regulations.[69] An agency statement that it intends to allow state coregulation is not dispositive when "the agency's position is inconsistent with clearly expressed congressional intent," or when "subsequent developments reveal a change in that position."[70] However, as agencies have numerous ways to make their preemptive intention clear, such as "regulations, *preambles*, interpretative statements, and responses to comments," the Court will not lightly infer preemptive intent, in the face of agency silence "solely from the comprehensiveness of federal regulations."[71] The plain implication is that an agency's recourse to one of the listed regulatory instruments should materially change the preemption analysis.

In *Medtronic*, a patient injured by a failed pacemaker sued the manufacturer of a critical pacemaker component in Florida state court, setting forth both negligence and strict liability claims. After removing the case to federal court, the component manufacturer asserted that plaintiffs' claims were prohibited by the express preemption provisions of the Medical Device Amendments (MDA) to the FDCA.

The Supreme Court held that none of the claims were preempted. First, the Court held that the FDA's determination that the manufacturer's device was "substantially equivalent" to an existing device did not constitute a

"specific, federally enforceable design requirement" that would justify federal preemption of state-law defective-design claims.[72] Second, the Court
determined that the preemption provision of the MDA did not prohibit the
states from providing damages remedies for violation of state-law duties that
were equivalent to FDA requirements. Third, the Court held that the preemption provision of the MDA did not encompass claims based on state
manufacturing and labeling requirements. The Court emphasized that
the "generality" of the federal device manufacturing and labeling requirements "make this quite unlike a case in which the federal government has
weighed the competing interests relevant to the particular requirement in
question, reached an unambiguous conclusion about how those competing
considerations should be resolved in a particular case or set of cases, and
implemented that conclusion via a specific mandate on manufacturers or
producers."[73]

Here, the natural inference is that an FDA drug approval decision—
which necessarily rests on a determination that the drug's benefits outweigh
its detriments—should carry preemptive weight. As noted earlier, FDA
decisions intrinsically, and by statutory mandate, constitute an effort to
establish a sensible trade-off among competing considerations, rather than
a mere "floor." The *Geier* case, rightly recognized by several contributors as
crucial to an understanding of preemption law, powerfully reinforces the
notion that agency determinations of optimum (rather than minimum)
standards deserve judicial respect.

In *Buckman*, a class of plaintiffs sued a consulting company involved in
the FDA's decision to approve certain orthopedic bone screws for use in the
arm and leg long bones. The plaintiffs, who had claimed injury from the
off-label use of these screws in their spines, alleged that the consulting company had made fraudulent representations to the FDA in the course of
obtaining this device approval.[74] The Supreme Court held that state law
claims alleging fraud on the FDA were preempted by federal law. Such
claims, the Court said, would interfere with the FDA's discretionary enforcement authority. They would discourage the manufacturers from seeking
approval of those devices that had potentially beneficial off-label uses, on
the ground that this could expose the manufacturer to state-law claims.
Moreover, concern that "disclosures to the FDA, although deemed appropriate by the Administration, [might] later be judged insufficient in state

court" would provide an incentive for manufacturers to burden the agency with "a deluge of information that the Administration neither wants nor needs."[75]

Several general principles can be drawn from these decisions. First, both preambles and *amicus* briefs can demonstrate agency preemptive intent to a degree requiring courts to consider deferring to the agency's judgment.[76] Second, situations where an agency has balanced competing interests are more likely to result in preemption than situations in which an agency has simply set a minimum standard.[77] Third, the Court is likely to find preemption when state-law claims implicate an agency's discretionary authority over regulated parties. Each of these principles provide support for preemption of state-law claims. The FDA has made its preemptive intent clear in both a preamble and in numerous *amicus* briefs. The agency's labeling decisions involve an effort to balance adequate warnings with appropriate availability and usage of beneficial drugs. And FDA authority over drug advertising involves discretionary oversight of regulated parties.

The direct result of recognizing the preemptive effect of FDA rulings would be nationally uniform drug labels on which both patients and manufacturers can rely.[78] A great deal of the uncertainty involved in distributing drugs would be removed with the threat of failure-to-warn suits, as would a great deal of the uncertainty in prescribing drugs (because labels would better differentiate between more significant and less significant risks). The FDA's ability to achieve its mission of protecting and promoting public health would be increased, and patients would receive the benefits of drugs that strike what the FDA has determined to be the optimal balance of safety and efficacy.

As the expert federal agency charged with regulation of prescription drugs, the FDA is ideally placed to make the risk-benefit determinations required for effective pharmaceutical regulation. Courts and juries applying state law, presented only with the facts of a specific case, do not have the same ability to see the broad landscape. Decisions that may seem "right" to a jury in an individual case—such as requiring a drug manufacturer to compensate an injured individual for a rare, genetically determined negative reaction to an otherwise beneficial drug—can have severe, unintended consequences for individuals who are not parties to the case. Importantly, even compensatory damage awards can have these adverse effects.

Although punitive damage awards severely increase the undesirable incentives affecting the pharmaceutical industry, mass tort claims would be exceedingly expensive to defend even without the possibility of punitive damages. As a matter of public health policy, it is both appropriate and necessary to reduce the negative effect of individual compensation decisions on the development, availability, and price of pharmaceuticals for other patients.[79]

Effects on nonparties may be uniquely harmful to public health in the context of pharmaceutical liability. Recall that prescription drugs, at our current state of technological achievement, can be modified only in limited ways. In most cases, the beneficial properties of a particular drug are simply not available without the possibility—or even the certainty—of some adverse effect. The FDA will approve an individual drug when the agency believes that the benefits of having the drug available to prescribers outweigh the adverse effects that the substance may have in some patients. Such an outcome is clearly desirable. For a dramatic example, it is difficult to imagine that any serious person would suggest that the world would be better off without the oral polio vaccine, even though that vaccine is known to cause polio in some individuals who would not otherwise have been exposed to the disease.[80]

The increasing tendency of courts to allow state-law suits to proceed, even when those suits attempt to hold drug manufacturers to standards of conduct that would contravene federal-law obligations, threatens the FDA's ability to regulate pharmaceutical manufacturers. The FDA initially defended its mandate through intervention in individual state-law suits. However, it soon became clear that use of the rulemaking process would allow the agency to protect its statutory mandate more effectively and at a lower cost than intervention alone. The FDA will likely continue to participate in product-liability lawsuits brought under state law as necessary to safeguard its considerable expertise in regulating the content of drug labeling and advertising. Nonetheless, this is not a complete solution to the problems created by inappropriate pharmaceutical-liability rules, as the FDA lacks the resources to use court submissions as a mechanism for defending its statutory mandate against all cases of state encroachment.

Neither the statement of preemptive intent in the Physician Labeling Rule nor the *amicus* briefs filed by the U.S. Department of Justice on behalf of the FDA were strictly necessary to establish preemption of state tort claims. (Should a future administration decide—perhaps as a favor to the plaintiff's bar—to attempt to disavow preemptive authority, it would and should have a hard time doing so.) The FDA statements of preemptive intent are useful primarily as an aid to courts in understanding the proper interpretation of the FDCA and its accompanying regulations. By clearly setting forth the FDA's preemptive authority in a document readily available to courts and litigants, the Physician Labeling Rule may make it less necessary for the FDA to file individual briefs. Even if some courts fail to give sufficient deference to the FDA's "fair and considered judgment,"[81] the new rule should, at the least, remove any question as to whether the FDA intends for its rules to preempt state tort actions.[82]

Notes

1. FDA, "Mission Statement," www.fda.gov/opacom/morechoices/mission.html (accessed December 12, 2006); see also 21 U.S.C. § 393(b) (setting out the FDA's statutory mission to both "promote the public health by promptly and efficiently reviewing clinical research and taking appropriate action on the marketing of regulated products in a timely manner" and "protect the public health by ensuring that . . . drugs are safe and effective").

2. John P. Swann, "History of the FDA," FDA History Office, www.fda.gov/oc/history/historyoffda/fulltext.html (accessed December 12, 2006).

3. FDA, "Requirements on Content and Format of Labeling for Human Prescription Drug and Biological Products" ("Physician Labeling Rule") (revising 21 C.F.R. §§ 201, 314, 601), at 37–47, 169–76. The page citations in this chapter refer to the signed version of the final rule dated December 7, 2005. This document is available at http://www.fda.gov/bbs/topics/news/2005/NEW01272.html (accessed March 4, 2007). For accounts of the controversy see, e.g. Lisa Brennan, "New FDA Rule's Preamble Stirs Up Bar on Both Sides," New Jersey Law Journal, February 1, 2006; Gardiner Harris, "New Drug Label Rule Is Intended to Reduce Medical Errors," New York Times, January 19, 2006.

4. As an additional disclaimer, my current practice includes the representation of companies facing state-law claims that could be affected by FDA preemption.

5. While I do not extensively address preemption issues in the context of medical devices (because an express preemption provision in the Medical Device Amendments to the FDCA makes the legal issues very different), many of the policy issues are the same.

6. Tufts Center for the Study of Drug Development, "Total Cost to Develop a New Prescription Drug, Including Cost of Post-Approval Research, is $897 Million," press release, May 13, 2003, http://csdd.tufts.edu/NewsEvents/NewsArticle.asp?newsid=29.

7. 21 U.S.C. § 355(d).

8. Physician Labeling Rule, supra note 3, at 39.

9. Ibid.

10. Am. Med. Ass'n, Reporting Adverse Drug and Medical Device Events: Report of the AMA's Council on Ethical and Judicial Affairs, 49 Food & Drug L.J. 359, 359–60 (1994).

11. Ibid. at 360 (footnote omitted).

12. Ibid.; accord Institute of Medicine, Vaccine Supply and Innovation (1985), 8 ("[T]here is no way totally to avoid injuries caused by current vaccines manufactured according to approved procedures and administered in accordance with recommended medical practices short of the total suspension of vaccine use, which is unacceptable because of the increased risk of morbidity and mortality.").

13. See Cass R. Sunstein, Administrative Substance, 607 Duke L.J. 625 (1991).

14. United States v. Evers, 453 F. Supp. 1141 (1978). The case discussed prescriptions for off-label use and held that "Congress did not intend to empower the FDA to

interfere with medical practice by limiting the ability of physicians to prescribe according to their best judgment." The court cited the lack of coverage for physician actions in the list of prohibited actions under the Federal Food, Drug, and Cosmetic Act, 21 U.S.C. § 331(k), as evidence of Congressional intent.

15. Physician Labeling Rule, *supra* 3 at 41–42; See also, *Geier v. American Honda Motor Co.*, 529 U.S. 861, 875–76, 868 (2000) (distinguishing for preemption purposes between "minimum safety standard" and a standard intended to balance competing factors); Michael D. Green, *Statutory Compliance and Tort Liability: Examining the Strongest Case*, 30 U. Mich. J. L. Reform 461, 468–69 (1997).

16. Physician Labeling Rule, *supra* 3 at 171. This position of the FDA is not new. See, *e.g.*, Labeling and Prescription Drug Advertising; Content and Format for Labeling for Human Prescription Drugs, 44 Fed. Reg. 37434, 37436 (1979) ("[S]tatutory scheme for drug labeling is intended to provide physicians, in straightforward and concise terms, with the information they need to prescribe a drug under conditions that maximize the drug's effectiveness and minimize its risks.").

17. 21 C.F.R. § 314.70. Courts and plaintiffs rely on § 314.70(c)(6)(iii)(A) to support their argument that a defendant manufacturer could have revised the risk information in its package insert without explicit permission from the FDA; however, manufacturers seldom, if ever, add or revise risk information unilaterally, preferring to consult with the FDA first. See Richard M. Cooper, *Drug Labeling and Products Liability: The Role of the Food and Drug Administration*, 41 Food & Drug L.J. 233, 238 (1986); Thomas Scarlett, *The Relationship Among Adverse Drug Reaction Reporting, Drug Labeling, Product Liability, and Federal Preemption*, 46 Food & Drug L.J. 31, 36 (1991). See also Physician Labeling Rule, *supra* 3 at 40 ("[I]n practice, manufacturers typically consult with FDA prior to adding risk information to labeling.").

18. Physician Labeling Rule, *supra* 3 at 171.

19. Terence Dungworth, *Product Liability and the Business Sector* (Santa Monica, CA: RAND Institute for Civil Justice, 1988), 38.

20. See Melissa Nann Burke, *Philadelphia Sees 10,000 Fen-Phen Cases in 2004*, Nat'l L.J., July 20, 2005.

21. *Bradley v. Weinberger*, 483 F.2d 410, 415 (1st Cir. 1973). This case, involving treatments for diabetes, was one of the most contentious episodes in the FDA's administration of the federal drug law. Physicians had sued the FDA, alleging that proposed labeling was misleading because of a failure to show the existence of debate within the scientific community. After winning the case, the FDA promulgated a regulation, 21 C.F.R. § 1.21 Labeling; Failure To Reveal Material Facts, 40 Fed. Reg. 28582 (1975)), stating that "[w]here potential danger is the statutory standard, a warning must be unencumbered and unambiguous . . . where warnings are required, disclamatory opinions necessarily detract from the warning in such a manner as to be confusing and misleading." Ibid.

22. AMA Board of Trustees, "Impact of Product Liability on the Development of New Medical Technologies," American Medical Association (1988), 1.

23. See Amy Finkelstein, "Health Policy and Technological Change: Evidence from the Vaccine Industry" (working paper no. 9460, National Bureau of Economic Research, Cambridge, MA, January 2003). Finkelstein's research focused on the Vaccine Injury Compensation Fund (VICF), a no-fault product liability system paid for by excise taxes on certain childhood vaccines. That system took the place of tort remedies stemming from those vaccines and applied a fixed payment schedule for claims. It had the salutary effects of reducing risk by normalizing payments and reducing expected liability costs. The result was stark: institution of the fund led to a statistically significant increase in new clinical trials. Ibid. at 22–24.

24. Michael J. Moore and W. Kip Viscusi, *Product Liability Entering the Twenty-first Century: The U.S. Perspective* (Washington, D.C.: AEI-Brookings Joint Center for Regulatory Studies, 2001), 25, 27.

25. *Browning-Ferris Indus. of Vt., Inc. v. Kelco Disposal, Inc.*, 492 U.S. 257, 282 (1989) (O'Connor, J., concurring in part and dissenting in part).

26. See, *e.g.*, Bernard Wysocki, Jr., "Fearing Avian Flu, Bioterror, U.S. Scrambles to Fill Drug Gap," *Wall Street Journal*, November 9, 2005 ("Vaccine makers point to the heavy costs of litigating suits alleging a link between vaccines and autism. Despite scholarly studies that have found no link, some 350 lawsuits have been filed, costing $200 million, industry executives say. None has yet gone to trial.").

27. Steven Garber, *Product Liability and the Economics of Pharmaceuticals and Medical Devices* (Santa Monica, CA: Rand, Institute for Civil Justice, 1993), 167.

28. John P. Wilson, *The Resolution of Legal Impediments to the Manufacture and Administration of an AIDS Vaccine*, 34 Santa Clara L. Rev. 495, 505 (1994); W. Kip Viscusi and Michael J. Moore, "Rationalizing the Relationship Between Product Liability and Innovation," in *Tort Law and the Public Interest: Competition, Innovation, and Consumer Welfare*, ed. Peter H. Schuck (New York: Norton, 1991) 111.

29. Institute of Medicine, *supra* note 12 at 2.

30. Viscusi & Moore, *supra* note 28 at 111; see also, Patricia Danzon and Nuno Sousa Pereira, "Why Sole-Supplier Vaccine Markets May Be Here to Stay," *Health Affairs* 24, no. 3 (2005): 694.

31. See Jon Cohen, "Is Liability Slowing AIDS Vaccines?" *Science*, April 10, 1992. See, *e.g.*, Linda Johnson, "Wyeth Won't Resume Norplant Sales," July 26, 2002, http://www.nwcn.com/sharedcontent/business/topstories/072602ccbiznorplant.2af08 712.html; Gina Kolata, "Will the Lawyers Kill Off Norplant?" *New York Times*, May 28, 1995; see generally Luigi Mastroianni, Jr. et al., eds., *Developing New Contraceptives: Obstacles and Opportunities* (Washington, D.C.: Institute of Medicine & National Research Council, 1990), 118–43.

32. See, *e.g.*, E. Patrick McGuire, "The Impact of Product Liability" (research report no. 908, The Conference Board, 1988), 17 (quoting a drug manufacturer: "We have been forced to discontinue sale of therapeutically beneficial drugs because of excessive product liability costs.").

33. Marvin E. Jaffe, "Regulation, Litigation. and Innovation in the Pharmaceutical Industry: An Equation for Safety," in *Product Liability and Innovation: Managing Risk in an Uncertain Environment*, eds. Janet R. Hunziker and Trevor O. Jonas (Washington, D.C.: National Academy Press, 1994), 126. As a result, it was reported in 1994 that "treatment for severe nausea during pregnancy now accounts for nearly $40 million of the nation's annual hospital bill." Ibid. at 126.

34. See Determination That Bendectin Was Not Withdrawn From Sale for Reasons of Safety or Effectiveness, 64 Fed. Reg. 43190 (Aug. 9, 1999); see also Louis Lasagna, "The Chilling Effect of Product Liability on New Drug Development," in *The Liability Maze: The Impact of Liability Law on Safety and Innovation*, eds. Peter W. Huber and Robert E. Litan (Washington, D.C: Brookings Institution, 1991), 337–41.

35. Lasagna, *supra* note 34 at 341–45.

36. Ibid. at 344.

37. *E.g.*, Anthony S. Fauci, "A Risky Business," *Washington Times*, November 30, 2004 (column by the director of the National Institute of Allergy and Infectious Diseases at the National Institutes of Health).

38. See, *e.g.*, Richard L. Manning, *Changing Rules in Tort Law and the Market for Childhood Vaccines*, 37 J. L. & Econ. 247, 273 (1994) (noting the "dramatic" effect of liability costs on vaccine prices); Richard L. Manning, *Products Liability and Prescription Drug Prices in Canada and the United States*, 40 J. L. & Economics 203, 234 (1997); Garber, *supra* note 27 at 122 (concluding that a high perceived liability potential results in "substantially higher" product prices).

39. Manning, *Changing Rules*, *supra* note 38 at 257; Gina Kolata, "Litigation Causes Huge Price Increase in Childhood Vaccines," *Science*, June 13, 1986.

40. Manning, *Changing Rules*, *supra* note 38 at 254–55, 257.

41. Ibid. at 257.

42. Ibid. at 254–55, 257–60.

43. Physician Labeling Rule, *supra* note 3 at 42–43 ("FDA has previously found that labeling that includes theoretical hazards not well-grounded in scientific evidence can cause meaningful risk information to 'lose its significance'. . . . Overwarning, just like underwarning, can similarly have a negative effect on patient safety and public health. . . . Similarly, State-law attempts to impose additional warnings can lead to labeling that does not accurately portray a product's risks, thereby potentially discouraging safe and effective use of approved products or encouraging inappropriate use and undermining the objectives of the act.") (citing Prescription Drug Advertising; Content and Format for Labeling for Human Prescription Drugs, 44 Fed. Reg. 37434, 37447 (June 26, 1979)); see also Lars Noah, *The Imperative to Warn: Disentangling the "Right to Know" from the "Need to Know" About Consumer Product Hazards*, 11 Yale J. on Reg. 293, 374–91 (1994).

44. See Physician Labeling Rule, *supra* note 3 at 37 ("In comments, some manufacturers expressed concerns that, by highlighting selected information . . . to the exclusion of information not highlighted, they make themselves more vulnerable to product

liability claims. . . . FDA acknowledges the comment's concerns and, as discussed more fully in response to comment 13, believes that under existing preemption principles such product liability claims would be preempted.").

45. *Feldman v. Lederle Labs.*, 125 N.J. 117, 128 (1991).

46. Ibid. at 154.

47. Ibid. at 123.

48. Ibid. at 147, 152–153.

49. See ibid. at 130. The FDA also addresses this issue in the new Physician Labeling Rule, squarely rejecting the myth that manufacturers are free to add or revise risk information without first obtaining FDA approval. Although the agency has not revised the relevant portion of the NDA regulations, 21 C.F.R. § 314.70, it does make clear in the preamble that manufacturers generally consult with FDA and await specific authorization before supplementing risk information in labeling. The agency also twice points out that changes-being-effected (CBE) supplements may not be used under the final rule to make changes to the "Highlights" section. Physician Labeling Rule, *supra* note 3, at 32, 40.

50. Justice Robert L. Clifford, writing for the majority of the New Jersey Supreme Court, suggested that compliance with the FDA determination was motivated by an irresponsible focus on profit above patient interest. Ibid. at 127. Justice Marie L. Garibaldi said in dissent, "[t]he majority unfairly casts Lederle as a scheming dissembler that provided evasive answers and caused some sort of knowing delay in FDA decisions by suppressing information. Were that true, my position here might be different." Ibid. at 170.

51. *Levine v. Wyeth*, 2006 Vt. 107 (Vt. 2006).

52. *Accord*, Levine, 2006 WL at ¶ 63 (Reiber, C.J., dissenting) ("While a state-court jury presumably shares the FDA's concern that drugs on the market be reasonably safe, the jury does not assess reasonableness in the context of public health and the associated risk-benefit analysis. A jury does not engage in a measured and multi-faceted policy analysis. Rather, a jury views the safety of the drug through the lens of a single patient who has already been catastrophically injured.").

53. FDA Commissioner Young to California Governor George Deukmejian, letter, August 28, 1987, in *Food and Drug Law, Cases and Materials*, eds. Peter B. Hutt and Richard A. Merrill (New York: Foundation Press, 2d ed. 1991), 1021.

54. See, *e.g.*, Lester M. Crawford, commissioner of food and drugs, to Bill Lockyer, attorney general of the state of California, letter, August 12, 2005, http://www.cfsan.fda.gov/~dms/fl-ltr65.html.

55. *Dowhal v. SmithKline Beecham Consumer Healthcare*, 88 P.3d 1, 4 (Cal. 2004) (citing minutes of the FDA Nonprescription Drug Advisory Meeting, April 19, 1996).

56. Ibid. at 46.

57. See Madhukar H. Trivedi et al., "Evaluation of Outcomes with Citalopram for Depression Using Measurement-Based Care in STAR*D Implications for Clinical Practice," *American Journal of Psychiatry* 163 (2006): 28; Gregory E. Simon et al.,

"Suicide Risk During Antidepressant Treatment," *American Journal of Psychiatry* 163 (2006): 41.

58. FDA, "Public Health Advisory: Worsening Depression and Suicidality in Patients Being Treated with Antidepressant," March 22, 2004, http://www.fda.gov/cder/drug/antidepressants/AntidepressanstPHA.htm.

59. Simon et al., *supra* note 27 at 44–45.

60. FDA, "FDA Alert: Suicidal Thoughts or Actions in Children and Adults," July 2005, http://www.fda.gov/cder/drug/infopage/sertraline/default.htm.

61. Memorandum of Decision, *In re Paxil Litigation*, No. CV 01-07937 MRP (C.D. Cal. Oct. 18, 2002).

62. *Motus v. Pfizer, Inc.*, 196 F. Supp. 2d 984, 1092 (2001).

63. *Motus v. Pfizer, Inc.*, 358 F.3d 659, 660 (9th Cir. 2004)

64. Amicus Brief for the United States, *Kallas v. Pfizer, Inc.*, No. 2:04-cv-998 (D. Utah filed Sept. 15, 2005), at 37.

65. 471 U.S. 707 (1985).

66. 518 U.S. 470 (1996).

67. 531 U.S. 341 (2001).

68. 529 U.S. 861 (2000).

69. *Hillsborough*, 471 U.S. at 716.

70. Ibid. at 714–15.

71. Ibid. at 718 (emphasis added).

72. *Medtronic*, 518 U.S. at 492.

73. Ibid. at 501 (1996).

74. *Buckman*, 531 U.S. at 343. The company obtained separate approval of the device's two parts for arm and leg use after twice failing to obtain approval of the full device for use in the spine. Ibid. at 346.

75. Ibid. at 351.

76. *Hillsborough*, 471 U.S. at 718; *Geier*, 529 U.S. at 881.

77. See *Medtronic*, 518 U.S. at 501; *Geier*, 529 U.S. at 881.

78. The FDA recognized the benefits of uniform warnings as early as 1982, when it promulgated over-the-counter labels for pregnant women: "A single national warning will help ensure that consumers receive clear, unambiguous, and consistent information . . . [d]iffering State requirements could conflict with the Federal warning, cause confusion to consumers, and otherwise weaken the Federal warning." Pregnant or Nursing Women; Amendment of Labeling Requirements for Over the Counter Human Drugs, 47 Fed. Reg. 54750 (Dec. 3, 1982).

79. This of course begs the question of how injured individuals *should* be compensated. An alternative, across-the-board compensation system does not appear to be politically feasible at this time. It bears mention, however, that in the related context of medical malpractice, the current liability regime poorly aligns compensation decisions with actual determination of fault. See, *e.g.*, Troyen A. Brennan et al., "Relation Between Negligent Adverse Events and the Outcomes of Medical-Malpractice

Litigation," *New England Journal of Medicine* 355 (1996): 1965 (noting that the one factor predicting whether a patient would be compensated was not negligence, but severity of the injury); David M. Studdert et al., "Claims, Errors, and Compensation Payments in Medical Malpractice Litigation," *New England Journal of Medicine* 354 (2006): 2024 (in a study touted as casting doubt on claims that frivolous medical malpractice suits are common, indicating that 28 percent of claims not involving errors resulted in compensation and that when compensation for such claims was paid, it averaged nearly 60 percent of the value of payments for claims involving medical errors).

80. See Centers for Disease Control and Prevention, "Polio Vaccine: What You Need To Know," January 1, 2000, http://www.cdc.gov/nip/publications/VIS/vis-IPV.pdf (noting that the oral polio vaccine causes polio in approximately 1 in 2.4 million people who receive it). The polio shot does not carry a risk of causing polio but is less effective as a public health measure in areas where polio is prevalent. Ibid.

81. *Geier*, 529 U.S. at 884 (quotation omitted).

82. See, *e.g.*, *Bates v. Dow Agrosciences LLC*, 544 U.S. 431, 453 (2005) (Breyer, J., concurring) ("In *Medtronic, Inc. v. Lohr*, 518 U.S. 470 (1996), I pointed out that an administrative agency, there the Food and Drug Administration, had the legal authority within ordinary administrative constraints to promulgate agency rules and to determine the pre-emptive effect of those rules in light of the agency's special understanding of 'whether (or the extent to which) state requirements may interfere with federal objectives.'")

4

Federal Preemption in Cellular Phone Regulation

*Thomas W. Hazlett**

Cellular phone service depends on spectrum policies enacted by the federal government. The basic market structure questions—how many firms compete, what technologies they use, how much bandwidth they access, and how they interconnect with other networks—are determined by the Federal Communications Commission (FCC). Still, state regulation of wireless phone systems has collided with federal jurisdiction in many respects. The Omnibus Budget Reconciliation Act of 1993 (OBRA) established that "no State or local government shall have any authority to regulate the entry of or the rates charged by any commercial mobile service or any private mobile service."[1] This effectively preempted state regulation of cellular rates with a one-year phase-in, meaning that there has been no federal or state regulation of wireless telephone charges since August 1994. However, states were left with jurisdiction over "other terms and conditions of commercial mobile services."[2] How much regulatory authority this provision cedes to the states is legally uncertain.[3] (It appears clear that there will be some shared responsibilities, with federal jurisdiction for key economic regulations including spectrum-related issues, and state authority over matters that are traditionally decentralized, such as the resolution of contractual disputes in municipal and state courts.) The Telecommunications Act of 1996 (1996 Act) instituted further preemption, particularly of local zoning restrictions, which inhibited the siting of towers for wireless networks. Again, the extent to which state and local authorities are prohibited from regulating is under debate. Portions of this question have been decided in favor of federal jurisdiction, while other responsibilities have been given to state law.[4]

The political wrangling over the scope of preemption under OBRA and the 1996 Act have continued to this day. Some states are considering new regulations for wireless telephone service, and federal legislation has been introduced to achieve similar objectives.[5] Proposed rules would potentially change marketing practices, alter the information conveyed in newspaper, radio, or TV ads, and stretch the "free trial" periods before "early termination fees" would kick in. Where, as a matter of public policy, should one draw the line regarding consumer protection regulations? From the perspective of consumer welfare, and assuming a possible role for regulatory standards, would the standards be most efficiently set and applied by the several states or at the federal government level? Two broad sets of marketplace evidence help to answer these questions, and both suggest that federal jurisdiction is relatively efficient.

The first concerns the efficiency of national scope in wireless networks. The economics of wireless telephony suggest that regardless of the jurisdiction selected for rulemaking, diverse local rules will not effectively determine standards. Rather, nationally integrated network operators will choose to conform to those regulations that allow them the best opportunity to offer nationwide service. This undermines incentives for states to create efficient rules. Either such rules will have little practical impact, or they will create large *external* effects on consumers and suppliers outside the political jurisdiction where policies are crafted. Such effects are typically discounted in the decisions of policy makers, resulting in rules that are relatively inefficient.

The second set of data is derived from a natural experiment involving the 1994 federal preemption of cellular rate regulation by the states. State controls demonstrably failed to lower rates for customers. Nonetheless, strenuous arguments were made at the time by several state regulatory commissions that such controls were efficient and should be permitted to continue. This speaks directly to the effectiveness of state regulation of wireless telephone service.

Trade-Offs: State vs. Federal Jurisdiction

The Case for Regulation: Market Failure. Government regulation provides two possible forms of protection for consumers, both related to the concept of market failure. The first is to constrain monopoly pricing. When successful, regulation can lower prices and increase output. The second general aim of economic regulation is to remedy externality problems. These develop when costs or benefits do not accrue to the decision makers who cause them and are external to economic calculations. This results in a misallocation of resources, yielding pollution and various public good problems. Efficient economic activities fail to take place because payoffs cannot be captured by those who would shoulder the costs of provision. Free-rider problems deny consumers useful products.

Regulation, of course, is neither free nor perfect. Market failure is necessary in an argument for government intervention, but it is insufficient without a convincing case that regulation will itself produce net consumer benefits. Even when market failure has been addressed by, for instance, rate regulation of monopoly cable television systems, policy remedies can prove counterproductive.[6] The case for regulation fundamentally depends on the likelihood of increased consumer welfare.

Monopolistic market power is not a compelling rationale for wireless telephone regulation. For some time, cellular telephone markets were dominated by duopoly licensees, and market power clearly existed.[7] But with the emergence of personal communications services (PCS) and enhanced specialized mobile radio (ESMR) competition and the emergence of strong national networks that aggressively rival each other, government regulators declared the market to be highly competitive. In abolishing the "spectrum cap" (effective January 2003), federal regulators certified that market rivalry was effectively protecting consumers from excessive prices.

The case for efficient government regulation in wireless must therefore point to market failure in the supply of consumer information. Consumers make choices based on their preferences and product expectations. The data on which purchasing decisions are based flows from a variety of sources: experience and research by the consumer, marketing campaigns waged by sellers, reputational capital of sellers, publicity and product evaluations provided by news organizations and third parties, and word of mouth. In some instances, however, reliable information is underprovided because suppliers are not remunerated for supplying it. Alternative market mechanisms for discovering which products best satisfy preferences are available, but they may leave a gap unfilled. The rationale for government regulation is then to encourage the supply of valuable information that consumers would gladly pay the market cost of providing.

A related rationale for government regulation arises in the context of fly-by-night operations. When firms supply goods without sinking capital, they may be tempted to cheat on performance. This behavior may include misleading advertising, hidden charges, or the delivery of goods or services that are less valuable than anticipated by the customer.[8] Cheating vendors may be able to escape with profits, as consumers have difficulty in identifying such behavior prepurchase. A legal intervention to improve quality ascertainment, perhaps through means such as direct regulation or binding rules that force firms to commit irreversible investment capital, may improve efficiency. This rationale, however, is unpersuasive in the wireless context. Wireless network owners commit very substantial resources to establishing infrastructure, and these assets will only prove profitable where long-run economic viability is maintained. These firms are unlikely to fly by night, leaving enormous capital assets behind.[9] This makes the argument for regulatory intervention weaker than in services where market forces do not similarly punish opportunistic behavior by sellers.

Optimal Jurisdiction. The question of optimal jurisdiction commonly arises when overlapping regulatory interests are present, as in antitrust law, cable television regulation, food labeling—and wireless telephony. State regulation is typically preferable when local markets are relatively idiosyncratic, when the benefits of diverse rules are large relative to the costs of nonuniformity, when the rules adopted in one state are largely contained within that jurisdiction, and when state utility commissions or local franchising agents are as technically competent as federal regulators. (For example, local utilities have traditionally been regulated as monopoly franchises by state commissions.) The advantage of differentiation lies in the informational efficiencies local regulators enjoy relative to the advantages of scale economies they sacrifice (or disrupt). Diverse state rules allow for trial and error, allowing different approaches to be tested over time. Yet, conflicting rules and regulations can clog the wheels of commerce, introducing inefficiencies that lower consumer welfare. When economies of scale stretch beyond state borders, decentralized regulations lack effective feedback. State regulators have little direct information regarding costs imposed on consumers in other states, and they have little reason to acquire this information. Even assuming that state regulators are well-informed as to costs and benefits within their political jurisdiction, an important externality issue is introduced courtesy of economies of scale, including network effects. The key economic issue concerns the costs and benefits of rule diversity. While consumers may have heterogeneous interests that return some informational advantage to state jurisdictions, the lack of coordination with other states can create costs for local consumers that outweigh these advantages.

Selection of the optimal jurisdiction largely reduces to a search for the smallest unit of government (lowest tier) that substantially avoids "beggar thy neighbor" outcomes from decentralized policy making. These results occur when nonuniformity is relatively costly and when the advantages of diverse rules are relatively unimportant. Under such circumstances, several problems can develop with decentralization, most of which are associated with free riding.

An example is the funding of such public goods as national defense. Because voters tend to prefer low taxes, elected state or local officials do too. If taxpayers in jurisdictions contributing little in taxes cannot be excluded from the defensive services provided by the nation's armed forces, decentralized provision would be predicted to lead to underprovision. This means that citizens would get less investment in national defense than they would be willing to pay if an effective payment collection mechanism were in place. In the absence of such, local and state officials predictably have incentives to limit taxes in their jurisdiction by free riding on the burdens shouldered elsewhere, a paradigmatic example of a governmental function most efficiently supplied through the central authority. This aspect of national defense extends to other domains. While not perfectly "nonrivalrous," network industries that depend on national economies of scale exhibit similar economic characteristics.

In markets where economies of scale or scope are important, it is possible for decentralized policy makers to effectively free-ride on investments undertaken by consumers in other jurisdictions. This occurs when a system is built to serve a large regional or national market, and state or local policy makers impose expensive regulations over a subset of that system. These regulations impose a tax, which may or may not be efficient for local consumers. Given that costs and/or benefits spill over to other jurisdictions, effects of local regulatory decisions will likely escape the attention of policy makers. Analogous to a "race to the bottom," state regulators search for rules that will bestow benefits locally while shifting costs to network investments that enable local benefits to be subsidized by users elsewhere.

Suppose a rule is imposed by Idaho regulators mandating that wireless carriers send each Idaho subscriber a monthly statement comparing the customer's billing with what identical service would cost on five other carriers. Assume that this "full disclosure" act costs ten dollars per subscriber per month, while the benefit to customers is just fifty cents per month (meaning that each subscriber would agree to pay just six dollars per year to receive such a statement). The rule is highly inefficient, imposing costs twenty times the level of benefits, but state regulators may still impose the rule, even under the assumption that Idaho regulators are perfectly loyal to the interests of Idaho residents.

If wireless telephone service is efficiently provided by national networks (as opposed to local systems), and if providing those networks entails the use of standardized national calling plans, then customizing a separate pricing structure for Idaho customers may prove more trouble than it is worth for wireless carriers. Carriers would then provide the monthly statements to Idaho subscribers without a differential charge, and competition would drive these costs to customers in other states. The charges would be imperceptible to users in Idaho or elsewhere. But the incentives thereby created would lead to regulatory free riding across all states, and costs would accumulate.

Three outcomes would result: First, inefficiency would result from rules that imposed costs in excess of the benefits delivered. Second, the decline in network profitability (associated with the inefficiency of the regulations imposed in Idaho) would lower investment in network infrastructure nationally. The magnitude could be modest, but the direction of change is unambiguous: with higher costs, the value of acquiring subscribers is lower.[10] Third, state regulators elsewhere would be tempted to do what Idaho regulators have done, pursuing ways to impose nationwide costs that only benefit in-state subscribers. This results in "beggar thy neighbor" policies that reduce the quality of services for consumers nationwide.

The problem is not that ripple effects occur, but that state regulators have no reason to take into account what ripples across state borders. Even with a best-case scenario, inefficiencies arise when the costs imposed on wireless users by regulators in one state spill over to subscribers elsewhere. To comply with diverse state rules, firms have three options. They can choose to sacrifice economies of scale, producing custom services state by state. Alternatively, they can choose to provide a national plan, tailoring it to comply with the most stringent state requirements. This may be impossible if state rules actually conflict; balkanized service plans would be required. This raises compliance costs and, ironically, eliminates the effectiveness of most states' regulations. That is because the most stringent rules will be set by regulators in another state, except in the special case when most people live in states where regulators reach precisely the same set of "toughest" rules. Finally, firms can adopt a hybrid approach where they maintain a national standard for most markets but customize local service where state regulation is onerous. This sacrifices some, if not all, scale economies while providing a safety valve to mitigate very expensive regulations that may be assessed in some jurisdictions. Some rules can prompt suppliers to tailor state level offerings by simply exiting some markets altogether. While that is unlikely in wireless telephony due to demands for ubiquitous coverage, firms can partially exit high-cost markets, investing less in cell sites, base stations, marketing, and other inputs.

In short, economic externalities imply that state decision making is ineffective. When integrated national networks are key both to suppliers, who seek scale economies, and to consumers, who desire nationwide coverage, the competition between the states results not in diverse standards but "winner take all"—the "winner" being the state with the most restrictive regulations. In situations where state regulations contradict each other, even this effort to smooth out differences in state laws will be stymied and the costs of balkanization further increased. Wireless communications regulation provides a powerful illustration.

Building Wireless Networks

Cellular phone service began with the issuance of two competing licenses, mostly by lottery, in each of 306 metropolitan service areas (MSAs) between 1984 and 1986 and in 428 rural service areas between 1988 and 1989. This was the result of a rulemaking process formally initiated by the FCC in 1968. The long delays involved regulatory debate over many issues, including how many companies should be licensed and how much spectrum should be allocated for use. The FCC, on an assumption of natural monopoly, initially decided to license just one operator, but became persuaded that some competition was possible and that licensing two rivals in each service area would still allow for economies of scale to be realized by each. It allocated various increments of bandwidth, finally deciding to allot 25 MHz (about the same used for four television channels) to each license.

The potential of wireless telephone service was vastly underestimated. Through the mid- to late 1980s, prices for actively traded cellular licenses increased almost monotonically. Beginning trades were just $12 "per POP" (price of the license divided by total population in the market area covered by the license), but by 1988, prices exceeded $135.[11] By 1990, the aggregate nationwide value of the licenses just in the MSAs (covering about 80 percent of U.S. population) was estimated at close to $80 billion. These large market capitalizations were driven by strong customer demand for wireless phone service, enhanced network coverage, rapidly falling handset costs, and rapidly increasing handset functionality (including miniaturization and increased battery life).[12]

Prices were much higher than fixed-line service, however, and they had exhibited no substantial decline since the initiation of cellular systems. The duopoly market structure imposed on the industry had established reasonable service, but it was expensive and extremely fragmented owing to the FCC's 734-market licensing grid. This would change as competition and consolidation dramatically restructured the industry.

Entry was primarily achieved in two regulatory proceedings, the most important being for PCS. PCS used smaller cells than traditional cellular systems, as well as digital formats that improved capacity and performance. Formally initiated in 1990, the Commission allocated 120 MHz to six new licenses. Two licenses were issued in each of 51 major trading areas (MTAs). These licenses were auctioned, pursuant to new federal legislation, in 1995. Four remaining PCS licenses were assigned in each of 493 basic trading areas (BTAs). Auctions for these licenses were held in 1996 and 1997.[13] With simultaneous auctions, PCS bidders could aggregate permits to create regional or national service territories, as Sprint PCS did, for example, in winning licenses covering close to the entire country.

PCS licensees began constructing competing wireless telephone systems just as Fleet Call, now Nextel, was deploying a nationwide wireless network using specialized mobile radio (SMR) licenses. The plan actually used licenses for local dispatch services (taxis, pizza delivery, etc.), which by means of a strategic regulatory waiver was permitted to provide wireless phone competition.[14] By accumulating thousands of licenses for such local-ized services and creating a national network with the right to offer service to the general public, a new coast-to-coast wireless competitor was created.

Ironically, just as entry was deconcentrating the industry, hundreds of mergers were stitching together regional and national networks. These rein-forced the roaming agreements and joint ventures that had been launched to create mobile services, giving customers the ability to move with their telephones and yet receive cellular service through far-ranging local con-nections. By 2001, when merger activity hit a lull, six national networks—AT&T Wireless, Cingular (a joint venture of SBC and BellSouth), Nextel, Sprint PCS, T-Mobile (Deutsche Telekom), and Verizon Wireless—emerged dominant, accounting for about 85 percent of U.S. subscribers. The net-works were pieced together from 3,642 separate licenses issued by regula-tors, and this omits the 41,833 SMR licenses that Nextel pieced together to construct its national wireless network. Economic rationalization via merg-ers, joint ventures, and marketing agreements has driven the aggregation of disparate franchise areas into nationwide systems.

TABLE 4-1
FCC LICENSE AGGREGATION IN WIRELESS TELEPHONY (2003)

	Number of Licenses			
	Cellular	PCS	SMR	Total
AT&T	56	282	0	338
Cingular	132	89	104	325
Nextel	0	0	41,833	41,833
Sprint PCS	0	163	0	163
T-Mobile	0	269	13	282
Verizon	165	117	0	282
Nextwave	0	95	0	95
Others	1,434	1,660	5,185	8,279
Total	**1,787**	**2,675**	**47,104**	**51,597**

SOURCE: Universal Licensing System, at http://wireless2.fcc.gov/UlsApp/UlsSearch/searchAdvanced.jsp.
Information was collected on July 31, 2003, by running searches in each license category.

Out of the consolidation arose competition. The emergence of nationally integrated networks and calling plans demonstrated that consumers were demanding services most economically provided on a broader scale. As larger networks formed, prices plummeted and demand skyrocketed. Between 1995 and 2002, the average price per minute fell from fifty-one cents to twelve cents; minutes of wireless use rose sixteen-fold (see table 4-2). Industry consolidation was marked during this period. The top six wireless operators served about 55 percent of U.S. subscribers in the mid-1990s and nearly 80 percent in 2000. Concentration did not rise in local markets (where, in any event, the FCC's "spectrum cap" constrained mergers). Instead, fragmented wireless operators were forming national networks. Intense competitive pressure made profits elusive, and efficiency gains are apparent.

TABLE 4-2
GROWTH IN U.S. WIRELESS TELEPHONE SERVICE, 1991–2002

Survey Period	Minutes of Use (MOU)	Subscribers	MOU/ Sub. per Month	Total Service Revenue ($000s)	Cost per Minute	Pene- tration Rate
1991	11,154,015,983	7,557,148	123	5,708,522	$0.51	2.9%
1992	13,567,533,156	11,032,753	102	7,822,726	$0.58	4.2%
1993	19,160,964,277	16,009,461	100	10,892,175	$0.57	6.1%
1994	26,950,000,239	24,134,421	93	14,229,922	$0.53	9.1%
1995	37,767,122,723	33,785,661	93	19,080,239	$0.51	12.6%
1996	51,970,200,176	44,042,992	98	23,634,971	$0.45	16.3%
1997	62,923,082,455	55,312,293	95	27,485,633	$0.44	20.2%
1998	89,010,438,637	69,209,321	107	33,133,175	$0.37	25.1%
1999	147,725,958,780	86,047,003	143	40,018,489	$0.27	30.9%
2000	258,854,860,127	109,478,031	197	52,466,020	$0.20	38.3%
2001	456,964,165,225	128,374,512	297	65,015,885	$0.14	44.4%
2002	619,000,000,000	140,766,842	366	76,508,187	$0.12	47.7%

SOURCE: Data from Cellular Telecommunication & Internet Association, "CTIA's Wireless Industry Indices Semi-Annual Data Survey Results: A Comprehensive Report from CTIA Year-End 2001 Results, An Analysis of the U.S. Wireless Industry," August 2002.

Plainly, the U.S. market gravitated to national networks because of economic efficiency, not due to regulatory constraints or path dependency. Indeed, regulators initially allotted thousands of local licenses, resisting any bias to impose national scope on service providers. No other Organization for Economic Co-Operation and Development (OECD) country had more than the eleven franchise areas used by Canada. The great majority of countries are issued national licenses for mobile wireless, on the presumption that wide area networks are efficient. In the United States, in contrast, national networks came to dominate from a radically fragmented starting point.

Regulators did not believe that this consolidation would, or should, occur. In 1995, in fact, the FCC theorized that national wireless service could be efficiently provided by local suppliers. Coordination between independent carriers could be arranged through roaming agreements and other contractual devices. But investors saw this differently. Between 1992 and 2002, substantial consolidation of the wireless telephone sector took place, even as new PCS and SMR entrants were introduced. The largest U.S. network in 1992 covered just a quarter of potential subscribers; a decade later, each of the top six networks covered nearly 75 percent or more.

The sharp drop in wireless telephone rates in the mid-1990s appears to be a deviation from the preexisting trend. State regulatory authorities told the FCC in 1994 that cellular rates had been fairly stable since the initiation of service in the mid-1980s.[15] Also in 1994, economist William Shew observed that the "average price of cellular service, in nominal terms, has exhibited a mild downward trend."[16] Rates plummeted only after PCS entry and the consolidation of national networks. As consolidation increased, prices declined.

The importance of national scope in service provision is clear. Seven years after the FCC hypothesized that local wireless operations might be competitive with national networks, market evidence clearly indicated the reverse: subscribers wanted the lower prices and ease of use, including roaming, made possible by consolidation and uniform national services. Key to this conclusion was the popularity of AT&T's "Digital One Rate" plan, a service offering that obliterates regional differences. When first brought to market in May 1998, AT&T's move was considered a risky gamble, but competitors rushed to offer similar plans of their own. The success of AT&T's uniform nationwide offer with customers was lost neither on market rivals nor on the FCC, which acknowledged the importance of unified national networks in numerous regulatory findings.[17]

These developments are fundamental in evaluating the optimal regulatory jurisdiction in wireless telephony. Because "seamless" operations are crucial to the competitiveness of wireless operators, these firms naturally strive to homogenize their offerings and to exploit economies of scale in advertising and marketing. In this marketplace, nonuniform offerings are inefficient, and wireless carriers will naturally gravitate to standard packages in order to deliver the efficiencies demanded by their customers.

Observed characteristics of the mobile telephone services market suggest that economies of scale and scope are important to consumers and that the licensing scheme instituted by the FCC imposed costs on the market by issuing licenses that unnecessarily fragmented networks. The FCC itself noted that cellular markets had been atomized with licenses issued by lotteries in 734 franchise areas.[18] It sought to promote aggregation both by licensing larger service territories in PCS and by awarding licenses via simultaneous auctions in which bidders could easily aggregate wireless service areas. But the basic marketplace dynamics were not driven by regulators or imposed by firms. They were the outcome of a competitive discovery process in which underlying efficiencies have proven themselves via the market test.

Gaining national geographic scope has also allowed competing wireless networks to better pursue technological upgrades and to roll out a richer mix of services. The result is that the quality of wireless service has improved markedly with the emergence of wider area networks. Uniform systems, governed by uniform rules, have contributed substantially to this crucial dimension of consumer satisfaction. The integration of local systems into nationwide networks allowed for economies of scale in developing advanced applications and in deploying new technologies. Efficiencies were realized in research, in marketing, and in purchasing of equipment for both operators (for example, base stations) and individual customers (for example, handsets). In piecing together disparate network elements, the coordination afforded the larger network often resulted in cost savings and improved functionality. In analyzing the merger between Bell Atlantic and GTE, which was one of several major mergers creating a national wireless network, the FCC predicted just this result.[19] Some evidence also suggests that consolidation has been associated with marked increases in the quality of mobile phone service.[20]

The implications for federal regulatory preemption are straightforward. To cede jurisdiction to state commissions risks undoing national network offerings that have taken years to construct and that deliver demonstrable benefit to users. Firms could relocalize service offerings, with the industry returning to its roots as a costly patchwork of small-area networks. Roaming was initially difficult and expensive, national marketing campaigns impractical, and competitive forces weak. Both users and carriers have benefited from the economies of scale and scope that came with national pricing of national networks, a development that is very far along and closely observed by FCC regulators. To force firms to readjust to locally diverse regulatory constraints would be to undo the proconsumer investments made over the past two decades.

A Natural Experiment

In exploring the optimal jurisdiction question, direct evidence revealing relative regulatory competencies is valuable but rare.[21] Fortunately, there exists a case study that puts the issue to the test. During the federal deregulation of cellular telephone rates in 1993 and 1994, alternative jurisdictions took different sides of the issue. In that instance, federal rules trumped those of state commissions, preempting rate regulations that many states were imposing and sought to continue to impose. Because we can observe what happened to cellular rates following that federal preemption of state regulation, it is possible to contrast the rival regulatory positions. This is direct evidence as to which jurisdiction has most effectively protected economic efficiency, and thus, consumer interests.

As noted, the Omnibus Budget Reconciliation Act of 1993 preempted regulation of cellular rates by the states as of August 10, 1994, one year from the day of enactment.[22] The rationale for preemption was that the FCC was responsible for spectrum allocation and licensing and, in this capacity, was the logical locus of authority for related regulatory decisionmaking. Specifically, in licensing other wireless entrants, only the FCC could create consistent rules for direct competitors. Because asymmetric regulation by the several states could clearly disrupt competitive forces, Congress vested the national regulatory agency with control over rates.

States that had been regulating cellular prices, however, were given one year to petition the FCC to request authority to continue regulating. Twenty-three states regulated rates in some way, and petitions to continue rate regulation were filed by eight states. All were denied, and state regulation was preempted. The arguments employed by the states, however, are of interest.

The petitioners argued that cellular telephone service was not fully competitive; competitive entry would eliminate the need for regulation, but not until competition actually arrived in the market. There was no telling how long it would take the upcoming PCS licensees to become full-fledged wireless telephone competitors, and until they were, state-level rate controls were needed to protect consumers.[23] As the state of New York argued, "the market for cellular services is not fully competitive, and, therefore, state regulation, as it is employed in New York, serves as a deterrence to anticompetitive and discriminatory practices."[24]

Curiously, evidence that state regulation proved ineffectual was introduced—and then ignored. New York regulators conceded that, "In general, cellular companies have been lightly regulated by this Commission."[25] Cellular operators did file tariffs with the New York State Public Service Commission, but regulators engaged in no substantial review of such rates (established by the firms themselves). The appeal to postpone preemption was made, therefore, on the grounds that continuing the threat of substantive regulatory intervention was constraining duopoly cellular pricing.[26] The California petition made similar claims, complaining that state rate regulation had failed to suppress prices but pleading for the opportunity to continue setting "just and reasonable" rates. In particular, the California Public Utilities Commission (CPUC) paradoxically based its request for continued rate regulation on the finding that, "Cellular rates in California are among the highest in the nation, and have failed to decline commensurate with substantial declines in capital and operating costs of providing cellular service."[27] CPUC noted that it "allowed the cellular industry to set retail rates for any service plan based on what the market would bear and not on cost."[28] This regulatory approach was adopted due to the fact that state regulators had limited knowledge about how to deal with an evolving market. "Because the cellular market was relatively new at the time, the CPUC adopted a hands-off approach to rate regulation, hoping the rates would come down in time as economies of scale occurred and the cost of doing business declined. Unfortunately, this has not occurred."[29]

Whatever the merits of state rate regulation in 1994, we now have an opportunity to test the hypothesis advanced by state commissions that regulated rates. Elimination of state rate regulation allows us to evaluate whether postregulation market evidence indicates that proconsumer regulation was, in fact, applied.

Aggregate National Price and Usage Trends. If state regulators effectively limited quality-adjusted prices, then releasing this constraint would result in a price increase. Costs would quickly rise for consumers, and subscriber growth would slow or reverse. (This could be true even if the observed price differences across states did not favor consumers in regulated jurisdictions.) With state regulators powerless to roll back rates because of federal preemption, cellular rates would be predicted to increase noticeably. This increase would manifest itself in two ways: a sharp rise in cellular rates, and a decline in consumer growth.

Rather than raise rates over an extended period of time, cellular operators would set prices at market levels with state regulatory constraints removed.[30] Rate increases should be visible in aggregate national data during the 1993–95 period surrounding rate deregulation via federal preemption (effective August 10, 1994). Given the negative relationship between price and quantity demanded, consumers should respond to rate increases by reducing the amount of wireless service purchased. This is probably best measured by minutes of use (MOU), which reflects consumption by both new and existing subscribers. Subscriber growth also reflects changes in service quality, providing an important cross-check on rate data.[31]

In fact, however, average national cellular rates declined appreciably in the immediate postregulation period. In 1993, the average price per MOU was fifty-seven cents. In 1995, it declined to fifty-one cents, a reduction of nearly 11 percent (see table 4-3). The reduction does not appear to have been due to long-term trends preceding rate deregulation. In fact, during the 1991–93 period, the average price per MOU increased 11.76 percent.

Output growth, whether measured by total U.S. MOU or by subscribership, also appears strong in the period following deregulation. MOU, in percentage terms, grew 36 percent faster in the two-year period straddling federal preemption of state regulation than in the same period preceding deregulation. Given the higher base from which they started, it is surprising that both usage and subscribership grew faster in percentage terms in the later period.

TABLE 4-3

RATES AND USAGE AROUND 1994 FEDERAL PREEMPTION OF STATE REGULATION OF CELLULAR TELEPHONE RATES

Metric	1991	1993	1995	1991–1993 (% change)	1993–1995 (% change)
Price (dollars)/MOU	0.51	0.57	0.51	11.76%	–10.53%
MOU (billions)	11.20	19.20	37.80	71.43%	96.88%
Subscribers (millions)	7.60	16.00	33.80	110.53%	111.25%

SOURCE: Data from Cellular Telecommunication & Internet Association, "CTIA's Wireless Industry Indices Semi-Annual Data Survey Results: A Comprehensive Report from CTIA Year-End 2001 Results, An Analysis of the U.S. Wireless Industry," August 2002.

There is no evidence that the national wireless market suffered ill effects from federal preemption of state rate regulation in 1994. At an aggregated, national level, price and output both responded positively. The proconsumer improvements may not be due to deregulation, and FCC reports tend to attribute the rate declines beginning about the time of federal preemption to the anticipated entry of PCS competitors. What can be said, however, is that state regulation did not generally lower rates or benefit consumers.

It is important to remember that this test of state jurisdiction takes place prior to the entry of new PCS licensees, which began providing service in a few markets in late 1995 or early 1996. The proconsumer outcomes cannot be directly ascribed to a change in market structure. While the coming of PCS was quite possibly a factor motivating service improvements by cellular operators bracing for intensifying competitive pressures, state regulators pleaded for continued rate regulation authority knowing that the PCS rulemaking was proceeding and that new licenses were likely to be issued.[32] Yet, the California petition saw state regulation as keeping rates at levels that were "just and reasonable," and predicted that were state controls not to continue, consumers would be adversely affected. The national data appear to contradict this view. Prices declined rapidly after preemption, belying the predictions of price increases made by state regulatory commissions attempting to extend controls. These included the best-staffed and most expert of the state commissions, those of California and New York.

California regulators argued in August 1994 that high prices were no more of a problem to consumers than rising prices. As the CPUC put it, "the presence of [state] rate regulation has probably prevented rates from being even higher and certainly has not contributed to higher rates."[33] But that claim—unaccompanied by any analysis—is clearly false. California consumers are not compensated for the higher prices they paid by the knowledge that at least these high prices were stable. Under a regime of deregulated federal preemption, on the other hand, California consumers have been compensated in cash. With nationwide service plans, and rapidly falling prices among national networks, they have had the opportunity to save money along with consumers in other states. State rate regulation had no effect, at best. At worst, it actually raised rates by reducing competitive forces and introducing incentives for firms to delay price reductions.

More dramatic still were the improvements in price, usage, and functionality that drove the wireless telephone market in the late 1990s. With the arrival of new competitors, prices declined to 11.5 cents per MOU in 2002 (see table 4-2), and total annual MOU rose to over 600 billion. Given that regulators in California and other states established pre-1994 cellular rates as "just and reasonable," it now appears that regulation was entirely ineffective—relative to procompetitive policies instituted at the federal level—in protecting consumer interests.

Cross-Sectional Analysis of State Rate Regulation. As some states regulated cellular rates and others did not, observing differences in pricing between the jurisdictions may show the effectiveness of state regulation. In general, rates appear to have been higher in regulated markets. The key question is how to interpret the causal connection between the two variables of regulatory status and market prices.

William Shew compared prices across regimes. He adjusted for demographic and economic characteristics of local markets while examining rates charged in ninety-five cellular markets for the years 1985, 1988, and 1991. He discovered prices were typically higher when regulated, but not (in two of three regressions) by statistically significant margins. He found "no evidence that customers have benefited from price regulation."[34] Another study, by Tomaso Duso, uses a distinct data set to arrive at roughly similar conclusions. Duso examined cellular telephone service charges across 122 U.S. markets during the December 1984 to July 1988 period.[35] He found that prices in regulated markets were somewhat higher than those found in unregulated markets, but that these differences are generally not statistically significant. Moreover, the "cost drivers" that appear significant in explaining prices in estimated regressions were usually slightly higher in regulated markets. This begs the question of causality, which cannot be answered directly by statistical analysis. Yet, the evidence tends to reject the hypothesis that rate regulation is associated with gains for consumers.

One issue brought up in the Duso study is whether or not states that were regulated prior to 1994 were systematically different from states that were not. If so, and if these differences were entirely independent of the regulatory regimes implemented, then the positive correlation between higher rates and state regulation would not suggest that the latter caused the former. One way to shed light on this question is to see how prices or subscriber growth perform in the postregulation period.

Table 4-4 summarizes the quarterly wireless subscriber data for the top ten U.S. markets in 1990, 1996, and 2000. These data allow for an analysis that abstracts from complex pricing issues. Subscriber levels are a rough indicator of consumer satisfaction. The higher the growth rate relative to an underlying trend determined by nonregulatory variables, the better the bundle delivered to customers, as evaluated by customers themselves (taking prices, service quality, customer service, and all other product dimensions into account).[36] Two things are apparent. First, penetration (subscribers as a percent of local market population) in regulated markets was considerably below the levels in unregulated markets in 1990 and 1996. Second, penetration in regulated markets had nearly caught up to levels in other markets by 2001. This broadly supports Shew's conclusion that regulation was associated with higher rates.

In the states with regulation, three impediments to price competition existed. First, when tariffs were publicly filed, changes would quickly be

TABLE 4-4

PENETRATION RATES IN DEREGULATED VS. UNREGULATED
Top Ten Cellular Markets, 1990-2001

Weighted Avg.	March 1990	September 1996	2000 Census
Markets in Regulated States	1.96%	9.64%	47.00%
Markets in Unregulated States	2.95%	19.27%	49.50%

SOURCE: Data from Herschel Shosteck Associates, "CMRS Seventh Annual Report," appendix C, table 3. Data Flash: The Cellular Market Quarterly Review 10 (September 1996).

communicated to competitors, often by law, and in advance of actual price reductions. Shew found this had a very large potential effect on prices, and it is easy to see how this would reduce incentives to engage in price competition.[37] Second, requiring tariff changes to be approved by utility commissions deters firms from lowering rates because operators face a cost in requesting permission to raise rates back to previous levels, should demand conditions change. Third, since operators working under rate-of-return or price cap regimes have substantial input as to where price levels are initially set, they will tend to favor higher prices when they believe that price reductions will be easier to obtain than rate increases. Effectively, high rates become an insurance policy against "get tough" policies by regulators.

The difference in the ratio of penetration rates (regulated to unregulated markets) narrows considerably during the seven years following federal preemption, as is shown in figure 4-1.[38] By December 2001, previously regulated markets have about 47 percent mobile phone penetration, while the never-regulated markets have penetration rates of about 49.5 percent. The factors limiting wireless phone use appear to have faded not immediately but over time. A factor that may explain this pattern is the initial tardiness of the cellular operators to offer service in regulated markets. By the time that the last regulated system in the sample, the nonwireline licensee in Los Angeles, began serving customers in March 1987, nonwireline licensees in unregulated states had been operating for an average of 20 months. The average time in the regulated sample was 10.75 months. Two of the four regulated nonwireline licensees opened for business after all six unregulated systems had begun operations, mirroring the relative entry delay among wireline licensees.

FIGURE 4-1

WIRELESS SUBSCRIBER PENETRATION GROWTH BEFORE AND AFTER FEDERAL PREEMPTION OF STATE RATE REGULATION

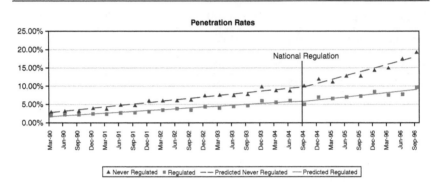

SOURCE: Author's calculations.

This substantial head start clearly put the unregulated systems in the pole position in the race for subscribers. Whether the regulated system lag was related to state rate regulation is unknown. What is known, as illustrated in figure 4-1, is that subscriber growth across both sets of markets is higher in the postpreemption years. If the quarterly data are truncated at September 1994 (the first month federal cellular deregulation was imposed on the states), it is seen that both regulated and unregulated markets experience higher penetration gains in percentage terms. An important argument for this policy reform was that eliminating state-by-state rate regulation would result in greater efficiencies in the provision of regional or national networks and that such economies would result in consumer gains. The observed increases in subscriber growth are consistent with this view.

They are also consistent with the hypothesis that state regulation of wireless telephony has effects that spill over into other states. National wireless penetration appears to respond positively to federal preemption, providing a strong argument that the policy was efficient. It is buttressed by the fact that subscriber growth is higher everywhere after preemption, not just in deregulated states. Subscriber growth in states that were unregulated exceeds growth in states deregulated through federal preemption, through 1996. This supports the view that wireless telephone regulation is properly based at the federal level.

Conclusion

Consumers did not benefit from state regulation of cellular telephone rates. During the period prior to federal preemption, rates tended to be higher in regulated markets, and some of this difference may have been due to inefficiencies imposed by state rules (including higher lag times for market entry). After federal preemption, rates did not shoot up in regulated states, or across markets generally. This surge in rates would have occurred if state regulation, or the threat of state regulation, had constrained prices for customers. But even in markets where incumbent duopoly providers possessed substantial pricing power, state regulators proved unable to (a) protect consumers via rate regulation, and (b) learn from their policy experiment, arguing for a continuation of price controls and against federal preemption.

The federal preemption of state cellular rate regulation shows that decentralized political decisionmaking did not add value for customers. Today's market, which has generated great increases in efficiency by developing competing national networks, owes much to regulatory harmonization, suggesting that the results of a reverse experiment today would likewise underscore the deleterious effects of balkanization.

Substantial public policy responsibility remains vested in state governments even after regulatory authority for consumer protection issues— rates, quality of service, contract disclosure—is placed in a federal agency. For the policy interventions now under consideration by regulators at the state and federal level, however, it is possible to categorize the efficiency implications of alternative jurisdictions. In general, the major regulatory proposals involve substantial jurisdictional externalities, due to the strong influence of national network economies in the wireless telephone sector.

Advertising Regulations. National marketing campaigns, including commercial messages distributed to nationwide audiences and high-visibility national events sponsored by wireless carriers, could be seriously affected by advertising regulations. To introduce nonuniformity in such rules would lead competitors to shy away from national advertising, reducing any efficiencies to be gained in this realm.

Disclosure Rules. The importance of national one-rate plans in promoting competition and network growth is substantial. Disclosure rules can disrupt such marketing efficiencies by imposing different point-of-sale procedures and conflicting requirements for what information must be conveyed. Because some proposals (such as California's) consider mandating lengthy written agreements and/or third-party verification to ensure that subscribers understand contract terms, marketing practices could be forced offline. Nonuniformity would reduce efficiencies associated with telephone or Internet sign-ups, undermining investments in these arrangements.

Minimum Trial Periods. The national carriers currently offer free trial periods of fourteen to thirty days, during which telephone service can be terminated without payment of an "early termination fee." Terms extending this period in some states would alter carriers' incentives to offer free or discounted telephones, lowering network utilization and, in the long term, network development.

Each of these proposals has the potential to impose costs on wireless subscribers outside the state in which the costs are levied. It would be ironic that, after spending more than a decade piecing thousands of fragmentary cellular telephone licenses into efficient national networks, resulting efficiencies could be at least partly undone by disparate state regulatory regimes that left the industry with a patchwork of conflicting rules.

Notes

*A longer version of this article appeared in 56 Fed. Comm. L.J. 155 (2003-2004).

1. Omnibus Budget Reconciliation Act of 1993, 47 U.S.C. § 332(c)(3)(A) (2000). The language of this section has been taken by some to include federal preemption of local zoning authority involving wireless base stations, towers, and antennas. See Office of Tech. Assessment, U.S. Cong., Pub. No. OTA-ITC-622, Wireless Technologies and the National Information Infrastructure 209 (1995). In addition, federal law preempted states from levying property taxes on wireless phone licenses.

2. 47 U.S.C. § 332(c)(3)(A).

3. For an excellent discussion see Leonard J. Kennedy and Heather A. Purcell, *Section 332 of the Communications Act of 1934: A Federal Regulatory Framework That Is "Hog Tight, Horse High, and Bull Strong,"* 50 Fed. Comm. L.J. 547, 547 (1998).

4. *Rancho Palos Verdes, Cal. v. Abrams*, 544 U.S. 113 (2005).

5. See, *e.g.*, S. 1216, 108th Cong. § 1 (2003).

6. Thomas W. Hazlett and Matthew L. Spitzer, *Public Policy Toward Cable Television: The Economics of Rate Controls* (Washington D.C.: AEI Press, 1997), 208–12.

7. Thomas W. Hazlett, "Market Power in the Cellular Telephone Duopoly" (paper submitted to the Federal Communications Commission on behalf of Time Warner Telecommunications, August 1993), 1–2.

8. Benjamin Klein & Keith Leffler, *The Role of Market Forces in Assuring Contractual Performance*, 89 J. Pol. Econ. 615 (1981).

9. The possibility that a network service provider could exit the retail market and yet use its nonsalvageable capital to provide wholesale services to resellers means that infrastructure investments may not be totally sunk. Yet, the gap in value between a network that integrates retail services and one that relies exclusively on resellers is likely substantial. This is implied by the observation that no successful U.S. wireless network executes this business model. Hence, the capital value at stake in preserving a reputation in the market for retail services is also likely to be substantial.

10. The increase in costs is not offset by higher demand, and hence higher prices, for two reasons. First, national pricing is efficient, and the great majority of customers do not receive any benefit from the costs imposed in Idaho. Second, Idaho customers are not willing to pay as much as the regulations cost, such that increased demand would not entirely offset the higher costs even if optimally configured networks served Idaho alone.

11. Thomas W. Hazlett & Robert J. Michaels, *The Cost of Rent-Seeking: Evidence from Cellular Telephone License Lotteries*, 59 S. Econ. J. 425, 427 (1993).

12. Nat'l Telecomm. & Info. Admin., U.S. Dep't of Commerce, U.S. Spectrum Management Policy: Agenda for the Future D-5 (1991).

13. Bankruptcy disputes arose with respect to many PCS-C licenses, and more than 80 percent of these licenses (adjusted for population) were as yet undeployed as of

July 1, 2003. See Thomas W. Hazlett & Babette E.L. Boliek, *Use of Designated Entity Preferences in Assigning Wireless Licenses*, 51 Fed. Comm. L.J. 639, 649 (1999).

14. The entrepreneurial vision driving Nextel was provided by a former FCC attorney, Morgan O'Brien. See Thomas W. Hazlett, *The Wireless Craze, the Unlimited Bandwidth Myth, the Spectrum Auction Faux Pas, and the Punchline to Ronald Coase's "Big Joke": An Essay on Airwave Allocation Policy*, 14 Harv. J.L. & Tech. 335, 426–28 (2001).

15. Petition of the People of the State of California and the Public Utilities Commission of the State of California to Retain State Regulatory Authority over Intrastate Cellular Service Rates, PR 94-108, at 12 (Aug. 8, 1994) (CPUC filing) notes that the commission allowed duopoly cellular carriers "to set retail rates for any service plan based on what the market would bear and not on cost." Implementation of sections 3(n) and 332 of the Communications Act, Petition to Extend Rate Regulation, PR No. 94-108, at 3 (Aug. 9, 1994) (citation omitted) (New York FCC Filing), CPUC Filing. To enhance competitive pressures, however, the CPUC mandated wholesale access to networks at rates which were projected to be profitable for resellers. After setting up a system in 1990 to monitor the results of the regulatory plan, the commission determined in 1993 that "Three years later virtually none of the Commission's expectations [of reducing cellular rates] have been met by industry performance." Ibid. at 17 (citation omitted). New rate controls were then crafted, but the following year the CPUC found that "none of the new or existing plans experienced any permanently lowered wholesale or retail rates" under them. Ibid. at 18.

16. William B. Shew, "Regulation, Competition, and Prices in the U.S. Cellular Telephone Industry" (paper presented at the ENSAE-CREST Conference on the Economics of Radio-Based Communications, June 23–24, 1994), 4.

17. See, *e.g.*, Implementation of Section 6002(b) of the Omnibus Budget Reconciliation Act of 1993, *Seventh Report*, 17 F.C.C.R. 12985, app. C, table 4, (2002), at 12997–98.

18. "[T]he transaction costs associated with license resales after [cellular license] lotteries have been quite significant. For example, for the year 1991, these costs have been estimated at $190 million." FCC Rpt. to Congress on Spectrum Auctions, *Report*, WT Dkt. No. 97-150 (Oct. 9, 1997) (footnote omitted), available at http://wireless.fcc.gov/auctions/data/papersAndStudies/fc970353.pdf.

19. "Combining these wireless businesses will likely produce . . . system-wide efficiencies through the common network engineering, management, purchasing, and administrative functions, leading to earlier and broader deployment of advanced wireless services." Application of GTE Corp. and Bell Atl. Corp., *Memorandum Opinion and Order*, 15 F.C.C.R. 14032, para. 377, 20 Comm. Reg. (P & F) 989 (2000).

20. Mobile EcoSystem 2003, an industry advisory and consulting firm, publishes the results of tests administered by Telephia, an engineering firm, on the proportion of calls blocked or dropped by wireless telephone subscribers. Although only data from the last two years (2001 and 2002) have been posted, they indicate that sharp improvements are being made in wireless telephone reliability. See Mark Lowenstein

and Mobile EcoSystem, "State of the Wireless Industry" (paper presented at the Pacific Research Institute Conference, April 15, 2003), 5.

21. Indirect evidence is more likely to be available, but it is also inconclusive. The FCC does enjoy certain economies of scale in evaluating nationwide data with a larger base of policy experts. It enjoys a work force of over 2,000 full-time employees; has a Wireless Telecommunications Bureau with staff attorneys, economists, engineers, and industry analysts knowledgeable about mobile telephony; and issues detailed annual reports evaluating the commercial mobile radio service (CMRS) market for Congress. No state possesses comparable resources. But how important is the federal regulatory advantage in crafting policies that help consumers? After all, dispersed experiments among the fifty states could contribute to a process that overcomes the disadvantage attendant to any one state commission's analysis by using trial and error to discover better modes of regulation.

22. Petition of N.Y. State Pub. Serv. Comm'n to Extend Rate Reg., *Report and Order*, 10 F.C.C.R. 8187, paras 2-3, 78 Rad. Reg.2d (P & F) 251 (1995).

23. See, *e.g.*, CPUC filing, *supra* note 15 at 19, 67.

24. New York FCC filing, *supra* note 15 at 3. The petition also stated: "[A]bsent a fully competitive market, continued light rate regulation is required to ensure that rates do not become discriminatory, unjust or unreasonable." Ibid. at 4 (footnote omitted). Similarly, California regulators conceded that, despite rate regulation, "[p]rices of wholesale cellular carriers [i.e., cellular networks] in California are highest in the nation and have remained high despite declining capital and operating costs." Ibid. at 7. This did not dissuade the CPUC from arguing that regulation was "necessary to protect cellular consumers from unjust and unreasonable rates." Ibid. at 64.

25. Ibid. at app. III, p. 5.

26. Ibid. at app. III, p. 5.

27. CPUC filing, *supra* note 15 at ii.

28. Ibid. at 12.

29. Ibid. at 38–39.

30. In some contexts, it is argued that firms price strategically to prevent regulation, but this is implausible in this instance. The national market was highly deconcentrated, and the probability that an individual operator's price increase would result in reregulation was virtually nonexistent. As Shew notes, the cable industry faced the threat of federal reregulation in 1992, but rates appeared unaffected through debate and passage of the Cable Television Consumer Protection and Competition Act of 1992. See Shew, *supra* note 16 at 29, note 27.

31. That is because falling rates may be associated with quality reductions (or increasing rates with quality improvements). All else remaining constant, demand exhibits a negative relationship between price and quantity, but price and quantity can be positively correlated without violating the law of demand when quantity is changing. Examining subscriber (or MOU) growth in response to regulatory changes allows consumers to respond to both price and quality changes.

32. California's petition stated: "We envision that in the not too distant future market forces of competition will police the mobile market and allow for an orderly withdrawal of government oversight." CPUC Filing, *supra* note 15 at 80 (footnote omitted).

33. Ibid. at 46.

34. Shew, *supra* note 16 at 35.

35. Tomaso Duso, "Lobbying and Regulation in a Political Economy: Evidence from the US Cellular Industry" (Discussion Paper FS IV, Wissenschaftszentrum Berlin, 2001): 8. http://skylla.wz-berlin.de/pdf/2001/iv01-03.pdf (accessed Mar. 7, 2007).

36. One weakness of the penetration metric is that it does not reflect changes in usage by inframarginal customers. So, if subscribers use their wireless telephones more, but not many new individuals subscribe, consumer gains may not be evident. There is little evidence that trends in minutes of use and subscriber levels actually diverge, however, so it is reasonable to use either as proxies for consumer preferences.

37. Shew, *supra* note 16 at 35–37.

38. The data for this graph are taken from Herschel Shosteck Associates, "Data Flash: The Cellular Market Quarterly Review," 10 *Quarterly Rev.* (September 1996).

5

Federalism and Financial Regulation

Hal S. Scott

The American system of dividing regulatory authority between the states and the federal government takes on a very different cast for three important financial sectors: banking, securities, and insurance.[1] In banking, federal regulatory power wholly preempts state authority over nationally chartered banks; while state power is, in principle, primary for state-chartered banks, state banks have increasingly become subject to significant federal constraints on risk and certain disclosure obligations. In insurance, "reverse preemption" governs: state regulatory power preempts federal authority for all insurance firms. In between these poles, securities offerings and securities firms are subject to concurrent state and federal regulation, with a recent trend of increasing federal preemption.

It seems odd that we have three different approaches to preemption for three different activities, all of which are increasingly offered by integrated financial service firms. Due to economic integration in the financial sector and other factors (such as sharper international competition in capital markets), the preemption regimes in all three sectors have become subjects of intense political and legal controversies. This chapter briefly describes the origins and contours of the varying preemption regimes, as well as the disputes over those arrangements. It then sketches the contours of a preemption regime that is better suited to the demands of modern financial markets. The principal elements of that improved system are a further expansion of federal preemption for securities offerings and firms; and a dual federal and state system for insurance, with complete federal preemption for nationally chartered insurance firms.

Banking

The dual banking system was created during the Civil War, through the enactment of the National Currency Act of 1863 and the National Bank Act of 1864 (NBA), primarily to promote the financing of the war through the creation of a national currency.[2] Until that time, private banks had been exclusively state chartered. The NBA created the possibility of chartering national banks.[3] Banks have since had the choice of whether to be chartered by the national government or by the states. This arrangement has become known as the dual banking system.

The NBA entrusts the chartering and supervision of national banks to the Office of the Comptroller of the Currency (OCC), part of the Treasury Department, and entrusts the OCC with the power to issue regulations that can have the effect of preempting state law. The statute grants the OCC comprehensive rulemaking authority to further its responsibilities: "Except to the extent that authority to issue such rules and regulations has been expressly and exclusively granted to another regulatory agency, the Comptroller of the Currency is authorized to prescribe rules and regulations to carry out the responsibilities of the office. . . ."[4] That grant of authority has far-reaching implications for preemption. In *Barnett Bank v. Nelson* (1995), the Court stated that "normally Congress would not want states to forbid, or to impair significantly, the exercise of a power that Congress specifically granted," and that "where Congress has not expressly conditioned the grant of 'power' upon a grant of state permission, the Court has ordinarily found that no such condition applies."[5] In addition, the NBA grants the OCC exclusive "visitorial powers" over national banks—that is, the authority to examine, supervise, and regulate a corporation: "No national bank shall be subject to any visitorial powers except as authorized by Federal law, vested in the courts of justice or such as shall be, or have been exercised or directed by Congress or by either House thereof or by any committee of the Congress or of either House duly authorized."[6] The "courts of justice" exception has become a matter of debate, as briefly discussed below. In recent years, both the OCC's rulemaking authority and its visitorial powers have become intensely controversial. Much of that controversy has focused on two preemption rules promulgated by the OCC in January 2004.[7] The first rule sought to clarify the applicability of state law to the operations of national banks and their subsidiaries. It preempted state laws with respect to real estate lending, deposit-taking, non–real estate lending, and other federally authorized activities of national banks. In particular, it set federal requirements for consumer lending that were intended to preempt state laws and regulations of this field. This was against a legal background in which courts had almost invariably sustained the exercise of preemptive rulemaking by the OCC.[8] The rule does not intend to preempt general-purpose state laws on contracts, rights to collect debts, acquisition and transfer of property, taxation, zoning, crimes, and torts.[9] While the OCC rule generally preempts state consumer protection laws, there remain some uncertainties on the margins as to exactly which state laws are preempted.

The second rule defined the scope of visitorial powers protection for national banks and their subsidiaries. It provides that unless otherwise provided by federal law, the OCC has exclusive visitorial authority "with respect to the content and conduct of activities authorized for national banks under federal law." Such authorizations are then enumerated, the right of state officials to inspect shareholder lists or to review bank records in connection with unclaimed property. The rule also interprets the aforementioned "courts of justice" exception:

> This exception pertains to the powers inherent in the judiciary and does not grant state or other governmental authorities any right to inspect, superintend, direct, regulate or compel compliance by a national bank with respect to any law, regarding the content or conduct of activities authorized for national banks under Federal law.[10]

The preemption rules have sparked an extensive debate, both in the literature[11] and in the courts, as to whether the OCC has exceeded its authority in promulgating the rules. Most of the opposition has been based on the concern, voiced primarily by state regulators, that the OCC has not been sufficiently committed to consumer protection and to fighting discrimination through its rules and enforcement policies. The OCC has vigorously defended its record in these areas.[12]

Three principal issues are being contested: (1) the extent to which the OCC can preempt state regulation of subsidiaries of national banks as distinct from the banks themselves; (2) whether the visitorial powers protection precludes states from civilly enforcing state statutes not preempted by federal law; and (3) whether the exception to exclusive federal visitorial powers for powers "vested in the courts of justice" applies to enforcement actions against national banks brought in courts, as well as administrative actions taken outside the courts. An additional important question is the extent to which state criminal proceedings—as distinct from civil actions—are preempted by the visitorial power provisions.

OCC Preemption: The Subsidiary Question. Much of the debate over the OCC's preemptive authority has focused on its 2004 determination that the subsidiaries of national banks, as well as the banks themselves, enjoy protection against state regulation. To date, four separate appellate courts have sustained the OCC's authority; none have denied it.[13] Nonetheless, the U.S. Supreme Court has granted certiorari in one of those cases, *Wachovia Bank, N.A. v. Watters* (2005). Wachovia Bank sought a declaratory judgment that Michigan law was preempted as applied to its operating subsidiaries, including Wachovia Mortgage. The Michigan law required Wachovia Mortgage to register with the state but did not require a license to operate. It also permitted the state to investigate consumer complaints not otherwise being pursued by federal regulators, and it required the registrant to file annual financial statements with the state, pay an annual operating fee, and make certain documents available for state examination. The Court of Appeals for the Sixth Circuit sustained the OCC regulation, holding that it preempted the Michigan law. Relying heavily on the *Chevron* doctrine, the Court found that the OCC's conclusion that it had the power to preempt state law applicable to operating subsidiaries was a reasonable interpretation of the NBA, especially in light of the fact that national banks had the power to create operating subsidiaries under their incidental powers. The Supreme Court granted certiorari to resolve whether the OCC properly relied on *Chevron* and, moreover, whether the regulation, by equating a national bank operating subsidiary with its parent national bank, violates the Tenth Amendment to the U.S. Constitution.[14]

Visitorial Powers and Nonpreempted State Statutes. In *Office of Comptroller of the Currency v. Spitzer* (2005), the U.S. District Court for the

Southern District of New York held that the OCC had exclusive authority to enforce state civil law against national banks even in the absence of a federal law or regulation preempting the state law that was being enforced. In an ancient case, *First National Bank in St. Louis v. Missouri* (1924),[15] the Supreme Court had held that because federal law did not permit intrastate branches, a Missouri law prohibiting branches was not preempted and could be enforced against national banks. The *Spitzer* court, however, distinguished *St. Louis* on the grounds that, in that case, the national bank was acting entirely outside the powers granted by federal law. At the time, the OCC had no clear authority to enforce national banks' compliance with applicable state banking laws. Now, the court reasoned, the OCC does possess that authority, and its exercise is entitled to *Chevron* deference.[16]

As a matter of policy, one could argue that enforcement authority should follow preemption: if Congress decides not to preempt a state law, or if the OCC has authority to preempt and does not exercise such authority, states should be free to enforce state law. However, the problem of having multiple states enforce state law against national financial institutions exists even in the absence of federal preemption. It seems sensible for national authorities to be generally entrusted with the enforcement of state law since they can coordinate state law enforcement on a national basis. *Spitzer* reaches the right policy result.

The Courts-of-Justice Exception. The second issue in *Spitzer* was whether the exception to exclusive federal visitorial powers for powers "vested in the courts of justice" applies to enforcement actions against national banks brought in courts, as well as administrative actions taken outside the courts such as administrative subpoenas or cease-and-desist orders. The *Spitzer* court held it did. Again, the primacy of national policy requires that all state enforcement, whether administrative or in the courts, be preempted. This would, of course, leave a court with powers to enforce its own jurisdiction in ordinary litigation, as where a private plaintiff sued a national bank for damages for breach of contract.

Criminal Enforcement. An unresolved issue requiring clarification is the applicability and enforcement of state criminal laws against national banks. The concern is that enforcement of criminal law can implicate broad national concerns that states, and state attorneys general in particular, do not share. State attorneys general are generally charged with enforcing antifraud, consumer protection, and antidiscrimination statutes. In this effort, they have the discretion to use various enforcement approaches, including corporate criminal prosecution that (as in the case of Arthur Andersen) can spell a corporation's death. If that weapon were applied to a national financial institution, it might not only cause the failure of that institution but others in a knock-on effect.

Under the OCC's preemption rule, national banks are subject to state criminal laws of general application. This leaves states free to argue that criminal fraud statutes can be applied to national banks or other financial institutions. It seems unwise, however, to leave the stability of the nation's financial system to the discretion of state attorneys general. Federal prosecutors can also use criminal weapons, but they function within an overall federal governmental structure. The U.S. Department of Justice must attend to the concerns of other agencies such as the Treasury, and is ultimately responsible to the president. Justice Department guidelines, in the form of a memorandum from Deputy Attorney General Larry Thompson (January 20, 2003) on whether to criminally prosecute corporations, take into account the "collateral consequences" to the public of such prosecutions, a process that has recently been applied in deciding what remedies to seek against KPMG in connection with its promotion of abusive tax shelters.[17] It would make sense to give the federal government exclusive jurisdiction over the criminal prosecution of financial institutions, at least in areas of overlapping jurisdiction—for example, where an institution could be prosecuted for violating state or federal antifraud statutes.

In the shadow of these battles over the OCC's preemptive authority looms another important regulatory and economic issue—the status of state banks. Those institutions are chartered and supervised by the states, but they are still subject to significant federal authority, and state powers over state banks have been significantly preempted by federal law. State banks that are members of the Federal Reserve System are regulated and supervised (including examination) by the Fed as well as the states. State-chartered non-member banks are supervised (again including examination) and regulated by the Federal Deposit Insurance Corporation (FDIC), as well as the states. In addition, the Fed regulates bank holding companies on a consolidated basis, thus giving it indirect authority over the state bank subsidiaries of such holding companies. Moreover, federal law places statutory limits on the activities of state banks. For example, FDIC-insured state banks and their subsidiaries (meaning virtually all state banks) "may not engage as principal in any type of activity that is not permissible for a national bank unless— (1) the Corporation has determined that the activity would pose no significant risk to the appropriate deposit insurance fund; and (2) the State Bank is, and continues to be, in compliance with capital standards prescribed by the appropriate Federal banking agency."[18] These federal constraints are largely based on the responsibility of the FDIC, through its insurance fund, for the failure of state banks, as well as the larger concern with systemic risk—that is, the possibility that the failure of state as well as national banks could impact the banking system as a whole. Furthermore, state banks in many states are permitted to engage in any activities permissible for national banks under so-called wild card statutes, further narrowing differences between permitted activities for state and national banks.[19]

State banks are examined by their primary federal regulator (state-member banks by the Federal Reserve; state nonmember banks by the FDIC). To avoid duplication, state and federal examinations are normally conducted in alternate years. There is, however, a difference between the cost of examination for state and national banks. Although state banks pay an assessment for supervision by their chartering state, they are not charged for supervision by either the FDIC or Federal Reserve, since these two agencies fund their own costs—the FDIC through the premium assessments on insurance; the Federal Reserve, through earnings on assets it purchases through interest-free reserves that must be held by banks. The OCC, on the other hand, has no internal source of funds and must rely on assessments on the examined institutions. Viewed in this perspective, the choice between federal and state charters is mainly based not on differences between the states and federal government but rather on differences between federal regulators.[20] State banks may prefer a partial state examination system to the complete federal system for national banks; however, state examination can be burdensome when state banks operate in several states and are then exposed to multiple state examination systems.

The national banking system is increasingly attractive to banks. From 1995 to 2000, state banks maintained a 45 percent share of all deposits. By

2005, this share had fallen to under 40 percent, and only one of the ten largest U.S. banks (the ninth largest) was state-chartered.[21] In 2004, two of the largest state banks, J.P. Morgan Chase & Co. and HSBC Bank, both in New York, switched to national charters. These developments have prompted the FDIC to propose that state charters be made more attractive by adopting the European Union's approach to interstate banking, making the operations of interstate state banks and their subsidiaries subject only to the laws of their home states.[22] This would establish a system of inter-state preemption. The FDIC proposal is based mainly on its authority under the Riegle-Neal Amendments to the Federal Deposit Insurance Act (FDI Act), which effectively provides that host-state law applies to an out-of-state state bank only to the extent it applies to a branch of an out-of-state national bank.[23] This provision was intended to create parity in interstate operations between state and national banks. (Without it, national banks would have a significant advantage insofar as they are subject only to fed-eral law, while state banks would be subject to their home state law and the law of each other state in which they established a branch.) Given that most host-state law for national banks is preempted by the NBA and the OCC's implementing regulations, the net effect of the Riegle-Neal Amendments is that home-state law applies to the interstate branches of state banks. The FDIC has broad authority to implement the FDI Act through regulation. Its proposed rule defines some key concepts in the statute, like what it means to conduct an activity at a branch. However, the proposal's real import is the determination of the FDIC to fully enforce the provisions of the statute.

The Riegle-Neal Amendments and the proposed FDIC rule come up short, however, in putting state banks completely on par with national banks. First, state banks are subject to their home-state law—the state in which they are chartered—that might not be as favorable as federal law. This problem might be ameliorated by changing one's charter to a state with the most favorable law. If the FDIC proposal were enacted, we might see state bank charter competition along the lines of corporate charter compe-tition, although the parameters of that competition would be constrained by federal rules (a phenomenon increasingly true with respect to corporate charters as well).[24] Second, the FDIC's proposal fails to discuss whether state banks would be subject only to the visitorial powers of their home state or rather of all states in which they operate. Without visitorial powers preemption, out-of-state banks operating in New York would be fully subject to the powers of the New York attorney general while national banks would not. It might be argued, however, that the Riegle-Neal Amendments would permit the FDIC to provide that interstate branches of state banks were only subject to the visitorial powers of their home states since branches of national banks were not subject to host-state visitorial powers. This would make state chartering competition highly dependent on state enforcement policies. Under current circumstances, New York state chartered banks would probably incorporate elsewhere and reorganize their New York operations into branch form. Not surprisingly, New York Attorney General Eliot Spitzer, representing himself and the attorneys general of six other states, has opposed the FDIC rule.

As already noted, the federal preemption system for national banks is not uncontroversial. Some members of Congress, as well as Attorney General Spitzer, have complained that preemption has been used as a tool to protect national banks from what would otherwise be violations of state consumer protection and antidiscrimination laws. This is coupled with the charge that the OCC is not vigilant in enforcing parallel federal law protections. While no convincing evidence has been adduced to prove these charges, they persist nonetheless, and the antipreemption forces, having largely lost their battles in courts, are seeking to roll back preemption through new legislation. Bills introduced in the House of Representatives and in the Senate in 2005 would significantly curtail the federal preemption of state law and state visitorial powers.[25] State consumer protection laws (including laws on "predatory" lending) and other state laws that do not specifically conflict with federal law would not be preempted. National bank protection against state visitorial powers would not extend to actions by state law enforcement officials (as compared with state bank regulators). Indeed, such state officials would be empowered to enforce both state *and federal* laws.

A recent proposed state boycott of national banks that allegedly fail to comply with state predatory lending statutes raises additional troublesome issues. Michael Madigan, the speaker of the Illinois House of Representatives (and father of the state's attorney general) has asked fifty state agencies, pension funds, and universities to stop doing business with national banks unless these banks comply in writing with a state "predatory lending" law—which has been preempted by the OCC.[26] Madigan proposed that these agencies require lenders to certify their compliance with the state law. National banks have stated that they voluntarily comply with the state law but will not sign certifications. Madigan's initiative raises serious legal questions. In *Crosby v. National Foreign Trade Council* (2000),[27] the Supreme Court held that a Massachusetts law restricting the authority of state agencies to purchase goods or services from companies doing business with Burma was preempted by a federal statute delegating to the President the control over economic sanctions against Burma. Given that the Illinois predatory lending statute is validly preempted by the OCC, any imposition of state boycott sanctions on national banks failing to comply with the preempted state law should also be preempted.

Securities

Regulation of securities firms has followed a different path from that of banks. Federal regulation in this area started much later in our history, in response to the Great Depression. The 1933 Securities Act[28] regulated the participation of securities firms as well as issuers in the offering of securities. The 1934 Securities Exchange Act[29] regulated reporting of public companies, the trading of securities, and the securities firms themselves. When enacted, these two cornerstone acts did not preempt state law. The states continued to have concurrent power to regulate offerings and firms, as provided in "savings clauses" in both acts. For example, the 1934 Securities Exchange Act provided that it would not "affect the jurisdiction of the securities commission (or any agency or office performing like functions) of any State or Territory of the United States . . . over any security or any person."[30] While this language has since been eliminated in connection with the preemption of state "Blue Sky" laws (discussed below), the 1933 Securities Act also provided, and still provides, that its "rights and remedies . . . shall be in addition to any and all other rights and remedies that may exist at law or equity" and that "[t]he securities commission (or any agency or office performing like functions) of any State shall retain jurisdiction under the laws of such State to investigate and bring enforcement actions."[31] Yet another section of the act, entitled "Preservation of Authority," provides that "[c]onsistent with this section, the securities commission (or any agency or office performing like functions) of any State shall retain jurisdiction under the laws of such State to investigate and bring enforcement actions with respect to fraud and deceit, or unlawful conduct by a broker or dealer, in connection with securities or securities transactions."[32] Similarly, the Securities Exchange Act provided that "nothing in this chapter shall affect the jurisdiction of the securities commission (or any agency performing like functions) of any State over any security or any person insofar as it does not conflict with the provisions of this chapter or the rules and regulations thereunder."[33] This language lives on in the current Securities Exchange Act, although it is now subject to the proviso, "[e]xcept as otherwise specifically provided in this chapter."[34] Manifestly, federally licensed securities firms were not thought of as federal instrumentalities in the same way as were national banks.

In recent decades, however, the trend has been toward increased federal preemption, as Congress has concluded that state regulation was interfering in the functioning of an efficient national capital market. In 1975, the 1934 Securities Exchange Act was amended to give the U.S. Securities and Exchange Commission (SEC) authority to create a national market system for the trading of securities and to end fixed commission rates.[35] As part of these amendments, the 1934 Securities Exchange Act was amended to preempt certain state taxes on the transfer of securities and to provide a "safe harbor" for soft dollar payments—that is, arrangements by which brokers charge customers higher-than-normal commissions in exchange for providing research or other noncash benefits. The preemption language here is somewhat curious, providing that persons using soft-dollar arrangements will not be deemed "to have acted unlawfully or to have breached a fiduciary duty under State or Federal law unless expressly provided to the contrary by a law enacted by the Congress or any State *subsequent to the date of enactment of the Securities Act Amendments of 1975*."[36] In other words, Congress preempted past but not future state laws. Even so, the preemption was probably quite powerful: most challenges to soft dollar arrangements were based on fiduciary duties under state common law, which necessarily preceded the new federal enactment. The 1975 amendments also authorized the SEC "to remove impediments to and perfect the mechanisms of a national market system for securities and a national system for the clearance and settlement of securities transactions." They further directed the SEC "having due regard for the public interest, the protection of investors, and the maintenance of fair and orderly markets to use its authority under [the 1934 Securities Exchange Act] to facilitate the establishment of a national market for securities. . . ."[37]

Pursuant to these provisions, in 1977 the SEC adopted a rule that required certain disclosures in confirmation statements regarding payment for order flow—that is, arrangements under which brokers receive payments for directing customer orders to particular trading venues. The SEC further amended that rule in 1994 and, in addition, adopted a new rule governing disclosure of order flow arrangements on customer account statements. Following the promulgation of those rules, several class actions were filed challenging payment for order flow arrangements under various theories (including state fiduciary duty law), claiming that the brokers were required to pass on any payments to their customers. The SEC rule contained no language specifically preempting any state law. Still, in the two leading cases, the courts decided that application of state fiduciary duty law would conflict with the purpose of the 1975 amendments and the SEC rules, and thus there was implied conflict preemption of the state law.[38] The Pennsylvania Supreme Court took an even more expansive field preemption approach, finding that federal regulation of the "narrow subject of disclosure of order flow payments is so thorough that we have no difficulty in finding the 'reasonable inference'. . . that no room has been left for a state to impose additional requirements."[39]

In 1996, the National Securities Markets Improvements Act (NSMIA) amended the 1933 Securities Act to preempt the states' "Blue Sky" laws over the distribution of stock of publicly listed and certain other companies, so-called "covered" securities. However, NSMIA preserved the right of a state "to investigate and bring enforcement with respect to fraud or deceit, or unlawful conduct by a broker or dealer, in connection with securities or securities transactions."[40] (This preservation of state authority did not extend to actions against issuers.) NSMIA also preempted certain state regulation of securities firms, in language that seems to preempt not only state laws but also state *enforcement* in these areas.[41] For example, state prosecution of a broker-dealer under general fraud laws for failure to maintain adequate capital, a specific area enumerated under NSMIA, would be preempted.

Another step toward federal preemption was taken in the Securities Litigation Uniform Standards Act of 1998 (SLUSA), which requires that securities fraud class actions generally be brought in federal court under federal law. SLUSA was intended to ensure that federal protections against abusive class actions, enacted in the Private Securities Litigation Reform Act of 1995, could not be circumvented by bringing such actions in state courts. In *Merrill Lynch, Pierce, Fenner & Smith v. Dabit* (2006), the Supreme Court has broadly interpreted the scope of this act.

Federal power over class actions was further bolstered by the enactment of the Class Action Fairness Act of 2005 (CAFA). CAFA adopted a minimal diversity standard for federal court jurisdiction so that federal courts can hear class actions if any member of the plaintiff class is a citizen of a state different from that of any defendant. It also provides that the requirement that the matter in controversy exceed $5 million can be satisfied by aggregating the claims of class members.[42]

Overall, there is partial federal legislative preemption of state securities laws and enforcement, but clearly no overall legislative field preemption.[43] Perhaps the most important unresolved issue in the current environment is whether the SEC has the authority to preempt state law through regulation in the way the OCC has under the NBA. Notwithstanding the savings clauses in the federal securities statutes, the SEC is given broad rulemaking authority under both the 1933 and 1934 acts.[44] And certainly, the Congress has charged the SEC with a very broad mandate. Thus, the 1934 Securities Exchange Act (as amended) provides:

> [T]ransactions in securities as commonly conducted upon securities exchanges and over-the-counter markets are affected with a national public interest which makes it necessary to provide for regulation and control of such transactions and of practices and matters related thereto, including [a wide range of matters] . . . and to impose requirements necessary to make such regulation and control reasonably complete and effective, in order to protect interstate commerce, the national credit, the Federal taxing power, to protect and make more effective the national banking system and Federal Reserve System, and to insure the maintenance of fair and honest markets in such transactions.[45]

A strong case can be made that the SEC's broad rulemaking authority includes the preemption of state law, where the commission feels such action is necessary to protect the "national public interest" in efficient capital markets. The fact that Congress has found it necessary to preempt state law in particular areas is not dispositive of the issue as to whether the SEC could do so through rulemaking. For example, then-SEC Chairman Richard Breeden considered in the early 1990s whether the SEC should preempt Blue Sky laws but decided not to do so—not because he thought he lacked authority but because he believed it was more appropriate for Congress to do so.[46] Also, the savings clauses are not necessarily a bar to preemption: they can be read as preserving state authority absent SEC rulemaking that would put state law in conflict with federal law.[47]

In the absence of broader preemption by legislation or the SEC, Attorney General Eliot Spitzer and other state attorneys general have been relatively free to use state civil and criminal antifraud statutes (such as New York's Martin Act[48]) to attack allegedly fraudulent business practices of securities firms. Unlike federal securities fraud standards, the Martin Act does not require a showing of intent to defraud. This authority has not only enabled Attorney General Spitzer to bring actions against individual firms, it has also given him a seat at the table in formulating regulation of the securities industry as a whole. To a large extent, this "regulation" has taken place through "global" settlements of state and federal charges. The most important example is the so-called "Global Research Analyst Settlement," concluded among the major investment firms and state and federal agencies in December 2002.[49]

Insurance

Federal preemption with respect to insurance followed an altogether different path. Up until 1945, insurance was entirely regulated by the states, largely due to an 1869 Supreme Court decision (*Paul v. Virginia*)[50] that held that issuing a policy of insurance is not a transaction of commerce. Since insurance did not involve interstate commerce, the Court concluded, the federal government had no constitutional authority to regulate it. In 1944, however, the Supreme Court in *United States v. South-Eastern Underwriters*

Ass'n overruled *Paul v. Virginia* (1868) and held that insurance companies are in interstate commerce and thus subject to federal antitrust laws.[51] This decision threatened the entire state regulatory system, under which rate regulation and state-encouraged collusion among carriers was designed to keep insurance prices high and thus to avoid "ruinous" competition. (This policy had evolved when insolvent insurance companies had defaulted on their obligations as a result of urban disasters like the great Chicago fire of 1871 and the San Francisco earthquake and fire of 1906.)

In 1945, one year after the decision in *South-Eastern Underwriters*, Congress passed the McCarran-Ferguson Act, to make sure that insurance continued to be regulated by the states and not be subject to antitrust laws. McCarran-Ferguson is a kind of reverse preemption. The law provides that "the business of insurance . . . shall be subject to the laws of the several States," and that "no Act of Congress shall be construed to invalidate, impair, or supersede any law enacted by any State for the purpose of regulating the business of insurance." It further provides that the Sherman Act, the Clayton Act, and the Federal Trade Commission Act apply to the business of insurance only "to the extent that such business is not regulated by State law."[52] By the time of passage of the legislation all states already had or had recently enacted some form of rate regulation to qualify for the exemption. Courts have had to interpret when and to what extent particular state laws govern. Generally, state law preemption has been broadly interpreted.[53]

In one important respect, there is now significant *federal* regulation of insurance: national banks are permitted, under the Gramm-Leach-Bliley Act of 1999,[54] to engage in insurance through financial holding company affiliates, and to a lesser extent through subsidiaries (subsidiaries cannot do underwriting). State law restrictions on affiliations of banks and insurance companies were generally preempted, as were state restrictions on bank sales of insurance, subject to the enumeration of thirteen specific prohibitions states may impose. State laws on matters other than sales were not preempted. Subject to these constraints, state insurance regulators generally have authority to regulate and enforce regulations against financial holding companies and national bank subsidiaries. However, for insurance activities within a given bank, the full national bank preemption regime would seem to apply. Thus, with respect to insurance activities conducted by financial holding companies or national banks or their subsidiaries, the pure state regime envisioned by McCarran-Ferguson no longer exists.

This system of state regulation has raised a number of problems for insurance carriers—most notably rate regulation, a form of regulation now largely absent from other areas of financial services (an exception being SEC regulation of access and data fees of stock trading venues), and conflicting and overlapping state laws on product introduction and innovation. To some extent these problems have been dealt with by coordinated state action through the National Association of Insurance Commissioners (NAIC). Most insurance carriers, however, believe that NAIC has failed to alleviate the most burdensome aspects of state regulation. As a result, two reforms have been considered in recent years: significantly enhanced federal involvement in the coordination of state policies; or an optional federal chartering system, much like the banking approach. The coordination approach is embodied in the Oxley-Baker draft legislation, the State Modernization and Regulatory Transparency (SMART) Act.[55] In 2006, Congresswoman Ginny Brown-Waite introduced part of the SMART Act, H.R. 5637, dealing with the regulation of reinsurance and so-called nonadmitted insurance (or surplus lines), which provides coverage for unique or hard-to-place property and casualty risks when such coverage is unavailable or unaffordable in the traditional, licensed, or "admitted" insurance market. The bill streamlines surplus lines and reinsurance regulation by making the insured's home state the principal regulator and preempts state laws in some limited areas. While this initiative seems to be supported by industry, NAIC has yet to weigh in.

All large insurance carriers have come to support the chartering option, and corporate support for that alternative has increased since Attorney General Spitzer entered the insurance scene. In October 2004, Spitzer filed a civil suit for fraud and antitrust violations against Marsh & McLennan Companies, charging that Marsh illegally steered clients to insurers that paid it the highest contingent commissions and, moreover, that Marsh solicited rigged bids for insurance contracts. The heavy impact of this action was reflected in the immediate loss of $15 billion by Marsh shareholders and an almost immediate change in brokerage commission practices. The New York action triggered similar actions by attorneys general in other states. Not surprisingly, state regulators generally oppose both increased federal preemptive coordination and the chartering option. In November 2004 congressional hearings, Spitzer called for greater federal oversight of the insurance industry but without preemption of state laws.[56]

There could be many versions of a federal chartering alternative. The American Bankers Association, the American Council of Life Insurers, and the American Insurance Association agree on certain principles for a chartering system for life and property/casualty insurers: (1) federal regulation of solvency, market conduct, and accounting; (2) no prior approval of rate regulation and forms; (3) preemption of state rules; (4) participation of federally chartered insurers in state guaranty funds subject to federal minimum standards (based on a concern that exits from the fund would put some funds in jeopardy); (5) repeal of antitrust exemptions; and (6) payment of state premium taxes.[57]

Senator John Sununu's S. 2509, introduced in 2006, sets forth a complete scheme for federal chartering largely modeled on the National Bank Act. The proposed legislation would establish a comprehensive system of federal chartering, licensing, regulation, and supervision for insurance companies and agents. State regulation would be preempted except in a few areas such as taxation or required participation of national insurers in state guaranty funds. The commissioner of national insurance, a counterpart to the comptroller of the currency, would have the power to implement the act through regulation and would "have exclusive authority to determine whether a person subject to this Act has complied with the Act or the application of any State law to matters regulated under this Act, including the determination of any complaint raised by any person."[58] This provision would appear to be the equivalent of visitorial protection for national banks, although its scope needs some clarification.

Federal Primacy and Preemption Reform: A Modern Necessity

For several important reasons, the federal government should have primacy in financial regulation. Foremost, the rules governing U.S. capital markets have a profound effect on national and international economic growth through their impact on the cost of capital. U.S. rules do not exist in an international vacuum. If U.S. regulation makes it difficult for foreign financial firms or issuers to do business in the United States, it may decrease competition in the U.S. capital market and result in a loss of U.S. business activity, together with employment and taxes, to foreign markets. Onerous rules may even lead to economic retaliation.[59] State-based financial regulation makes it difficult for the United States to speak with one voice abroad.

Within the United States, most large financial firms operate in several states; several operate in most. Left to their own devices, states may impose conflicting or unnecessarily duplicative regulation on these multistate financial institutions. The cost of multiple state regulations was a major reason why the OCC promulgated its 2004 preemption rule.[60] The experience in insurance has been similar, and regulatory balkanization is a continuing problem for state-chartered banks. These risks have been widely recognized. Indeed, Eliot Spitzer himself has stated that fifty different investigations of financial practices would balkanize regulation.[61] Furthermore, one state's efforts to regulate the economic activity of national firms within its jurisdiction can interfere with the policy choices of other states in which those firms operate. Given the fact that most national financial institutions operate in New York, New York can trump federal regulatory policy in areas currently not preempted. A case in point was Spitzer's influence over the research analyst settlement in 2002. New York should not be controlling national policy with respect to insurance or securities markets. National economic activity and national financial institutions are most appropriately regulated at the national level.

An important feature of the federal system is that regulation is *typically* left to independent agencies, most notably the Federal Reserve and the SEC. While the Office of the Comptroller of the Currency is part of the Treasury, it is treated within the Treasury as a largely independent office. Its independence is reinforced by a specific statutory prohibition on the secretary of Treasury delaying or preventing the issuance of OCC regulations.[62] While the SEC and the Fed are part of the national government, they are somewhat insulated from political pressure through a combination of devices, such as terms of office that do not fully correspond to presidential elections and the power to issue rules without review by the White House. State regulatory officials often do not enjoy this kind of political independence, and state attorneys general are often elected officials, in some cases seeking higher office. Independent federal agencies, insulated from political pressure, are in a better position to reach *sensible* trade-offs between consumer protection and efficient markets.

Our current approach to a different mix of state and federal power in different financial sectors is becoming rapidly outmoded because financial firms may now combine banking, securities, and insurance activities within a single business organization, a practice legalized by the Gramm-Leach-Bliley Act. Banks, for example, engage in some insurance and securities activities in the bank and others through affiliates. Activities within the bank or in operating subsidiaries of the bank are subject to national regulation with preemptive effect on the states, but activities engaged in by bank sister affiliates are subject to a fuller reach of state regulation in the case of securities and exclusive state regulation in the case of insurance. Regulation should not depend on the choice of corporate form for doing business.

Banking. A threshold issue for preemption policy is whether there is a need for a state regulatory option in a dual banking system and, by extension, a state choice for other financial firms. One might design an exclusively federal system, at least for banks with national scope, on the theory that for these important banks federal policy should prevail. Historically, the dual banking system was based on a model of competitive federalism, in which competition between federal and state charters would lead to a race to the optimum level of regulation. Leaving aside whether such a result was achieved, we have seen an increasing federalization of state bank supervision and regulation, and thus there is little remaining scope today for competition. Nonetheless, there is little harm (except for duplicative costs) in preserving the existing state banking option, and there would be enormous state opposition to abolishing it, as this would require the dismantling of significant state bureaucracies. As we have also seen, large banks with national scope have increasingly chosen federal charters. This trend is likely to continue even with the adoption of the FDIC preemption rule, both because the FDIC cannot give state banks visitorial-powers protection and because there will be difficulties in working out home-state preemption of host-state laws.

The state bank charter option should not, however, be propped up by federal subsidization of the state examination process, as is the case today.

As discussed, state banks do not pay the costs of Federal Reserve and FDIC examinations (which substitute periodically for state examinations), while national banks do pay the cost of OCC examinations. Either OCC examinations should be similarly subsidized, or the Federal Reserve and the FDIC should charge for their services.[63] With this reform, attrition from the state banking system would likely continue for banks that operate in more than one or a few states. The dual banking system would die a natural death for all significant national institutions.

Securities. The case for preemptive regulation of securities firms and offerings is quite strong given the national and international character of capital markets. Securities regulation of both securities firms and offerings is primarily federal already. Unlike banking or insurance, where firms can conduct exclusively local business, the U.S. capital markets in primary issues and secondary trading link all participants. This is indeed why the Congress mandated a national market system of regulation in 1975. The only legitimate scope of state regulation is the relatively narrow case of unlisted intrastate offerings. Securities firms should be regulated entirely by the federal government through the SEC, and the SEC should be given explicit authority to preempt state law (its powers at present are, at best, implicit). Federal preemption thus needs to be extended beyond the areas dealt with in NSMIA and the same visitorial powers protection in banking and proposed for insurance should be adopted for securities firms.[64]

Insurance. In light of the policy concerns discussed earlier, there is clearly a need for federal insurance chartering, along the lines of S. 2509. However, it is not clear that the largely moribund dual chartering system of banking should be extended to insurance. It might be preferable to require insurance firms and agencies with national or even regional scope to be nationally regulated and to require firms and agencies that operate in only one or a few states (the line would have to be clearly drawn) to be state-regulated. This would be a dual chartering system without chartering competition. On the other hand, I am persuaded that the argument could be made that insurance differs from banking, where state regulation became federalized due to concerns about systemic risk and the federal cost of poor state supervision and regulation. Real differences in state and federal regulation can be tolerated because of the lack of a systemic risk concern over the failure of an insurance firm and because of the dominance of the state guaranty funds. Indeed, under the existing system, the states bear the cost of their own regulatory failure through these guaranty funds. And under S. 2509, as under most federal chartering proposals, the state guaranty systems would continue, and even be joined by the new nationally chartered insurers. Under this view, dual chartering of insurance makes more sense today than it does for banking.

Investor and Consumer Protection. A major problem with the federal preemption approach, and particularly with visitorial powers protection, is the void left when federal regulators do not do their jobs. State attorneys general have argued that they have remedied inadequate SEC enforcement in Enron and subsequent scandals and that their efforts are needed in banking because the OCC has inadequately enforced federal consumer protection and antidiscrimination laws. Proposals for a federal insurance charter have likewise met with fears of inadequate federal enforcement.

In assessing the adequacy of federal enforcement, one needs to look at the whole picture. In banking, federal supervision is largely effected through the examination process. Large national banks have teams of examiners that are permanently installed at the banks. Issues that arise in the examination process can be resolved without need of public enforcement mechanisms like cease-and-desist orders or injunctions. Bank regulators can issue a range of private enforcement orders, such as safety and soundness orders, prompt corrective-action directives, capital directives, or memoranda of understanding. The mere mention of a problem in an examination report is often sufficient to get the bank to remedy a problem. The SEC has, and the new federal insurance regulator would have, similar *low-visibility but highly effective* enforcement powers.

States should be given access to information about all forms of federal enforcement so they can reach informed judgments as to the degree of and effectiveness of federal enforcement. If state officials perceive a lack of enforcement, they should bring the matter to the attention of Congress, which has the power to do something about inadequate federal enforcement. Congressional criticism of the OCC's enforcement efforts in the consumer protection area has already resulted in a strengthening of those efforts. It was Congress that reacted to Enron by enacting Sarbanes-Oxley in 2002, and it is Congress that has put pressure on the SEC to be more vigorous in enforcing securities laws, but Congress, and not the states, should exercise oversight over the OCC and SEC and over a newly created federal insurance agency.

If the issue is truly inadequate enforcement, backup enforcement capabilities could be created at the federal rather than the state level. S. 2509, for example, would establish a federal chartering option for insurance companies and, along with it, the Office of the Ombudsman within the Office of the Commissioner, the new federal regulator. The ombudsman would act as a liaison between the office "and any person adversely affected by the Office's supervisory or regulatory activities, including the failure of the Office to take a requested action." Thus, any person who believed the commissioner was not responding to a problem could direct complaints to the ombudsman. S. 2509 does not give the ombudsman enforcement powers independent of the Office of the Commissioner, but this could be changed if enforcement redundancy were truly a concern. The concept might be extended to an Office of the Ombudsman for financial services to provide backup enforcement for banking and securities as well as insurance.

Concerns over a federal enforcement deficit in financial industry regulation are real but manageable. The fragmentation of regulatory and enforcement functions is more serious. Thus, we need a stronger federal role in the regulation of national and international financial service activities.

Notes

1. According to the Federal Reserve, at the end of 2005, total assets held by these three types of firms were $11.82 trillion, $10.5 trillion, and $5.6 trillion, respectively. Testimony of Randal Quarles, under secretary for domestic finance, U.S. Department of the Treasury, before the U.S. Senate Committee on Banking, Housing, and Urban Affairs, July 18, 2006.

2. Bray Hammond, *Banks and Politics in America: From the Revolution to the Civil War* (Princeton, NJ: Princeton University Press,1957) , 720–25.

3. The constitutional foundation for the power of the federal government to establish national banks had been established over fifty years earlier when the Supreme Court in *McCulloch v. Maryland*, per Chief Justice John Marshall, upheld the legitimacy of the Second Bank of the United States under the "necessary and proper" clause, 17 U.S. (4 Wheat.) 316 (1819).

4. 12 U.S.C. § 93a. In addition, 12 U.S.C. § 371 gives the OCC specific authority to preempt state laws applicable to national banks with respect to real estate activities.

5. *Barnett Bank of Marion Cty. N.A. v. Nelson*, 517 U.S. 25, 33–34 (1995) (Breyer, J., for a unanimous Court).

6. 12 U.S.C. § 484(a). For the common law origin and the scope of "visitorial powers," see *Guthrie v. Harkness*, 199 U.S. 148, 157 (1905).

7. Bank Activities and Operations; Real Estate Lending and Appraisals, 69 Fed. Reg. 1904 (January 13, 2004).

8. See, *e.g.*, *Wells Fargo Bank v. James*, 321 F.3d 488 (5th Cir. 2003) (preemption of state prohibition on check cashing fees); *Cline v. Hawke*, 51 Fed. Appx. 392 (4th Cir. 2002) (preemption of state insurance laws affecting national banks), cert. denied by Ind. Ins. *Agents v. Hawke*, 540 U.S. 813 (2003); *Bank of Am. N.A. v. San Francisco*, 309 F.3d 551 (9th Cir. 2002) (preemption of municipal ordinances prohibiting national banks from charging automatic teller machine (ATM) fees to nondepositors).

9. Testimony of John D. Hawke, Jr., comptroller of the currency, before the Committee on Banking, Housing, and Urban Affairs of the U.S. Senate, April 7, 2004, 6–7 (Hawke testimony).

10. Bank Activities and Operations, 69 Fed. Reg. 1895, 1904 (Jan. 13 2004) (amending 12 C.F.R. § 7.4000(b)(2)).

11. Compare A. Wimarth, Jr., *The OCC's Preemption Rules Exceed the Agency's Authority and Present a Serious Threat to the Dual Banking System and Consumer Protection*, 23 Ann. Rev. of Bnk'g & Fin. Law 225 (2004) with H. Cayne & N. Perkins, *National Bank Preemption: The OCC's New Rules Do Not Pose A Threat to Consumer Protection or the Dual Banking System*, 23 Ann. Rev. of Bnk'g & Fin. Law 365 (2004).

12. Hawke testimony, *supra* note 9 at 12–25.

13. *Wachovia Bank, N.A. v. Watters*, 431 F.3d 556 (6th Cir. 2005), cert. granted, 126 S.Ct. 2900 (2006); *Wachovia Bank, N.A. v. Burke*, 414 F.3d 305 (2nd Cir. 2005); *Wells*

Fargo Bank v. Boutris, 419 F. 3d 949 (9th Cir. 2005); and *National City Bank of Ind. v. Turnbaugh*, 463 F.3d 325 (4th Cir. 2006).

14. *Chevron v. NROC*, 467 U.S. 837 (1984). On this second issue, the lower court had briefly noted that Congress assumed the authority to regulate national banks under the Commerce Clause. Thus, the Tenth Amendment, reserving to the states those rights and powers not enumerated, was not applicable.

15. 263 U.S. 640 (1924).

16. *Office of Comptroller of the Currency v. Spitzer*, 396 F. Supp.2d 383 (2005). The Court might have also pointed to the provision of the Riegle-Neal Interstate Banking and Branching Efficiency Act of 1994, P.L. 103-328, 108 Stat. 2338, which provides in Section 101(f)(B) that "the provisions of any State law to which a branch of a national bank is subject under this paragraph [community reinvestment, consumer protection and fair lending] shall be enforced, with respect to such branch, by the Comptroller of the Currency."

17. Larry D. Thompson, deputy attorney general, U.S. Department of Justice, to head of department components and U.S. attorneys, memorandum, "Principles of Federal Prosecution of Business Organizations," January 20, 2003, http://www.usdoj.gov/dag/cftf/corporate_guidelines.htm (accessed Mar. 1, 2007).

18. Section 303(a), (d), Federal Deposit Insurance Corporation Improvement Act (FDICIA), 12 U.S.C. § 1831a (1991).

19. Christian Johnson, *Wild Card Statutes, Parity and National Banks—The Renascence of State Banking Powers*, 26 Loyola U. Chi. L.J. 351 (1995).

20. Christine E. Blair and Rose M. Kushmeider, "Challenges to the Dual Banking System: The Funding of Bank Supervision," *FDIC Banking Review* 18, no. 1 (2006): 1.

21. See P. Strahan, "Financial Openness and Regulatory Competition" (presentation at the Chicago Federal Reserve Bank Structure Conference, May 2006). http://www.chicagofed.org/news_and_conferences/conferences_and_events/files/2006_bsc_strahan.pdf.

22. Federal Deposit Insurance Corporation, Notice of Proposed Rulemaking, 70 Fed. Reg. 60019 (October 14, 2005).

23. 12 U.S.C. § 1831a(j)(1): "The law of a host State, including laws regarding community reinvestment, consumer protection, fair lending, and establishment of intrastate branches, shall apply to any branch in the host State of an out-of-State State bank to the same extent as such State laws apply to a branch in the host State of an out-of-State national bank. To the extent host State law is inapplicable to a branch of an out-of-State State bank in such host State pursuant to the preceding sentence, home State law shall apply to such branch."

24. See M. Roe, *Delaware's Politics*, 118 Harv. L. Rev. 2491 (2005).

25. See *Preservation of Federalism in Banking Act*, H.R. 3426 and S. 1502, 109th U.S. Congress, 1st sess., 151 Congr'l Rec. E1625 (July 27, 2005).

26. Barbara A. Rehm, "Preempted, Illinois Backs Up Predator Law with Boycott," *American Banker*, April 27, 2006, 1–7.

27. 530 U.S. 363 (2000).

28. 15 U.S.C. § 77a *et seq.*

29. 15 U.S.C. § 78a *et seq.*

30. Securities Exchange Act of 1934, 15 U.S.C. § 78 (1934).

31. Securities Act of 1933, 15 U.S.C. § 77p(a), (e) (1933).

32. 15 U.S.C. § 77r.

33. 15 U.S.C. § 78.

34. 15 U.S.C. § 78bb(a).

35. Securities Act Amendments of 1975, Pub. L. No. 94-29, 89 Stat. 97 (1975).

36. 15 U.S.C. § 78bb.

37. 15 U.S.C. §§ 78b, 78k-1(a)(2).

38. *Guice v. Charles Schwab & Co.*, 674 N.E.2d 282 (N.Y. Ct. App. 1996); *Dahl v. Charles Schwab & Co.*. 545 N.W.2d 918 (Minn. 1996).

39. *Shulick v. PaineWebber*, 722 A.2d 148, 151 (1998) (citing *Fidelity Fed. Sav. & Loan Ass'n v. de la Cuesta*, 458 U.S. 141 (1982)).

40. 15 U.S.C. § 77r(c).

41. 15 U.S.C. § 78o(h): "No law, rule, regulation, or order, or other administrative action of any State or political subdivision thereof shall establish capital, custody, margin, financial responsibility, making and keeping records, bonding, or financial or operating reporting requirements for brokers, dealers, municipal securities dealers, government securities brokers or government securities dealers that differ from, or are in addition to, the requirements in those areas established under this title. . . ." (emphasis added).

42. See E. Sherman, *Class Actions After the Class Action Fairness Act of 2005*, 80 Tulane L. Rev. 1593 (2006).

43. F. Facciolo & R. Stone, *Avoiding the Inevitable: The Continuing Viability of State Law Claims in the Face of Primary Jurisdiction and Preemption Challenges under the Exchange Act of 1934*, 1995 Columbia Bus. L. Rev. 525, 547 (1995).

44. 15 U.S.C. § 77s(a) ("The Commission shall have authority from time to time to make, amend, and rescind such rules and regulations as may be necessary to carry out the provisions of this title, including rules and regulations governing registration statements and prospectuses for various classes of securities and issuers, and defining accounting, technical and trade terms used in this title." Similarly broad regulatory authority is provided under Section 23(a)(1) of the Securities Exchange Act, 15 U.S.C. § 78w(a)(1)).

45. See 15 U.S.C. § 78(b). Additional preemptive authority for the SEC is found in Section 11A of the 1934 Securities Exchange Act, also part of the 1975 amendments, where Congress describes its interest in having a national market system. See J. Mathiesen, *Dr. Spitzlove or: How I Learned to Stop Worrying and Love Balkanization*, 2006 Colum. Bus. L. Rev. 311 (2006).

46. Facciolo & Stone, *supra* note 43 at 562–63.

47. Mathiesen, *supra* note 45 at 341–42.

48. N.Y. Gen. Bus. Law Art. 23-A, § 352 *et seq.* (McKinney 1996).

49. SEC, "SEC, NY Attorney General, NASD, NASAA, NYSE and State Regulators Announce Historic Agreement to Reform Investment Practices," press release 2002-179, Dec. 20, 2002, http://www.sec.gov/news/press/2002-179.htm (accessed Mar. 1, 2007); this agreement in principle was finalized by the United District Court for the Southern District of New York on October 31, 2003. SEC, "Federal Court Approves Global Research Analyst Settlement," litigation release no. 18438, Dec. 31, 2003, http://www.sec.gov/litigation/litreleases/lr18438.htm (accessed Mar. 1, 2007).

50. 75 U.S. 168 (1868).

51. *United States v. S.-E. Underwriters Ass'n*, 322 U.S. 533 (1944) (overruling *Paul v. Virginia*, 75 U.S. 168 (1868)).

52. McCarran-Ferguson Act of 1945, 15 U.S.C. §1012 (1945).

53. J. Macey & G. Miller, *The McCarran-Ferguson Act of 1945: Reconceiving the Federal Role in Insurance Regulation*, 68 N.Y.U. L. Rev. 13, 30–31 (1993).

54. See Graham-Leach-Bliley Act, Pub. L 106-102, 113 Stat. 1338 (Nov. 12, 1999); see generally L.Broome & J. Markham, 25 Iowa J. Corp. L. 723 (2000).

55. For a copy of the discussion draft from 2004, see "The SMART Act– Oxley/Baker Draft Legislation," http://www.aba.com/ABAI/ABAI_Reg_Mod_Page.htm (accessed Mar. 1, 2007).

56. New York Attorney General Eliot Spitzer, Testimony before the Subcommittee on Financial Management, the Budget, and International Security, U.S. Senate Committee on Governmental Affairs, November 16, 2004.

57. Scott Harrington, Statement before the U.S. Senate Committee on Banking, Housing, and Urban Affairs, July 18, 2006, 9–10, http://banking.senate.gov/_files/Harrington.pdf (accessed on Mar. 1, 2007). For a similar proposal, see Statement of the Shadow Financial Regulatory Committee, No. 232, "Federal Preemption for Financial Firms," May 8, 2006, http://www.aei.org/research/shadow/publications/pubID.24338,filter.pub_detail.asp (accessed Mar. 1, 2007).

58. National Insurance Act of 2006, S. 2509, National Insurance Act of 2006, 109th Cong., 2nd sess. (April 5, 2006): S2901.

59. The preemption issue needs to be seen in the larger context of various U.S. policies that currently make our capital market uncompetitive, see H. Scott and G. Dallas, "End of American Dominance in Capital Markets," *Financial Times*, July 19, 2006.

60. Hawke testimony, *supra* note 9 at 27.

61. Patrick Healy, "Spitzer, in a Shift, Will Yield Inquiries to U.S. Regulators," *The New York Times*, December 25, 2004.

62. 12 U.S.C. § 1.

63. See J. Hawke, Jr., "Deposit Insurance Reform and the Cost of Bank Supervision," (remarks made at the Exchequer Club, Washington, D.C. , December 20, 2000); Blair & Kushmeider, *supra* note 19.

64. H.R. 2179, the Securities Fraud Deterrence and Investor Restitution Act of 2003, would have expressly limited the ability of states to impose disclosure or conflict-of-

interest requirements on broker-dealers beyond those required by the SEC. The bill languished after heavy criticism from state officials. See Christopher Lane, *Halting the March Toward Preemption: Resolving Conflicts Between State and Federal Securities Regulators*, 39 New Eng. L. Rev. 317 (2005).

6

Preemption in Environmental Law: Formalism, Federalism Theory, and Default Rules

Thomas W. Merrill*

The jurisprudence of preemption is basically formal: it isolates particular federal statutes and asks whether the statute fits into one of several abstract categories of laws that have been deemed to be preemptive. The categories are broadly divided into express and implied. Implied preemption is further subdivided into field preemption, conflict preemption, and obstacle (or frustration of purpose) preemption. This yields four principal categories of preemptive statutes: express, field, conflict, and obstacle. The task in each case is to determine whether a particular statute or provision within a statute fits into one of these categories. If yes, the statute preempts; if no, it does not. This pigeon-holing exercise produces myriad interpretational issues, including disputes about the relationship among the categories. And if this were not frustrating enough, it is also unclear whether or in what context there should be a presumption against preemption.

Yet dissatisfaction with preemption doctrine runs deeper than the usual irritation with indeterminacy of verbal formulas invented by judges. The root of the problem, I believe, can be traced to the very formality of the doctrine. Preemption doctrine is at once too abstract and too particular. It is too abstract because the doctrine is framed in a way that is neutral as to subject matter. The same formal categories apply to deciding whether federal law preempts state efforts to engage in foreign diplomacy as apply to state rules of inheritance. At the same time, the doctrine is too particular. The cases proceed by examining each statute—or more often particular sections of statutes—in splendid isolation from the surrounding statutory framework or the history of regulation in the area. In other words, there is no context. The net effect is a doctrine empty of any conception of the appropriate spheres of federal and state authority. We have a doctrine of preemption—a set of mechanical instructions for deciding cases—but no theory of preemption.

To illustrate the emptiness of preemption law, consider the venerable presumption against preemption.[1] This seems to invoke a conception of federal-state relations: in cases of doubt, the state always wins. But such a conception makes little sense. A federal system, like ours, is one in which certain governmental functions are assigned to the federal government, and other governmental functions are assigned to the state and local governments. The task of courts is to police the boundaries between federal and state power and to assure that the proper allocation is respected. But to say the states always win in cases of doubt means that in a certain percentage of cases authority will be assigned to the states that should properly be assigned to the federal government. This makes no more sense than to say that in cases of doubt, the federal government always wins, which of course would produce mistakes in the other direction.[2]

In order to develop a meaningful preemption doctrine, we need a substantive conception of those areas of regulation in which uniform rules of federal law should prevail and those areas in which diverse state standards and approaches should be allowed to flourish. It is tempting to say that what we need is Federalism Theory. Such a theory might contain propositions like the following:[3] uniform national rules should prevail when state regulation would yield significant interstate externalities or would give rise to destructive interstate competition (races to the bottom or the top), or would interfere with important economies of scope or scale. Conversely, diverse state rules should prevail when there are regional divergences in policy preferences, or there is substantial uncertainty about the correct regulatory strategy suggesting the need for experimentation, or when competition among states and localities is likely to yield superior policy outcomes over time.

But Federalism Theory, like the Court's formal preemption doctrine, also suffers from being at once too abstract and too particular. Its propositions are highly abstract—if anything, even more abstract than the Court's categories of preemption. What is more, in order to apply these propositions to particular problems, courts would have to make extensive findings of legislative fact that are difficult even for administrative agencies to assemble.[4] Thus, if the propositions of Federalism Theory ever caught on with judges, they would generate as much indeterminacy as the empty formalisms we contend with today. One person's healthy regional diversity is another's interstate externality.

What we need is an approach to preemption that charts an intermediate course between formal categories divorced from any conception of federalism and abstract theories of federalism unlikely to gain traction in specific cases and controversies. This chapter outlines a possible approach for generating propositions of this intermediate quality. I propose to resolve preemption disputes based on default rules that would apply to recurring problems.

Default Rules

Both formal preemption doctrine and high Federalism Theory apply a single standard to all preemption questions. The default rules I propose, in contrast, would arise out of and would apply only in particular subject matter areas.[5] I will use recurring problems in environmental law as a model for how this approach might be developed. I do not suggest that the default rules I discuss are in any sense exhaustive of the defaults that would apply in environmental law or in any other context. Because default rules, as I conceive of them, are subject-matter specific, it is quite likely that some or all of those rules would have no precise analogue in other areas of the law. Still, environmental law is an especially auspicious field for such a thought experiment: it is an area where both federal and state law have a significant presence; where propositions of Federalism Theory will lead to contested conclusions about the appropriateness of federal or state law; and where bruising battles between tort lawyers and corporate interests have featured less prominently than elsewhere, and hence have had less opportunity to distort judicial outcomes.

By "default rule," I mean a legal presumption applied by courts to reach a decision about the preemptive effect of a federal statute in the absence of a discernable intention of Congress directing a different result. The concept is similar to the understanding of default rules in the law of contracts—off-the-rack rules that courts apply in the absence of a manifestation of intent to the contrary.[6] Thus, default rules do not challenge the proposition that Congress has the last word on whether state law should be preempted in any given context, any more than the formal categories currently used by the Court challenge that understanding. Rather, they are tools for imputing an intent to Congress when Congress is silent or speaks indistinctly. My central claim is that default rules would be a better tool for resolving preemption questions than the formal categories, because they would be drawn from experience with how federalism values have played out in the past in particular areas, rather than from an abstract categorization of statutes based on legislative form or general theory divorced from context.

Default rules in contract are frequently justified on the ground that they are the rules most people would agree upon if they attended to the issue. This does not mean that any particular pair of contracting parties would agree to these rules; we do not know, because by hypothesis they did not speak to the issue. Similarly, I cannot say that my default rules for resolving preemption controversies correspond to what any particular Congress or any particular members of Congress would "intend" with respect to a given preemption question. The defaults are derived from history and traditions. They reflect the legal status quo, as it has emerged over time and has become more or less settled. In this sense my defaults, like the majoritarian defaults of contract law, correspond to what most legal actors over time would agree should be the allocation of governmental authority. But this does not mean they necessarily correspond to what the enacting Congress would have intended if it had spoken to the issue or to what Congress would want if it legislated today. Default rules impute to the relevant actors what most people would want (or in my version, what history and tradition suggest), leaving them free to specify a different result by express language if this is not what they in fact intend.

A default rule, as I conceive of it, is stronger than a canon of interpretation. Canons are relatively weak sources of interpretational authority, often balanced against other factors such as plain meaning, inferences from statutory design, evidence of intent, and rival canons. A default rule is more than a factor for consideration; it is a rule of decision. It would thus function like a clear statement rule—a principle that dictates a result unless Congress overrides the outcome with a specified degree of clarity.[7]

In practice, I admit, there is no bright-line distinction between canons and default rules. Canons and default rules exist on a continuum. Preemption law, in my view, would benefit most from decisional rules toward the strong default end of the spectrum. But one cannot expect courts grown accustomed to formalism divorced from federalism values to leap in one bound to a regime of strong defaults. It is more realistic to think that courts might begin developing canons of interpretation for resolving preemption problems in particular subject-matter areas. Over time these canons might solidify into something closer to a genuine default rule.

In terms of methodology, courts should derive preemption default rules inductively rather than by trying to deduce them from abstract constructs of Federalism Theory. Specifically, I suggest that preemption defaults be developed by examining patterns of decisions reached by authoritative decisionmakers in contexts closely analogous to the particular preemption problem under consideration. That is essentially the methodology of the common law, where courts review past precedents, generalize from those precedents, and then extend them by analogy to new situations.[8] The process of drawing from past experience should not, however, be confined to judicial experience. After all, federal judges render common law decisions having preemptive effect only in unusual contexts, like the federal common law or the dormant Commerce Clause, and they do so only in default of action by Congress. Congress makes judgments about whether to preempt state law much more frequently, and so it would be desirable if courts could also draw upon the patterns of preemption decisions reached by Congress in formulating preemption default rules. Specifically, courts should examine the pattern of outcomes Congress has reached in legislating express preemption clauses in order to develop default rules to apply either in interpreting other express preemption clauses, or in considering implied preemption claims. The justification for this approach is that any responsible institution that has been repeatedly exposed to a problem, whether it be an appellate court or a legislative body, is likely to devise solutions to the problem that reflect a balance of competing factors, which in this case includes substantive federalism values.

Federal Common Law Defaults

One source of preemption default rules is judicial decisions applying common law to resolve particular kinds of disputes. The potentially relevant type of common law confronts the question whether *federal* common law should apply to particular kinds of disputes. Federal common law is by its nature preemptive: when federal common law applies it is because state common law would be inappropriate and hence cannot apply.[9] Hence, if we can discern a category of environmental disputes in which the Court has concluded with some consistency that federal common law must govern, this could establish a core of situations in which federal preemption should presumptively apply.

To be sure, the matter is complicated by separation-of-powers considerations. Under the U.S. Constitution, federal courts are assumed to have very limited authority to develop primary norms of behavior, unless they have been delegated such power by Congress.[10] This constraint means that the scope of federal common law is unlikely to exhaust the circumstances in which federal preemption is appropriate. But the very reluctance of federal courts to resort to federal common law[11] suggests that if we can identify a category of disputes that have been governed by federal common law, the case for adopting a preemption default rule for that type of dispute should be especially powerful.

One category of environmental disputes that historically has been governed by federal common law is transboundary nuisance disputes.[12] Early in the twentieth century, the Supreme Court adjudicated a series of transboundary-pollution disputes as part of its original jurisdiction. The first such case involved a suit by Missouri against Illinois for reversing the flow of the Chicago River and sending sewage down the Mississippi toward St. Louis.[13] Other prominent suits involved air pollution along the Tennessee-Georgia border and garbage and sewage dumping disputes between New York and New Jersey.[14] In each of these cases, the Court took jurisdiction, found the facts or directed a special master to find the facts, and applied a version of public nuisance law of its own making, without reference to the law of either state.

Although the Court did not use the term "federal common law" to describe its decisional rules, that is unmistakably what it created. The claim might be made that these decisions applied general common law rather than *federal* common law. After all, the decisions were rendered before *Erie R. Co. v. Tompkins*,[15] at a time when federal courts regarded themselves as free to depart from state common law rulings which they found contrary to correct principles. But this hypothesis would be mistaken. A careful reading of Justice Holmes's foundational opinion in *Missouri v. Illinois* shows that he fully understood that the "principles of law" articulated by the Court to resolve transboundary-pollution controversies could not be revised by either of the contesting states.[16] He agonized over the possibility that Congress could not revise these principles either—this was an era when the Commerce Clause was read a good deal more narrowly than today.[17] But his conclusion was that the Court needed to proceed with "caution" in laying down the applicable rules of decision, not that state law would govern the outcome. Other decisions of the era are fully consistent with this analysis.[18]

After a hiatus of several decades, transboundary cases returned to the Court in the early 1970s. In contrast to the earlier cases, the Court declined to take jurisdiction over these disputes, primarily on the ground that the issues were intensely factual and the Court, as an appellate tribunal, was poorly situated to resolve them.[19] The cases were therefore remanded for adjudication in federal district court. But after a false start,[20] the Court reaffirmed in *Milwaukee I* that such transboundary-pollution disputes had to be tried under federal common law.[21]

After an elaborate trial, the case returned to the Supreme Court and was reviewed again in *Milwaukee II*. This time around, the Court held that the federal common law of water pollution had been eliminated by comprehensive amendments to the Clean Water Act, adopted after the original suit was filed. The Court explained that the act contained a regulatory mechanism that allowed Illinois to intervene in the proceedings to establish discharge limits on Milwaukee sewage plants and found that this administrative remedy had effectively displaced liability under federal common law. Importantly, the opinion in no way questioned the importance of providing a federal forum applying federal law to resolve transboundary-pollution disputes. It merely held that judge-made law had to give way to legislatively made law, once it was clear that Congress had entered the field to address the problem.

Two propositions emerge from the transboundary cases. First, the Court has consistently affirmed the necessity of providing some federal forum for adjudicating transboundary nuisance disputes. Second, when an environmental controversy involves sharply conflicting interests between two or more states, it is inappropriate to resolve the case by applying the law of one of the contesting states. To adopt the law of either the source state or the affected state would allow one of the contestants to jigger the rules to affect the outcome. Ever since *Missouri v. Illinois* the Court has recognized that the only plausible source of law to be applied in these disputes—absent intervention by Congress—is a set of principles articulated by the Court itself, which the Court eventually identified as "federal common law."

The more general point that can be synthesized from these propositions may be stated as follows: where pollution-creating activity generates significant interstate friction between two or more states, it is important that the federal government provide a neutral forum in which the friction can be resolved peaceably and in a manner consistent with norms of fair adjudication. The danger of allowing individual states or state law to apply has been expressed in terms of partiality:

> The object of vesting in the courts of the United States jurisdiction of suits by one State against the citizens of another was to enable such controversies to be determined by a national tribunal, and thereby to avoid the partiality, or suspicion of partiality, which might exist if the plaintiff State were compelled to resort to the courts of the State of which the defendants were citizens.[22]

This gives us our first preemption default rule for environmental controversies, which I will call the *partiality rule*: state law is presumptively preempted when its application to an interstate dispute would present serious danger of partiality toward one state or another, and hence would pose a threat to the stability of the federal system.

So formulated, the scope of the rule is still uncertain. A narrow version would limit the rule to transboundary-pollution disputes that could be adjudicated under the Supreme Court's original jurisdiction—basically interstate disputes in which at least one state is a party. A broad version would extend the rule to any dispute in which a molecule of pollution crosses a state line. My sense is that something intermediate between these extremes is called for. I would suggest that the rule should apply when the costs of pollution are primarily borne in one or more states other than the source state, or when the benefits of the pollution-generating activity are primarily captured by the state that is the source of the pollution to the exclusion of one or more other states that incur the costs of the pollution.[23] In other words, the partiality rule would apply whenever the costs or benefits of pollution-generating activity are sharply asymmetrical across state lines. This rule admittedly has some imprecision about it, but it strikes me as being faithful to the central judgment the Court has reached over time in transboundary-pollution disputes.

Dormant Commerce Clause Defaults

The principles that govern the dormant Commerce Clause are a type of common law—constitutional common law, if you will.[24] Like federal common law, these principles have built up over time by a process of accretion likely to capture important insights about the appropriate division of authority between the federal government and the states.

While commerce is usually thought of as the buying and selling of goods, the Supreme Court has consistently held that the Commerce Clause also applies to state laws that affect the interstate disposal of "bads." One can think of these cases as involving "purchases" of transportation and disposal services, as opposed to "sales" of garbage.[25] Whatever the characterization, the movement of waste material can and often does cross state lines, making the disposal industry a commercial service with genuine and important interstate implications.

In its foundational decision in *City of Philadelphia v. New Jersey*,[26] the Court held that the Commerce Clause prohibits states from imposing an embargo on out-of-state waste. The Court concluded that such an embargo was "basically a protectionist measure" designed to favor in-state waste generators at the expense of those living elsewhere. "The New Jersey law blocks the importation of waste in an obvious effort to saddle those outside the State with the entire burden of slowing the flow of refuse into New Jersey's remaining landfill sites."[27] This type of economic isolationism was impermissible. The Court subsequently expanded this principle of free trade in waste to strike down laws imposing differential taxes or fees on waste produced out-of-state relative to in-state wastes,[28] laws designed to encourage each county in a state to dispose of its own waste,[29] and laws requiring that all waste be pretreated locally without regard to its eventual destination for disposal.[30]

The Court's free-trade-in-waste decisions reflect a formalism analogous to the formalism of its preemption doctrine—the relentless search for some element in a state legal regime that explicitly differentiates between in-state and out-of-state producers or service providers, to the disadvantage of the out-of-staters. That search can perhaps be justified here, given the difficulties courts would encounter if they undertook a kind of incidence analysis of the interstate effects of local laws. But putting exclusive weight on explicit discrimination leads to anomalous outcomes, as when the Court strikes down all fees charged to out-of-state waste generators, who typically pay fewer state taxes than in-state generators, while permitting a small non–oil-producing state to prohibit refinery-owned filling stations, on the ground that the law is "neutral" in its application as between domestic and foreign firms.[31]

Yet notwithstanding the over- and underinclusion created by the Court's preoccupation with explicit discrimination, it is reasonably clear what the explicit discrimination formalism is a proxy for: the Constitution forbids state and local laws designed to export costs to other states.[32] In particular, laws that interfere with free trade in waste are impermissible because they seek to export the costs of transporting and landfilling such wastes to persons in other states. Thus, we have a second preemption default rule, which I will call the *cost-exporting rule*: state law is presumptively preempted when its application to interstate commercial activity presents a serious danger that the state is seeking to export a disproportionate share of the costs of environmental regulation to other states.

This default, like the partiality rule, requires specification before it can be used to resolve preemption controversies. One critical question here is whether we are concerned only with cost-exporting, or also with benefit-importing. The two are, of course, often the opposite sides of the same coin. States seek to export the bad in order to preserve more of the good, or to capture more of the good in order to keep out the bad. But the Supreme Court has drawn a distinction between attempts by states to regulate the bad as opposed to subsidizing the good and has often immunized the latter under the market-participant exception to the dormant Commerce Clause.[33] So I would err on the side of caution and confine the cost-exporting default to efforts to use state regulation to thrust a disproportionate share of the bad on other states.

The relevant sphere of behavior is roughly coincident with "not in my backyard" (NIMBY) laws that seek to fence out environmentally unwanted processes, without forgoing the benefits associated with such processes. NIMBY laws present a classic example of the prisoners' dilemma: everyone has an incentive to export the costs of an activity, but if everyone pursues this strategy, the benefits associated with the activity are lost to all. Federal regulation that permits a weighing of the costs and benefits of the activity in question as part of an overall strategy seems to be a logical response. Thus, states' NIMBY laws should presumptively be preempted by federal statutes that arguably foreclose such behavior.

Express Preemption Defaults

A third source of preemption default rules, and the most innovative from a methodological perspective, considers the pattern of judgments reached by Congress in statutes in which it has expressly considered whether to preempt certain kinds of state and local regulation. Here, we find a pronounced imbalance in environmental law. Federal environmental statutes are chock full of express savings clauses and antipreemption clauses;[34] in contrast, they contain relatively few express preemption clauses.

There is reason to be skeptical about the value of savings clauses as sources of preemption default rules. They have the quality of boilerplate, being cut and pasted from one enactment to another with little evidence that Congress has given any thought to their meaning or significance.[35] They date from the 1970s, when the reigning attitude was that one could never have too much regulation of polluters, and little or no thought was given to calibrating optimal regulation. Perhaps most importantly, the many savings clauses fail accurately to capture the enormous and pervasive role of federal law in environmental regulation. The environmental revolution of the 1970s was achieved primarily through conditional spending and conditional regulation, rather than by direct congressional mandates, which obscured the momentous nature of the shift in the allocation of power.[36] The federal piper made the states dance to its tune. One should not read too much into statutory clauses professing to preserve state authority.

Express preemption clauses are more unusual, but the ones that exist may provide a more promising basis for identifying an additional preemption default rule. They bear evidence of being carefully considered and carefully limited. They run counter to the tenor of the times, which was to impose multiple sources of liability on polluters. They may provide some further clues to the circumstances that Congress regards as warranting the exclusion of state law remedies.

Federal Insecticide, Fungicide, and Rodenticide Act. The Federal Insecticide, Fungicide, and Rodenticide Act (FIFRA) contains an express environmental preemption provision that has attracted a significant amount of litigation. FIFRA combines an express savings clause with an express preemption clause:

> A State may regulate the sale or use of any federally registered pesticide or device in the State, but only if and to the extent the regulation does not permit any sale or use prohibited by this subchapter.

> Such State shall not impose or continue in effect any requirements for labeling or packaging in addition to or different from those required under this subchapter.[37]

In other words, the statute expressly saves state regulation of the sale or use of pesticides, provided it adds to, rather than subtracts from, any federal prohibition on sale or use. But the statute expressly preempts any and all state regulation of labeling or packaging of pesticides, without regard to whether the regulation amplifies federal regulation. With respect to labeling and packaging, there is to be one uniform federal rule throughout the country.

Toxic Substances Control Act. The Toxic Substances Control Act (TSCA) gives preemptive effect to U.S. Environmental Protection Agency (EPA) regulations of chemicals promulgated under TSCA. Since the EPA has issued relatively few TSCA regulations, the clause has generated few lawsuits. The gist of it is that state and local governments are authorized to ban the local sale or use of TSCA regulated chemicals but may not attempt to regulate the manufacture, processing, or (presumably) distribution for sale in interstate commerce of TSCA-regulated chemicals.[38]

Clean Air Act. The Clean Air Act (CAA) contains a general preemption of any state standards for new motor vehicles or engines subject to regulation under federal provisions. But there is an interesting "waiver" provision, which can be claimed by "any State" that regulated motor vehicle emissions "prior to March 30, 1966," provided such state standards are "at least as stringent as the comparable applicable Federal standard."[39] Due to this California exception—California being the only state that had such a standard in effect in 1966—the CAA establishes a two-tier system of auto-emissions standards, a general national standard and a more stringent California standard. The act was subsequently amended to allow any state out of compliance with one or more ambient air standards to opt in to the more stringent standard, provided it gives two years' advance notice and its standards are identical to the California standards.

While it is always hazardous to try to generalize from a small sample of observations, it takes no great flight of imagination to perceive that FIFRA, TSCA, and the CAA aim to eliminate state regulation where it would undermine the efficient scope of markets for particular commercial commodities. TSCA and FIFRA draw a distinction between local sale or use of chemicals, where state and local regulation is permitted, and other activities like manufacturing or processing (TSCA) or packaging and labeling (FIFRA) where state and local regulation is preempted. Congress perceived that states could regulate local sale or use without appreciably undermining the efficient scope of the markets for the chemicals regulated under these acts. But allowing states to mandate different types of packaging and labeling for products distributed throughout the United States, or to demand that products distributed throughout the United States be formulated in different ways, would require integrated manufacturing firms to produce multiple products for different states and quite likely would interfere with the efficient scope of operations.

The point is even clearer with respect to automobile-emissions standards. When the express preemption clause was first adopted in 1967, the Senate report explained that permitting each state "to have a variation in standards and requirements" could "result in chaos insofar as manufacturers, dealers, and users are concerned."[40] This was hyperbolic. The result would not be chaos—just a great deal of additional expense which would not be commensurate with the benefits of allowing free experimentation with tailpipe standards by fifty states.

The California exception can be explained in part by the historical quirk that California, alone of all the states, was ahead of the federal government in mandating tailpipe standards. But perhaps more importantly, California is such a huge market for automobiles that allowing variation in this one state does not appreciably undermine the economies of scope associated with automobile manufacturing and distribution.[41] Once the California exception was established, it was relatively easy to see that a two-tiered system for tailpipe standards, tough (federal) and tougher (California), could be extended throughout the country. This presented greater logistical challenges for Detroit, particularly because cross-border sales are much more common in smaller states in the eastern part of the country.[42] But after considerable litigation and a nudge from EPA, the two-car strategy has been institutionalized on both coasts.

We can thus see in the express preemption clauses a different rationale for adopting uniform federal standards than the one at work in the transboundary or cost-exporting contexts. The concern here is that there are too many states, many of which cover too little territory given the exigencies of modern commercial enterprise. This gives us a third preemption default principle—the *anti-balkanization rule*: state law is presumptively preempted when its application to interstate enterprises presents a serious danger of interfering with the ability of those enterprises to exploit economies of scope.

The anti-balkanization default rule, like the others, presents challenges in extending it to new cases and controversies. Here, the challenges are not so much interpretational as they are factual. How is a court supposed to know when permitting fifty different regulatory standards would interfere with economies of scope and when it would not? Consider the question whether states should be permitted to regulate the chemical ingredients that go into pesticides. The attentive reader may have noticed that FIFRA's hybrid savings clause/preemption clause is silent on this point. The answer may depend on facts about the real world that can only be learned by investigating the way the industry operates. Are pesticides typically manufactured in central plants and then distributed to farm supply stores throughout the country? Or do pesticide manufacturers ship raw chemical ingredients to more localized assembly plants, where they are mixed in different combinations to accommodate local conditions? Without the answer to this question, a court cannot know whether allowing state standards to apply to pesticide ingredients does or does not present a balkanization problem. But at least the anti-balkanization default tells us that the question needs to be asked. The Supreme Court, in its recent decision in *Bates v. Dow Agrosciences LLC*,[43] did not even ask. It simply observed the silence of Congress, applied the presumption against preemption, and held that pesticide manufacturers therefore can be sued under state products liability law for design defects in the way their pesticides are formulated.

Applications

I have suggested three preemption default rules that could be applied in resolving preemption controversies in environmental law. In this part, I consider how those rules might assist in resolving specific preemption controversies in environmental law.

The Partiality Rule: Transboundary Pollution. In *Milwaukee II*, the Court held that the federal common law of nuisance, which previously had governed transboundary-water-pollution disputes, had been extinguished when Congress enacted the Clean Water Act of 1972 (CWA), which included a comprehensive federal administrative scheme for dealing with such pollution. The Court's focus was exclusively on whether federal legislation had supplanted federal common law; no issue about the availability of *state* nuisance law remedies for interstate pollution was presented. But that issue inevitably arose after the case was decided and it returned to the Court in the form of a preemption controversy. Since federal common law had preempted state common law, and federal common law had in turn been extinguished by the CWA, were state common law actions directed at transboundary pollution still preempted? Or did the presence of express savings clauses in the Clean Water Act mandate the conclusion that such actions had been expressly authorized by Congress?

In *International Paper Co. v. Ouellette* (1987), the Court provided a surprising answer: state nuisance law had been half preempted and half saved.[44] Drawing upon his greatest powers of legal legerdemain, Justice Louis Powell, Jr., writing for the Court, concluded that the state law of the *source state* could continue to apply to transboundary pollution, but the state law of *affected states* was preempted. Thus, property owners on the Vermont side of Lake Champlain could sue a paper mill located on the New York side under the common law nuisance of New York, but they could not sue for injuries sustained to their property in Vermont under the common law of Vermont.

Ouellette sought to strike a compromise between two difficulties created by *Milwaukee II's* elimination of federal common law as an available option. One difficulty was legal. The Clean Water Act included savings clauses that seemed to preserve state authority over waters of the state, including boundary waters. The other difficulty was practical. The Court thought it would invite undue harassment for industrial sources of pollution if their activities could give rise to liability under the law of more than one state. Hence the solution: state law was preserved, but only with respect to the source state.

The problem with this solution, viewed through the lens of the partiality rule, is that it sanctions the continued application of state law in a context that is likely to produce partial results. States that both export and import pollution might adopt relatively balanced common law nuisance rules. But an upwind or upriver state that saw much of the pollution it generates transported to downwind or downriver states would have an incentive to adopt unduly lax common law rules, while downwind or downstream states might adopt unduly harsh common law rules. And since states can always modify the common law with targeted police-power legislation, nothing would stop them from adopting particular rules that would dictate the outcome in particular anticipated pollution controversies in ways that would be partial to the state's own interests.

Assuming *Milwaukee II* was rightly decided, the correct result under the partiality rule is that all state law is preempted with respect to transboundary pollution disputes. To apply either the law of the affected state or the law of the source state runs an intolerable risk of partiality in the adjudication of a suit that implicates a sensitive interstate controversy. If *Milwaukee II* is correct that the Clean Water Act creates a fully adequate federal administrative remedy to handle such disputes, then the application of the state law of either of the contesting states runs an unacceptable risk of biased decisionmaking that could trigger intolerable friction among the states. The more difficult question is whether *Milwaukee II* was in fact correct in its determination that the administrative remedies created by the Clean Water Act are an adequate substitute for the federal common law regime the Court had previously recognized. The question is a close one.

Under the CWA, "an affected State only has an advisory role in regulating pollution that originates beyond its borders."[45] The act gives an affected state the right to submit "written recommendations" to the permitting authority in the source state. If the recommendations are not accepted, then the source state must notify the affected state in writing the reasons for the rejection.[46] But "an affected state does not have the authority to block the issuance of the permit if it is dissatisfied with the proposed standards. An affected state's only recourse is to apply to the EPA Administrator, who then has the discretion to disapprove the permit if he concludes that the discharges will have an undue impact on interstate waters."[47]

An opportunity for notice and comment followed by a discretionary appeal to the EPA seems like a dubious substitute for a common law public nuisance action adjudicated by a federal court. However, the EPA has interpreted a related provision of the CWA (involving federally licensed facilities) as prohibiting any discharge from a source state that would result in a "detectable violation" of water quality standards in other states, and this policy has been sustained by the Supreme Court.[48] Assuming the same policy would apply to sources not federally licensed, this administratively generated policy appears to give a significant measure of substantive federal protection to affected states—probably more protection than would be afforded by the federal common law of nuisance. On this slender reed of probable administrative policy, therefore, I would conclude that the conclusion of *Milwaukee II* is sound. The federal common law of interstate water pollution was correctly found to be extinguished by the Clean Water Act, which provides an adequate administrative remedy to substitute for the federal common law. And since the original recognition of federal common law preempted the state law of nuisance, under the partiality rule state law should remain preempted.

The last step in the inquiry is whether the savings clauses of the CWA are sufficiently ambiguous to permit such an interpretation. The critical language provides:

> Except as expressly provided in this chapter, nothing in this
> chapter shall . . . be construed as impairing or in any manner

affecting any right or jurisdiction of the States with respect to the waters (including boundary waters) of such States.[49]

Justice Powell in *Ouellette* did not suggest that this language unambiguously requires that state law remain available to combat interstate pollution. To the contrary, he conceded that "[t]his language arguably limits the effect of the clause to discharges flowing *directly* into a State's own waters, i.e., discharges from within the State." This is surely correct. I would add that it is also unclear whether the savings clause extends to pollution that affects some *other* state's waters. Moreover, we have seen that for many decades before the CWA was enacted, such pollution was governed exclusively by federal common law, and Congress is presumed to legislate against the background of established law. Since the clause is ambiguous as to whether the "right or jurisdiction of the States" extends to pollution that originates in some other state or that affects some other state, there is room for interpretation, meaning room to apply a relevant preemption default rule. Applying the partiality rule to the CWA's savings clauses, the correct result is that any application of state common law to transboundary pollution—whether it be the law of the source state or the affected state—is preempted.

The Cost-Exporting Rule: State Vetoes of Hydroelectric Dams. The default rule that emerges from the dormant Commerce Clause cases is that a state's attempt to impose a disproportionate share of environmental costs on other states, while continuing to partake of the benefits associated with the activity that generates these costs, is presumptively preempted by relevant statutory language. This rule can be helpful in resolving a variety of environmental preemption controversies. Consider the question whether the construction of new hydroelectric dams, which must be licensed by the Federal Energy Regulatory Commission (FERC), may be vetoed by states on the ground that they modify in-stream water flows and compromise state water quality standards.

Although this was not always the case, new hydro dams are increasingly viewed with hostility by local residents, especially in Western states where most potential dam sites are located. Dams modify in-stream river flows, which can be detrimental to fish populations and hence also to sport fishermen, and they can affect the use of rivers for water-based recreation like rafting. Most of these activities are performed by, or inure to the commercial advantage of, local residents. Of course, hydro dams also create benefits in the form of additional electric energy, which bolsters the supply of power in regional power pools. And since the energy they produce entails no burning of carbon fuels, dams reduce the nation's dependence on oil imports and contribute to the effort to combat global warming. Since the costs of new dams are primarily local (reduced in-stream flows), while the benefits are regional or national (more clean power), a rational but self-serving state response is to try to block the construction of new dams within the state, in the hope that future power needs will be met by dams or other types of power plants constructed in other states.

When the issue of state vetoes of new dams came before the Court in *California v. FERC* (1990), it held that the Federal Power Act (FPA) preempts state regulations designed to impose minimum-flow requirements on rivers stricter than FERC standards. The Court followed earlier precedent that had construed a savings clause in the FPA as preserving only state authority over proprietary rights in water, such as rights to water for irrigation and municipal uses.[50] The Court had held that all other state authority over water, including environmental concerns, was preempted by the comprehensive nature of the regulatory scheme adopted by the FPA. This long-standing interpretation was reinforced by recent amendments directing FERC to consider the impact of dams on fish and wildlife in determining whether to issue a license.[51]

Given this holding, it is more than a little surprising that just four years later, in *PUD No. 1 of Jefferson County v. Washington Department of Ecology*,[52] the Court construed the Clean Water Act as giving back to the states the veto power taken away in the Federal Power Act. The Court framed the issue as one of statutory construction; indeed, the word "preemption" does not appear in its opinion. Under the CWA section allowing states to set "Water Quality Standards" for different bodies of water, the Court held, states were authorized not only to regulate the quality of the water but also the *quantity* of in-stream flows. Hence, a state could impose standards for in-stream flows at a level that would render construction of a new hydro dam impossible, thereby neatly reversing the result that *California v. FERC* had held to be required by the Federal Power Act.[53]

The juxtaposition of *California v. FERC* and *PUD No. 1* starkly reveals the impoverished state of the Court's preemption jurisprudence—all the more so because both majority opinions were written by Justice Sandra Day O'Connor. Each opinion addresses a different statute—the Federal Power Act in the first opinion, and the Clean Water Act in the second. Each opinion carefully attends to the details of its statutory scheme. Each respectfully addresses the litigants' arguments as to why states either do or do not have the authority to veto hydroelectric dams under either of these respective schemes. But there is virtually no acknowledgment that the Court is giving its blessing to diametrically opposite results in terms of the underlying dispute about the appropriate roles of the federal government and the states with respect to a critical policy issue. This is all the more astonishing given that the CWA provision that *PUD No. 1* held had restored veto power in the states was enacted eighteen years *before* the decision in *California v. FERC*, holding that the veto had been taken away; thus, there could be no claim that Congress had changed its mind in the interval between the two decisions.[54]

Missing from both decisions is any consideration of the cost-exporting dangers associated with giving states a veto over the construction of new dams. States like California and Washington have incentives to try to block new dam construction within their borders, just as New Jersey has an incentive to block the importation of garbage into New Jersey landfill sites. Once that underlying dynamic is discerned, the holding in *California v. FERC* begins to make much more sense, and its undoing in *PUD No. 1* seems highly questionable. Congress had established a scheme whereby FERC, a federal agency, would gather evidence relevant to both power needs and the value of in-stream uses. FERC was to license new dams in such a way as to maximize the net benefits from competing uses of the resource. The Court's blindness to the substantive federalism values at stake allowed it casually to destroy through one exercise in statutory construction what it had previously recognized in another.

The Anti-Balkanization Rule: State Fleet Purchase Mandates. The anti-balkanization rule tells us that preemption should be presumed when state intervention would create submarkets that are inefficiently small in scope. This default rule is tricky, because its application turns on legislative facts about the efficient scope of markets and about the potential benefits of competition among jurisdictions over standards. These legislative facts are difficult, to say the least, for courts to determine with any confidence. But at least where Congress has already made a determination that balkanization beyond a certain point is undesirable, this default can help resolve related preemption issues.

My illustration involves a recent controversy over state rules mandating that fleet operators purchase only certain types of low-emission vehicles. The express preemption provision of the Clean Air Act bars state and local governments from adopting or enforcing "any standard relating to the control of emissions from new motor vehicles or new motor vehicle engines."[55] This clearly preempts state standards that direct manufacturers to produce only certain types of low-emission vehicles. But what if a state adopts a rule requiring that fleet operators *purchase* only certain low-emission vehicles? Is such a proscription on consumer behavior, as opposed to manufacturing standards, a "standard relating to the control of emissions from new motor vehicles?"

In *Engine Manufacturers Ass'n v. South Coast Air Quality Management District*,[56] the Supreme Court held that fleet purchase rules are in fact preempted. Justice Antonin Scalia's opinion for the Court is the very model of what I have called the formal approach to preemption law. He considers only express preemption, and in determining whether express preemption applies, he refuses to go beyond a textual analysis. There is no reference to any conception of the appropriate division of authority between the federal government and the states. The word "standard" is interpreted as including mandates on purchasers as well as mandates on manufacturers, because dictionary definitions support this broad reading and because a limitation to manufacturers would "confuse" standards with methods of enforcement of standards.[57] Justice David Souter's dissent was also largely an exercise in formalism; he would come out differently, primarily by applying the presumption against preemption.[58]

How would a court proceed if it sought to determine the validity of fleet purchase requirements under the anti-balkanization rule? The question would be whether the requirements will have the effect of creating a new submarket for vehicle manufacturers. We know from the anti-balkanization rule that Congress is frequently concerned about the impact of state laws that create submarkets having an inefficiently small scope. And we know more particularly from the Clean Air Act that Congress regarded submarkets equal to or smaller than individual states to be suboptimal for the distribution of motor vehicles.[59] The relevant question then is whether fleet purchase rules create de facto submarkets having these suboptimal dimensions.

The answer is factual, not definitional. Fleet purchase rules do not cover all vehicles offered for sale in a jurisdiction, only those vehicles purchased by fleets. With respect to some kinds of vehicles, such as street sweepers and garbage trucks, the only purchasers may be fleet purchasers. In these contexts, a mandate on fleet purchasers is tantamount to the creation of a new submarket for manufacturers—a de facto balkanization of the market of the sort Congress clearly sought to avoid. But with respect to other types of vehicles, such as passenger cars, fleet purchases will represent only a fraction of the purchases in the market.[60] Mandating that fleets purchase only low-emission passenger cars thus would not necessarily compel manufacturers to modify their product line in order to sell in the market where the purchase rule is imposed. There would be some commercial pressure to modify vehicles to be able to compete for fleet sales, but this would also be true if the state offered subsidies to consumers who purchase low-emission vehicles, and the Court seemed to acknowledge that subsidies would not be preempted.[61]

So under the anti-balkanization rule the proper disposition of *Engine Manufacturers Ass'n* was a remand for specific factual findings about the percentage of the market for each type of vehicle foreclosed by a fleet purchase rule. The majority and the dissent in that case both wanted to decide the issue as a matter of law, but the anti-balkanization rule reminds us that questions about the proper allocation of responsibilities between the federal government and the states often turns on questions of fact. To the extent legislative facts are key, courts need to take their cues from politically accountable bodies that historically have been charged with finding such facts, which in this context primarily means Congress. To the extent more particular adjudicative facts are at issue, they should be resolved by trials. Under the Court's preemption jurisprudence, all too often contested issues of fact are resolved by manipulating competing formalisms, which is not a sensible way to make either type of determination.

Conclusion

The Supreme Court's preemption doctrine has few fans. The core defect, I have argued, is that the doctrine is oblivious to the appropriate division of federal and state authority. The remedy is to identify default rules in specific subject-matter areas for determining the preemptive effect of federal statutes. Such default rules, derived from the experience of courts and Congress in dealing with related issues about the role of the federal and state governments, would provide a basis for resolving preemption disputes that is sensitive to, rather than oblivious of, the underlying federalism values. Environmental law illustrates how such default rules might be identified and how they might be used in resolving specific preemption controversies. The illustrations I have offered are not intended to be exhaustive, but I hope they are sufficient to suggest a better approach to preemption controversies than the Supreme Court's empty exercise in formalism.

Notes

*Charles Keller Beekman Professor, Columbia Law School. Mina Farbood provided excellent research assistance.

1. See *Rice v. Santa Fe Elevator Co.*, 331 U.S. 218, 230 (1947) ("We start with the assumption that the historic police powers of the States were not to be superseded by the Federal Act unless that was the clear and manifest purpose of Congress.").

2. See Viet D. Dinh, *Reassessing the Law of Preemption*, 88 Geo. L. J. 2085 (2000).

3. For some notable contributions to such a theory, pitched at the subject of environmental law, see, *e.g.*, Henry N. Butler & Jonathan R. Macey, *Externalities and the Matching Principle: The Case for Reallocating Environmental Regulatory Authority*, 14 Yale L. & Pol'y Rev. 23 (1996); Daniel C. Esty, *Revitalizing Environmental Federalism*, 95 Mich. L. Rev. 570 (1996); Richard L. Revesz, *Federalism and Environmental Regulation: A Public Choice Analysis*, 115 Harv. L. Rev. 553 (2001); Richard B. Stewart, *Pyramids of Sacrifice? Problems of Federalism in Mandating State Implementations of National Environmental Policy*, 86 Yale L.J. 1196 (1977). For more general treatments of federalism theory, pitched at lawyers, see David L. Shapiro, *Federalism: A Dialogue* (Evanston, Ill.: Northwestern University Press, 1995); Jacques LeBoeuf, *The Economics of Federalism and the Proper Scope of the Federal Commerce Power*, 31 San Diego L. Rev. 555 (1994); Michael McConnell, *Federalism: Evaluating the Founders' Design*, 54 U. Chi. L. Rev. 1484 (1987).

4. See Frank B. Cross, *The Folly of Federalism*, 24 Cardozo L. Rev. 1, 56 (2002) ("Courts are inferior institutions when dealing with polycentric policy problems and therefore not the ideal institution for allocating governmental decisionmaking authority."); Larry Kramer, *Understanding Federalism*, 47 Vand. L. Rev. 1485, 1503 (1994) ("judges lack the resources, know-how, and flexibility to make dependable decisions about the level at which to govern in today's complex and rapidly evolving world.").

5. For similar suggestions, advanced in the context of statutory interpretation, see William N. Eskridge, Jr., *No Frills Textualism*, 119 Harv. L. Rev. 2041, 2074 (2006); Jonathan R. Siegel, *Textualism and Contextualism in Administrative Law*, 78 B.U. L. Rev. 1023 (1998).

6. See, *e.g.*, Ian Ayres & Robert Gertner, *Filling Gaps in Incomplete Contracts: An Economic Theory of Default Rules*, 99 Yale L.J. 87 (1989); Richard Craswell, *Contract Law, Default Rules, and the Philosophy of Contracting*, 88 Mich. L. Rev. 489 (1989).

7. See Thomas W. Merrill, *Rescuing Federalism After Raich: The Case for Clear Statement Rules*, 9 Lewis & Clark L. Rev. 823 (2005).

8. The hypothesis that this method would generate sensible default rules is analogous to the hypothesis that the common law tends to evolve in ways that favor efficient outcomes. See, *e.g.*, George L. Priest, *The Common Law Process and the Selection of Efficient Rules*, 6 J. Legal Stud. 65 (1977); Paul Rubin, *Why is the Common Law Efficient?* 6 J. Legal Stud. 51 (1977).

9. *Milwaukee v. Illinois* (*Milwaukee II*), 451 U.S. 304, 314 n.7 (1981); Thomas W. Merrill, *Global Warming as a Public Nuisance*, 30 Colum J. Envtl. L. 293, 306–07 (2005).

10. See *Milwaukee II* at 312–13; Thomas W. Merrill, *The Common Law Powers of Federal Courts*, 52 U. Chi. L.Rev. 1 (1985).

11. See, *e.g.*, *Texas Indus., Inc. v. Radcliff Materials, Inc.*, 451 U.S. 630, 640 (1981) (recognizing courts' ability to create federal common law in "few and restricted" (quoting *Wheeldin v. Wheeler*, 373 U.S. 647, 651) instances where a federal rule is "necessary to protect uniquely federal interests" (quoting *Banco National de Cuba v. Sabbatino*, 376 U.S. 398, 426) or when authorized by Congress).

12. See generally Robert V. Percival, *Environmental Federalism: Historical Roots and Contemporaneous Models*, 54 Md. L. Rev. 1141 (1995).

13. *Missouri v. Illinois*, 200 U.S. 496 (1906); *Missouri v. Illinois*, 180 U.S. 208 (1901).

14. *Georgia v. Tenn. Copper Co.*, 206 U.S. 230 (1907); *New Jersey v. New York*, 283 U.S. 336 (1931); *New York v. New Jersey*, 256 U.S. 296 (1921).

15. 304 U.S. 64 (1938).

16. *Missouri*, 200 U.S. at 517–21.

17. See ibid. at 520 ("If we suppose a case which did not fall within the power of Congress to regulate, the result of a declaration of rights by this court would be the establishment of a rule which would be irrevocable by any power except that of this court to reverse its own decision, an amendment of the Constitution, or possibly an agreement between the States sanctioned by the legislature of the United States.").

18. See, *e.g.*, *Hinderlider v. La Plata Co.*, 304 U.S. 92, 110 (1938) (apportionment of interstate streams governed by federal common law); *Kansas v. Colorado*, 206 U.S. 46, 98 (1907) (apportionment of interstate rivers governed by "interstate common law").

19. *Ohio v. Wyandotte Chemicals Corp.*, 401 U.S. 493 (1971) *Illinois vs. Milwaukee* (*Milwaukee I*), 406 U.S. 91.

20. *Wyandotte*, 401 U.S. at 498 n.3 ("So far as it appears from the present record, an action such as this, if otherwise cognizable in federal district court, would have to be adjudicated under state law.") (citing *Erie R. Co. v. Tompkins*, 304 U.S. 64 (1938)).

21. *Milwaukee I*, 406 U.S. at 101–7.

22. *Wisconsin v. Pelican Ins. Co.*, 127 U.S. 265, 289 (1888).

23. *Cf.* Thomas W. Merrill, *Golden Rules for Transboundary Pollution*, 46 Duke L.J. 931 (1997).

24. See Henry Paul Monaghan, *Foreword: Constitutional Common Law*, 89 Harv. L. Rev. 1 (1975).

25. See *Fort. Gratiot Sanitary Landfill, Inc. v. Mich. Dep't of Natural Res.*, 504 U.S. 353, 359 (1992). The equation of bads and goods under the dormant Commerce Clause is questioned in Richard A. Epstein, *Waste & the Dormant Commerce Clause*, 3 Green Bag 2d 29 (1999). For a defense, see Jonathan H. Adler, *Waste & the Dormant Commerce Clause—A Reply*, 3 Green Bag 2d 353 (2000).

26. *Philadelphia v. New Jersey*, 437 U.S. 617 (1978).

27. Ibid. at 629.

28. *Or. Waste Sys., Inc. v. Dep't of Envtl. Quality*, 511 U.S. 93 (1994); *Chem. Waste Mgmt., Inc. v. Hunt*, 504 U.S. 334 (1992).

29. *Fort Gratiot*, 504 U.S. 353.

30. *C & A Carebone, Inc. v. Clarkstown*, 511 U.S. 383 (1994).

31. Compare *Or. Waste Sys.*, 511 U.S. at 103, with *Exxon Corp. v. Gov. of Md.*, 437 U.S. 117 (1978).

32. See Thomas W. Merrill, *Toward a Principled Interpretation of the Commerce Clause*, 22 Harv. J. L. & Pub. Pol'y 31, 40 (1998).

33. See, *e.g.*, *Hughes v. Alexandria Scrap Corp.*, 426 U.S. 794 (1976).

34. See, *e.g.*, Clean Air Act, 42 U.S.C. § 7416 (2000); Clean Water Act, 33 U.S.C. § 1370 (2000); Oil Pollution Act of 1990, 33 U.S.C. § 2718(c) (2000).

35. See *Milwaukee II*, 451 U.S. at 329 n.22 ("The fact that the language of [the savings clause] is repeated *in haec verba* in the citizen-suit provisions of a vast array of environmental legislation indicates that it does not reflect any considered judgment about what other remedies were previously available or continue to be available under any particular statute.").

36. See generally E. Donald Elliott, Bruce A. Ackerman, & John C. Millian, *Toward a Theory of Statutory Evolution: The Federalization of Environmental Law*, 1 J.L. Econ. & Org. 313 (1985); Stewart, *supra* note 3.

37. FIFRA, 7 U.S.C. § 136v(a), (b) (2000).

38. TSCA, 15 U.S.C. § 2601 (1976).

39. 42 U.S.C. § 7543(b).

40. S. Rep. No. 89-192, 6 (1965).

41. Reflecting on the 1967 Clean Air Act, former Senator Muskie observed: "Since the size of the California auto market would prevent this from being too much of a hardship for manufacturers, it was agreed that the state could have such an exemption, and it stands today." Edmund S. Muskie, *The Clean Air Act: A Commitment To Public Health*, Envtl. F. 13, 14 (1990). Whether this prediction was accurate in all cases is open to doubt. With respect to some California standards, the benefits of scale economies and the reduction of distribution costs from having a single technology have been substantial enough to induce manufacturers to certify *all* vehicles to the stricter California standard, even in states that did not opt-in to California standards. See Board on Environmental Studies and Toxicology, "State and Federal Standards for Mobile-Source Emissions" (report, The National Academies, Washington, D.C., 2006) 157.

42. Auto manufacturers were concerned that dealerships near the borders of states with disparate emissions standards would have to stock different versions of the same models and would be unable to transfer inventory across state lines as demand changed. By contrast, most of California's population centers are located far enough away from state borders that the California standards did not pose that problem. Taly L. Jolish, note, *Negotiating the Smog Away*, 18 Va. Entl. L.J. 305, 320 (1999).

43. *Bates v. Dow Agrosciences LLC*, 544 U.S. 431 (2005).

44. *Int'l Paper Co. v. Ouellette*, 479 U.S. 481 (1987).

45. *Ouellette*, 479 U.S. at 490.

46. 33 U.S.C. § 1342 (b) (5). This subsection applies to states that administer their own permitting systems (the NPDES system), but 33 U.S.C. § 1342 (a) (3) provides that permitting systems administered by the federal government are "subject to the same terms, conditions, and requirements as apply to a State permit program" and so presumably these procedural rights apply in federally administered permits as well.

47. *Ouellette*, 479 U.S. at 490-91.

48. *Arkansas v. Oklahoma*, 503 U.S. 91 (1992). The result may not be generalizable to the more common case of sources not federally licensed, because Section 401(a)(2) instructs EPA in the case of transboundary pollution caused by sources federally licensed to "condition such license or permit in such manner as may be necessary to insure compliance with applicable water quality standards." 33 U.S.C. § 1341 (a)(2). No such instruction appears in Section 402 (33 U.S.C. § 1342), which applies to other sources. Still, it is not clear as a matter of policy why EPA should apply different transboundary-pollution standards to nonfederally licensed as opposed to federally licensed sources, so there is reason to believe EPA would adopt the *Arkansas v. Oklahoma* standard in the more familiar context.

49. 33 U.S.C. § 1370. The Court also discussed another savings clause, 33 U.S.C. § 1365, but as the Court correctly observed, this clause only disclaims any inference that the creation of a citizens' suit remedy should be regarded as preempting the application of state law. *Ouellette*, 479 U.S. at 493.

50. See *First Iowa Hydro-Electric Coop. v. FPC*, 328 U.S. 152 (1946).

51. See *California v. FERC*, 495 U.S. 490, 499-500 (1990).

52. 511 U.S. 700 (1994).

53. The Court reaffirmed *PUD No. 1* in *S.D. Warren Co. v. Maine Bd. Of Env. Protection*, 126 S.Ct. 1843 (2006). *S.D. Warren* explicitly holds what was assumed in *PUD No. 1*, namely that the discharge of water from a federally licensed dam triggers Section 401 of the CWA, which in turn activates Section 303 (the Water Quality Standards).

54. What in fact appears to have happened is that the Executive Branch changed its mind. In 1990, the Bush administration was still interested in building hydro dams. FERC was thus allowed to defend its regulatory role in the Supreme Court. By 1994, the Clinton administration had decided that hydro dams were passé and protecting fish habitat was a more compelling value. Thus, the solicitor general filed an *amicus* brief supporting state regulation, and FERC silently acquiesced. See *PUD No. 1*, 511 U.S. 722 ("at oral argument the Deputy Solicitor General stated that both EPA and FERC were represented in this proceeding, and that the Government has no objection to the stream flow condition. . . .").

55. 42 U.S.C. § 7416.

56. 541 U.S. 246 (2004).

57. Ibid. at 252–54.

58. Ibid. at 266 (Souter, J. dissenting).

59. Like the Court, I ignore the complication that the case involved California, and hence tougher standards were theoretically possible under the California exception. The fleet purchase rule was imposed by a regional agency (South Coast Air Quality Management District, or SCAQMD), and the exception applies only to statewide rules.

60. The SCAQMD purchase rules for passenger cars in fact only applied to public agency fleets, not private fleets, which further minimizes the impact of this rule on the market. See ibid. at 249 (summarizing the Fleet Rules).

61. *Engine Mfrs.*, 541 U.S. at 258.

7

Supreme Court Preemption: The Contested Middle Ground of Products Liability

*Samuel Issacharoff and Catherine M. Sharkey**

Preemption cases are generally described as a "muddle,"[1] seemingly defying attempts at categorization. While the cases fit uncomfortably into the high-voltage area of federal-state relations, they do not lend themselves to the easy liberal or conservative framework that typifies discussions of the Eleventh Amendment and sovereign immunity. Moreover, since preemption is invariably invoked to defeat a state law claim asserted by a plaintiff, the effect of preemption would seem to be most appropriately analyzed as an effective weapon in the defense arsenal in an era increasingly hostile to recovery in the courts.

We offer a different take on preemption, focusing primarily on the most difficult cases in which Congress has sought to regulate a discrete aspect of nationwide economic activity rather than seeking to regulate an entire field or, alternatively, leaving regulation in the hands of the states. Our best examples come from the universe of cases that concern products liability, where Congress has often sought to define the regulatory standards that products must meet while leaving intact the background state tort law for remedies. Rather than standing alone as strange outliers in the contested terrain between federal and state regulation, these preemption cases occupy a difficult middle ground. At one pole are the areas of law that Congress has sought to capture altogether, such as under Employee Retirement Income Security Act (ERISA)[2] or the Copyright Act.[3] In these areas of "field preemption," the statutes typically announce the exclusive sway of federal law and typically provide for exclusive jurisdiction in the federal courts as well. At the other pole stand the dormant Commerce Clause cases, typified by a judicial determination that Congress's silence as to both substantive law and federal jurisdiction should nonetheless be seen as an exercise of federal power to keep states from regulating in a discriminatory fashion.

The products liability cases present themselves as a particularly propitious area of inquiry in which two of the great themes in preemption law come together. Because tort law is so thoroughly a traditional area of state governance, the federalization of this branch of the common law threatens a serious reallocation of power in our delicate system of dual sovereignty. At the same time, the sweep of the market for products undermines any realistic sense that the individual states are the optimal level of regulatory authority for what is increasingly an undifferentiated national, and indeed international, market. Products liability preemption cases thus form a natural environment for a hesitant federalization of American law. When applied properly, preemption can foster predictability in the manufacture of products and permits prices to be set in anticipation of known liability risks.

We contend that despite the common law origin of products liability law, the unmistakable evolution has been toward the development of national law for a national market. By examining the tort-based preemption cases that have come to the Supreme Court in the past two decades, we demonstrate how the Rehnquist Court, contrary to its billing as a proponent of state autonomy from federal regulation, was actually a critical ally in expanding the reach of federal law. Further, and contrary to the more facile political explanations of the Court's behavior and to the claim that all is hopelessly muddled, we contend that the Court is highly attentive to two problems that ultimately drive its move toward "federalization," the term we apply to the nationalizing impulse in this area of law. The first is the need for coordination among the states. In the absence of federal regulation, it is difficult for anything from safety standards to environmental impact to be addressed comprehensively. Absent coordination, there is the risk that states with the greatest taste for regulation or with disproportionate liability rules will come to define the product market, regardless of the overall efficiencies or fairness of the rules they set. Second, there is the risk of predation when states use their power to impose liability or even assess punitive damages on out-of-state enterprises whose long-term viability may be of insufficient concern to them.

Our approach draws in part from a broader study of the way in which the jurisprudence of expanding federal substantive law and expanding federal jurisdiction over state law matters work in tandem to frontload the work of the federal judiciary as a federalizing agent for national market concerns.[4] We have examined a range of preemption cases decided by the Rehnquist Court to discern a trend, over the long haul, in the direction of reading the claims of congressional authority broadly and correspondingly narrowing the field for permissible state conduct.[5] While our sample is necessarily partial, the overall long-term trend is sufficiently compelling to mute overblown claims of antipathy to regulation.

Federal Interests in Preemption

Two types of preemption, corresponding roughly to field preemption and conflict or obstacle preemption, need to be distinguished: vertical and horizontal. Perhaps the strongest case for national uniformity is found along the vertical dimension of federalism, mediating the role between the national and state governments in dealing, for example, with foreign relations. But the cases that interest us the most involve horizontal preemption, where the assertion of a federal interest emerges as a necessary default to prevent states from imposing externalities on each other or to overcome the inability to rationalize coordinated national standards for goods and services. Congress frequently regulates activities because state regulation, or lack thereof, imposes external costs on neighboring states. Building on this insight, Roderick Hills has noted that "[t]he whole point of the federal scheme is to suppress states' creativity, which might consist only in creatively achieving benefits for their own citizens at the expense of nonresidents."[6] As Justice Brandeis recognized, experimentation—a "chief virtue" of federalism—may nonetheless have nefarious spillover effects upon "the rest of the country."[7] By spillover effects, we simply mean state law that, by its operation, shifts costs away from and favors its own citizens while disproportionately affecting out-of-state interests, or what economists would term the imposition of externalities on others. As Michael Greve colorfully puts it, "Preemption is a way of arresting [states'] perennial quest for a free lunch."[8]

Field Preemption along the Vertical Axis. The quintessential case for vertical uniformity arises in the international context, where the power of the federal government largely occupies the entirety of the field at the expense of any claimed state autonomy. The cases defining field preemption offer the most direct and readily comprehensible account of the conflict between federal and state power over the regulation of an entire area of law. Typically these cases turn on an interpretation of the extent of congressional action to determine how completely Congress sought to clear the terrain of impeding state intervention.

In cases applying broad field preemption, the Court seems to go out of its way to emphasize that these are not areas where states have traditionally regulated. Seldom does the "presumption against preemption" rear its head where, for example, there is an overriding federal interest in trade or foreign relations. Consider, for example, the Ports and Waterways Safety Act (PWSA),[9] which establishes standards for the design and maintenance of ships, the reporting of accidents, and the condition of ships that vessels must meet before entering a U.S. port. Despite the existence of a federal statute, Washington state enacted its own set of regulations, providing a number of standards that vessels were required to meet in order to enter the state's waters. In *United States v. Locke* (2000), the Court unanimously determined that these state-imposed requirements were preempted by the PWSA.[10] Highlighting the importance of the national interest at stake with respect to regulation of ports and waterways, the Court explained that Washington had enacted "legislation in an area where the federal interest has been manifest since the beginning of the Republic and is now well established. . . ." Accordingly, "we must ask whether the local laws in question are consistent with the federal statutory structure, which has as one of its objectives a uniformity of regulation for maritime commerce."[11]

The Court essentially loads the preemption dice by framing the question as whether the states have traditionally regulated interstate navigation and commerce among the states. (Consider, instead, how the Court might have asserted that the "traditional" role of states is to provide remedies for their citizens; or alternatively, that the states have "traditionally" regulated the ships that leave their ports.) Posed in the Court's fashion, though, the preemptive interest of the federal government is clear. State-level efforts to augment or otherwise alter federal standards would, in the Court's view, impede the certainty and uniformity necessary to promote free international commercial trade. Federal authority, therefore, is deemed necessarily exclusive:

> [T]he Supremacy Clause dictates that the federal judgment that a vessel is safe to navigate United States waters prevail over the contrary state judgment. Enforcement of the state requirements would at least frustrate what seems to us to be the evident congressional intention to establish a uniform federal regime controlling the design of oil tankers.[12]

The vertical preemption cases apply beyond the prototypical field of foreign relations. A substantial percentage of the Court's regulatory preemption cases involve ERISA, a "comprehensive statute for the regulation of employee benefit plans" with "an integrated system of procedures for enforcement."[13] The issue in ERISA preemption is not so much the primacy of the federal government's interest as in the field of foreign relations but the federal role in providing uniformity. Thus, ERISA's broad preemption is directly linked to the statutory interest in uniformity.[14]

In case after case dealing with the inevitable tension between ERISA and state common law tort and contract obligations, the Rehnquist Court consistently preempted state tort suits that threatened the uniform character of benefit plan regulation. In *Ingersoll-Rand Co. v. McClendon* (1990), most notably, the Court foreclosed common law wrongful termination claims as inconsistent with ERISA's comprehensive civil enforcement regime, characterizing the potential for conflict as "[p]articularly disruptive." The Court envisioned an employer with operations and employees across many states whose benefit plans, accordingly, would be subject to "different substantive standards," necessitating "the tailoring of plans and employer conduct to the peculiarities of the law of each jurisdiction." The Court viewed this as "fundamentally at odds with the goal of uniformity that Congress sought to implement."[15]

The contested issues in field preemption cases—where the overriding federal interest is plain—pertain to setting the boundaries of the putative field. A useful example is *English v. General Electric Co.* (1990), involving a claimed conflict between federal standards for the nuclear industry and state law claims for intentional infliction of emotional distress resulting from the retaliatory firing of a whistleblower. In mediating the conflict between federal control over nuclear emissions and state employment law, the Court found that state laws should only be preempted to the extent they tried to impose their own standards on radiological safety levels. The Court read the federal interest as requiring only uniform, predictable emissions rules for a national nuclear power industry, not a comprehensive scheme of labor relations in nuclear power plants. While recognizing that a whistle-blower's claim for intentional infliction of emotional distress might have some tangential effect on the operation of nuclear power plants, the Court concluded that "this effect is neither direct nor substantial enough to place petitioner's claim in the preempted field."[16] We are left with a strong sense that the Court simply believed that the connection between the state tort suit and the uniform standards established by the law was simply too atten-uated: the one was unlikely to alter in any meaningful way the obligations imposed by the other.

Conflict Preemption along the Horizontal Axis. Whereas vertical pre-emption aims to achieve federal-state uniformity, horizontal preemption serves to develop coordinated solutions to matters that cross state lines. Necessarily, these are cases in which state law is the prime regulator of the underlying conduct, but in which disparate state standards are potential sources of drag in a unified national market.

Environmental pollution may present the clearest case of national hor-izontal coordination impelled by significant interstate externalities. The Clean Water Act (CWA),[17] for example, prohibits the discharge of effluents into navigable waters unless the point source has obtained a permit from the Environmental Protection Agency. The act also allows a state in which the point source is located to impose more stringent discharge limitations than the federal ones, and even to administer its own permit program if cer-tain requirements are met. By contrast, "affected" states that are subject to pollution originating in source states have only the right to notice and com-ment before the issuance of a federal or state source permit.

While the CWA establishes federal regulatory authority, it leaves open the question of the relationship between regulation and potential common law claims arising out of the same events. In *International Paper Co. v. Ouellette* (1987), the Supreme Court held that the CWA preempted a property owner's common law nuisance claim (brought in Vermont state court) for discharges from a New York–based paper company into Lake Champlain, which his property abutted on the Vermont side. Unchecked, the common law could as easily alter the regulatory framework as formal participation in the administrative regulatory scheme. The Court was therefore "convinced that if affected States were allowed to impose separate discharge standards on a single point source, the inevitable result would be a serious interference with the achievement of the 'full purposes and objectives of Congress.'"[18] The assertion of state common law claims would invariably compromise the federal purpose. "The inevitable result of such suits," the Court concluded, "would be that Vermont and other States could do indirectly what they could not do directly—regulate the conduct of out-of-state sources." Moreover, and most critically, "a source would be subject to a variety of common law rules established by the different States along the interstate waterways."[19]

Worker safety is another area that implicates coordination concerns, as evidenced by the Occupation Safety and Health Act (OSHA).[20] Here, too, we find a strong impulse toward using broad preemption as a tool to coordinate national standards. In *Gade v. National Solid Wastes Management Ass'n* (1992), for example, the Court held that OSHA preempted state regulations dealing with worker safety that had not been submitted and approved according to the act. The Court explained that:

> [t]o allow a State selectively to "supplement" certain federal regulations with ostensibly nonconflicting standards would be inconsistent with this federal scheme of establishing uniform federal standards, on the one hand, and encouraging States to assume full responsibility for development and enforcement of their own OSHA programs, on the other. [21]

In the Court's view, the act mandated cooperation between state and federal authorities: the federal standard provided a benchmark, which the states would then have power to implement or enforce on their own, complementing federal enforcement but not dislodging the federal coordination of standards. The act's cooperative federalism objective would be frustrated by state regulations that imposed substantive obligations that were not authorized under federal law. State requirements that might attempt to tighten or loosen the federal benchmark standard threatened the uniformity with which multistate employers regulate their workplaces.

Products Liability: The Contested Middle Ground

The concept of horizontal preemption is perhaps best elucidated in areas where the direct federal interest is weakest, such as in the standards governing tort liability for the manufacture of products placed on the national market. Unlike the modern regulatory state, which developed in tandem with the expansion of federal power, "[t]ort law in America is built on the bedrock of state common law."[22] Not only is tort liability an area traditionally controlled by state law, but the ready sources of potential tort cases—such as laws governing automobiles, landowners, or medical malpractice—generally concern matters that are quite localized in their impact. Seen through the lens of extraterritorial effects, however, the products liability strain of tort law stands as a striking counter-example.[23] It may be possible to hold off property claims as subject to local authority and to preserve state autonomy in the limited context of state governmental conduct of its own affairs.[24] But in the rich regulatory environment of commercial exchange and the production of goods, a potential federal interest is never too far at bay, creating a contested terrain between field and conflict preemption.

Products liability claims raise two types of problems that might warrant federal intervention: coordination problems and spillover problems. Coordination problems arise from the fact that most products are mass produced and mass distributed. They might end up anywhere in the national market, and the need for federal uniformity would thus seem especially pressing. Mass production means that goods and services are produced for potential distribution and sale anywhere demand might arise, without a particular purchaser in mind. In the case of the prototypical widget manufactured for a national market, not only is the ultimate buyer unknown, but so is the particular state in which the ultimate sale may occur—except in some actuarial sense by which California may historically have been the market for 30 percent of national widget sales, for example. This mass production and distribution of products cast significant doubt upon the propriety of individual state courts as the sources of liability rules. Given vexing choice-of-law issues, it is virtually impossible for manufacturers to adjust the price of products they sell in various states to take account of different liability standards.[25] The upshot is that manufacturers design and market uniform products rather than different products for each state and, correspondingly, design their products to the specifications of the largest states or to the jurisdiction with the most stringent liability standards, regardless of whether they represent either an efficient solution or the national consensus.[26]

Products liability law raises the specter of spillover effects because a state may be tempted to use its liability regime to benefit in-state residents with larger compensation payments and/or export the costs of its regulation to out-of-state manufacturers and product consumers in the rest of the nation.[27] Alan Schwartz has termed this the "cost externalization constraint" on federalism.[28] Elected state officials could well respond to their constituents' political preferences, and, in the process, sacrifice "interjurisdictional efficiency" to "intrajurisdictional efficiency."[29] The end result could be underregulation or overregulation, with states either deregulating to favor an entrenched local industry or overregulating to impose costs on out-of-state actors. Overregulation poses the most serious interstate risk if a state with little industry of a certain kind imposes high liability on an out-of-state industry—whether due to pandering to native competitors, the local trial bar, state courts seeking fees, or local plaintiffs seeking damages.[30] The West Virginia Supreme Court case of *Blankenship v. General Motors Corp.* (1991) offers an unusually candid portrayal of this issue:

> West Virginia is a small rural state with .66 percent of the population of the United States. Although some members of this Court have reservations about the wisdom of many aspects of tort law, as a court we are utterly powerless to make the overall tort system for cases arising in interstate commerce more rational: Nothing that we do will have any impact whatsoever on the set of economic tradeoffs that occur in the national economy. And, ironically, trying unilaterally to make the American tort system more rational through being uniquely responsible in

West Virginia will only punish our residents severely without, in any regard, improving the system for anyone else.[31]

Per *Blankenship*, no state has an incentive to rein in the recoveries of its citizens so long as there is no corresponding diminution by other states (the coordination problem) and the costs are borne out of state (the spillover effect). It is therefore not surprising to see several pivotal preemption cases articulating a need for the coordinated power of the federal government to oust state courts of their traditional jurisdiction over common law tort actions.

Vacillating Approaches: Field Preemption, Conflict Preemption. Reflecting the tension between state tort law and national interests, the Supreme Court's approach in products liability preemption cases has vacillated between a field preemption and conflict preemption analysis. This is partly explained by the reluctance of federal courts to interfere by way of preemption in an area of traditional state authority—that is, common law torts. Inevitably, when the Court does act in the name of creating a common national baseline, the dissenters inveigh against "giv[ing] unelected federal judges carte blanche to use federal law as a means of imposing their own ideas of tort reform on the States."[32] Federalism concerns loom large in the background, often deployed via the controversial "presumption against preemption."[33]

A useful contrast can be drawn between an impulse toward preserving the integrity of the common law in cases such as *Medtronic v. Lohr* (1996) and a more expansive account of the federal interest in a distinct line represented by *Buckman Co. v. Plaintiffs' Legal Committee* (2001). *Medtronic* involved negligence and strict liability claims by a plaintiff injured by a pacemaker, which had been approved by the FDA under the Medical Device Amendments Act of 1976.[34] As is typical, neither the statutory language (nor the legislative history) of the MDA is explicit about barring tort claims. A sharply divided Court held that common law claims concerning the design of medical implements were not preempted by the MDA. The plurality rejected as unpersuasive and implausible Medtronic's argument that *any* common law claim altered incentives and imposed additional duties. The case shows the Court's hesitation to move toward the ultimate logic of the national marketplace—the complete displacement of state tort law. The plurality relied on a "sliding scale" field preemption approach that factored in the breadth of the unwinding of the tort law system: preemption is more likely when the field preempted is narrow and when there is some potential alternative legal remedy available to individuals.[35] By contrast, where a statute covers an entire field, like the design of medical devices, and where a broad reading of the statute would invariably and completely supplant the states' traditional ability to provide remedies for their injured citizens, the Court will shy away from preemption.[36] It is noteworthy that *Medtronic* ultimately involved a claim for personal injury that would have gone unaddressed under the MDA's regulatory scheme.

Buckman Co. v. Plaintiffs' Legal Committee (2001) pushes in the other direction, with the Court showing far greater concern for the potential balkanization of federal regulatory authority. There, a state common law claim was premised upon allegedly false representations made to the Food and Drug Administration in the course of obtaining approval for orthopedic bone screws. The question presented was whether the state common law could be used to oversee enforcement of federal regulations, a far cry from the issue in *Medtronic* involving a personal injury about whose remedy the federal regulation was silent. From a field preemption perspective, here (unlike in *Medtronic*) one might argue that the Court was content to treat the FDA as the master of its domain, given that "policing fraud against federal agencies is hardly a field which the States have traditionally occupied."[37] For this reason, too, the presumption against preemption need not rear its head. But an exclusive field preemption lens misses a significant portion of the case. In adopting more of a conflict preemption analysis, the Court emphasized the functional consequences of allowing such a claim to proceed:

> As a practical matter, complying with the FDA's detailed regulatory regime in the shadow of 50 States' tort regimes will dramatically increase the burdens facing potential applicants. . . . Would-be applicants may be discouraged from seeking . . . approval of devices with potentially beneficial off-label uses for fear that such use might expose the manufacturer or its associates . . . to unpredictable civil liability.[38]

Buckman vacillates between field and conflict preemption approaches; it seemingly crowns the FDA king of its federal domain, while simultaneously reaffirming the need for horizontal integration to coordinate the liability standards of goods manufactured for the national market.

The Preemption Dilemma: Federal Regulation, State Remedies. In part, the difficulty faced by the Court is the byproduct of the source of the preemptive authority. Unlike in vertical preemption cases, where the Court responds to an assertion of a direct federal interest that claims to occupy the entire field, products liability cases typically present themselves as part of an incomplete federal regime. Most often the cases arise under statutes that attempt to establish national regulatory objectives that come to govern liability. The remedial schemes of those statutes, however, do little more than hearken back to the same state laws that are being preempted on substantive grounds.[39] Thus, federal preemption must be implied against a poorly elaborated regulatory patchwork that assumes the continued operation of both state and federal law.

At first blush, the Court's approach in the products domain appears to be a highly fact-dependent, case-by-case inquiry into congressional purpose and the language employed to effectuate that purpose. As has been oft-remarked, however, "[f]or a variety of reasons, Congress often does not make its intention known so clearly that one can say with confidence whether it had in mind to statutorily preempt state tort law."[40] The opinions are context-driven exercises in statutory exegesis, typically weighted down by numerous dissents and concurrences that defy the traditional liberal-conservative split on the Court. Any attempt to derive from them a uniform set of guiding principles would thus seem futile. We nonetheless wish to press our thesis in this realm: in preemption cases dealing with state products liability suits, the Supreme Court acts to protect the national market from externalities and spillover effects, albeit in a more tentative, less comprehensive fashion than in cases involving state statutes. While spillover effects would compel a broader swath of preemption in the products liability area, the Court is no doubt constrained by the absence of comprehensive national legislation and by the absence of a remedial scheme that matches the potential field-clearing sweep of the federal regulatory interest.

Consider, for example, *Geier v. American Honda Motor Co., Inc.* (2000). The Court was asked to decide whether the National Traffic and Motor Safety Act preempted a state common-law tort action against a defendant car manufacturer that equipped its cars with passive restraints, as required by a regulation promulgated under the act, but not air bags (which were not required). The act provided a clear statement of the extent of the federal interest. Its preemptive clause decreed that "no State . . . shall have any authority . . . to establish . . . any safety standard . . . which is not identical to the federal standard." Yet the accompanying savings clause took away any ostensible clarity by directing that "[c]ompliance with any Federal motor vehicle safety standard . . . does not exempt any person from any liability under common law."[41] An injured motorist sued under state tort law, claiming that the manufacturer was negligent in not protecting him with airbags. Either the claim was barred for claiming a safety standard different from the federal standard, or the claim was protected by the statutory savings clause. In holding that the regulation (promulgated pursuant to the act) impliedly preempted state-common-law tort claims for a manufacturer's failure to provide state-of-the-art passenger protection, the Court reasoned that, absent preemption, "state law could impose legal duties that would conflict directly with federal regulatory mandates."[42] The policy concern here went beyond a mere ephemeral concern that imposition of tort liability would increase the cost of making cars. Rather, the Court was concerned that state tort suits themselves would have the perverse effect of limiting the choices available to automobile manufacturers. The regulatory standard itself explicitly invited federal nonuniformity, but a single state's imposition of tort liability would impose a significant spillover effect because of the interstate mobility of cars. Even if manufacturers limited the distribution of cars to conform sales to the requirements of a particular state, they would remain exposed to suit should an accident ensue after the car had been driven to another state where a different restraint system was required. Because automobile manufacturers cannot restrict the freedom of movement of end purchasers of their cars, the only way to avoid massive tort liability would be to adopt an airbag-only policy. But, as the Court explained, "[t]he standard deliberately provided the manufacturer with a range of choices among different passive restraint devices. Those choices would bring about a mix of different devices introduced over time; and . . .

would thereby lower costs, overcome technical safety problems, encourage technological development, and win widespread consumer acceptance."[43] In this instance, state law "would have presented an obstacle to the variety and mix of devices that the federal regulation sought."[44]

The point is confirmed by *Cipollone v. Liggett Group* (1992), a watershed decision in which a divided Court signaled a broader approach to preemption and a willingness to set aside state common law in the name of federal objectives. At issue was the claim of a long-term smoker that the obfuscations of tobacco companies were responsible for her ultimately fatal lung cancer. A plurality of the Court held that the 1969 Public Health Cigarette Smoking Act expressly preempted a number of state tort claims that were based on the failure to provide information about the health consequences of cigarette smoking.[45] The technical issue that divided the Court was whether common law causes of action were "requirements" (akin to state statutory and administrative regulations) within the meaning of the 1969 statute's express preemption provision. Although this division could be placed within a traditional statutory interpretation framework, the resulting opinions are far from an homage to textualism. Absent some overriding theory of the relation between federal integration and the risk of conflict among state commands, it is difficult to lend any coherence to the Court's approach to preemption.

Not surprisingly, we find room for a more functionalist account, much in line with the views of the late Gary Schwartz. Schwartz provided a favorable account of the result in *Cipollone* by emphasizing the undesirability of allowing nonuniform rulings from state to state to control the extent of cigarette companies' warning obligations:

> The federal interest in a coherent warning program would be unduly impaired if a jury in Massachusetts could find that the warning should mention addiction while an Oregon jury rules that the warning should include a skull-and-crossbones and a Florida jury concludes that the warning should set forth actual data on the probability of disease.[46]

Thus the Court found that a state tort claim that was premised upon the notion that the manufacturer "should have included additional, or more clearly stated, warnings" could not survive.[47] By contrast, the Court let stand a state law claim for fraudulent misrepresentation on the grounds that fraud did little to disrupt national uniformity: "[u]nlike state-law obligations concerning the warning necessary to render a product 'reasonably safe,' state-law proscriptions on intentional fraud rely only on a single, *uniform* standard: falsity."[48] In the wake of *Cipollone*, lower courts have read the fraud exception narrowly and followed a trend to infer broad preemption of state law.[49]

Nonetheless—as we must concede—the federalization process moves by fits and starts and corresponds to the central problem: incomplete federal regulation. Oddly, and perhaps as a residual hangover of *Erie v. Tompkins* (1938), the Court seems less willing to displace state common law than positive (statutory or regulatory) enactments.[50] And, as we saw in *Geier*, many federal statutes claim the field with regard to liability standards but leave intact state law remedies. Most notably, in *Bates v. Dow Agrosciences* (2005), the Court confronted once again the preemptive effects of federal labeling requirements, presented here by the Federal Insecticide, Fungicide and Rodenticide Act (FIFRA).[51] A number of farmers contended that the product label falsely stated that use of the pesticide was appropriate for all peanut crops, and they asserted state law claims for strict products liability, negligence, fraud, and breach of warranty. In a 7–2 decision, the Court reaffirmed that "requirements" embraces both positive enactments and common-law duties, but it rejected the notion that defective design, defective manufacture, negligent testing, and breach of express warranty claims were premised on requirements for *labeling or packaging*. Reasoning that the manufacturer's mere motivation to change its label based on the farmers' state law claims did not amount to a state labeling requirement, the Court held that these claims were not preempted. It remanded the fraud and failure-to-warn claims to determine whether they imposed additional duties.

As an initial matter, the Court seemed to breathe new life into the presumption against preemption.[52] It is also curious that the decision restricts itself to the realm of express preemption; at no point does the majority attempt to expand the scope of the congressional preemption by employing principles of field and conflict preemption. This time, and perhaps in tension with *Cipollone*, the Court relied on a "parallel requirements" reading of federal law to hold that FIFRA could coexist with common law claims. The Court concluded that since the common law did not expressly alter the labeling requirements under federal law but simply added another level of remedial penalties, it did not necessarily do violence to congressional regulation. In other words, states may provide their own forms of redress for violations of federal standards, standards from which they are unable to add or subtract. The court is essentially requiring a more in-depth inquiry into the nature of the state law claim, one which identifies whether the existence of the state law imposes standards up-front with which the manufacturer would be forced to comply. Of course, any business performing the familiar cost-benefit analysis associated with changing behavior (like deciding to change a label) is likely to include the potential for a jury award on nonpreempted claims into its calculus. But while the existence of the remedy might well affect business decisions, the court has directed that such calculations are not proper in the preemption inquiry: a change in market incentives that attach to business decisions in the Court's view produces no conflict in the commands that companies are compelled to follow. In that latter regard, the Court makes clear, FIFRA retains preemptive force:

> In the main, it preempts competing state labeling standards—imagine 50 different labeling regimes prescribing the color, font size, and wording of warnings—that would create significant inefficiencies for manufacturers.[53]

The distinction between liability and remedies in *Bates* is conceptually unsatisfying but reflects the tension in areas where the Court wants to promote uniformity in the absence of a complete regulatory framework.

Conclusion

We have focused on the contested terrain of products liability to test the Court's preemption cases in their most difficult setting. There appear to be few federalism constraints in the Court's view of federal power over the traditional areas of exclusive federal authority, most notably foreign affairs.

Nor are there any significant constraints, as evident in the Court's expansive treatment of federal power in the medical marijuana setting,[54] when Congress flexes its considerable Commerce Clause muscles. The products liability area is one in which congressional action is typically partial, most often seeking to find a coordinated liability standard across a national market but leaving in place a stratified world of state law remedies. The lack of an integrated products liability regime for the national market forces the Court to rely on some interpretive metric to make sense of the resulting patchwork regulatory environment. Our claim is that the resulting case law draws heavily from a surprisingly simple approach: the need for national product standards for products that must move freely across the national market. It is this impulse toward what we term "federalization" that provides a basic organizing logic to the messy world of horizontal preemption. The imprecision that remains in this area, of which there is concededly quite a bit, owes to something beyond the Court's control: it is ultimately difficult to reconcile subnational levels of regulation with a fully integrated national market for products.

Notes

*This chapter is inspired by Samuel Issacharoff & Catherine M. Sharkey, *Backdoor Federalization*, 53 UCLA L. Rev. 1353 (2006). We thank Rodman Forter for extraordinary research assistance.

1. Caleb Nelson, *Preemption*, 86 Va. L. Rev. 225, 232 (2000) ("Most commentators who write about preemption agree on at least one thing: Modern preemption jurisprudence is a muddle.").

2. Pub. L. No. 93-406, 88 Stat. 829 (1974) (codified in scattered sections of 26 U.S.C. & 29 U.S.C.).

3. Pub. L. No. 94-553, 90 Stat. 2541 (1976) (codified as amended at 17 U.S.C.).

4. Issacharoff & Sharkey, *supra* note *. A vivid example is provided in *Merrill Lynch, Pierce, Fenner & Smith, Inc. v. Dabit*, 126 S. Ct. 1503 (2006), where the Court adopted a broad reading of the preemptive effect of the Securities Litigation Uniform Standards Act of 1998, and in so doing, emphasized the "magnitude of the federal interest in protecting the integrity and efficient operation of the market for nationally traded securities." 126 S. Ct. at 1509. Our contention is that this federalizing impulse applies, albeit in a more implicit fashion, well beyond the context of "national standards for securities class action lawsuits involving nationally traded securities." Ibid. at 1514, quoting 112 Stat. 3227.

5. We derived our sample from the universe of cases analyzed by Michael Greve and Jonathan Klick. Michael S. Greve & Jonathan Klick, *Preemption in the Rehnquist Court: A Preliminary Empirical Assessment*, 14 Sup. Ct. Econ. Rev. 43 (2006).

6. See Roderick M. Hills, Jr., *Against Preemption: How Federalism Can Improve the National Legislative Process*, 82 N.Y.U. L. Rev. (forthcoming 2007).

7. *New State Ice Co. v. Liebmann*, 285 U.S. 262, 311 (1932) (Brandeis, J., dissenting).

8. Michael Greve, *Subprime but not Half-Bad: Mortgage Regulation as a Case Study in Preemption*, AEI Federalist Outlook No.19 (September-October 2003), 4, http://federalismproject.org/depository/FederalistOutlook19.pdf (accessed Feb. 22, 2007).

9. Ports and Waterways Safety Act, 33 U.S.C. §§ 1221–1232a (2000).

10. 529 U.S. 89 (2000). More precisely, the Court held that at least four of the requirements were preempted and remanded to determine whether any other requirements were also preempted. Ibid. at 112–16.

11. Ibid. at 99, 108.

12. Ibid. at 111, quoting *Ray v. Atlantic Richfield Co.*, 435 U.S. 151 (1978).

13. *Aetna Health v. Davila*, 542 U.S. 200, 208 (2004); 29 U.S.C. § 1144(a) (2000) (ERISA provisions "shall supersede any and all State laws insofar as they may now or hereafter relate to any employee benefit plan"). According to Greve and Klick, *supra* note 5, 435, of the 105 preemption cases (focusing only on preemption of state statutes) decided by the Rehnquist Court (from 1986–2003), labor and employment cases (in which ERISA predominated) comprised 32, or roughly one-third of the total.

14. *Ingersoll-Rand Co. v. McClendon*, 498 U.S. 133, 142 (1990) ("Section 514(a) [a preemption provision] was intended to ensure that plans and plan sponsors would be subject to a uniform body of benefits law; the goal was to minimize the administrative and financial burden of complying with conflicting directives among States or between States and the Federal Government"). See also *FMC v. Holliday*, 498 U.S. 52, 60 (1990) ("To require plan providers to design their programs in an environment of differing state regulations would complicate the administration of nationwide plans. . . .").

15. *Ingersoll-Rand*, 498 U.S. at 142. Similarly, in *Egelhoff v. Egelhoff ex rel. Breiner*, 532 U.S. 141, 148 (2002), the Court found a Washington state statute preempted not only by the express language of ERISA but also on implied or obstacle preemption grounds because the statute "interfere[d] with nationally uniform plan administration." The uniformity goal, the Court explained, would be thwarted "if plans are subject to different legal obligations in different States." Ibid.

16. *English v. General Electric*, 496 U.S. 72, 85 (1990).

17. 33 U.S.C. §§ 1251–1387 (2000).

18. *International Paper Co. v. Ouellette*, 479 U.S. 481, 493 (1987).

19. Ibid. at 495–96. Worse still, the Court continued: "These nuisance standards are often 'vague' and 'indeterminate.' The application of numerous States' laws would only exacerbate the vagueness and resulting uncertainty." Ibid. at 496.

20. 29 U.S.C. §§ 651–78 (2000).

21. *Gade v. Nat'l Solid Wastes Mgmt. Ass'n*, 505 U.S. 88, 103 (1992).

22. Robert L. Rabin, *Federalism and the Tort System*, 50 Rutgers L. Rev. 1, 2 (1997).

23. See Sherman Joyce, *Federal Product Liability Litigation Reform: Recent Developments and Statistics*, 19 Seattle U. L. Rev. 421, 427–28 (1996) (advocating federal products liability legislation in light of the fact that the U.S. economy is both national and global, and, according to a U.S. Department of Commerce report, over 70 percent of the goods manufactured in one state are shipped and sold out of that state) (citing Bureau of the Census, U.S. Dep't of Commerce, Pub. No. TC77-CS, Commodity Transportation Survey 1–7 (1981)).

24. See, respectively, *Kelo v. New London*, 545 U.S. 469 (2005); and *Bd. of Trs. of the Univ. of Ala. v. Garrett*, 531 U.S. 356, 363 (2001).

25. For creative choice-of-law proposals to address the spillover effects problem, see Michael McConnell, "A Choice-of-Law Approach to Products-Liability Reform," in *New Directions in Liability Law*, ed. Walter Olsen (New York: Academy of Political Science, 1988), 90–101; and Samuel Issacharoff, *Settled Expectations in a World of Unsettled Law: Choice of Law After the Class Action Fairness Act*, 106 Colum. L. Rev. 1839 (2006). The extent (and significance) of variation in state products liability law is subject to debate. Compare, *e.g.,* Gary Schwartz, *Considering the Proper Federal Role in American Tort Law*, 38 Ariz. L. Rev. 917, 929 (1996) ("Within products liability . . . the inter-state variations in common law doctrine are both more frequent and more significant than they are in other sectors of the common law of torts."), with, *e.g.,* Stephen D. Sugarman, *Should Congress Engage in Tort Reform?*, 1 Mich. L. & Pol'y 121, 127

(1996) ("state tort laws today are broadly the same in product injury cases," although there are differences "around the edges").

26. See, *e.g.*, Schwartz, *supra* note 25 at 927 ("Manufacturers . . . must distribute a uniform product on a nationwide basis and cannot modify the price they charge for each product to account for state-law variations in that product liability's exposure.").

27. Gary Schwartz terms this the "structural bias problem." Ibid. at 932. See also Robert M. Ackerman, *Tort Law and Federalism: Whatever Happened to Devolution*, 14 Yale J. Reg. 429, 451 (1996); John S. Baker, Jr., *Respecting a State's Tort Law, While Confining Its Reach to That State*, 31 Seton Hall L. Rev. 698, 704–6 (2001); Harvey S. Perlman, *Products Liability Reform in Congress: An Issue of Federalism*, 48 Ohio St. L.J. 503, 508 (1987).

28. Alan Schwartz, *Statutory Interpretation, Capture, and Tort Law: The Regulatory Compliance Defense*, 2 Am. L. & Econ. Rev. 1, 21 & n. 26 (2000) (specifying as a constraint on the pursuit of local values that "local regulation will not externalize costs to other states").

29. The terminology is from Robert P. Inman & Daniel L. Rubinfeld, *Making Sense of the Antitrust State-Action Doctrine: Balancing Political Participation and Economic Efficiency in Regulatory Federalism*, 75 Tex. L. Rev. 1203, 1234 (1997).

30. See, *e.g.*, Richard Neely, *The Product Liability Mess: How Business Can Be Rescued From the Politics of State Courts* (New York: Free Press, 1988) (demonstrating that state judges and legislators shape tort law to favor the interests of resident plaintiffs over nonresident manufacturers); William Powers, Jr., *Some Pitfalls of Federal Tort Reform Legislation*, 38 Ariz. L. Rev. 909, 910 (1996) ("[I]n a classic example of the tragedy of the commons, each state may have a bias in favor of products liability rules that increase recovery.").

31. *Blankenship v. General Motors Corp.*, 406 S.E.2d 781, 783 (W.Va. 1991).

32. *Geier*, 529 U.S. 861 at 894 (Stevens, J., dissenting).

33. Ibid. at 887 (Stevens, J., dissenting) ("This is a case about federalism," that is about respect for "the constitutional role of the States as sovereign entities") (quoting, inter alia, *Alden v. Maine*, 527 U.S. 706, 713 (1999)). Justice Stevens is clearly the justice the most concerned with preempting state common law remedies through broad federal preemption. His opinions in *Cipollone v. Liggett Group,* 505 U.S. 504 (1992), *Medtronic v. Lohr*, 518 U.S. 470 (1996), and *Geier* are the most clear statements of the role of federalism in preemption decisions, and he is the most consistent and outspoken justice in favor of the presumption against preemption.

34. 21 U.S.C. §§ 360c–379a (2000).

35. Justice Stevens created a new sort of balancing test: the preemptive statute in *Cipollone* was targeted at a limited set of state requirements—those "based on smoking and health"—and then only at a limited subset of the possible applications of those requirements—those involving the "advertising or promotion of any cigarettes the packages of which are labeled in conformity with the provisions of" the federal statute.

In that context, giving the term "requirement" its widest reasonable meaning did not have nearly the preemptive scope nor the effect on potential remedies that *Medtronic's* broad reading of the term would have in this suit. *Medtronic*, 518 U.S. at 488.

36. The dissent understood the same tension in federal-state relations but would have preempted any claim that might potentially alter incentives or impose additional requirements upon entities covered by the statute. See ibid. at 509 (O'Connor, J., dissenting).

37. *Buckman*, 531 U.S. at 347 ("To the contrary, the relationship between a federal agency and the entity it regulates is inherently federal in character; the relationship originates from, is governed by, and terminates according to federal law.").

38. Ibid. at 350.

39. For an express recognition that common law damages are an integral part of the Court's understanding of legal requirements or prohibitions, see *Cipollone*, 505 U.S. at 522 (relying in turn on W. Prosser, *Law of Torts* (4th ed. 1971), 4).

40. Robert L. Rabin, *Reassessing Regulatory Compliance*, 88 Geo. L.J. 2049, 2054 (2000). See also James A. Henderson and Aaron D. Twerski, *Products Liability: Problems and Process* (New York: Aspen Publishers, 5th ed. 2004), 424 ("Congress quite clearly has sought to placate both industry and consumers by speaking out of both sides of its mouth. And in the event that no one should understand how both [preemption and saving clauses] can work in tandem, that job is left to the United States Supreme Court, which does not have to face the wrath of political constituencies.").

41. *National Traffic and Motor Safety Act*, 15 U.S.C. 1392(d) (1988); 15 U.S.C. 1397(k) (1988).

42. *Geier*, 529 U.S. 861 at 871. The majority's decision prompted criticisms that the Court was imposing tort reform in disguise, ibid. at 894 (Stevens, J., dissenting).

43. Ibid. at 875.

44. Ibid. at 863. The solicitor general argued in *Geier* that the promulgation of the regulation (Federal Motor Vehicle Safety Standard 208) embodied an affirmative "policy judgment that safety would be best promoted if manufacturers installed alternative protection systems in their fleets rather than one particular system in every car," *Geier*, 529 U.S. at 881 (quoting Brief for the United States as *Amicus Curiae*, at 25)—offering up a possible ground by which to distinguish *Sprietsma v. Mercury Marine*, 537 U.S. 51 (2002). In *Sprietsma*, the Court held (unanimously) that a state common-law tort action seeking damages from the manufacturer of an outboard motor was not preempted either by the enactment of the Federal Boat Safety Act of 1971 or by the decision of the U.S. Coast Guard in 1990 not to promulgate a regulation requiring propeller guards on motorboats. Here, too, the interest in securing "uniformity of boating laws and regulations as among the several States and the Federal Government," ibid. at 57, would seem paramount. Unlike in *Geier*, however, here there was no definitive agency regulation—instead, the Court was asked to consider whether the Coast Guard's decision not to regulate propeller guards impliedly preempted any state law common law liability. Ibid. at 65 ("[H]istory teaches us that a Coast Guard decision not

to regulate a particular aspect of boating safety is fully consistent with an intent to preserve state regulatory authority pending the adoption of specific federal standards."). The Court, moreover, was likely heavily swayed by the fact that the solicitor general, joined by counsel for the Coast Guard, took the position that the agency did not view the 1990 refusal to regulate or any subsequent regulatory actions by the Coast Guard as having any preemptive effect. For an elaboration of the influence of agencies' views on the Supreme Court's preemption determinations in products liability cases, see Catherine M. Sharkey, *Preemption by Preamble: Federal Agencies and the Federalization of Tort Law*, 56 DePaul L. Rev. (forthcoming 2007).

45. A plurality of the Court (per Justice Stevens) held that petitioner's claims based upon express warranty and conspiracy were not preempted by the 1969 Act. *Cipollone*, 505 U.S. at 525–30. Justice Blackmun (writing for himself and Justices Kennedy and Souter) concluded that the 1969 Act did not clearly and manifestly exhibit a congressional intent to preempt common law damages actions, and therefore concurred in part that certain of the claims were not preempted. Ibid. at 533–34 (Blackmun, J., dissenting). Justices Scalia and Thomas concurred in part and dissented in part, arguing that all of the claims were preempted by the 1969 Public Health Cigarette Smoking Act, 15 U.S.C. § 1340 (2000), under ordinary principles of statutory construction. Ibid. at 548–54 (Scalia, J., dissenting). A majority (again, per Justice Stevens) also held that the previously enacted 1965 Federal Cigarette Labeling and Advertising Act (FCLAA), 15 U.S.C. § 1331, did not preempt state-law damages actions but preempted only positive enactments by state and federal rulemaking bodies in the areas of advertising and labeling cigarettes. Ibid. at 518–20.

46. Gary T. Schwartz, "Tobacco Liability in the Courts," in *Smoking Policy: Law, Politics, and Culture*, eds. Robert L. Rabin and Stephen D. Sugarman (Oxford: Oxford University Press, 1993), 131–60.

47. *Cipollone*, 505 U.S. at 524.

48. Ibid. at 529 (emphasis added).

49. See, *e.g.*, Robert J. Katerberg, *Patching the "Crazy Quilt" of* Cipollone: *A Divided Court Rethinks Federal Preemption of Products Liability in* Medtronic v. Lohr, 75 N.C. L. Rev. 1440, 1478 n. 260 (1997) (listing post-*Cipollone* cases broadly inferring preemption). See also *Lorillard Tobacco Co. v. Reilly*, 533 U.S. 525 (2001) (holding that Massachusetts state law cigarette advertising regulations were preempted by FCLAA, which prescribed mandatory health warnings for cigarette packaging and advertising).

50. The Court here has been persuaded that state law remedies (that is, damages) are distinct from pure regulatory law. Thus, for example, in *Silkwood v. Kerr-McGee Corp.*, 464 U.S. 238 (1984), the definitive early case in which the Court tackled the issue of the preemptive effect of federal law upon state tort law, the Court held that Silkwood's claim for punitive damages, arising out of radiation injuries from exposure to plutonium, was not preempted by the Atomic Energy Act (AEA)—despite the fact that in the previous term, the Court had held that the AEA preempted state safety regulation of nuclear power plants. See *Pacific Gas & Elec. Co. v. State Energy Res. & Conservation &*

Dev. Comm'n, 461 U.S. 190 (1983). The majority in *Silkwood* conceived punitive damages as distinct from pure regulatory law. Moreover, since the AEA did not provide for a private right of action, preemption in the case would have left victims wholly without legal remedy. The dissent ridiculed the majority's reasoning here, arguing that a punitive damages award would, in effect, allow a state to enforce a legal standard that was "more exacting than the federal standard." *Silkwood*, 464 U.S. at 265 (Blackmun, J., dissenting).

51. 125 S.Ct. 1788 (2005) at 1788. The express preemption provision at issue provided that "Such State shall not impose or continue in effect any requirements for labeling or packaging in addition to or different from those required under this subchapter." Federal Insecticide, Fungicide, and Rodenticide Act (FIFRA), 7 U.S.C. § 136v(b) (2000).

52. See *Bates*, 125 S.Ct. at 1801 ("Because the States are independent sovereigns in our federal system, we have long presumed that Congress does not cavalierly pre-empt state causes of action."). The Court, moreover, was clearly concerned by the fact that most farmers would be left without a remedy if state tort suits for misbranding were entirely preempted. Ibid. at 1801–2 ("The long history of tort litigation against manufacturers of poisonous substances adds force to the basic presumption against preemption. If Congress had intended to deprive injured parties of a long available form of compensation, it surely would have expressed that intent more clearly.").

53. Ibid. at 1803.

54. *Gonzalez v. Raich*, 125 S.Ct. 2195 (2005).

PART III

The Logic of Preemption

8

The Problem of Federal Preemption: Toward a Formal Solution

Robert R. Gasaway and Ashley C. Parrish

A workable implied preemption jurisprudence must draw nonarbitrary distinctions between areas in which state regulatory activity is permitted and those in which it is proscribed. Because the legislative, executive, and judicial branches of state governments are all subject to capture by factions and will inevitably take actions that seek to undermine or nullify federal policies that state actors oppose, a robust preemption doctrine is needed to control and discipline the states.[1]

Current preemption jurisprudence is both too malleable to inspire confidence and too feeble to protect federal policies from state encroachment. Reliance on express preemption alone does not work because any descent into congressional intent under current doctrine creates an intolerable risk of results-driven decisionmaking. Congress cannot possibly be expected to anticipate in advance or respond in timely fashion to all conceivable ways in which states might attempt to intrude on federal policies. And even if Congress could allot adequate attention to policing state encroachments,[2] current doctrine makes it harder, not easier, for Congress to express its intent to preempt. The often-invoked "presumption against preemption," for example, is so poorly delineated that no matter how insistently Congress says it intends to displace state law—at least in the area of health and safety regulation—it will risk being deemed not to have spoken clearly enough for courts predisposed to find against preemption.[3] Because Congress cannot possibly anticipate in advance or nullify afterward all the many state intrusions on federal policies, more robust *implied* preemption doctrines are required—doctrines that protect federal policies even in the absence of express congressional directives.

This chapter seeks to further the development of preemption rules that inhibit results oriented decisionmaking, while giving proper scope for the operation of in state, out of state, and federal law. To that end, we suggest that courts assign preemptive effect to individual collisions between state and federal law using differences in legal form—the alternative modes of framing a given substantive legal requirement. Every federal and state legal requirement necessarily involves legislative choices along several formal dimensions, including (1) the prescriptive or preclusive nature of the regulatory regime; (2) the decision to employ a rule, as opposed to a standard, as the form of the conduct governing requirement; and (3) the decision to employ a pure legal standard, a licensing standard, or an equitable standard as the mechanism for enforcing the substantive requirement. It is these critical, albeit implicit, choices to which courts already do look and to which they might look even more carefully in the future in determining the *implied* preemptive scope of federal legal requirements.

This chapter consists of two parts. Part one examines the formal distinction between affirmative (or prescriptive) legal requirements and negative (or preclusive) requirements. Courts have increasingly recognized that when federal decisionmakers make an *affirmative* judgment in favor of a certain, optimum level of regulation—that is, when a federal scheme reflects a regulatory "golden mean"—that judgment operates as a *negative* judgment on state law requirements that would strike an alternative regulatory balance. Unfortunately, courts have not yet been able to agree, even at a conceptual level, on the preemptive significance of negative (or preclusive) federal requirements. It is here that arbitrary or results-oriented decisionmaking too often holds sway. In order to develop a workable implied conflict preemption doctrine for prohibitory requirements, courts must evaluate those requirements along at least two formal dimensions: first, whether the substantive requirement governing primary conduct takes the form of a rule as opposed to a standard; and second, whether the substantive requirement is enforced through fines and damages, through a licensing scheme, or through an equitable regime of injunctive remedies.

In part two, we suggest doctrinal improvements intended to correct some of the more egregious excesses of present-day tort litigation. We begin by demonstrating that when Congress enforces standards of conduct through a federal licensing scheme, Congress has implicitly preempted any pure state law standard governing the same conduct. We then show how the rules versus standards distinction can be applied to view conflict preemption through a lens of conflicts-of-law doctrine. The upshot is a suggested response to abusive applications of state tort standards by cabining them along a horizontal dimension with the home-state standards of out-of-state defendants and along a vertical dimension with the substantive requirements of most federal licensing regimes. We offer these theoretical and doctrinal suggestions as balm for what too often has ailed implied conflict preemption doctrines over the course of the past century—more or less random presumptions either in favor of state authority or against it and, in some quarters, dissatisfaction to the point where the very legitimacy of impliedly preempting state laws is questioned.[4]

Identifying the Elements of Form

The best-understood element of legal form is the difference between affirmative (or prescriptive) requirements and negative (or prohibitory) requirements. Courts and agencies alike increasingly appreciate the significance of this distinction for preemption analysis. In particular, courts and agencies are increasingly confident in their ability to assign appropriate preemptive force to prescriptive requirements that embody a federally established "golden mean."

Affirmative (or Prescriptive) Regulations: The "Golden Mean." When federal decisionmakers make an affirmative judgment in favor of a specific legal requirement, that judgment necessarily makes a negative judgment on alternative requirements that may be imposed by state legislators, regulators, or courts. In the context of numerical requirements, the question can be phrased as the distinction between an optimum, on the one hand, and a maximum or minimum on the other.[5] In the context of nonnumerical requirements, the distinction can be described as the choice of a "golden policy mean" to the exclusion of alternative arrangements that would skew policy in either direction. When Congress establishes requirements that set a regulatory optimum, or "golden mean," the standards are impliedly preemptive because, viewed from the perspective of the regime as a whole, the requirements represent a federal affirmation of one policy to the exclusion of all alternatives.[6] In contrast, when Congress establishes minimum or maximum standards, the standards are generally viewed as nonpreemptive of state regulation on grounds that they reflect federally prescribed bounds on private conduct but not a definitive and affirmative judgment in favor of federal policy.[7]

Although long decisive in a variety of implied preemption contexts, the *magna carta* for the centrality of the prescription proscription distinction is Justice Stephen Breyer's opinion for the Supreme Court in *Geier v. American Honda Motor Co., Inc.* (2000). In *Geier*, the Court addressed whether regulations promulgated under the federal Motor Vehicle Safety Act, which permitted car manufacturers to choose whether to equip vehicles with driver side airbags, preempted "no airbag" tort suits brought under state law. The Court held that, although the Motor Vehicle Safety Act's preemption provision did not expressly preempt common-law claims, the plaintiffs' state-law tort suit was *impliedly* preempted because it "presented an obstacle" to the "accomplishment and execution" of the safety objectives of federal law regulating vehicle passive restraint systems. In reaching that conclusion, the Court emphasized that the expert federal agency, the Department of Transportation's National Highway Traffic Safety Administration (NHTSA), had "rejected a proposed . . . 'all airbag' standard," and instead had promulgated regulations that deliberately "sought a variety—a mix of several different passive restraint systems."[8] The Court further explained that the agency's regulations "deliberately sought a gradual phase-in of passive restraints"[9] as opposed to setting a minimum airbag standard. As the Court framed the issue, NHTSA had struck a precise balance that would be disrupted if state tort laws were permitted to impose duties on manufacturers to install airbags in *all*, as opposed to only *some*, of their vehicles. NHTSA's chosen percentages thus precluded states from effectively altering the federal passive restraint phase-in to require restraints in 100 percent of vehicles on an accelerated timetable.

Geier's doctrinal breakthrough is its explanation of how an *affirmative* federal judgment in favor of one numerical requirement operates as a *negative* judgment on alternative numerical requirements. The *Geier* Court concluded that NHTSA's selection of certain passive-restraint phase-in percentages affirmed those percentages *to the exclusion* of alternatives of any sort—including an implicit 100-percent airbags mandate. Significantly, the Court's discussion focused not so much on the narrow wording of particular Code of Federal Regulations provisions but on the integrity of the regulatory regime in which the phase-in percentages were embedded. The examination showed that NHTSA's regulatory regime contemplated optimum phase-in percentages intended to exclude alternative possibilities.

Geier constitutes a jurisprudential landmark because of the clarity and cogency of its logic. But its animating principle was subtly at work in earlier preemption cases, even cases set in the more difficult context of *nonnumerical* requirements. Perhaps the best example comes from the Supreme Court's longstanding recognition of what amounts to implied preemption under the National Labor Relations Act (NLRA).[10] Although the NLRA contains no express preemption provision, some of the most potent instances of federal preemption appear in the NLRA context.[11] A traditional explanation for this preemptive potency lies in the fact that the NLRA affirmatively seeks to strike a balance between the powers of unions and management in the collective-bargaining process.[12] States that try to upset that equilibrium—whether to the advantage of unions or management—necessarily encroach upon a field of economic activity impliedly reserved for federally ordered private conduct.

Courts hold that the NLRA precludes states from regulating conduct that is arguably protected or prohibited by federal labor law[13] or that falls within a zone of activity Congress intended to remain open to the "free play of economic forces."[14] When Congress enacted the NLRA, it created a "complex and interrelated federal scheme of law, remedy, and administration," and "entrusted administration of the labor policy for the Nation to a centralized administrative agency, armed with its own procedures, and equipped with its specialized knowledge and cumulative expertise."[15] Critically, the Supreme Court has recognized in the NLRA context that Congress intentionally left certain areas of conduct unregulated. It has concluded on this basis that states are precluded from intruding on the resulting preserve for the free play of private forces acting in presumed equilibrium.[16] In the NLRA context, as in *Geier*, Congress's affirmative judgment in favor of one set of regulations has been deemed a negative judgment on alternative regulatory regimes.

In contrast, the Federal Trade Commission's standards for business conduct promulgated pursuant to section 5 of the Federal Trade Commission Act of 1914 have been viewed as generally nonpreemptive of similar state laws. Those standards, unlike the somewhat analogous labor law standards, have been widely viewed as outlawing abusive practices but not as prescribing nonabusive ones. They have been deemed preclusive, not prescriptive.[17] An exception that proves this rule is a case where the Federal Trade Commission enters into a negotiated consent decree with a private party to govern its future conduct: such a consent decree may preempt state laws if it can be viewed as setting a federal regulatory optimum.[18]

In the wake of *Geier*, the significance of the prescriptive-preclusive distinction has been increasingly recognized by administrative agencies, which now understand that sound policy reasons counsel in favor of giving preemptive status to a regulatory golden mean. For example, NHTSA recently issued a notice of proposed rulemaking to amend the definition of "designated seating position" in the federal motor vehicle safety standards and to establish new procedures for determining the number of designated seating positions on bench or split bench seats in passenger vehicles.[19] In proposing these regulatory changes, NHTSA emphasized that the designation of vehicle seating positions is important for safety-related reasons and determined that, because differing "state requirements would 'prevent or frustrate the accomplishment of a federal objective,'" the proposed regulations would "preempt State statutes and regulations requiring the designation of more or different seating positions than those required" under federal law, as well as "any conflicting determinations in state tort law as to whether a location is or ought to be a designated seating position." In this latter regard, NHTSA took care to explain that a "tort determination premised on the designation of more designated seating positions than those required by the proposed definition could have a negative impact on safety." NHTSA thus made clear that its proposed rule contemplates a regulatory optimum: requiring either more or fewer "designated seating positions" would negatively "impact" safety. In other words, additional layers of state tort liability—an invitation for lay juries to pick winners from battles between so-called safety experts—could only "frustrate" NHTSA's own expert endeavors to strike a precise golden policy mean.

Negative (or Preclusive) Regulations: Outlawing the Outliers. Although courts and agencies now appreciate the preemptive significance of pre-scriptive federal regulation, they have yet to make equal progress in ana-lyzing the preemptive force of negative (or preclusive) federal requirements. It is widely recognized that regulatory prohibitions come in two general forms—rules and standards. But although academic discussions of rules and standards are voluminous, these discussions, at least to date, have had little influence on the development of judicial doctrine. Instead, lawyers and judges tend to employ and manipulate the rules-standards distinction under a set of terms, doctrines, institutions, and traditions that revolves around a traditional taxonomy involving common law, equity, and statute. Here, our embedded Anglo-American traditions of common law and equity are both an essential guide and a stumbling block. The result is a central tenet of legal theory, the rules-standard distinction, that is at once ubiqui-tously recognized, under-theorized, and almost completely disconnected from the work-a-day operations of legal institutions.

Rules vs. Standards: Governing Primary Conduct. In developing implied conflict preemption doctrines for prohibitory requirements, courts need to appreciate that, on a theoretical level, rules and standards are not limiting cases along a spectrum reflecting the relative ambiguity of legal requirements; rather, they are a paired set of labels used to express a logical or formal dif-ference in kind. In general, rules govern conduct as such, while standards govern conduct defined in terms of legal relationships.

In the years before *Erie*, a rough-and-ready version of the rules-versus-standards distinction was central to the task of integrating federal common law standards with states' retained authority over economic regulation. Before *Erie*, the Supreme Court interpreted the Federal Rules of Decision Act (now codified at 28 U.S.C. § 1652) to require federal courts to apply the *statutory* law of the appropriate state in diversity cases but to disregard state court judgments in matters of "general common law." In *Swift v. Tyson* (1842), Justice Story concluded that the act's reference to "laws of a state" referred only to "the rules and enactments promulgated by the legislative authority thereof, or long-established local customs having the force of laws." Hence, although federal courts sitting in diversity were obliged to apply state statutory law, they had no obligation to defer to state common law created by state courts, especially in cases raising "questions of general commercial law."[20]

This bygone doctrinal significance between statutory rules and common law standards is largely congruent with the technical usage in which a legal "rule" is viewed in contradistinction to a legal "standard."[21] This technical usage can frequently be a source of confusion, however, because the difference between rules and standards is frequently—and wrongly—viewed merely as a matter of degree.[22] From this perspective, legal rules and legal standards are both species of legal requirements; it just so happens that standards are framed in looser, vaguer, more elastic terms, a difference that gives rise to characteristic sets of advantages and disadvantages that apply to each form of legal requirement.

For purposes of implied preemption analysis, this received understanding does not suffice. For implied preemption to become workable, the rules-standards distinction must be sufficiently sharp to be operational. Rules must become sufficiently distinguished from standards for federal rules and standards to be given their proper (and differing) effects in displacing state rules and standards. The rules-standards distinction must be seen as one of kind, not degree.

In line with many scholars, Margaret Jane Radin disagrees that rules are inherently different from standards. She contends instead that "absolute ruleness is merely a heuristic device at the far end of [a] theoretical continuum."[23] She concludes, contrary to our hypothesis, that it is "incorrect to postulate 'logical' distinctions between rules and standards."[24] This view questioning the possibility of drawing "logical distinctions" between rules and standards is closely associated with the Critical Legal Studies movement,[25] as well as old-time legal realism. It is a serious point of view and likely the prevailing view in current legal scholarship.

That view is limited, however, in that it sees the rules-standards distinction as a technical difference elicited by lawyerly observation, rather than as a logical distinction that has appeared and reappeared for centuries in prominent treatments of law and logic. A presaging of the distinction appears at least as early as the medieval *Treatise on Law*, where Thomas Aquinas defines law as "a rule and measure (*regula . . . et mensura*) of human acts" whose "ultimate purpose (*finas ultimas*) is human happiness."[26] The conjunction of "rule and measure" is repeated throughout the

Treatise on Law, including the critical point where Aquinas turns to his discussion of the practicalities of lawmaking—the "framing" of law. Aquinas first says that "law is framed for what frequently happens," before going on to remark, in the disjunctive, that "law is *framed* as a *rule* or *measure of human acts*."[27] For Aquinas, rules differ from measures, and law is framed as a rule or a measure, not both. The point is that, in the strictest sense, a measure can be applied only to past or completed action. Before conduct is fully complete it cannot be measured in all its dimensions and consequences; it can only be anticipated, estimated, or hypothesized. A rule, by contrast, looks to the future and prescribes metes and bounds for conduct that has yet to occur. To be sure, a repealed rule may still bind in the sense that past actions taken during a repealed rule's effective period may give rise to present legal liabilities. But in a deeper sense a repealed rule is no longer a rule at all. Once it ceases to bind actions being taken *here* and *now*, the repealed rule (together with its associated limitations period) governs only the secondary conduct of the adjudicator. In this sense, repealed rules, together with their associated statutes of limitations, are akin to rules of judicial procedure as opposed to substantive rules for private, primary conduct. *The* central distinction involved in every requirement governing private conduct, the fundamental choice in the "framing" of law, is thus the choice between a rule that prescribes or proscribes some hypothesized course of future conduct, and a "measure" for conduct already completed.

The differences between prospectivity and retroactivity—a rule for the future and a measure for the past—are prominent in the received discussions of legal rules and standards. But to make the distinction operational for purposes of preemption doctrine an additional dimension to the distinction must be acknowledged: the relevant difference, we believe, is that rules govern conduct, pure and simple, whereas standards govern conduct defined in terms of *a relationship*. A standard thus defines the requirements governing actions taken by person A *in relation to* person (or thing) B. The nature of this relationship can and does vary: it can be one of cause and effect, of ownership, of endangerment, of deception, of some combination of the above, or of something else altogether. But the critical point in all these instances is that standards, unlike rules, govern conduct defined in relational terms.

The centrality of legal relationships to the functioning of legal standards can be seen in the legal "fictions" widely employed in defining legal standards. In cases where courts seek to apply a governing standard, but no second party to a relationship steps forward to present himself, courts routinely *hypothesize* such a party. Familiar cases of such legal sorcery include the hypothetical "reasonable person" who receives a potentially misleading solicitation; the hypothetical "foreseeable plaintiff" to whom a duty of reasonable care is owed; and the hypothetical "ordinary user" of products liability law. In each case, the hypothesized person is needed precisely because the existence of a legal relationship is the hallmark of any legal standard. It is needed precisely because the difference between rules and standards is the distinction between conduct that can be adjudged purely in relation to a single actor and conduct that can be adjudged only in context of a relationship between two or more persons or between a person and some other thing.

An assurance of the practicality of making distinctions in kind between legal rules and standards comes from the close interconnections between this distinction and the central insights of the nonmathematical branch of modern logic.[28] This philosophical branch of logic purports to go beyond the medieval reliance on Aristotle's categories to achieve what, in the view of thinkers like Immanuel Kant and Georg Hegel, is a higher logical plane. A central distinction in Kant's endeavor is the one between objects as they exist at a particular time and place (what he calls "mathematical" categories) and objects that exist "in relation to one another" or in relation to the observer (what he calls "dynamical" categories).[29] This central distinction becomes in Hegel a distinction between "qualities" (a category of "Being") and "properties" (a category of "Essence"). A quality "is the *immediate* determinateness of something," as opposed to a property, which is the "determinate relations of the thing to *another* thing."[30] A property thus exists "only as a mode of relationship." "A thing has the property of effecting this or that in another thing and of expressing itself in a peculiar manner in relation to it."

In more simple terms, what Kant and Hegel recognize is that a given fact usually can be expressed either as a "quality" or as a "property"—that is, either as an isolated characteristic or as a relational characteristic. One might say that skunks are capable of emitting a distinctive and distinguishing spray of a particular chemical composition; alternatively, one might say skunks have the capability of emitting noxious odors. Both statements are valid. Both describe the same underlying fact. But one describes skunks viewed in isolation; the other describes skunks viewed *in relation to* something else. The critical point is that an assertion of relation lies latent in any designation of an emission as "noxious." An emission can be "noxious," not in isolation, but only if it is actually or potentially perceived as such by someone or something else—for instance, an animal or human observer.

This linguistic and logical difference between expressing a fact as an isolated characteristic as opposed to a relational characteristic is closely related to the legislator's choice between casting legal requirements in the form of rules as opposed to standards. Legislators almost always enjoy the option of framing legal prohibitions in terms of qualities or properties; that is, in terms of rules or standards. A lawmaker might, for example, promulgate a legal rule prohibiting releases of specified chemicals as identified by a list of Chemical Abstracts Service numbers. Alternatively, the lawmaker might choose to promulgate a legal standard prohibiting emissions of *any* noxious odor. Shaping the requirement in the form of a standard (as opposed to a rule) means it will be at once less precise, more subject to interpretation, and potentially better tailored to the underlying harms at which it aims.[31] But these characteristic advantages and disadvantages, while important, are adventitious. They are not what constitutes the categorical difference between rules and standards—a difference that turns on the fact that standards are defined in relational terms, while rules are not.

Precisely because it is a ubiquitous logical and linguistic construct (as well as a legal construct), the rules-standards distinction is a frequently unacknowledged elephant in the room of legal discourse. The root of the *Miranda* controversy, for example, was the never properly attacked, never properly defended, never properly articulated proposition that constitutional doctrine under the relevant prong of analysis must evolve through the elaboration of standards, not rules. If the *Miranda* rule had been a *Miranda* standard ("no confession may be used unless a defendant is afforded prior, reasonably comprehensible notice of his or her constitutional rights") there would have been no controversy.

Likewise, Karl Llewellyn's most famous example of interpretive "antinomy"—a paired set of authoritative canons, each of which purportedly says precisely the opposite of the other—appears unremarkable if illuminated by the rules-standards distinction.[32] One may disagree with, but one certainly cannot find contradictory, the twin propositions that *rules* in derogation of the common law should be narrowly construed,[33] but remedial *standards* should be broadly construed to effectuate their purposes.[34] If ever one doubts the ubiquity of lawyers' unarticulated appreciation for the rules-standards distinction, one need only listen to everyday lawyerly conversation—a staple of which is an unspoken assumption that courts generally may draw doctrinal distinctions by elaborating legal standards, not legal rules.[35]

It is therefore not surprising that, even allowing for the unavoidable ambiguities that inhere in distinguishing rules from standards or, indeed, in drawing any distinction in law, most scholars acknowledge that the "contrast between rules and standards is quite useful."[36] One suggests that "it is possible to classify most legal pronouncements as standards or rules, based on their core characteristics."[37] Although all legal categorizations, at their margins, are ambiguous, Richard Epstein rightly reminds us that legal categories that work in a great majority of cases can be extremely useful.[38] No one need complain if in a few remaining cases—those that populate the law reviews—the categorization becomes ambiguous or even arbitrary.

Rules vs. Standards: Enforcement Mechanisms

A second underappreciated and underutilized element of legal form involves the nature of a lawmaker's chosen enforcement mechanism. In general, legislators may cast requirements in terms of public law or private law. In addition, they may punish conduct *after* it occurs, proscribe it from continuing *as* it occurs, or require its preapproval *before* it occurs. These modes of civil enforcement apply both to rules and to standards. As applied to legal rules, the differences are fairly straightforward: fines and damages punish past violations of rules; equitable injunctions restrain ongoing or imminently impending violations of rules; and licensing regimes can be used to precertify the legality of proposed conduct.

As applied to legal standards, the legislator's choice between enforcement alternatives carries a deeper level of implication. In that case, the alternative modes of enforcement can be seen in significant part as legislative determinations of the need to mitigate the potential unfairness of retroactively applying a loosely framed standard to govern private conduct. As in the case of legal rules, legal standards may be enforced either by public officials or by private actors. And, as with rules, the enforcement of legal standards comes in at least three familiar forms: (1) pure standards enforced through fines and damages; (2) licensing standards addressed initially to agency personnel that only derivatively govern private conduct; and (3) equitable standards addressed to the courts that will enforce those standards through prospective injunctions. But unlike with rules, the nature of the associated enforcement regime can affect the character of a legal requirement *as* a standard. A legislator's choice of a licensing standard or an equitable standard effectively injects some of the characteristic advantages of legal rules into regimes that ultimately set standards for private conduct.[39] Substantive requirements cast in the form of licensing or equitable standards must therefore be deemed an intermediate and distinct category of legal form. The alternative forms assumed by substantive legal standards are summarized below in table 8-1:

TABLE 8-1
STANDARDS ENFORCEMENT

	Pure Standards	Licensing Standards	Equitable Standards
Public Enforcement	Public Law Fines	Single Party Licensing	Public Law Injunctions
Private Enforcement	Private Damages	Contested Licensing	Private Injunctions

SOURCE: Authors' work.

The alchemy by which substantive legal standards come to be implemented like rules is one reflection of the close interconnections between substantive requirements and the procedures and remedies through which they are implemented. Meta-requirements such as rules of administrative agency and judicial practice entail significant, fully intended consequences for primary, private decisionmaking. Consider as an example "guidelines" governing the internal enforcement actions of an administrative agency. At one level, such guidelines are addressed only to agency enforcement personnel; involve only internal agency decisions; and bind no one outside the agency. They thus have no *direct* bearing on private conduct.[40] As a practical matter, however, the fact that agency personnel can be expected to attempt to penalize certain conduct has obvious and fully intended implications for private decisionmaking. These implications are so obvious that courts will, in appropriate cases, treat enforcement guidance statements as if they were substantive rules for private actors, even though they ostensibly are purely internal and nonbinding.[41]

A legislated or regulatory criterion governing agency licensing is a similar type of a meta-requirement, ostensibly internal, but in fact having determinative and fully intended implications for primary, private conduct. The typical federal licensing regime includes as its essential elements a legal rule prohibiting certain acts in the absence of a federally issued license, coupled with an administrative process for obtaining such a license. Pesticides must be registered with the Environmental Protection Agency. Drugs and medical devices are subject to preapprovals by the Food and Drug Administration. In struggling to determine the implied preemptive implications of these and similar licensing regimes, courts have often focused on whether supplementation of the federal regime is needed in order to ensure compensation for injured parties. But the perceived need for compensation of private harms (if indeed it exists in a given context) can almost always be accommodated by applying a state law requirement providing compensation for harms produced by activities undertaken in violation of a federal licensing regime,[42] plus a state court procedure requiring referrals to the federal agency's primary jurisdiction of questions whether a given activity is or is not violative of federal requirements.[43] More important than the compensation issue is Congress's underlying determination that (1) conduct should be precertified as adhering to an elastic, technically difficult standard before the conduct occurs and (2) this precertification process should be administered by a body with requisite expertise.

Somewhat akin to licensing regimes are federal remedial regimes enforced exclusively via injunctive remedies.[44] These arrangements, too, can be viewed as grounded entirely on a meta-requirement, albeit one directed to Article III judges as opposed to Article II administrators. The law of equity is characterized by specified jurisdictional grants, an admonition to do equity in accordance with maxims framed at extremely high levels of generality, and a strict requirement that equitable injunctions apply only prospectively and only to specific parties and specific conduct.[45] It can appear to casual observers that the law of equity imposes the loosest of legal standards. In fact, from the point of view of private actors, the law of equity operates in some significant part as a law of prospective rules. Like a licensing regime, an enforcement regime that relies purely on injunctive remedies empowers a government agency (a court of equity) to frame prospective, case- and party-specific rules to govern private conduct.

Although at one time the federal courts entertained the misimpression that it was the business of legislators to frame substantive requirements and that of the courts to devise the procedures and remedies for implementing those requirements, that day is now largely past.[46] Beginning with the Supreme Court's landmark decision in *Cort v. Ash* (1975), the Court has come to appreciate that remedial questions are themselves important issues of federal policy that should be guided by the intentions of Congress as expressed in law. This respect for Congress's remedial choices appears in a preemption context in *Buckman Company v. Plaintiffs' Legal Committee* (2001), where the Court determined that federal law impliedly preempts state-law tort claims alleging fraud on the FDA during the regulatory process for obtaining prior FDA clearance for medical devices.[47] The Court explained that "[t]he conflict stems from the fact that the federal regulatory scheme amply empowers the FDA to punish and deter fraud against the Administration, and that this authority is used by the Administration to achieve a somewhat delicate balance of statutory objectives."[48] The Court emphasized that the balance sought by FDA could be skewed by allowing fraud-on-the-FDA claims under state tort law. This holding in *Buckman*, together with *Cort v. Ash* and related cases, establishes the principle that Congress's substantive and remedial choices must be viewed as a coherent whole, including in preemption cases. Any other approach skews a court's assessment of the Congress's intent as embodied in law.

In summary, every Congressional decision to impose standards of conduct is inherently two dimensional. Most importantly, Congress must ask itself whether a given substantive standard, as stated and without further elaboration, is concrete enough to be fairly applied directly to private conduct by lay judges and juries. If not, then the substantive requirement can be maintained in the form of a legal standard, while its unfairness is mitigated or avoided through enforcement via an equitable or licensing regime. Given the policy significance of these formal determinations, the Supreme Court has rightly recognized that remedial choices such as those between pure standards, equitable standards, and licensing standards are themselves legislative decisions of the highest order.

The Problem of State Law Standards. We emphasize the dual dimensions of the rules-standards distinction because we believe that these aspects of legal form can help courts better evaluate federal statutes' potency in preempting as well as state statutes' implicit susceptibility to being preempted. We offer below two illustrations of analysis based on these formal differences as an indication of how form-of-law distinctions might be employed to determine the implied preemptive scope of federal requirements and the implied limitations on the effectiveness of state-law standards.

Illustration No. 1: The Implied Preemptive Force of Federal Licensing Regimes. The typical federal licensing scheme establishes elastic standards of conduct enforced by expert agency personnel and provides for fines only when regulated parties fail to obtain a license or abide by a license already issued. Where Congress has provided for fines in such regimes but limited their imposition to instances where the licensing regime is violated, it can be inferred that Congress has implicitly (indeed, almost expressly) rejected the option of establishing a pure standard of conduct.

The critical point for implied conflict preemption is that plaintiffs suing manufacturers of federally licensed products under state tort law effectively try to undermine Congress's implicit decision rejecting the option of a pure standard of conduct—a decision Congress presumably has taken in view of the licensing agency's specialized expertise or to mitigate the unfairness of standards cast in their pure form. One could imagine, for instance, a federal regime that enforces the same substantive standard in two different ways. Under such a regime, federal enforcement officials, either in the agency itself or in the Department of Justice, might be permitted to second-guess or reassess an agency's initial decision in issuing or framing a federal license by seeking to impose fines for conduct that should not have been but in fact was preauthorized by license. That is, the law might deem the procuring of a license a necessary but not a sufficient condition for avoiding liability. A regime of that nature would effectively establish a pure regulatory standard in addition to, as opposed to in lieu of, a licensing standard. In the more common case, of course, the Executive Branch of the United States government, including its executive departments and "independent" agencies, renders a unitary decision as to what primary conduct is permitted or proscribed, and federal enforcement decisions must adhere to, not second guess, those determinations.

But precisely because one can imagine such "nonpreclusive" licensing regimes, a Congressional choice in favor of unitary determinations of adherence to substantive licensing requirements carries important preemption implications. The fundamental preemption avoidance contention of state-law tort plaintiffs is that, although Congress has specifically declined to give enforcement authority to federal officials acting under federal law, it has nonetheless allowed such authority to be wielded by private parties acting under state law. They essentially contend that private tort plaintiffs, unlike federal enforcement officers, may second guess federal agency determinations.

The federal statutory scheme and state law claims at issue in *Bates v. Dow Agrosciences* (2005) provide a helpful example. Under the Federal Insecticide, Fungicide, and Rodenticide Act, a pesticide may not be sold or distributed unless it is registered with the Environmental Protection Agency. The agency will register a pesticide only if it determines that the pesticide is efficacious; that it will not cause unreasonable adverse effects on humans and the environment; and that its label complies with the statute's prohibition on misbranding. Once a pesticide is registered by the agency, manufacturers have a continuing obligation to adhere to the statute's labeling requirements and to report incidents involving a pesticide's toxic effects not adequately reflected in its label's warning. The EPA may institute cancellation proceedings and take other enforcement actions if it determines that a registered pesticide is misbranded. In addition, it may impose fines for any violation of the statute, including selling unregistered pesticides or selling pesticides with labels that are "false or misleading in any particular." Under this statutory regime, Congress has permitted public enforcement through public-law fines for misbranding violations but not instances where the safety or efficacy of the product itself is in question. In our nomenclature, Congress has determined that safety and efficacy determinations may be made only in accordance with licensing standards as opposed to pure standards.

To see the practical importance of this Congressional determination, consider the many different state law causes of action the Supreme Court analyzed in *Bates*—almost all of which were cast in the form of pure standards for primary conduct. Farmers allegedly injured by Dow Agrosciences' Strongarm herbicide product pleaded state law claims for (1) negligence (for testing and failure to warn); (2) violation of the Texas Deceptive Trade Practices Consumer Protection Act; (3) breach of contract; (4) breach of implied and express warranties; (5) strict liability for defective design and defective manufacture; (6) fraud and fraud in the inducement; and (7) estoppel and waiver. The farmers characterized their claims as "centered" on the allegedly "defective design and negligent testing of Strongarm for soils in western Texas."[49] Putting aside the contractual causes of action, each of these claims rested on a state law standard, not a state law rule.[50] Moreover, by seeking private penalties and damages, the *Bates* plaintiffs were seeking enforcement of those state law standards in their pure form.

Allowing state law plaintiffs, like those in *Bates*, to proceed under pure state law standards is necessarily inconsistent with Congress's decision to reject pure standards in favor of federal licensing standards. Whether the reason for Congress's decision was to provide room for the play of expertise or to mitigate the potential unfairness and retroactivity of loosely framed requirements, by casting the requirement in the form of an exclusive licensing standard Congress can be presumed to have considered and rejected practically the precise scheme advocated by those who would leave state law unpreempted. A state tort suit questioning the safety or efficacy of a federally registered pesticide must, by definition, rest on the improbable proposition that Congress intended for state tort plaintiffs to have greater authority to look behind safety and efficacy determinations made in the EPA registration process than federal enforcement officials. In order to find implied conflict preemption, all a court need do is to reject this improbable proposition.[51]

Illustration No. 2: Projection of State Standards onto Out-of-State Corporations. Conflict preemption issues are rarely analyzed from the standpoint of their interrelationships with conflicts of law doctrines. The best synthetic treatment of implied preemption in relationship to other doctrine, that of Viet Dinh, extensively examines doctrines of federal common law, express preemption, implied preemption, and the dormant Commerce Clause, but not conflicts of law.[52] Caleb Nelson rightly emphasizes that the text of the Supremacy Clause itself points to the problem of reconciling conflicting laws but then concludes (wrongly) that courts should hew narrowly to Congress's express preemptive intentions and largely decline to enforce implied preemption doctrines.[53] The failure of commentators to discuss the relationship between conflicts of law and conflict preemption doctrines is all the more perplexing, in that courts' typical task in conflict preemption cases is not to facially invalidate all operation of a state law but simply to limit the state law's scope and deny its effectiveness as applied to a particular case. Such reconciliations are almost precisely analogous to the task of courts facing conflicts of law problems, save for the fact that in federal preemption cases the laws of the two sovereigns do not stand on equal footing.

A consequence of courts' underappreciation of the elements of legal form, and their importance for related common law, conflicts of law, and conflict preemption doctrines, is courts' resulting inability to define conflict preemption doctrine in terms concrete enough to be used as a baseline for measuring Congress's express preemption decisions. In *Bates*, for example, conflict preemption doctrines played no role in the Supreme Court's decision; rather, the case was litigated and resolved by the Supreme Court exclusively under an express preemption analysis. The express preemption question presented in *Bates* accordingly was *not* addressed through a natural analytical progression—by first ascertaining the implied preemptive scope of a statute, then assuming Congress was aware of that scope, and finally examining whether the preemption frontier may have been pushed forward or pulled back by Congress via express preemption. Precisely because the formal dimensions of implied preemption analysis are dimly understood, implied conflict preemption cannot practically serve as the starting point for express preemption analysis.

Instead of addressing conflict preemption, *Bates*'s core analysis began by rejecting the admonition of Justice Clarence Thomas's separate opinion[54] and citing a canon of interpretation that demands a "clear and manifest" Congressional intention as a prerequisite for displacing state law in "areas of traditional state regulations"[55] *Bates* then cited what it termed the "long history of tort litigation against manufacturers of poisonous substances."[56] An alternative question *Bates* might have asked, however, is whether states have traditionally enjoyed authority to apply pure legal standards to regulate the health and safety aspects of in-state commercial behavior of out-of-state corporations. It also might have inquired whether states have traditionally enjoyed such authority in the face of a comprehensive federal licensing regime that itself seeks to reconcile commercial and health and safety implications of the same course of conduct.[57] Had it framed the questions presented in this fashion, *Bates* would have arrived at much different answers.

In fact, prior to the Court's decision in *Erie*, states enjoyed only very limited authority to enforce health and safety standards (as opposed to substantive rules) against out-of-state corporations, and even this limited authority was severely circumscribed in cases where the federal government had entered the regulatory picture.[58] To understand the likely fate of pre-*Erie* "tort litigation against manufacturers of poisonous substances," consider the fate under *Swift* of a tort suit brought, as in *Bates*, by a Texas plaintiff against an Indiana corporate defendant. If the suit were filed in Texas state court, the Indiana defendant would be permitted to remove to federal court. Under *Swift*, that removal would free the Indiana defendant from Texas substantive law, except in areas (such as property law) whereas *federal* choice-of-law rules determined what conduct was appropriate for state regulation by Texas. Alternatively, the Texas plaintiff could sue the Indiana defendant in Indiana. Because in-state defendants have never been permitted to remove to federal court on diversity grounds, the Indiana defendant would have no choice but to litigate in Indiana courts.

A critical aspect of the *Swift* regime was thus its function, together with rules governing diversity jurisdiction and removal to federal courts, as a system for handling choice-of-law disputes in tort litigation between citizens of different states. If a plaintiff sued in his home state and the defendant declined to remove, the law of the plaintiff's state would govern by acquiescence of both parties. If the plaintiff sued in the defendant's home state, the defendant could not remove and the law of the defendant's home state would govern by acquiescence of both parties. If, and only if, the parties could not agree in this fashion would their dispute end up in federal court and be governed by a substantive federal common law of tort.

Erie changed this regime, of course, by interpreting the Rules of Decision Act to require federal courts to apply state common law standards (as well as statutory requirements) in diversity cases, absent federal preemption. In steering the Court into this sea change, Justice Brandeis's *Erie* opinion raised qualms over the fact that, under *Swift*, the rights of citizens "var[ied] according to whether enforcement was sought in the state or in the federal court, and the privilege of selecting the court in which the right should be determined was conferred upon the non-citizen."[59] The most perplexing aspect of Justice Brandeis's statement is not that his forecast was woefully wrong in predicating that *Erie* would mitigate (as opposed to exacerbate) forum shopping.[60] It is that he failed to view some degree of concurrent state and federal jurisdiction as a natural consequence of the Framers' decision to "split the atom of sovereignty."[61] Putting federal preemption aside, there is nothing surprising in a corporation's legal duties being subject to definition by both the federal government and the government of its home state.

The upshot for conflict preemption analysis is twofold. Most immediately, the assertion of the tort plaintiffs in *Bates* (and similarly situated plaintiffs in other cases) that states have traditionally enjoyed authority to adopt and enforce tort-law standards, such as standards governing the manufacture of poisons, must be qualified by a bold asterisk. The tort standards of care that states adopted and enforced for a hundred years under *Swift* could be applied, without consent, only to *in-state* corporations. That is, under *Swift*, corporations could be held liable under principles of general common law only if those principles had been embraced either in federal law or in the law of the corporation's home state. Cases like *Bates*, where plaintiffs seek without even tacit consent to apply state tort standards to out-of-state corporations, are largely a post-*Erie* feature of the legal landscape.

More fundamentally, the *Erie* revolution, together with courts' failure to view the rules-standards difference as an operative distinction, has prompted courts to overlook *Swift*'s latent wisdom. Precisely because legal rules address conduct characterized as occurring at a given time and place, differing state law *rules* may apply, prospectively, to different conduct in different states without colliding with one another. By contrast, state law *standards* govern legal relationships, and the relationship between an interstate business and its interstate customers is not easily divvied up along state territorial boundaries.

In *Bates*, for example, the relationships at issue were those between, on the one hand, an Indiana corporation, and, on the other hand, its nationwide customers and potential customers; the persons nationwide who might foreseeably use its products; the persons nationwide who might foreseeably be exposed to its products and so forth. The question presented in *Bates*, from a conflicts of law standpoint, was whether the law of Indiana, the business's home state, should or should not displace the law of Texas, the customer's home state—an analysis analogous to conflict preemption analysis, albeit in a context where the relationship between sovereigns is horizontal, not vertical.[62]

If the *Swift* regime were based merely on a distinction between judge-made common law and legislatively enacted statutes, it could not readily be defended. In today's terms, there is little reason why a state common law action for misrepresentation should have a differing range of effect in relation to federal or foreign-state law than to a similar action brought under a state unfair trade practices statute. *Swift* makes eminent sense, however, if it is viewed as resting not on the institutional source of a legal requirement, but on the legal form in which the requirement is cast. A critical element of the *Swift* regime was its rough-and-ready distinction between state statutory rules and state common law standards, together with common law courts' tacit understanding that they may promulgate doctrine only in the form of standards, not rules. That constraint was tacit, of course, because courts, both then and now, did not consciously call to mind the technical differences between rules and standards we outline above, but the constraint is nonetheless effective.

Most any common law court, then or now, would view a litigant's proffered substantive *standard* (say, that vehicles must provide "reasonable safety to occupants") as a potentially legitimate grounds of decision, while viewing a judge-made *rule* in the technical meaning of the term (say, a requirement that rear seats in vehicles have a precise number of "designated seating positions") as exceeding the court's authority. Viewed from this perspective, the *Swift* regime maintains that the *conduct* of an interstate commercial enterprise may be regulated through rules enacted by the state in which such conduct occurs, but the enterprise's legal *relationships*, at least as defined by judge-declared tort standards, may be governed solely by the enterprise's home state, together with the federal government. *Swift* used the latent logic embodied in the rules-standards distinction to protect the integrity of the nationwide marketplace.

In the wake of *Erie*, and the mounting distress over judicial discretion and power, it is impossible to imagine a return to an all-embracing federal common law for interstate commerce in the manner of *Swift*. What is easy to imagine, however, is a reaffirmation of *Erie*'s fundamental holding in favor of state common law, coupled with a retreat from federal courts' absolutist embrace of state conflict of law principles. Under such an approach, federal courts would continue to apply state tort *standards*—whether grounded in legislated statutes, administrative regulations, or common law judicial decisions—but would take better care in deciding *which* state's standards to apply. Specifically, the federal courts could and should exclusively apply the commercial common law of a federal defendant's home state, absent congressional direction to the contrary.

In sum, the fundamental and still valid premise of *Swift* is that states need not apply pure regulatory standards to out-of-state corporations in order to protect their citizenry. That premise is itself grounded on an assumption that in-state citizen-consumers or citizen product-users will be fully protected by the combination of federal law, plus the pure regulatory standards of a corporation's home state (which apply nationwide of constitutional necessity[63]), plus those of the citizen's home state laws that have been cast in forms that are readily limited geographically—equitable standards, licensing standards, and above all legal rules. This conflicts-of-law result becomes even more compelling, of course, in those many instances in which the federal government maintains its own extensive regulatory regime. In those instances, consumers nationwide will be afforded a full three layers of protection—federal requirements, the corporation's home state standards, plus fifty states' worth of geographically cabined licensing standards, equitable standards, and legal rules. Absent Congressional direction to the contrary, three overlapping layers of protection should be enough.

Conclusion

A dozen years ago, Stephen Gardbaum remarked that "preemption has largely been ignored by constitutional law scholars."[64] The intervening years have undoubtedly seen this neglect being remedied. Scholars have since questioned "the easy assumptions that inform much of the seemingly settled, black-letter law of preemption,"[65] and preemption analysis has become increasingly sophisticated. Amidst this burgeoning inquiry, we suggest both a theoretical and a practical step forward. Our proposed theoretical advance maintains that legal requirements reflect formal differences in kind between rules, pure standards, licensing standards, and equitable standards. Our suggested practical innovation addresses the problem of cabining otherwise omnivorous state tort standards. We suggest in this latter regard that pure state standards be displaced along a horizontal dimension by the home-state standards of out-of-state defendants and along a vertical dimension by the substantive requirements of most federal licensing regimes. We believe, taken together, these innovations could go far in curing the most egregious excesses of present-day tort litigation.

Notes

1. See generally Robert R. Gasaway, *The Problem of Federal Preemption: Reformulating the Black Letter Rules*, 33 Pepp. L. Rev. 25 (2005).

2. But see St. Thomas Aquinas, "Question 96, Article 6," in *Treatise on Law*, ed. R.J. Henle S.J. (Notre Dame: University of Notre Dame Press, 1993), 339 ("[N]*ullius hominis sapientia tanta est ut posit omnes singulares casus excogitare; et ideo non potest sufficienter per verba exprimere ea quae convenient ad finem intentum. . . .*" [No man is so wise that he can take into account every single case, and, therefore, he cannot sufficiently express in words everything that is conducive to the end he intends].

3. See Caleb Nelson, *Preemption*, 86 Va. L. Rev. 225, 290–91 (2000) (noting that "the presumption has taken on a life of its own, and is now being applied even to federal statutory provisions that plainly do manifest an 'inten[t] to supplant state law'"); see also Gasaway, *The Problem of Federal Preemption*, 33 Pepp. L. Rev. at 35–36.

4. See *Cipollone v. Liggett Group, Inc.*, 505 U.S. 504, at 517 (1992) (suggesting that perhaps express preemption should operate to the exclusion of implied preemption); but see *Freightliner Corp. v. Myrick*, 514 U.S. 280, 289 (1985) ("At best, *Cipollone* supports an inference that an express pre-emption clause forecloses implied pre-emption; it does not establish a rule."); see also Nelson, *supra* note 3 at 231, 290–303 (arguing that "constitutional law has no place for the Court's fuzzier notions of 'obstacle' preemption").

What we mean by "implied conflict preemption" is what is known in the cases as both "direct conflict preemption" and "obstacle preemption." For a more detailed discussion of the different categories of preemption and the reasons why the implied preemption analyses carried out under the "direct conflict" and "obstacle" preemption categories should be merged into a unified inquiry, see Gasaway, *supra* note 3 at 33–34.

5. See, *e.g.*, *Norfolk Southern Ry. Co. v. Shanklin*, 529 U.S. 344, 359 (2000) (Breyer, J., concurring) (noting the difference between federal optimum and minimum standards).

6. See, *e.g.*, *Transcontinental Gas Pipe Line Corp. v. State Oil & Gas Bd.*, 474 U.S. 409 (1986) (congressional determination to allow market forces to set price preempts state regulation that would upset intricate cost relationships of the market); *Mich. Canners & Freezers Ass'n., Inc. v. Agric. Mktg. & Bargaining Bd.*, 467 U.S. 461 (1984) (Agricultural Fair Practices Act preempts state marketing statutes that undermine the balanced relationship Congress sought to establish between agricultural producers and "handlers"); *Edgar v. MITE Corp.*, 457 U.S. 624 (1982) (plurality opinion) (the Williams Act struck a careful balance between the interests of offerors and target companies, and state statute that "upset" this balance was preempted).

7. For example, the numerical standards prescribed by minimum wage and maximum hour regulation have been viewed as nonpreemptive. See 29 U.S.C. § 218 (2007) ("No provision of this chapter or of any order thereunder shall excuse noncompliance with any Federal or State law or municipal ordinance establishing a minimum wage higher than the minimum wage established under this chapter or a maximum workweek lower than the maximum workweek established under this

chapter"); see also *Williams v. W.M.A. Transit Co.*, 472 F.2d 1258, 1261 (D.C. Cir. 1972) (noting that section 218 "expressly contemplates that workers covered by state law as well as FLSA [the Fair Labor Standards Act] shall have any additional benefits provided by the state law-higher minimum wages; or lower maximum workweek").

8. *Geier v. American Honda Motor Company, Inc.*, 529 U.S. 861, at 878 (2000).

9. Ibid. at 879.

10. See, *e.g.*, *Wis. Dep't of Indus., Labor, & Human Relations v. Gould, Inc.*, 475 U.S. 282, 288–89 (1986).

11. See, *e.g.*, *Livadas v. Bradshaw*, 512 U.S. 107 (1994) (holding California Labor Commissioner's policy preempted by federal law); *Nash v. Florida Indus. Comm'n*, 389 U.S. 235 (1967) (holding that Florida's refusal to pay unemployment insurance frustrated congressional purpose and was therefore preempted).

12. See, *e.g.*, *Golden State Transit Corp. v. Los Angeles*, 494 U.S. 103, 109 (1989) (the National Labor Relations Act "creates rights in labor and management both against one another and against the State"); *Allis-Chalmers Corp. v. Lueck*, 471 U.S. 202, 210–11 (1985); *Local 174, Teamsters v. Lucas Flour Co.*, 369 U.S. 95, 104 (1962); see also *Chamber of Commerce of the United States v. Reich*, 74 F.3d 1322 (1996) (holding that a National Labor Relations Act provision guaranteeing management's right to hire permanent replacements during labor strikes preempted a conflicting executive order made under the Procurement Act).

13. See *San Diego Bldg. Trades Council, Millment's Union, Local 2020 v. Garmon*, 359 U.S. 236, 243 (1959).

14. *Lodge 76, International Ass'n of Machinists v. Wis. Employment Relations Comm'n*, 427 U.S. 132, 149–52 (1976); see generally Stephen F. Befort & Bryan N. Smith, *At the Cutting Edge of Labor Law Preemption: A Critique of Chamber of Commerce v. Lockyer*, 20 Lab. Law. 107, 110–15 (2004) (discussing *Garmon* and *Machinist* preemption).

15. *Garmon*, 359 U.S. at 243.

16. See *Golden State Transit*, 475 U.S. at 619.

17. *American Fin. Servs. v. FTC*, 767 F.2d 957, 989 n.41 (D.C. Cir. 1985) (noting that "[t]he expansion of the FTC's jurisdiction [over unfair and deceptive trade practices] is not intended to occupy the field or in any way preempt state or local agencies from carrying out consumer protection or other activities").

18. See *General Motors Corp. v. Abrams*, 897 F.2d 34, 39 (2d Cir. 1990) ("a consent order reflecting a reasonable policy choice of a federal agency and issued pursuant to a congressional grant of authority may preempt state legislation"). But see *Wabash Power Valley Ass'n, Inc. v. Rural Electrification Admin.*, 903 F.2d 445, 454 (7th Cir. 1990) (Easterbrook, J.) (noting that because "neither the state nor the consumers" are typically parties to the FTC's case, "it is hard to understand how" a consent decree may "blot out their claims based on state law").

19. See National Highway Traffic Safety Administration, *Federal Motor Vehicle Safety Standards; Designated Seating Positions and Seat Belt Assembly Achorages*, 70 Fed. Reg. 36,094 (June 22, 2005).

20. See, *e.g.*, *Swift v. Tyson*, 41 U.S. (16 Pet.) 1 (1842).

21. See, *e.g.*, Louis Kaplow, *Rules Versus Standards: An Economic Analysis*, 42 Duke L.J. 557 (1992); Kathleen M. Sullivan, *Foreword: The Justices of Rules and Standards*, 106 Harv. L. Rev. 24, 57 (1992); Duncan Kennedy, *Form and Substance in Private Law Adjudication*, 89 Harv. L. Rev. 1685 (1976).

22. See, *e.g.*, Margaret J. Radin, *Boilerplate Today: The Rise of Modularity and the Waning of Consent*, 104 Mich. L. Rev. 1223, 1227 (2006) ("rules and standards form a continuum based upon the degree of vagueness of a word or term, not a conceptual dichotomy"); Russell B. Korobkin, *Behavioral Analysis and Legal Form: Rules vs. Standards Revisited*, 79 Or. L. Rev. 23 (2000) ("The legal forms of rules and standards . . . are better understood as spanning a spectrum rather than as being dichotomous variables."); see also Sullivan, *supra* note 21 at 61 ("distinctions between rules and standards, categorization and balancing, mark a continuum, not a divide").

23. Margaret Jane Radin, *Presumptive Positivism and Trivial Cases*, 14 Harv. J.L. & Pub. Pol'y 823, 823-24 (1991).

24. Ibid. at 823.

25. Pierre J. Schlag, *Rules and Standards*, 33 U.C.L.A. L. Rev. 379 (1985).

26. Aquinas, *supra* note 2 at 131.

27. Ibid. at 316.

28. The central insight of modern mathematical logic, which is in some ways related to this discussion, is Gödel's theorem. See, *e.g.*, Kurt Gödel, "On Formally Undecidable Propositions of Principia Mathematica and Related Systems I," in Gödel's *Theorem in Focus*, ed. S. G. Shanker (New York: Croom Helm, 1988), 30; see generally Mike Townsend, *Implications of Foundational Crises in Mathematics: A Case Study in Interdisciplinary Research*, 71 Wash. L. Rev. 51, 118–19 (1996).

29. Immanuel Kant, "The Critique Of Pure Reason," in *Kant*, ed. R.M. Hutchins (Chicago: Encyclopedia Britannica, 1952), 923 ("That sort of intuition which relates to an object by means of sensation is called an empirical intuition." Extension and shape "belong to pure intuition, which exists *a priori* in the mind, as a mere form of sensibility, and without any real object of the senses or any sensation.").

30. Georg W. F. Hegel, *Science of Logic*, trans. A. V. Miller (Amherst: Humanity Books, 1999), 672.

31. See Cass R. Sunstein, *Problems with Rules*, 83 Cal. L. Rev. 953, 992 (1995) (noting that rules are both over- and underinclusive); Russell B. Korobkin, *Behavioral Analysis and Legal Form: Rules vs. Standards Revisited*, 79 Or. L. Rev. 23, 36 (2000).

32. K.N. Llewellyn, *Remarks on the Theory of Appellate Decision and the Rules or Canons About How Statutes Are To Be Construed*, 3 Vand. L. Rev. 395 (1950).

33. *United States v. Texas*, 507 U.S. 529, 534 (1993) ("[s]tatutes which invade the common law . . . are to be read with a presumption favoring the retention of long-established and familiar principles, except where a statutory purpose to the contrary is evident"); *United States v. Fausto*, 484 U.S. 439, 454 (1988) (noting principle that "statutes in derogation of the common law will be strictly construed").

34. *Tcherepnin v. Knight*, 389 U.S. 332, 336 (1967) (noting "the familiar canon of statutory construction that remedial legislation should be construed broadly to effectuate its purposes"); *Stuart v. Kahn*, 78 U.S. 493, 504 (1870) (the "statute is a remedial one and should be construed liberally to carry out the wise and salutary purposes of its enactment").

35. See Neil S. Siegel, *A Theory in Search of a Court, and Itself: Judicial Minimalism at the Supreme Court Bar*, 103 Mich. L. Rev. 1951, 2017–18 (2005).

36. Cf. Sunstein, *supra* note 31 at 965.

37. Russell B. Korobkin, *Behavioral Analysis and Legal Form: Rules vs. Standards Revisited*, 79 Or. L. Rev. 23, 30 (2000).

38. Richard A. Epstein, *Simple Rules for a Complex World* (Cambridge: Harvard University Press, 1995), 21–49 (discussing attributes of rules and standards).

39. For example, it is likely no accident that some of the most elastic legal standards known to federal law are implemented through licensing regimes. Legal requirements that rates be just and reasonable, that broadcasts be in accordance with the public convenience and necessity, and that pharmaceuticals be safe and efficacious have all been enforced as a matter of federal law through licenses. Likewise, it appears that both the courts and the Federal Trade Commission have been more willing to enforce the loosely framed prohibition on false and deceptive advertising through prospective injunctions while reserving retrospective penalties for instances of particularly egregious conduct.

40. See *Heckler v. Chaney*, 470 U.S. 821, 830–35 (1985).

41. See *U.S. Tel. Ass'n v. FCC*, 28 F.3d 1232 (1994).

42. See, *e.g.*, *Hinojosa v. Guidant Corp.*, No. Civ.A. C-06-159, 2006 WL 903720, *2 (S.D. Tex. Apr. 7, 2006) (remanding to state court for consideration of allegations that defendants failed to comply with "duties to Plaintiff under Texas law as established by Defendants' failure to meet federal standards and violations of federal regulations and procedures" concerning preapproval of medical devices under federal law).

43. *Reiter v. Cooper*, 507 U.S. 258, 268–70 (1993) (discussing doctrine of primary jurisdiction); *Kappelmann v. Delta Air Lines, Inc.*, 539 F.2d 165 (D.C. Cir. 1976) (holding that the Federal Aviation Administration has primary jurisdiction over issues raised in action brought by a passenger allegedly exposed to radiation leaking from an improperly shielded container in the cargo section of a commercial airliner).

44. See Deep Water Port Act of 1934, § 16(a)(2), 33 U.S.C. § 1515(a) (authorizing citizen suits seeking only injunctive relief against any person in violation of the act or any condition of a license issued under the act); Ocean Thermal Energy Conservation Act of 1980, § 114(a), 42 U.S.C. § 9124(a) (authorizing citizen suits for only injunctive relief against any person in violation of the act or "any regulation or condition of a license issued" under the act). Cf. 15 U.S.C. § 1125(c) (permitting only injunctive relief for dilution of famous marks unless the trademark owner can prove that the unauthorized user acted with "willful intent").

45. See Fed. R. Civ. P. 65; *IDS Life Ins. Co. v. SunAmerica Life Ins. Co.*, 136 F.3d 537, 543 (7th Cir. 1998) (injunctions must be "both specific and self-contained").

46. See Thomas W. Merrill, *The Common Law Powers of Federal Courts*, 52 U. Chi. L. Rev. 1 (1985).

47. *Buckman Company v. Plaintiffs' Legal Committee*, 531 U.S. 341 (2000) at 348.

48. Ibid.

49. Appellant's Brief at 10, *Dow Agrosciences LLC v. Bates*, 332 F.3d 323 (5th Cir. 2003) (No. 02-10908).

50. Under Texas law, for example, liability for failure to warn "is imposed (like negligence liability) only for a failure to exercise reasonable care in discovering and warning of a danger." *Wood v. Phillips Petroleum Co.*, 119 S.W.3d 870, 873 n.6 (Tex. App.-Houston (14th Dist.) 2003). Similarly, strict liability for defective design claims under Texas law requires a showing that a product is "unreasonably dangerous as designed, taking into consideration the utility of the product and the risk involved in its use." *Turner v. General Motors Corp.*, 584 S.W.2d 844, 847 n. 1 (Tex. 1979).

51. In *Dow Agrosciences LLC v. Bates*, 544 U.S. 431 (2005) analyzing FIFRA's express preemption provision, the Supreme Court emphasized that state common-law rules that "require manufacturers to design reasonably safe products, to use due care in conducting appropriate testing of their products, [and] to market their products free of marketing defects" implicate express preemption because they do not require manufacturers to "label or package their products in any particular way." *Bates*, 544 U.S. at 444. But that express preemption conclusion does nothing to negate the fact that such common-law rules conflict directly and irreconcilably with the federal licensing standards, in particular, Congress's finely balanced regulatory scheme requiring that the safety and efficacy of pesticides be determined by an expert agency through a licensing process.

52. Viet D. Dinh, *Reassessing the Law of Preemption*, 88 Geo. L.J. 2085 (2000).

53. Nelson, *Preemption, supra* note 3.

54. *Bates*, 544 U.S. at 457. ("Our task is to determine which state-law claims § 136v(b) pre-empts, without slanting the inquiry in favor of either the Federal Government or the States.")

55. *Bates*, 544 U.S. at 449.

56. Ibid.

57. See generally Gasaway, *supra* note 3 at 35 (noting that "an obvious difficulty" with the presumption against preemption "is that its application can depend on how the inquiry is framed").

58. See *Missouri Pac. R. Co. v. Stroud*, 267 U.S. 404, 408 (1925) ("It is elementary and well settled that there can be no divided authority over interstate commerce, and that the acts of Congress on the subject are supreme and exclusive.")

59. *Erie*, 304 U.S. at 74–75.

60. Three years after *Erie*, in *Klaxon Co. v. Stentor Elec. Mftg. Co.*, 313 U.S. 487 (1941), the Court further required that state choice-of-law rules be applied by federal courts in diversity cases. As did the *Erie* court, the *Klaxon* court worried that absent the application of the *Erie* doctrine, "the accident of diversity of citizenship would constantly

disturb equal administration of justice in coordinate state and federal courts side by side."

61. *U.S. Term Limits, Inc. v. Thornton*, 514 U.S. 779, 838 (1995) (Kennedy, J., concurring).

62. The conflict-of-law question ought to be answered in favor of the home state law of the business. If a business's home state standards plus federal standards, and only those standards, define the rights and duties entailed by relationships such as those at issue in *Bates*, the unity of the nationwide market is maintained. Under such circumstances, the same dual standards would govern the corporation's commercial relationships with all of its multistate constituencies. The corporation would thus be subject to the same standards (and only those standards), wherever it conducted business within the United States.

63. Constitutional doctrines such as the dormant Commerce Clause and privileges and immunities clause insure that Indiana law would be barred from giving Indiana's citizens greater protection than citizens of other states. See *Granholm v. Heald*, 544 U.S. 460 (2005) (striking down Michigan and New York laws that allowed in-state wineries to sell wine directly to consumers in the state but prohibited out-of-state wineries from doing so); *Saenz v. Roe*, 526 U.S. 489 (1999) (striking down California statute limiting the maximum welfare benefits available to newly arrived citizens on grounds that it deprived them of their constitutional right to travel).

64. Stephen Gardbaum, *The Nature of Preemption*, 79 Cornell L. Rev. 767, 768.

65. Kenneth W. Starr, *Reflections on Hines v. Davidowitz: The Future of Obstacle Preemption*, 33 Pepp. L. Rev. 1, 1 (2005).

9

Federal Preemption and State Autonomy

*Ernest A. Young**

Federalism has two faces: one limits the authority of the central government, the other checks the power of the states. Most observers of the Rehnquist Court's "Federalist Revival" have focused on the first aspect, embodied in cases limiting Congress's authority to legislate under the Commerce Clause, to mandate state enforcement of federal law, or to subject the states to damages liability in federal lawsuits. A growing literature, however, addresses the absence of any corresponding move to loosen federalism-based constraints on *state* authority.[1] A solid majority of the Court has rejected calls to roll back the "dormant" commerce power doctrine, which limits state action that discriminates against or burdens interstate commerce, and the Court has interpreted the preemptive reach of federal law broadly in a wide variety of statutory decisions.[2] Given the evidently limited ambitions of the Court's decisions on federal powers,[3] the Court's most important contributions are likely to be along federalism's nationalist dimension.

Many of the contributors to this volume seem to favor vigorous judicial enforcement of both aspects of federalism. They seem generally to approve the Court's efforts to limit the national commerce power and to wish those efforts would go somewhat further. At the same time, however, they enthusiastically endorse the judge-made dormant Commerce Clause doctrine and an expansive reading of federal statutes as preempting state regulation. This "libertarian vision" sees federalism as a tool of deregulation with the potential to keep both national and state governments within relatively narrow bounds. The state-limiting face of federalism, in particular, serves to enforce a nationwide free-trade area by squelching burdensome or discriminatory state regulation.

I want to offer a different, "state autonomy" vision of federalism. That vision is agnostic on whether more or less regulation is generally a good or bad thing. Instead, it emphasizes the importance of allowing individual states to make their own policy choices in response to the democratic desires of their respective peoples. By protecting the role of the states as autonomous political communities, this vision hopes both to ensure that states are vital enough to preserve liberty by checking central power and to push our institutional arrangements back in the direction of the Constitution's command of balance between national and state authority.

The libertarian and state autonomy approaches to federalism are both centrally concerned with the preemptive effect of federal law, both in its "dormant" aspect and in its active or statutory aspect. Where the libertarian approach frequently welcomes preemption, however, the state autonomy approach seeks to limit it. Lacking the space for a comprehensive discussion here, I shall make three primary points about preemption doctrine: First, if we look at federalism doctrine from the standpoints of the values we are trying to protect and the institutional constraints on judicial enforcement, preemption emerges as the most promising focus. Second, a look at preemption cases in particular statutory contexts demonstrates that existing doctrinal limits on preemption are not consistently enforced, that this failure to limit preemption has implications inconsistent with standard assumptions about the political valence of federalism, and that disputes about federalism within the Rehnquist Court are more complex than is sometimes thought. Third, I propose to strengthen doctrinal limits on federal preemption by reviving the traditional presumption against preemption and by developing rules to limit which federal actors can preempt state law.

Preemption and the Imperatives of Federalism Doctrine

Conventional wisdom makes several assumptions about federalism doctrine. The first is that a strong federalism requires relatively firm substantive limits on Congress's authority. A second assumption, following closely on the first, is that the judiciary must choose either to enforce those substantive limits or to abdicate judicial review of federalism issues entirely. Those who choose enforcement often make a third assumption—namely, that the most important thing in constructing limits on Congress's authority is to protect state governmental institutions themselves from federal interference. This may be done through tools like the *National League of Cities* doctrine, which sought to exempt state entities from federal regulation altogether,[4] or, more recently, through state sovereign immunity.[5] Finally, most people attach a relatively determinate political valence to federalism issues: conservatives back the states, while liberals promote national power.[6]

Not everyone shares these assumptions. Federalism scholars are somewhat less likely to share them than nonspecialists in the academy or the profession.[7] Nonetheless, the conventional wisdom has an important effect in limiting debate about federalism issues to options that are, on the whole, less promising than approaches that would challenge these assumptions. To give just one example, conservative scholars and justices who seek a strong federalism have been exceptionally suspicious of process-oriented approaches to federalism doctrine, which focus on enhancing the political representation of states at the national level and the burdens of inertia that impede national action—even though those approaches show significant potential for protecting state autonomy.[8]

A more constructive approach would assess federalism doctrine from two perspectives: the underlying values that federalism is supposed to protect, and the institutional constraints that courts confront in developing workable doctrinal limits on national power. While I do not undertake a normative defense of federalism *per se*, identifying the primary values on which such defenses have rested can help focus doctrine, as not all approaches protect these values in equal measure. Federalism doctrine must also be shaped, however, by the comparative institutional competences of courts. Simply put, some doctrinal approaches are likely to be more sustainable than others from the perspective of the judiciary as an institution.

Federalism Values. The most important values that state autonomy is thought to promote fall into two groups. The first set emphasizes regulatory diversity: where states are allowed to adopt different regulatory regimes, they are likely in many instances to satisfy a greater proportion of diverse citizen preferences, and they may achieve *better* policies through experimentation and competition among states. The second set focuses on the value of state political institutions independent of regulatory outcomes. State institutions provide opportunities for citizen participation and the accumulation of social capital. They also foster political competition and, as a result of that competition, help to maintain checks on the central government.[9]

All these values arise out of regulatory autonomy: they depend on an institutional space in which the states are free to make their own policy choices. We obviously will not get satisfaction of diverse preferences, or regulatory experimentation and competition, if the states are *not* free to make their own regulatory choices. Likewise, state governments cannot provide opportunities for citizen participation or for opposition politicians to demonstrate leadership and policy credibility if those governments are not entrusted with meaningful responsibilities.

If preservation of regulatory autonomy is the critical factor in federalism, then preemption is the critical issue. Federal preemption, after all, is "jurispathic"—it kills off state regulatory authority in the areas where it occurs.[10] Other aspects of federalism doctrine—such as whether the states will be subject to federal law (*National League of Cities*) or subject to certain remedies when they break it (state sovereign immunity)—do not address this central issue of the state's freedom to make its own regulatory choices. These other doctrinal approaches thus bear a much more tenuous relationship to the reasons why we value federalism in the first place.

Institutional Constraints and Opportunities. Federalism doctrine should also be shaped by the institutional constraints confronting the courts, as well as the relationship of judicial review to other enforcement mechanisms built into the constitutional system.[11] The relevant factors here are both historical and theoretical. On the historical side, the Court has a long and troubled history of enforcing (and not enforcing) federalism. One fairly obvious lesson of that history is that the Court ought to minimize its confrontations with Congress. One would not want to take this lesson too far, and strong theories of limited "institutional capital" are controversial. But it seems safe to say that, all else being equal, an approach to federalism doctrine that avoids direct confrontations with Congress is preferable to one that does not.

Historical experience also speaks directly to doctrine. Justice Souter has warned that renewed attempts to enforce federalism through the courts raise a "portent of incoherence," based on the doctrinal disarray that resulted from the courts' previous forays into the area.[12] Doctrinal incoherence, the history suggests, worked to undermine the legitimacy of the Court's enterprise. The troubled story of "dual federalism," which contemplated fixed and exclusive spheres of state and federal regulatory authority, suggests that rigid subject-matter categories are unstable over time. The Court's attempts to maintain limits on national power *without* such categories, by inquiring much more directly whether good reasons existed for national action, were likewise unsuccessful. That in turn suggests that direct value-application tests—modeled, perhaps, on the European Union's notion of subsidiarity—are unlikely to work well today.[13]

This troubled history has led many to conclude that the judiciary should get out of the federalism business and leave its preservation to various institutional mechanisms built into the constitutional scheme. Self-enforcement has an important place in the Framers' political theory, and it of course provides the centerpiece for Herbert Wechsler's seminal argument about the "political safeguards of federalism."[14] James Madison's earlier theory of political safeguards, developed in *The Federalist* Nos. 45 and 46, held that the federal balance would largely come down to a competition for loyalty between state and national institutions.[15] State governments would have a critical advantage in this competition, he thought, because they held primary responsibility for the regulatory concerns that mattered most in the daily lives of their citizens. This analysis prefigured aspects of the "economic theory of regulation" in modern political science, which assumes that voters and interest groups trade political support for beneficial regulation and that different political institutions will generally compete to offer that regulation to their common constituents.[16]

Madison's theory puts the focus squarely on state regulatory autonomy: states can compete for the loyalty of their citizens only if they retain the authority to do good things for them. It also suggests a basic problem with Wechsler's focus on the representation of the states in Congress. After all, in Madison's theory (and in modern political science), members of Congress will often be competitors to state politicians rather than to their ambassadors in Washington, D.C. This and other relatively familiar criticisms of Wechsler's analysis suggest that, to the extent that federal representation *does* protect the states, that protection may be owing as much to the *procedural* constraints on congressional action as to the political representation that the states enjoy there.[17] It also suggests that relying on the composition of Congress *alone* to protect state autonomy would be misguided.

"Political safeguards" arguments, however, can play a role without total judicial abdication. John Hart Ely's process-based vision of individual rights,[18] for example, hardly left protection of those rights entirely to politics. Rather, it called for a fairly aggressive role for judicial review to enforce and enhance those aspects of the political process that promote individual liberty. At least some versions of the political safeguards of federalism argument are susceptible to a similar reading. Wechsler himself, for example, never denied a judicial role, and Justice Blackmun's opinion in *Garcia* left the door open for judicial enforcement that is "tailored to compensate for possible failings in the national political process."[19]

All this suggests a set of criteria for federalism doctrine: (1) Such doctrine should minimize direct confrontations with the political branches; (2) it should avoid rules that place too much weight on subject-matter categories, on the one hand, or direct value-application, on the other; (3) it should seek to guarantee and enhance three separate aspects of the constitutional structure—the political representation of the states in Congress, the procedural hurdles and burdens of inertia that impede the creation of federal law, and the underlying ability of the states to generate loyalty by providing services and regulation to their citizens; and finally, (4) it should be designed to operate in a world where state and federal regulatory jurisdiction are largely concurrent.[20]

A preemption-focused doctrine best fits these criteria. That doctrine has generally employed rules of statutory construction—the traditional "presumption against preemption"[21]—rather than hard limits on Congress's authority. For that reason, its application leaves Congress a final say and minimizes direct confrontation. Moreover, preemption doctrine has *not* traditionally applied the sort of subject-matter categories or policy-laden value application that failed in the past. Clear statement rules provide notice that may enhance political representation, and they raise drafting and associated costs that buttress procedural hurdles to federal action. Most important, preemption doctrine focuses the courts' energies where they can do the most good: on protecting the basic regulatory autonomy of the states. And because preemption is the classic problem of concurrent power, preemption doctrine is well-suited to the realities of the post–1937 legal environment.

The Libertarian Vision

The argument thus far presupposes that state autonomy is, by and large, a good thing. To borrow the editors' terms, it views the states as "'benevolent despots' who supply locally desired public goods" rather than "Leviathans whose basic purpose and function is to serve as opportunity points for rent-seeking factions."[22] The "libertarian" vision of federalism, of course, tends to take the latter view. This alternate view of federalism pairs a healthy skepticism of national legislation with Madison's yearning for a federal censor to head off exploitative impulses at the state level. Libertarian federalists emphasize federalism's competitive dimension: states compete with one another to produce the most efficient (and therefore attractive) regulatory policies, and they likewise compete with the national government along the same lines. Federal courts, on this view, play a role as antitrust enforcers that check monopolistic tendencies at both levels. Rather than attempt a thorough critique of the libertarian model (or an analysis of its many virtues) in this essay, I confine myself to three points.

First, the competitive dynamic at the heart of the model presupposes the existence of strong, viable state governments. Libertarian federalists thus cannot be indifferent to the core concerns of state regulatory autonomy. If those regulatory functions are continually ceded to the federal government or simply foreclosed by federal judicial action, the capacity of state governments to serve as competitive counterweights to one another and to the feds will decline over the long term. Libertarians should be willing to sacrifice some measure of efficient policy in the short term in order to assure a healthy competitive dynamic down the road.

Second, regulatory minimalism is not a goal of constitutional policy. The Constitution, as Justice Holmes pointed out, does not enact *laissez faire* economics; it *does* enact a basic balance of authority between state and federal governments.[23] Whereas the libertarian model seems to see two layers of regulators as a threat to liberty, the state autonomy model holds that sometimes it takes a government to check a government.[24] The point of strong, viable state governments with important responsibilities is thus not simply to provide policy competition, but also to stand as intermediary bodies between the national government and the individual.[25] The authority of the people of each state, acting through their own democratic processes, to make their own policy choices in areas not constitutionally committed to the national government may likewise be viewed as an end in itself, whether or not the choices actually made amount to efficient policies.[26]

Third, institutional considerations favor a role for courts as defenders of state autonomy over a role as antitrust enforcers in the libertarian model. The pure case of the latter model occurs when courts employ the dormant Commerce Clause to enforce limits on state regulation entirely in the absence of national legislation. Use of that doctrine to police burdensome state regulation, however, involves the courts in much the same sort of policy judgments as the discredited *Lochner* doctrine under the Due Process Clause. Even the nondiscrimination branch of dormant Commerce Clause doctrine often involves such fine distinctions as to make one wonder whether the judges have not crossed over into policymaking.[27] A rule of deference to state governments obviously eases these institutional concerns.

The institutional considerations are somewhat more complex in preemption cases. Interpreting federal statutes broadly cannot be considered a matter of deferring to Congress. Close preemption cases are close, after all, because Congress's intent is unclear, and the question is what default rules should control in the absence of a clear statement from the national legislature. The institutional advantage of an antipreemption default is that of deference to a democratically elected *state* legislature. (I discuss the case of state *judicial* decisions below.) That advantage, in turn, must be measured against a judge-made antiregulatory presumption or, what is often the case, deference to a federal administrative agency. As also discussed below, significant deference to federal agencies is virtually inevitable due to the significant legislative discretion delegated to them under current law and the difficulty of applying the presumption against preemption in the administrative context. Given the low risk of unduly discounting agency policy and the attenuated connection between agency action and the democratic process, courts should defer where possible to state legislative judgments.

It is worth noting that the range of disagreement here is somewhat smaller than it may appear at first glance. Libertarian federalists generally stop short of advocating a wholesale broadening of the dormant Commerce Clause doctrine. State autonomy advocates, on the other hand, are resigned to according preemptive effect to national legislation when Congress's intent (or a functional conflict) is clear. The disputed ground concerns how to handle ambiguities concerning preemptive intent. That is a debate primarily about the validity of the traditional "presumption against preemption" as a canon of statutory construction. However, ambiguity concerning preemptive intent is sufficiently pervasive that this presumption may make a substantial difference in the overall balance of authority between the states and the nation.

Preemption in Statutory Context

Most preemption scholarship falls into one of two groups: a large number of studies that address preemption under particular statutes (such as ERISA or banking law) or preemption of state tort claims by federal safety regulation; and a second, much smaller group that addresses general issues in preemption law—for example, the scope of implied preemption or the validity of the presumption against preemption—without paying a great deal of attention to the statutory contexts in which these issues arise.[28] Both types of studies have made very helpful contributions, but I think something can be gained from trying to combine them. Here I seek some general conclusions from preemption cases under two sets of statutory regimes: safety regulation and environmental protection. My approach is doctrinal rather than quantitative; it seeks to outline the major features of preemption doctrine in each area that are relevant to the more general concern of preserving state regulatory autonomy. Perhaps unsurprisingly, the relationship between state and federal law is quite different in each area, and those differences have resulted in substantial variance in the way that preemption operates.

Congress often expressly preempts state law in the text of a statute. Courts have also recognized *implied* preemption where federal regulation is so pervasive as to "preempt the field," or where particular aspects of state law conflict with the federal scheme. The obvious conflicts occur where compliance with both federal and state law is impossible; more difficult judgment calls arise when state law arguably "stands as an obstacle" to federal purposes.[29] All of these wrinkles, however, are merely conceptual tools that assist courts in divining the intent of Congress. Moreover, they are (supposedly) applied through a particular lens—the rule of statutory construction that, at least in cases implicating the states' "historic police powers," state law is "not to be superseded by the Federal Act unless that was the *clear and manifest* purpose of Congress."[30] This much is hornbook law. But preemption doctrine in particular regulatory contexts presents a considerably more complex picture.

Safety Regulation. Safety regulation is one of the most traditional functions of the states' police power; during the reign of dual federalism, such regulation was reserved to the states. State primacy is now, however, significantly qualified—if not reversed altogether—by important federal statutes concerning occupational safety and health; automobile, traffic, and railroad safety; atomic energy; medical devices; pesticides; and cigarettes. These statutes have generated a higher proportion of major preemption decisions at the Supreme Court in recent years than any other area of regulation.[31]

Most federal statutes in this area entrust enforcement to a federal administrative agency, which is charged with developing federal standards on particular issues. The Traffic Safety Act, for example, instructs the Secretary of Transportation to establish motor vehicle safety standards. Where the agency has not yet promulgated a standard, the states remain free to regulate. Once a federal standard is in place, however, the Act preempts any safety standard imposed by a state that is not "identical" to the relevant federal standard.[32] In many of the Court's recent cases, a key question has been whether a state *tort* claim for design defect, failure to warn, or some similar theory amounts to a state "standard" that would be preempted by the federal scheme.[33] Others have considered whether the federal scheme allows states to supplement federal restrictions; on this question, the answer has usually been "no."[34]

The safety cases highlight two important aspects of preemption law that are not immediately obvious from boilerplate statements of general principles. The first is that preemption in this area is not a choice of which legislative body—Congress or the state legislature—will set the governing rules. Rather, it is often a choice between a bureaucratic process (agency standard-setting) at the federal level and a judicial one (common law claims) at the state level. The agency's role at the federal level means that the scope of preemption is fluid over time, as the agency develops standards on more and more issues. It also means that the political and procedural safeguards of federalism are unlikely to operate in the way that Wechsler and others have anticipated.

At the state level, on the other hand, the fact that many of the relevant standards are set by courts may undermine some of the advantages of state autonomy deriving from political participation and political competition.[35]

The second point is that preemption is generally deregulatory in its effect. Typically, the preemption claim is raised by a regulated entity to challenge a state requirement that is stricter in some way than the relevant federal standard. An important caveat is that in the state common law cases, the operative question is whether the plaintiff's claim can go forward notwithstanding the federal regime, not whether state law is really as strict as the plaintiff makes it out to be. Once the preemption defense is out of the way, many state courts might still reject plaintiffs' argument that, say, state products liability law required installation of airbags in situations where federal law did not.[36] This caveat notwithstanding, however, it seems safe to say that preemption simply does not come up if a regulated entity has failed to comply with federal standards. The cases arise, then, when state law is alleged to require something more. Federal preemption is thus a favorite theory of businesses seeking regulatory relief.

Environmental Protection. The regulation of air and water pollution has been thought to be primarily a federal responsibility since enactment of the key provisions of the Clean Air Act and the Clean Water Act in the late 1960s and early 1970s. Those statutes are generally thought to have been enacted in response to decades of state regulatory failure, although the history is not uncontested and there is at least some evidence that industry pressed for federal regulation to avoid nonuniform (and possibly more rigorous) standards at the state level.[37]

Environmental statutes created perhaps the classic examples of "cooperative federalism," under which most standards are set at the federal level but much of the implementation and enforcement is carried out by state governments. The statutes reserve the right of the Environmental Protection Agency to implement federal standards itself if states fail to do so adequately.[38] In most instances, however, federal officials are so dependent on the states for information and enforcement resources that they could not realistically carry out this option.[39]

The pattern of cooperative federalism in environmental law arguably bears out several observations from the more general theoretical literature.

First, as Larry Kramer has suggested in his updating of Herbert Wechsler's "political safeguards" argument, the interlocking state and federal bureaucracies in environmental law do seem to provide a mechanism for state input into federal regulatory policy.[40] Second, the pattern likewise seems to fit Jonathan Macey's argument that federal regulators will defer to state officials when particular states have invested heavily in expertise, where solutions must be tailored to local conditions, and where potentially unpopular choices can be delegated away.[41] In particular, it seems likely that federal politicians find attractive the prospect of enacting popular goals at the federal level ("Clean air!") while leaving unpopular implementation decisions ("Must I really have my car inspected *again*?") to state officials.

Finally, the Rehnquist Court's anticommandeering doctrine, which holds that the national government may not require states to implement federal law,[42] is of limited practical relevance to the environmental regime. The environmental statutes, after all, have secured massive state enforcement of federal law through the carrot of conditional spending and the stick of conditional preemption. The Court has explicitly approved each of these mechanisms as an instrument for securing state implementation of federal law.[43] While Congress may not *compel* state enforcement, then, it frequently makes states offers that they cannot refuse.

The relationship between state and federal law is generally more complex in the environmental field than in the safety cases. Most provisions of the Clean Air Act and the Clean Water Act set a federal "floor" on a particular issue, leaving the states free to impose more rigorous standards above that level. Others, such as the mobile source provisions of the Clean Air Act, impose nondiscretionary standards that set both a floor and a ceiling. Sometimes these nondiscretionary standards come with provisions allowing the EPA to issue waivers, generally for more demanding state standards; sometimes they do not. Importantly, the courts sometimes *create* nondiscretionary arrangements through theories of conflict preemption. Where the courts interpret a federal standard as balancing environmental protection against cost or uniformity concerns, for example, they are likely to bar state deviation in either direction on grounds of "conflict" or "obstacle" preemption.[44]

Perhaps the most interesting aspect of the Clean Air regime is California's exemption from the mobile source provisions, which allows California to set significantly more stringent standards for emissions by autos and other vehicles than would otherwise be permitted under federal law.[45] The exemption illustrates two central federalism values: the value of state experimentation (the exemption is based in part on California's pioneering efforts in the field), and the need to tailor regulatory solutions to local conditions (such as Los Angeles's smog problem). Other aspects, however, are less in keeping with the conventional wisdom. State experimentation, for example, is usually thought to be important for its *informational* value; if the experiment works out, then the nation as a whole may benefit through its adoption at the federal level. But California is so big that its policies have an impact even if they are never adopted outside the boundaries of the Golden State. California on its own outpaces most of the world's nations in energy consumption, and its auto market is sufficiently large that no automaker, even foreign ones, can afford to ignore its requirements.[46] Moreover, California has the political clout (sometimes) to secure a shield against preemption for its own policies; no other state has secured a similar exemption. (Other states may adopt California's rules; they may not adopt their own standards.) This suggests that in a system where the balance of federalism is left in large part to politics, some states will emerge as more autonomous than others.

Finally, the environmental experience reinforces the impression that preemption is generally deregulatory in nature. While the federal statutes may originally have been enacted as responses to state inaction, state governments today often seek to go further in protecting the environment than federal law provides.[47] Where this is *not* the case, preemption rarely comes up; rather, the issue is simply enforcement of the federal "floor." Preemption becomes important where the states have gone further and regulated entities seek relief from these additional regulatory burdens by invoking federal law.[48]

The State of Preemption. Important differences exist concerning the operation of federal preemption under different statutory regimes. Many of these differences arise from the particulars of the underlying federal statutes, and these sorts of differences suggest important limitations on the project of developing a "unified" preemption doctrine. Nonetheless, important commonalities also emerge.

One is simply that there's a lot of preemption. We are no longer in the world of Hart and Wechsler's first edition, which stated that "[f]ederal law is generally interstitial in its nature."[49] In auto and railroad safety, for example, federal law is clearly primary; state law governs only if the relevant federal agency has not gotten around to promulgating a standard. In environmental law, the states are relegated primarily to an enforcement role, and state efforts to innovate often meet with fierce resistance.[50]

It is harder to say whether the courts' willingness to *find* preemption in close cases is likewise increasing.[51] The safety cases provide some tentative evidence for that proposition, at least at the Supreme Court, but some of the developments in other areas, such as ERISA law, seem to cut the other way.[52] There is no evidence, though, that the Court's "federalist revival" on issues like the Commerce Clause and state sovereign immunity has spilled over into preemption doctrine. More important still, the pervasive scope of federal preemption suggests that the primary threat to state autonomy lies here, and not in the more peripheral areas on which the Court has chosen to focus.

Second, the preemption cases also suggest that the traditional *Rice* presumption—that federal statutes should not be read to preempt state law unless Congress has indicated a "clear and manifest" purpose to do so—is not consistently enforced. Decisions differ about *when* it applies (only in areas of traditional state regulation, or across the board?) and how it interacts with express preemption clauses (do such clauses overcome the presumption, or is it relevant to their scope?). A fair number of opinions fail to mention the presumption at all or, even worse, set its application aside as a controversial matter unnecessary to the result.[53] Probably more important, but also more difficult to measure, are differences in the *weight* that courts give the presumption. Some opinions treat it as a genuine clear statement rule, while others give it considerably less weight than that. And, the decisions diverge as to whether *other* federal actors, such as administrative agencies, can provide the requisite clear statement if none is forthcoming from Congress.

These inconsistencies obviously pose a threat to state autonomy, given the pervasive scope of federal preemption and its direct bearing on the states' ability to protect themselves in the political process by earning the loyalty of their citizens. But the inconsistencies also create an opportunity. As I discuss further below, one could do a lot for state autonomy without creating any innovative new doctrines, simply by enforcing the presumption against preemption with a little more rigor. Many of the important cases seem close enough on the merits for modest differences in application to make an important difference in results.[54]

Third, the cases confirm the intuition that preemption will generally have a deregulatory impact. Although we occasionally see litigation about Congress's power to enact a given statute,[55] no one doubts that federal laws that fall within Congress's power must be complied with, state laws that fail to regulate or even purport to deregulate the matter in question notwithstanding. The contested questions arise when state law seeks to go *further* than federal law. In those cases, the regulated entities typically raise federal preemption as a defense to more rigorous state regulation. Although federalism was once a shield against rigorous economic regulation in the years prior to 1937, now it is national power that frequently operates to reduce regulatory burdens.

Finally, we should note the voting alignments in the Rehnquist Court's preemption cases. In "classic" federalism cases like *Lopez* or *Seminole Tribe*, we see an almost completely static division between five "conservative" or "states' rights" justices (Rehnquist, O'Connor, Scalia, Kennedy, and Thomas) and four "liberal" or "nationalist" justices (Stevens, Souter, Ginsburg, and Breyer). The pattern in preemption cases is very different. First of all, it is not nearly so static. Perhaps due to the variety of the underlying statutory schemes, it is not uncommon to see a given justice voting for preemption in one case but against it in another. There is, however, a pattern, and it is not what one would expect. It is generally the "liberals" who favor state law in close cases like *Lorillard* or *Geier*, while the "conservatives" insist on national power.[56]

Why do the conservatives ignore federalism in preemption cases? Why do the liberals suddenly discover it? It is tempting to offer purely political explanations.[57] If preemption is generally deregulatory in its impact, it should not be surprising that conservatives favor it and liberals oppose it. And the many cases that involve state tort claims even implicate the time-honored political divide between the plaintiffs' and defense bars. These sorts of arguments no doubt have some explanatory power, but I am distrustful of purely political explanations. For one thing, too many of the cases are hard to categorize in this way.[58]

Other possible explanations might emphasize disagreements among the justices on matters of statutory construction. Strong textualists like Justice Scalia, for instance, may have little use for presumptions and canons, even when they favor the states. Likewise, cross-cutting issues like the scope of *Chevron* deference or other aspects of separation of powers may explain some subset of the results. A broader possibility, however, has more central implications for my project: disagreement in preemption cases tracks the basic divide in *Garcia* over the legitimacy and prospects of process federalism.[59] The conservatives accept no substitutes for strong *substantive* limits on national power, in keeping with the conventional wisdom. The liberals, in contrast, may be offering a new vision of federalism doctrine that is more process-based in its means and more focused on state regulatory autonomy in its ends.[60]

Whether these patterns will hold under the new Roberts Court is, of course, anyone's guess. As I have argued elsewhere, we should not assume too quickly that the two new additions, Chief Justice John Roberts and Justice Samuel Alito, will be solicitous of state autonomy simply because they are considered to be politically conservative.[61] The new Chief's decision to join Justice Scalia's dissent in the Court's first major federalism case, the Oregon right-to-die decision in *Gonzales v. Oregon*,[62] suggests that he may be willing to construe federal regulatory broadly at the expense of state prerogatives. Given the Court's apparent unwillingness to impose meaningful substantive limits on national *power* in *Gonzales v. Raich*,[63] however, what the Court does in preemption cases is likely to take on even greater importance.

Limiting Preemption

What sort of preemption regime can reinforce and enhance the existing political and procedural safeguards of state autonomy? I focus on two sorts of doctrines: the traditional "presumption against preemption" exemplified by the Court's 1947 decision in *Rice v. Santa Fe Elevator Corp.*, and rules about which federal actors can preempt state law. I reject a third alternative, tightening substantive limits on federal regulatory jurisdiction, as unlikely to provide meaningful relief for state autonomy in the foreseeable future.

The Presumption Against Preemption. Four problems have recurred under the traditional presumption against preemption. First, that presumption recently has been attacked as inconsistent with the judicial obligation to construe statutes in accord with Congress's intent. Second, courts have had difficulty organizing the relationship between express and implied preemption; the *Rice* presumption, after all, is framed as a way of reading ambiguous statutory texts and translates somewhat awkwardly into a rule for adjudicating functional conflicts between state and federal policies. Third, the Court has suggested in several recent cases that the presumption should not apply outside areas of traditional state regulatory primacy. A fourth issue arises out of Caleb Nelson's argument that the presumption is inconsistent with the Framers' understanding of the Supremacy Clause.[64]

The *Rice* presumption is best understood as a normative canon of statutory construction rather than as a descriptive canon designed to get at what Congress actually intended. As such, the presumption is vulnerable to attack as a betrayal of judges' obligation to act as faithful agents of the legislature. Viet Dinh, for example, has argued that the presumption against preemption encourages judges to "rewrite the laws enacted by Congress"; use of any interpretive rule not designed simply "to discern what Congress has legislated and whether such legislation displaces concurrent state law" risks "an illegitimate expansion of the judicial function."[65] I disagree. Normative canons in general, and federalism canons like the *Rice* presumption in particular, are legitimate ways of giving effect to underenforced constitutional principles. Such canons also perform the important function of buttressing political and procedural checks on national power and, as a result, reduce the need to rely on substantive constitutional limitations.[66]

The relation between express and implied preemption is complex, and I can summarize only imperfectly here. I reject suggestions that courts should not recognize *any* form of implied preemption: Congress often does not explicitly address preemption at all, and in any event it cannot realistically be expected to anticipate and address every conceivable barrier to federal policy. But this rationale has considerably less force where Congress *has* explicitly addressed a statute's preemptive effect in the text. In those circumstances, only extreme conflicts should be recognized as warranting preemption beyond the express mandate. I also suggest that courts should never find implied *field* preemption, since preemption of state laws that actually conflict with particular aspects of the federal scheme is enough to protect the workability of that scheme in light of unforeseen circumstances. Finally, courts should rarely construe federal statutes as striking an inflexible equilibrium between competing values, such as safety and cost. To do so has the effect of preempting *any* departure by state law, effectively creating a form of field preemption. Instead, conflict preemption should occur only where a state law conflicts with the federal statute's primary purpose.

Some recent decisions attempt to confine the *Rice* presumption to areas in which the states have traditionally legislated,[67] but I view those efforts as inconsistent with the way in which that presumption has generally been applied. Despite repetition of the "field which the States have traditionally occupied" language from *Rice*, in practice the presumption has applied virtually across the board.[68] More important, attempts to confine the presumption in this way reintroduce the concept of separate state and federal "spheres" of authority that proved to be unsustainable under dual federalism. *Rice* should govern *all* preemption cases.

A final question about the *Rice* presumption concerns whether it is consistent with the original understanding of the Supremacy Clause. Caleb Nelson has recently argued that it is not, because the Framers would have understood the concluding language of the Supremacy Clause—"any Thing in the Constitution or Laws of any State to the Contrary notwithstanding"—as a *non obstante* clause. Such clauses, he maintains, were used at the time to direct courts not to apply the customary canon against implied repeals of prior legislation. According to Nelson, "[t]he *non obstante* provision tells courts that even if a particular interpretation of a federal statute would contradict (and therefore preempt) some state laws, this fact is not automatically reason to prefer a different interpretation. It follows that courts should not automatically seek 'narrowing' constructions of federal statutes solely to avoid preemption."[69]

The short answer to Nelson's nuanced argument is that a strict originalist reading of the Supremacy Clause to invalidate limits on federal preemption fits poorly with the rest of contemporary federalism doctrine, which has departed radically from the Founders' vision of a national government of limited and enumerated powers.[70] Because we are unlikely to jettison the post–New Deal interpretation of the Commerce Clause, it becomes both necessary and legitimate for courts to formulate "compensating adjustments" to protect the federal balance under modern circumstances. To the extent that a canon of statutory construction disfavoring preemption may depart from the original understanding, it is nonetheless an adjustment that is modest, well-suited to the courts' institutional capacities, and likely to be efficacious in protecting state autonomy.

Who Can Preempt State Law? Most federal law is made not by Congress but by federal administrative agencies and—less frequently—federal courts making federal common law. Preemption doctrine has not traditionally distinguished between federal statutes, on the one hand, and federal agency action or federal common law on the other; all these forms are supreme under Article VI. That is a problem: however problematic reliance on political and procedural safeguards for federalism may be in the legislative context, those safeguards are largely illusory when we move to federal courts and administrative agencies. Constitutionally based limitations should ensure that the power to preempt state law remains with *Congress*.

Preemption by the independent action of federal courts would seem to be barred by *Erie*'s insistence that "[t]here is no federal general common law."[71] But federal common law survived and flourished after *Erie*, and it often preempts state law.[72] Indeed, in several contexts, the Court has suggested that in the areas of "uniquely federal interest" where federal common lawmaking is permitted, the ordinary *Rice* presumption is reversed. "[T]he fact that the area in question is one of unique federal concern," Justice Scalia has explained, "changes what would otherwise be a conflict that cannot produce preemption into one that can."[73] In my judgment, courts are unlikely to be able to define the boundaries of spheres of "unique federal concern" in a principled way. In any event, preemption by courts should always be *more* problematic than by Congress—in which the states are represented—rather than less so. The remedy is to insist, as many of the Court's federal common law cases have insisted, on a significant conflict with federal policy before preempting state law.[74]

Preemption by administrative agencies is the more pervasive problem, and the solutions are less obvious. Two different scenarios arise. In one, the agency interprets an ambiguous federal statute to preempt state law, and the question is whether deference to the agency under the *Chevron* doctrine should trump the *Rice* presumption that ambiguous federal statutes do not preempt state law.[75] *Rice* should prevail in these cases, but that resolution is not as significant as it might at first appear. Agency interpretations of what the federal statute actually *does* should still get *Chevron* deference;

otherwise, *Rice* would swallow the *Chevron* rule entirely. Deference should only be denied on the further, legal question of whether the statute, so interpreted, actually preempts state law. Unfortunately, what the statute does will often be the most important interpretive question, and once the agency interprets the statute broadly, preemption may follow unambiguously.

In the second scenario, the agency preempts state law through its own independent action rather than its interpretation of a federal statute. Sometimes Congress specifically delegates the authority to preempt state law; in other instances, agencies rely on broad delegations of all authority that is "necessary and proper" to their statutory responsibilities.[76] Rather than develop a comprehensive theory for limiting the preemptive effect of agency action in such circumstances, I hope simply to identify the problems and suggest a series of possible limiting principles. These principles, which I list in order of declining rigor, would each limit agency preemption at least to some extent.

The first possibility would be to hold that Congress simply may not delegate the authority to preempt state law. The problem is that *every* agency action is potentially preemptive in the conflict or obstacle sense. This makes it difficult to separate the agency preemption problem from more general issues concerning the scope of delegated authority, and doctrinal instruments to regulate such delegations have proven notoriously elusive.[77] A second option would limit agency preemption to the direct supremacy effect of the agency's substantive actions. Agencies, for example, would have authority to preempt state laws in direct conflict with their regulatory actions but would lack further authority to preempt a given field entirely.

The other possibilities involve a variety of "clear statement" rules. We might, for instance, insist that any freestanding preemptive authority delegated from Congress be accompanied by a clear statement of legislative purpose to that effect. Alternatively, courts might not require Congress to address preemption directly but, instead, limit the scope of agency preemption powers to situations where Congress has delegated authority to act with the "force of law."[78] Finally, we might simply insist that the agency actually exercise its preemptive authority, rather than inferring preemption from the mere fact of the delegation itself. Even this seemingly obvious requirement would cut back on some of the Court's recent holdings, which have found preemption even in the absence of executive action.[79]

Substantive Limits on National Power. Critics of the "presumption against preemption" tend to place their faith in substantive restrictions on Congress's regulatory jurisdiction as a limit on preemption. That is the explicit suggestion of Nelson and Dinh, both state-autonomy-minded scholars who have nonetheless attacked the presumption against preemption. I have already discussed why I think such limits are difficult for courts to enforce, and I have long expressed doubt that the Rehnquist Court would ever push them very far. Those doubts seem to have been confirmed by the Court's recent decision in *Raich*, in which Justices Scalia and Kennedy joined the Court's nationalists in declining to limit Congress's power over illegal drugs—notwithstanding that the drugs were produced and consumed wholly in-state, in the absence of any commercial transaction.[80] It is possible that the Roberts Court will take the steps that *Raich* eschewed, but we have little reason for confidence in that hope.

Conclusion

In the absence of meaningful substantive limits on Congress's powers, we need federalism doctrines designed for a world of concurrent authority. That is not to say that the Court should *never* enforce the limits of the Commerce Clause. Decisions like *Lopez* and *Morrison* may serve an important "cueing" function, reminding the political community that federalism is, in fact, a constitutional value that all political actors are bound to respect.[81] But we should not count on substantive limits for a great deal more than that. We need a "Democracy and Distrust" for federalism: an approach that does not pretend indifference to constitutional substance but that grounds the justification and shape of judicial review in the institutional relationships between the courts and the political process. Preemption doctrine is the most promising starting point for such a jurisprudence. Absent a true sea change in the Supreme Court's willingness to enforce substantive limits on Congress's enumerated powers, Justice Breyer is correct to insist that "the true test of federalist principle" comes in preemption cases.[82] If the Court is serious about protecting federalism, it will heed him.

Notes

*I am grateful to the American Enterprise Institute for the opportunity to partici-pate in the AEI conference on preemption, to Richard Epstein and Michael Greve for helpful comments on the manuscript, to Lisa Ewart, Liz McKee, and Garrick Pursley for research assistance, and to Allegra Young for Christian charity.

1. See, *e.g.*, Richard H. Fallon, *The "Conservative" Paths of the Rehnquist Court's Federalism Decisions*, 69 U. Chi. L. Rev. 429, 462 (2002); Erwin Chemerinsky, *Empowering States When It Matters: A Different Approach to Preemption*, 69 Brook. L. Rev. 1313 (2004); Calvin Massey, *Federalism and the Rehnquist Court*, 53 Hastings L. J. 431, 502–12 (2002); Ernest A. Young, *The Rehnquist Court's Two Federalisms*, 83 Texas L. Rev. 1 (2004).

2. See, *e.g.*, *Camps Newfound/Owatonna v. Town of Harrison*, 520 U.S. 564 (1997) (rejecting a call from Justice Thomas to junk the dormant commerce power doctrine); *Lorillard Tobacco Co. v. Reilly*, 533 U.S. 525 (2001) (holding Massachusetts' regulation of tobacco advertising directed at children preempted under federal law).

3. See, *e.g.*, *Gonzales v. Raich*, 545 U.S. 1 (2005) (upholding Congress's authority under the Commerce Clause to regulate the state-authorized use of home-grown mar-ijuana for medicinal purposes); *Central Virginia Community College v. Katz*, 126 S. Ct. 990 (2006) (holding that the Court's state sovereign immunity jurisprudence does not extend to the federal bankruptcy power). On *Raich*, see generally Ernest A. Young, *Just Blowing Smoke? Politics, Doctrine, and the Federalist Revival After Gonzales v. Raich*, 2005 Sup. Ct. Rev. 1.

4. *Nat'l League of Cities v. Usery*, 426 U.S. 833 (1976). The Court overruled *National League of Cities* nine years later in *Garcia v. San Antonio Metro. Transit Auth.*, 469 U.S. 528 (1985).

5. See, *e.g.*, *Seminole Tribe of Fla. v. Florida*, 517 U.S. 44 (1996) (holding that Congress may not override state sovereign immunity and subject the states to damages suits when they violate laws enacted under Congress's Article I powers). For a more extended critique of the Rehnquist Court's emphasis on sovereign immunity and a fuller exposition of the argument in this section, see Young, *Two Federalisms*, *supra* note 1.

6. See, *e.g.*, Harold J. Spaeth, "The Original United States Supreme Court Judicial Database, 1953–2003 Terms: Documentation," (database, Michigan State University, 2005), 53–55, http://www.as.uky.edu/polisci/ulmerproject/allcourt_codebook.pdf (accessed, March 8, 2007) (explaining that, under the coding conventions in the lead-ing political science database classifying Supreme Court decisions by ideological direc-tion, a vote to limit national power is "conservative").

7. See, *e.g.*, Vicki C. Jackson, *Federalism and the Uses and Limits of Law: Printz and Principle?* 111 Harv. L. Rev. 2180 (1998) (advocating a mix of substantive and process-based limits on federal power).

8. Compare, *e.g.*, Saikrishna B. Prakash & John C. Yoo, *The Puzzling Persistence of Process-Based Federalism Theories*, 79 Tex. L. Rev. 1459 (2001) (criticizing process federalism), with Bradford R. Clark, *Separation of Powers as a Safeguard of Federalism*, 79 Tex. L. Rev. 1321 (2001) (emphasizing process checks).

9. For a good overview of the extensive literature on values served by federalism, see Barry Friedman, *Valuing Federalism*, 82 Minn. L. Rev. 317 (1997); Michael McConnell, *Federalism: Evaluating the Founders' Design*, 54 U. Chi. L. Rev. 1484, 1491–1511 (1987) (book review); David L. Shapiro, *Federalism: A Dialogue* (Evanston, Ill.: Northwestern University Press, 1995).

10. S. Candice Hoke, *Preemption Pathologies and Civic Republican Values*, 71 B.U. L. Rev. 685, 694 (1991) (borrowing the term from Robert M. Cover, *The Supreme Court, 1982 Term: Foreword – Nomos and Narrative*, 97 Harv. L. Rev. 4, 40 (1983)).

11. For a more extended treatment, see Ernest A. Young, *Making Federalism Doctrine: Fidelity, Institutional Competence, and Compensating Adjustments*, 46 Wm. & Mary L. Rev. 1733 (2005).

12. *United States v. Morrison*, 529 U.S. 598, 647 (2000) (Souter, J., dissenting).

13. For examples of this sort of proposal, see, *e.g.*, Donald H. Regan, *How to Think About the Federal Commerce Power and Incidentally Rewrite* United States v. Lopez, 94 Mich. L. Rev. 554, 557 (1995) ("[I]n thinking about whether the federal government has the power to do something or other, we should ask what special reason there is for the federal government to have that power."); Stephen Gardbaum, *Rethinking Constitutional Federalism*, 74 Tex. L. Rev. 795 (1996) (invoking subsidiarity).

14. Herbert Wechsler, *The Political Safeguards of Federalism: The Role of the States in the Composition and Selection of the National Government*, 54 Colum. L. Rev. 543 (1954).

15. See Madison, *The Federalist* 45 and 46; see also Todd E. Pettys, *Competing for the People's Affection: Federalism's Forgotten Marketplace*, 56 Vand. L. Rev. 329 (2003).

16. See generally Jonathan R. Macey, *Federal Deference to Local Regulators and the Economic Theory of Regulation: Toward a Public-Choice Explanation of Federalism*, 76 Va. L. Rev. 265 (1990).

17. See generally Clark, *supra* note 8.

18. See John Hart Ely, *Democracy and Distrust: A Theory of Judicial Review* (Cambridge, Mass.: Harvard University Press, 1980).

19. See Wechsler, *supra* note 14 at 559; *Garcia*, 469 U.S. at 554.

20. The editors' conclusion suggests that one way to minimize confrontations and enhance the relationships of political accountability that undergird our federalism is to reject my fourth condition of concurrent jurisdiction (and implicitly my second as well, since a "dual" regime would surely entail a return to subject-matter categories). My own view is that such an approach would impose unmanageable line-drawing problems on the courts. In any event, a return to dual federalism is not the only way to meet my institutional conditions. For a more extended discussion, see Young, *Two Federalisms*, *supra* note 1 at 65–122.

21. See *Rice v. Santa Fe Elevator Corp.*, 331 U.S. 218, at 230–31 (1947), "We start with the assumption that the historic police powers of the States were not to be superseded by the Federal Act unless that was the clear and manifest purpose of Congress."

22. Richard A. Epstein and Michael S. Greve, *Federal Preemption: A Madisonian Perspective*, at 1.

23. See *Lochner v. New York*, 198 U.S. 45, 75 (1905) (Holmes, J., dissenting); Young, *Making Federalism Doctrine, supra* note 11 at 1765–71 (documenting the Framers' commitment to a federal balance).

24. Compare, *e.g.*, Douglas Laycock, "Protecting Liberty in a Federal System: The U.S. Experience," in *Patterns of Regionalism and Federalism: Lessons for the U.K.*, eds. Basil Markesinis and Jorg Fedtke (Oxford: Hart Publishing, 2005), with Ernest A. Young, *Welcome to the Dark Side: Liberals Rediscover Federalism in the Wake of the War on Terror*, 69 Brook. L. Rev. 1277, 1284–91 (2004).

25. See, *e.g.*, J. Harvie Wilkinson III, *Is There a Distinctive Conservative Jurisprudence?* 73 U. Colo. L. Rev. 1383, 1392–98 (2002).

26. By "constitutionally committed to the national government" I mean not only areas outside Congress's enumerated powers—if those areas exist anymore—but also areas in which no national proposal has managed to surmount the considerable barriers to national legislative action. The boundaries of the latter category are, of course, often precisely what is at stake in preemption cases.

27. See, *e.g.*, *Camps Newfound/Owatonna* 520 U.S. at 620 (Thomas, J., dissenting) (complaining that when the Court has applied the antidiscrimination rule in close cases, "the distinctions turned on often subtle policy judgments, not the text of the Constitution"); see also ibid. at 596 (Scalia, J., dissenting) ("Our cases have struggled (to put it nicely) to develop a set of rules by which we may preserve a national market without needlessly intruding upon the States' police powers, each exercise of which no doubt has some effect on the commerce of the Nation.").

28. See, *e.g.*, Caleb Nelson, *Preemption*, 86 Va. L. Rev. 225 (2000); Stephen Gardbaum, *The Nature of Preemption*, 79 Cornell L. Rev. 767 (1994).

29. For a general statement of these principles, see, *e.g.*, *Hillsborough Cty. v. Automated Medical Labs., Inc.*, 471 U.S. 707, at 713 (1985).

30. *Rice*, 331 U.S. at 230–31 (emphasis added).

31. See, *e.g.*, *Lorillard Tobacco Co. v. Reilly*, 533 U.S. 525 (2001) (cigarette advertising); *Geier v. American Honda Motor Co., Inc.*, 529 U.S. 861 (2000); *United States v. Locke*, 529 U.S. 89 (2000) (oil tanker safety); *Medtronic, Inc. v. Lohr*, 518 U.S. 470 (1996) (medical devices); *Cipollone v. Liggett Group, Inc.*, 505 U.S. 504 (1992) (cigarettes).

32. 49 U.S.C. § 30103.

33. See, *e.g.*, *Geier*, 529 U.S. 861; *Medtronic*, 518 U.S. 470; *Cipollone*, 505 U.S. 504.

34. See, *e.g.*, *Lorillard*, 533 U.S. 525; *Locke*, 529 U.S. 89.

35. The difference between state courts and state legislatures should not be overstated, however. First, many state judges are elected so that state courts share to some extent the legislature's democratic imprimatur. Second, to protect state causes of action

from federal preemption is often to protect the role of the jury—a democratic and participatory institution that loomed large in the Framers' political theory. See, *e.g.*, Akhil Reed Amar, *The Bill of Rights* (New Haven, Conn.: Yale University Press, 1998), 83. Finally, the burden of legislative inertia may be less at the state level, so that one may read some democratic endorsement into the failure of state legislatures to override state common law decisions.

36. See *Geier*, 529 U.S. 861 (holding that this theory was preempted, so that the question under state law was never reached).

37. See respectively, John P. Dwyer, *The Role of State Law in an Era of Federal Preemption: Lessons from Environmental Regulation*, 60 L. & Contemp. Probs. 203 (1997); and Richard L. Revesz, "Federalism and Regulation: Some Generalizations," in *Regulatory Competition and Economic Integration: Comparative Perspectives*, eds. Daniel Esty and Damien Geradin (Oxford: Oxford University Press, 2001), 3.

38. See, *e.g.*, 42 U.S.C. § 7410(c) (Clean Air Act provision providing for federal regulation in the event that a state implementation plan fails to meet federal requirements).

39. See, *e.g.*, Robert V. Percival, *Environmental Federalism: Historical Roots and Contemporary Models*, 54 Md. L. Rev.1141, 1175 (1995).

40. See Larry Kramer, *Understanding Federalism*, 47 Vand. L. Rev. 1485 (1994).

41. See Macey, *supra* note 16.

42. See *Printz v. United States*, 521 U.S. 898 (1997) (holding that Congress may not require state executive officers to implement federal law); *New York v. United States*, 505 U.S. 144 (1992) (holding that Congress may not require state legislators to enact laws that implement a federal program).

43. See *New York*, 505 U.S. at 167.

44. See, *e.g.*, *Gade v. Nat'l Solid Wastes Mgmt. Ass'n*, 505 U.S. 88, 102 (1992) (plurality opinion).

45. See 42 U.S.C. § 7543(b)(1). Similar waiver provisions for California exist for nonroad vehicle emissions, see 42 U.S.C. § 7543(e)(2), and for fuels and fuel additives, see 42 U.S.C. § 7545(c)(4).

46. See, *e.g.*, Pew Center on Global Climate Change, "California Climate Action," (report, June 3, 2005) http://www.pewclimate.org/what_s_being_done/in_the_states/cajune3targets.cfm (noting that if California were its own country, it would be the fifth largest consumer of energy in the world and the tenth largest emitter of greenhouse gases); *The Economist*, "Replacing Gas with a Gas" (July 19, 2001), http://www.economist.com/science/displaystory.cfm?story_id=E1_GJJVVT (accessed March 8, 2007).

47. See, *e.g.*, *The Economist*, "Grass-roots Greenery" (Jan. 18, 2003), 35; R. Steven Brown, "States Put Their Money Where Their Environment Is," *ECOStates* (Spring 2001), 22, 26, http://www.ecos.org/files/686_file_rsbrown.pdf (accessed October 30, 2006).

48. See, *e.g.*, *Cent. Valley Chrysler-Plymouth v. Calif. Air Res. Bd.*, No. CV-F-02-5017, 2002 U.S. Dist. LEXIS 20403 (E.D. Cal. June 11, 2002) (issuing a preliminary injunction, on preemption grounds, against California's new zero-emissions-vehicle rules).

49. Compare Henry M. Hart, Jr. and Herbert Wechsler, *The Federal Courts and the Federal System* (Mineola: Foundation Press, 1st ed. 1953) (quoted in the text), with Richard H. Fallon, Daniel J. Meltzer, and David L. Shapiro, *Hart and Wechsler's The Federal Courts and the Federal System* (Westbury: Foundation Press, 4th ed. 1996), 522 (acknowledging that "today federal law appears to be more primary than interstitial in numerous areas").

50. See, *e.g.*, Felicity Barringer, "California, Taking Big Gamble, Tries to Curb Greenhouse Gases," *New York Times*, Sept. 15, 2006 (noting legal challenges to California's efforts to cut carbon dioxide emissions).

51. See generally Michael S. Greve & Jonathan Klick, *Preemption in the Rehnquist Court: A Preliminary Empirical Assessment*, 14 Sup. Ct. Econ. Rev. 43 (2006) (discussing patterns in the Supreme Court's case law); David B. Spence & Paula Murray, *The Law, Economics, and Politics of Federal Preemption Jurisprudence: A Quantitative Analysis*, 87 Cal. L. Rev. 1125 (1999) (examining preemption cases in the lower federal courts).

52. See *e.g.*, *Rush Prudential HMO, Inc. v. Moran*, 536 U.S. 355 (2002) (rejecting preemption of a state second-opinion statute; until recently, the norm had been that ERISA preempts just about everything).

53. See, *e.g.*, *Gonzales v. Oregon*, 126 S. Ct. 904, 925 (2006).

54. See, *e.g.*, *AT&T Corp. v. Iowa Utilities Board*, 525 U.S. 366 (1999) (holding, despite any clear indication in the statute, that the 1996 Telecommunications Act transferred rulemaking authority over local telephone service from state utilities boards to the FCC).

55. See, *e.g.*, *United States v. Lopez*, 514 U.S. 549 (1995).

56. See, *e.g.*, *Lorillard*, 533 U.S. 525 (replicating the *Lopez* split but with the conservatives arguing for broad preemption and the liberals complaining about the intrusion on state autonomy); Greve & Klick, *supra* note 51 at 83–85 (observing that, with some qualifications, "[t]he coalitions [in preemption cases] look like the mirror image of the pro-state and anti-state blocs in straightforward federalism cases"). Greve and Klick go on to point out that the pattern of votes in preemption cases is considerably less predictable than in mainstream federalism cases and that "[i]t is very difficult to interpret the evidence as an indication of ideological bloc voting." Ibid. Nonetheless, their data seem to support the conclusion of other scholars that, by and large, the conservative justices are more friendly to preemption and the liberals are more skeptical of it. See also Fallon, *supra* note 1 at 471–72.

57. See, *e.g.*, Frank B. Cross, *Realism About Federalism*, 74 N.Y.U. L. Rev. 1304 (1999).

58. See, *e.g.*, *AT&T Corp. v. Iowa Utils. Bd.*, 525 U.S. 366 (1999) (preemption litigation over the allocation of rulemaking authority between the state utility commissions and the FCC, with "Baby Bell" local exchange carriers supporting state authority and long distance companies supporting federal agency).

59. See Dan T. Coenen, *The Rehnquist Court, Structural Due Process, and Semisubstantive Constitutional Review*, 75 S. Cal. L. Rev. 1281, 1377–81 (2002).

60. See generally Young, *Two Federalisms, supra* note 1 at 39–50.

61. See Young, *Just Blowing Smoke, supra* note 3 at 42–49.

62. 126 S. Ct. 904.

63. 545 U.S. 1 (2005) (upholding Congress's authority to regulate purely medicinal use of home-grown marijuana).

64. Nelson, *supra* note 28.

65. Viet D. Dinh, *Reassessing the Law of Preemption*, 88 Geo. L. J. 2085, 2092 (2000).

66. See generally Ernest A. Young, *Constitutional Avoidance, Resistance Norms, and the Preservation of Judicial Review*, 78 Tex. L. Rev. 1549 (2000) (discussing the constitutional basis of normative canons of statutory construction).

67. See, *e.g.*, *Locke*, 529 U.S. at 108 (holding that no presumption against preemption applies in the area of maritime commerce).

68. See, *e.g.*, *Medtronic*, 518 U.S. at 485 (suggesting that the *Rice* presumption should apply "in all preemption cases").

69. Nelson, *supra* note 28 at 232.

70. The argument summarized in this paragraph is developed at much greater length in Young, *Making Federalism Doctrine, supra* note 11.

71. *Erie Railroad v. Tompkins*, 304 U.S. 64, 78 (1938).

72. See, *e.g.*, *Boyle v. United Technologies Corp.*, 487 U.S. 500 (1988).

73. Ibid. at 508; see also *S. Pacific Co. v. Jensen*, 244 U.S. 205 (1917) (essentially creating a pro-preemption presumption in maritime cases). For a critique of Jensen and preemption of state law by maritime law, see Ernest A. Young, *Preemption at Sea*, 67 Geo. Wash. L. Rev. 273 (1999).

74. See, *e.g.*, *Atherton v. FDIC*, 519 U.S. 213, 218 (1997).

75. See generally *Chevron U.S.A., Inc. v. NRDC*, 467 U.S. 837 (1984) (holding that courts should defer to agency interpretations of statutes they administer where the statute is ambiguous and the agency's interpretation is reasonable); Damien J. Marshall, *Note, The Application of Chevron Deference in Regulatory Preemption Cases*, 87 Geo. L. J. 263 (1998).

76. See, *e.g.*, 47 U.S.C. § 303(5) (delegating to the FCC the authority to "[m]ake such rules and regulations . . . as may be necessary to carry out [the communications laws]").

77. See, *e.g.*, *Whitman v. Am. Trucking Ass'ns*, 531 U.S. 457, 474-75 (2001) ("[W]e have 'almost never felt qualified to second-guess Congress regarding the permissible degree of policy judgment that can be left to those executing or applying the law.'" (quoting *Mistretta v. United States*, 488 U.S. 361, 416 (1989) (Scalia, J., dissenting)).

78. *Cf. United States v. Mead Corp.*, 533 U.S. 218 (2001); *Christensen v. Harris Cty.*, 529 U.S. 576 (2000).

79. See *Crosby v. National Foreign Trade Council*, 530 U.S. 363 (2000) (inferring preemption from the mere fact that Congress had delegated authority to the president to preempt state trade sanctions on Burma, even though the president had been unwilling to exercise that authority).

80. See generally Young, *Just Blowing Smoke, supra* note 3 (discussing *Raich*).

81. See Philip C. Bobbitt, *Constitutional Fate: Theory of the Constitution* (Oxford: Oxford University Press, 1982), 191–95.

82. *Egelhoff v. Egelhoff*, ex rel. Breiner, 532 U.S. 141, 160 (2001) (Breyer, J., dissenting).

10

Supremacy and Preemption:
A View from Europe

*Anne van Aaken**

Questions and conflicts over the European Union's (EU's) and the member states' authority have arisen with great regularity. In fact, those questions—typically framed in terms of "supremacy" and "competences" (or powers, as Americans would say)—are one of the most contentious issues both in the legal debate and the political arena. Many believe that the European Community (EC) has all too often usurped competences, thereby eroding the member states' sovereignty. The EU, it is said, has a tendency to legislate in areas in which it is not legally competent, where central intervention is not appropriate, or in too detailed a manner. The delimitation of EU competences is also said to lack clarity and therefore to obscure responsibility. Following the 2001 Laeken Declaration on the future of the union, the draft treaty establishing a Constitution for Europe (CT) sought to clarify competences and to strengthen the subsidiarity principle first enacted as a general principle by the 1992 Maastricht Treaty. But the draft treaty still drew criticism, and after its rejection by the French and Dutch electorates, its prospects are unclear. Thus, Europeans are still in the middle of a constitutional debate over the alignment of competences between the national and the European level—maybe inevitably so in a project that calls for progressive integration and "ever closer Union."

Following other scholars, I here discuss the existing arrangements under the heading of "preemption."[1] Preemption doctrine is at the heart of the delineation of competences and the workings of the European model of federalism. While the term "preemption" is neither in the European treaties, that is most importantly the Treaty establishing the European Community as in force from 1 February 2003 as well as the Treaty on the European Union, nor used by the European Court of Justice (ECJ), misunderstandings are likely to arise not from the transposition of legal terms, but rather from an inadequate appreciation of the profound institutional differences between the United States and the European Union. Foremost among those differences is the central notion of federal supremacy.

Supremacy, European-Style

In contrast to the United States, the European Union does not have a "Supremacy Clause" as such. In fact, it was founded on international treaties that failed to declare clearly whether community law would enjoy supremacy among the member states. However, the ECJ decided very early that EC law is an autonomous legal order, supreme over the law of the member states. In *Costa v. ENEL* (1964), the seminal case, the ECJ construed community powers broadly by holding that community laws trump national laws, including national constitutional law.[2] A contrary holding, the ECJ argued, would risk the entire common market experiment.

The ECJ further strengthened the authority of community law by applying a doctrine of *direct effect* not only to regulations (as specified in Art. 249 EC) but also to other community acts, including directives under certain circumstances and provisions of the treaty itself. Departing from the public international law orientation of most treaties among states, the ECJ ruled that the European treaty system created a new legal order that gives rights and obligations not only to the state parties but also to individuals, without the nation-states' intervention. As early as 1963, the ECJ declared that individuals may be directly subject to all the provisions of the founding treaties that set out absolute conditions, are complete in themselves and self-contained in legal terms, and do not require further action on the part of the member states or community institutions in order to be complied with or acquire legal effect.[3] Most prominently, the four freedoms of the treaties—which guarantee the free movement of goods, persons, services, and capital—have direct effect. Other practically important principles with direct effect include equal pay for men and women (Art. 141 EC) and the general prohibition of discrimination (Art. 12 EC).[4]

This concept of supremacy, like its U.S. counterpart, allows the EU to preempt member state action that could conflict with a community measure, even if only indirectly. However, the European idea of supremacy differs from its U.S. equivalent in two crucial respects.[5]

First, the European Union combines features of a federal nation-state with features of an international organization, operating under international public law principles. The so-called "Kompetenz-Kompetenz" stays with the member states, meaning that they retain the authority to decide which legislative competences they want to confer on the European Union's institutions. Only through an intergovernmental conference (IGC) of the heads of state of the participating member states can the treaties be amended. Amendments enter into force after being ratified by all member states in accordance with their respective constitutional requirements.[6] In short, the creation of treaty or "primary" law follows international law principles. In contrast, the adoption of "secondary" legislation, or the creation of legal obligations by the European institutions, comes closer to the model of a traditional federal state. The Council of Ministers, whose members are dispatched by the member states, together with the European Parliament has the final responsibility for the adoption of most secondary legislation (some of it by qualified majority voting in the council, some of it still by unanimity). The interplay between primary and secondary law and their relationship with national law are crucial questions for European federalism. So long as unanimity voting prevails, otherwise unacceptable "preemption" seems acceptable. The shift to qualified majority voting in the Maastricht Treaty, which also signaled a move away from the international law principles of unanimous consent in secondary legislation, seemed to weaken the political-procedural safeguard. It was therefore counterbalanced by the introduction of the principle of "subsidiarity," which is discussed below.

Second, the union's federalism cannot easily be compared to America's "dual" federalism, where the federal government's power to legislate is generally accompanied by the power to enforce federal law directly against citizens. The EU follows a model of cooperative or "executive federalism,"[7] which emphasizes interconnections and interdependence among different levels of government and views the subordinate governments' authority to administer federal laws as an essential element of their autonomy.[8] In principle, executive and enforcement competences stay with the member states, which have to finance, implement, and apply European legislation in accordance with their respective constitutional rules, with due regard for the treaties, and subject to monitoring by the European Commission, the ECJ, and national courts. In other words, the EU assigns the implementation and application of "federal" norms to the lower levels and has no direct coercive power. Furthermore, the ECJ has no competence to invalidate national law and no jurisdiction to rule on the interpretation of national laws or regulations. Thus, unlike the U.S. Supreme Court, the ECJ does not rule directly on the validity of member state laws and cannot invalidate a member state measure as such. The ECJ can only supply the national court with a ruling on the interpretation of community law to enable that national court to resolve the legal problem before it. The national court must then interpret the national law in conformity with European law or not apply the law at all. Noncompliance with an ECJ ruling may carry fines and penalties.[9]

The different conception of federalism makes the exercise of supremacy and preemption under the European framework both more attenuated and potentially more intrusive than its U.S. equivalents. While European preemption lacks the immediate coercive force that attends to the exercise of congressional supremacy, it may carry with it affirmative obligations on the part of member states to carry EU measures into effect, a form of obligation that many American lawyers would associate with "commandeering" rather than preemption. "Violation" of EU law encompasses not only outright conflicts with EU regulations and the "frustration" of the EU's purposes through hostile national legislation (analogous to "obstacle preemption" in the United States); it also encompasses a failure to transpose an EU directive—a set of affirmative commands, unknown in the American federalism context—into national law through "transforming" or "implementing" legislation. These obligations flow from Art. 10 EC:

> Member States shall take all appropriate measures, whether general or particular, to ensure fulfilment of the obligations arising out of this Treaty or resulting from action taken by the institutions of the Community. They shall facilitate the achievement of the Community's tasks. They shall abstain from any measure which could jeopardise the attainment of the objectives of this Treaty.

National courts must tailor appropriate remedies if they find that EU law has been violated. In all events, national courts must ensure that the remedy provided is at least as generous as the remedy provided by an analogous national law. The remedy must be effective, irrespective of the remedy available for violation of the analogous provision of national law. The ECJ may determine whether the type of remedy available in the member states is adequate for community law purposes and may indicate as a matter of law that state measures of a certain kind or description run afoul of the EC.

In short, "commandeering" is perfectly admissible in the EU. It is even a basic principle, again on the theory that the member states participate directly *as states* in the EU law-making process and, moreover, enjoy a certain autonomy in administering and implementing EU norms. The adoption of the U.S. alternative of prohibiting commandeering in the EU would presuppose a total decoupling of the European level from the member state level and would entail the establishment of a functional EU administration in every member state.[10] It would also presuppose an EU power to tax, which it does not have now or, for political reasons, probably ever.

The Union's Powers

The notion of "preemption" in the United States is usually used for statutory law—as European lawyers say, the union's "secondary legislation." However, the questions of whether and how far the union's secondary legislation may preempt national law depend largely, though not exclusively, on primary law, that is, the treaty text. The intensity of European legislative action allowed depends on the range of the European competence as well as the legal instruments provided for in the treaties. Those, in turn, determine the preemption by secondary laws.

Every act of an EC institution needs a legal basis (enabling norm) in the treaties in order to be valid.[11] This principle of conferral (also known as the principle of attributed powers, *principe d'attribution*, or *Prinzip der begrenzten Einzelermächtigung*) is codified in Art. 5 (1) EC, a rough equivalent of the Tenth Amendment: "The Community shall act within the limits of the powers conferred upon it by this Treaty and of the objectives assigned to it therein." Theoretically, member states retain all residual competences, and a broadening of European competences is possible only by treaty amendment. In practice, however, the ECJ has been quite active in assigning—more diplomatically, in clarifying—competences in favor of the union.

The treaties usually do not empower the union as such but rather name one of its institutions (for example, "the Council shall adopt," "the Commission shall carry out" or "shall make recommendations," "the Council shall, on a proposal from the Commission . . . issue directives acting by a qualified majority"). No institution "is vested with the residual power to exercise a 'non-specified' vertical competence."[12] Moreover, under the so-called *Meroni* doctrine, the delegation of discretionary powers to institutions which are not fully legally responsible (that is, not named in the treaties) is prohibited.[13]

The original treaties generally conferred legislative competence upon the EC in terms of objectives to be attained and the means of doing so. Successive revisions of the treaties have replaced this method with precise definitions of the action to be taken by the community in certain areas, in some instances accompanied by specific exclusions of competence, but these distinctions are not clear-cut. In certain areas the union's legislative competence is defined both in terms of *objectives* (or functions) and *subject-matter*. There are functional competences with a cross-sectoral character, functional competences in a special policy field, and competences in a particular field without reference to functional elements. Competences based on EC objectives are particularly difficult to delineate, since the finality-driven structure of competences may broaden the scope of a field.[14] Neither the academic literature nor the case law presents a coherent and generally accepted system of competences.[15]

Art. 5 (2) EC distinguishes between exclusive and nonexclusive powers. The ECJ usually distinguishes exclusive from nonexclusive, or "shared," competences. It is not difficult, though, to draft a conceptual scheme that is both broader and more discriminating. At one extreme lie "negative" competences—that is, affirmative limits on the EU's powers. At the other extreme lie exclusive EU competences. In between lie nonexclusive powers, which can be separated into concurrent, parallel, and complementary competences.

Negative Competences. Negative competences encompass areas where the treaties (1) expressly exclude union competence or expressly recognize the competence of member states or (2) forbid the union or community to legislate (as opposed to using nonbinding instruments). They also include areas that are not referred to in the treaties and therefore, as a result of the principle of attribution of powers, are not within the competence of the EU/EC.

While the treaties contain no explicit prohibitions on the conferral of powers, some provisions are viewed as putting limits on the union's powers.[16] These clauses may be regarded as precautions against the EU's potential abuse of nonexclusive powers. On social policy, for example, Art. 137 (4) carves out pay, freedom of association, and the right to strike or impose lockouts. Similarly, there are harmonization prohibitions in fields where, in principle, the community has competence to act. For example, Art. 129 EC empowers the council, in a codecision procedure, to provide for incentive measures and promotion of cooperation between member states in the field of employment policy, while forbidding the harmonization of laws and regulations of the member states. Many other norms limit the powers of the community in detail.[17]

Exclusive Competences. Exclusive competences come in two forms: truly exclusive competences, where the competence *per se* excludes action of the member states, irrespective of whether the union has exercised its powers; and "latent exclusivity," where the exclusivity is created only by the activity of the union. This distinction between "primary" and "secondary" exclusivity matters because primary, truly exclusive competences are not subject to the subsidiarity principle, discussed below.

Primary exclusive competences authorize the community to act to block any legislative intervention by the member states. The treaties explicitly classify as an exclusive competence only monetary policy for the member states in the euro area.[18] Other exclusive competences, however, are commonly inferred either from the treaty text or from the ECJ's case law. One such competence is regulating fisheries, or more precisely, living marine resources in the zones covered by the treaty. Trade policy is to a wide extent also an exclusive competence, as is common customs tariff policy (Art. 26 EC). Furthermore, laws governing the European institutions fall undisputedly within the exclusive competence of the community, as these tasks by their very nature cannot be carried out by individual member states. The establishment of joint bodies (for example, the European Community Trademark Office) falls under exclusive competences if the subject-matter is within the frame of an exclusive competence. Elsewhere, identifying the areas in which the EC assigns exclusive powers to the community becomes more problematic. Not surprisingly, the most intensive debates over exclusive powers have been about foreign trade relations and the regulation of the internal market.

Secondary (or latent) exclusive powers are areas in which member states may legislate so long and insofar as the union has not legislated. They include agriculture and fisheries, excluding the conservation of marine biological resources; the environment; and transportation. Most important by far is the establishment and operation of the internal market (Art. 94, 95 EC), where it was much debated whether the internal market competence is of primary exclusivity. In principle, harmonization can be carried out only by the community. However, as long as the community has not fully exercised that competence, member states retain the capacity to legislate.

Harmonization of the internal market presents a clear parallel to the dormant Commerce Clause in the United States, especially with respect to the strong continuity between exclusivity doctrines and statutory preemption. European law on the four basic freedoms—that is, the elimination of barriers to the free movement of goods, persons, services, and capital—provides a good illustration. (I will here focus on the free movement of goods, but the principles hold also for the other freedoms.) Art. 23 EC requires member states to refrain from enacting or maintaining unjustifiable trade-impeding restrictions. By attributing direct effect to this provision, the ECJ enabled national courts to deny legal effect to member state measures containing such restrictions.

In the landmark ruling of *Cassis de Dijon* (1979),[19] the ECJ ruled that a product (in this case, the French black currant liqueur, "Cassis") sold lawfully in one member state may generally not be prohibited in another member state (in this case, Germany). Divergences from this so-called "principle of mutual recognition" are permitted only for overriding reasons in the public interest. *Cassis de Dijon* set an important precedent for future nontariff barriers to trade in goods (and to a lesser extent services). While member states may still decide on the degree of protection that they wish to afford to such legitimate public interests and on the way in which that protection is to be achieved, they may do so only within the limits set by the treaty and must, in particular, observe the principle of proportionality, which requires that the measures adopted be appropriate to secure the attainment of the objective they pursue and not go beyond what is necessary in order to attain it. However, in more recent decisions, the ECJ has sometimes tended to circumscribe the mutual recognition principle. Notably, in its *Keck* decision (1993), the ECJ distinguished between product-related rules and sales arrangements. Product-related rules continue to be subject to mutual recognition. In contrast, national rules on sales arrangements do not constitute an obstacle to trade as long as they apply to all traders without discrimination.[20]

Art. 94, 95 EC authorize the European legislator to enact "positive" legislation to facilitate the removal of nontariff barriers to trade. Generally, member states retain a safeguard competence if the implementation of the four freedoms endangers public health, the life of human beings and animals, or public safety. Nevertheless, in the broad realm of the internal market, the union may enact harmonizing laws in all policy fields unless the treaties specify an express limit or exception. Thus, the ECJ has decided that member states may not rely on safeguard competences to derogate from the four freedoms in areas where the EU has issued a harmonizing directive. In these cases, EU law is to be viewed as exhaustive, optimal, and therefore preemptive of national laws. For example, the ECJ declared that an EU measure on animal transport preempted a stricter national law on that same issue.[21] Where harmonization is fulfilled, member states may no longer evoke exemptions, and general preemption of an entire field is possible. If there is no harmonization or incomplete harmonization, the principle of mutual recognition holds.

Parallel Competences. Parallel competences, sometimes called "shared" or "cumulative" concurrent powers, allow the union and member states to exercise competences alongside one another. For the most part, such competences are found in areas where the levels of government—EU and member states—are not expected to be in opposition or conflict but rather reinforce each other. Usually the treaties speak of "complementing" member states' activities—for example, in employment policy, research and technological development, or industrial and development policy. The common foreign and security policy under the EU Treaty also falls in this category. In cases of conflict between rules of parallel competences (for example, when the union as well as the member states enact legislation containing rights and obligations for citizens), union law prevails. Thus, conflict preemption may significantly reduce the competences of member states even where general preemption of an entire field is not permitted. For example, national food laws that would impair the internal market in violation of Art. 28 EC (quantitative restrictions on imports) are prohibited, even though health is a shared competence. Likewise, conflicts of national law with secondary legislation are resolved in favor of union law. For example, a council directive obligating member states to foster gender equality in the labor market led to the change of the German Constitution so as to allow women into the military.[22]

A subset of parallel competences are those that allow the union to set minimum standards while allowing member states to take stricter measures. The most prominent examples are social policy, competition law, and especially environmental standards, where the delineation between minimum and total harmonization can be particularly difficult. Here again, the principle of primacy of union law holds. Parallel competences and minimum harmonization are a flexible way of integration: through the exclusion of field preemption as a hard constitutional constraint, they allow for regulatory competition on top of an EU floor.[23]

Complementary Competences. Complementary competences encompass the union's nonregulatory powers. They permit the union to supplement or support member states or to adopt measures of encouragement or coordination, while the primary power to adopt legislative rules remains in the hands of member states. Under normal circumstances, conflicts between member state law and union law cannot arise. The legal instruments used are usually decisions *sui generis* that are not addressed to particular persons and do not create any legal duties for citizens or for member states (although for governments, Art. 10 EC creates a general obligation to facilitate the achievements of the union's undertakings). Complementary competences are prominent in the areas of cultural policy, employment, education and vocational training, industrial policy, trans-European networks, research and technological development, and defense policy.

Apart from the difficulty of classifying particular competences as exclusive (or not), Europe has also encountered problems that broadly correspond to the perennial American debate over "implied" federal powers. The much-criticized "Subsidiary Competence" of Art. 308 EC—Europe's answer to the Necessary and Proper Clause[24]—allows the community to take the appropriate measures if that should prove necessary to attain one of the objectives of the EC Treaty. It is the sole competence norm where only an objective is needed in order to act, and it applies across area fields or policies, thus extending the competence potential of the union considerably. It can only be used by the council acting unanimously, thereby instituting a procedural safeguard. Art. 308 EC is not a treaty amendment norm and does not give the community "Kompetenz-Kompetenz," as it is not possible for community institutions to use powers for objectives that are not mentioned in the treaty. However, in the beginning of the communities, the European institutions used the norm extensively, without encountering resistance from the ECJ. With the expansion of explicit competences in the treaties, the use of Art. 308 EC has receded to some extent.

The community has also acquired implied powers under case law, now well established, to the effect that the community may adopt measures for which it is not explicitly empowered but without which an existing competence cannot be reasonably and appropriately used. This reasoning has been most important in the field of external trade policy. The court specified that EU member states were no longer allowed to adopt legislative measures or to independently conclude treaties with third countries, since the EC power was exclusive.[25] In the exclusive areas, the community has the power to enter into agreements with nonmember nations, which then become binding on both the community and the member states. However, the ECJ also held that certain competences concerning treaties were not exclusive.

The issue arose during the Uruguay round of the General Agreement on Tariffs and Trade (GATT) negotiations, which eventually led to the creation of the World Trade Organization. While the commission clearly had exclusive competence over certain aspects of the deal, most member states disputed the community's exclusive competence with respect to the General Agreement on Trade in Services (GATS) and the Agreement on Trade-Related Aspects of Intellectual Property Rights (TRIPs). The ECJ held that only those subjects in which the community had pursued total harmonization in the parallel internal fields fell under the EC's exclusive competence.[26] Under the ECJ's case law, the EC additionally possesses exclusive responsibility for external relations in those areas in which it has enacted secondary law.[27] Here, the exclusive external competence follows the latent exclusive internal competence as implied power.[28] The ECJ took the view that if a competence is to be found internally, it implies the equal range of competence with respect to external relations, even if that power is not explicitly assigned to the union.

Under this so-called *ERTA* principle, once the community adopts common rules, the member states no longer have the right, individually or collectively, to undertake obligations toward nonmember countries that affect those rules or alter their scope.[29] That holds not only where the community has achieved complete harmonization; it applies even in the absence of any express provision authorizing the community's institutions to negotiate with nonmember countries, where the common rules thus adopted could be "affected or altered."[30] The contours of that test have never been very clear. The court analyzes the scope of the relevant community legislation, either by using a quantitative approach (does secondary community law largely or entirely cover a certain subject matter?) or by using a formal test to determine whether a specific EC legislative act contains provisions relating to the treatment of non-EU nationals or authorization to negotiate with nonmember countries. In practice, the long-established quantitative approach has predominated.

Canons of Construction

As in the United States, much of the task of working out viable supremacy and preemption arrangements has fallen to the courts—in Europe, the ECJ. And in Europe, as in the United States, the interpretive canons have run in somewhat different directions. For the most part, the ECJ has extended— in much-criticized lines of decisions—the union's powers. However, principles of subsidiarity and proportionality—codified in the treaties—have exerted a gravitational pull in the opposite direction.

Given the treaty principle that nonenumerated powers stay with the member states, one would think that the burden of proof in questions of competences should in all events rest on the community in case of a legal conflict. Nevertheless, the Maastricht Treaty introduced subsidiarity as a justiciable principle along with a broadening of the union's competences and a further shift to qualified majority voting in the council. Community institutions are bound to observe subsidiarity and proportionality as general principles of decision.[31] For the member states, the principles constitute a judicially enforceable mechanism of self-defense against the risk that they are overruled in the council.[32] The principle, codified in Art. 5(2) EC, provides:

> In areas which do not fall within the exclusive competence, the Community shall take action, in accordance with the Principle of Subsidiarity, only if and in so far as the objectives of the proposed action cannot be sufficiently achieved by the Member States and can therefore, by reason of the scale or effect of the proposed action, be better achieved by the Community.

This language is not meant to reorganize the division of powers between the community and the member states. It operates only on the exercise of an already existing competence and, by its terms, applies only to nonexclusive competences. But as those powers predominate, the principle does affect the dividing line between the actual community powers and the residual powers of the member states.

Although the subsidiarity principle binds all European institutions, not merely the ECJ, much of the legal debate has focused on the Court. The ECJ has been presented with a variety of cases on the subject of subsidiarity, but only a few cases deal directly with the annulment of union law under Art. 5 (2) EC. Two seminal cases both held that the principle was not violated. In *United Kingdom v. Council* (1996), the United Kingdom sought annulment of parts of a directive containing minimum harmonization requirements for work time. The ECJ articulated a very limited and deferential scope of review: "[I]t is not the function of the court to review the expediency of measures adopted by the legislature. The review exercised must be . . . limited to the legality of the disputed measure."[33] In effect, the ECJ narrowed the practical significance of the subsidiarity principle to obvious violations and manifest error. The second case, *Federal Republic of Germany v. EP and Council* (1997), also dealt with minimum harmonization, this time concerning deposit guarantee schemes in a directive concerning the establishment of a Europe-wide market in financial services. The question was whether member states may require a stricter standard (which Germany had concerning deposit guarantee). Again, the ECJ deferred to the discretion of the union's law-making institutions.[34]

The proportionality principle complements the subsidiarity principle. It is codified in Art. 5 (3) EC, which requires that "any action by the Community shall not go beyond what is necessary to achieve the objectives of this Treaty." Unlike subsidiarity, the proportionality requirement applies to all EU competences, exclusive as well as nonexclusive. Proportionality had been well-accepted as a general principle of community law in the exercise of power vis-à-vis citizens;[35] Art. 5(3) extended it to the exercise of EU competences vis-à-vis member states. Where community institutions have a choice among several appropriate measures or instruments, recourse must be had to the least onerous, and the disadvantages caused must not be disproportionate to the aims pursued.

The ECJ usually follows a two-prong test. A community act that fails to satisfy either of those prongs must be ruled unproportional and void. The first test is the suitability of a community act, including the determination of a goal permitted by the treaties. The measure should be based on an empirical-prognostic evaluation of its likely effects. As with subsidiarity, however, the ECJ has been reluctant to declare an act invalid for a lack of suitability. It only examines whether the legislative intent of a community act was "obviously inappropriate for the realization of the desired objective."[36] The second test is the necessity of the act. If various suitable measures are available, "necessity" is determined by the least burdensome measure. The community legislator is not required to make use of a less efficient means. If a less burdensome measure, in principle, achieves the legislative intent but does not do so with the same level of certainty, the ECJ will sustain the more burdensome measure.[37] For the choice among equally suitable measures, the authorities are entitled to their own discretion and judgment.[38]

So far, the ECJ has never annulled a community measure on subsidiarity grounds. That has been explained by two factors. One factor is the general deference to the legislative powers of the union, as the principle is devoid of a clear legal concept and would need, for a proper assessment, some kind of in-depth social science prognosis which overburdens the capacity as well as the legitimacy of the court.[39] The second factor is the ECJ's political agenda, which is driven by the vision of integration.

Legal Instruments and Bases

For all its complexities, the American understanding of federal supremacy is, at its core, straightforward: any federal law, in whatever form and of whatever (lawful) provenance, trumps any state law in cases where the two conflict. The European understanding, in contrast, is highly sensitive both to the choice of the EU's legal instruments and to the specific legal basis on which any given act of legislation is presumed to rest. Art. 249 EC enumerates the standard legal instruments the community may use. They differ in their legal consequences and addressees, thereby creating different depths of intrusion into member states' sovereignty. For the purposes at hand, I put aside *decisions* (roughly, administrative acts addressed to particular member states or individuals) as well as nonbinding legal instruments, such as *recommendations*, *opinions*, and nonbinding instruments not foreseen in the treaty such as council resolutions and communications issued by the commission. I here focus on the legislative instruments that are of particular interest in the preemption context: *regulations* and *directives*.

Regulations are binding and directly applicable in all member states. They are of a general character and may be compared to ordinary national laws. Regulations are binding in their entirety, become part of the domestic national legal order of each country without needing transposing legislation, and are executed by national or state officials. Most union legislation takes the form of regulations.[40]

Directives are binding upon member states to which they are addressed as to the result to be achieved, but they leave the method and form of implementation to the member states. They entail an obligation to legislate on the part of the member states, which can be spelled out in detailed instructions. Directives usually set deadlines by which the member state needs to adopt national legislation or regulations to achieve the specified results. A national law transposing a directive must be interpreted, so far as possible, "in light of the wording and the purpose of the directive in order to achieve the result pursued by the latter."[41] Thus, when national courts apply domestic law, they are bound to interpret it, so far as possible, in the light of the wording and the purpose of the directive and in such a way as to achieve the desired result.[42] This obligation to interpret national law in conformity with community law concerns all provisions of national law, whether adopted before or after the directive in question.

In principle, directives are not directly applicable. Under some circumstances, however, unimplemented or inadequately implemented directives may have direct effect, at least against the defaulting state.[43] Community law requires the member states to make good damage caused to individuals through failure to transpose a directive, provided that three conditions are fulfilled. First, the purpose of the directive in question must be to grant rights to individuals. Second, it must be possible to identify the content of those rights on the basis of the provisions of the directive. Finally, there must be a causal link between the breach of the member state's obligation and the damage suffered.[44] An individual may essentially "leapfrog" national legislation and seek to rely upon the terms of the underlying directive. This option is a powerful tool in forcing states to uphold agreements made at the European level.

The founding treaties in some cases coupled enabling norms and legal instruments. Over time, however, competences and instruments have become more separated. The most prominent and important example is again the internal market. Art. 18 of the Single European Act of 1987 added Art. 100a EEC (now Art. 95 EC). Unlike the old Art. 100 EEC (now 94 EC), Art. 95 is not limited to directives but allows for all kind of measures to ensure the establishment and functioning of the internal market. Enabling norms requiring the use of a specific instrument are a largely anachronistic phenomenon. The general rule is that the empowered institution may choose the appropriate instrument itself. This gives large discretion to the European institutions, which in turn has affected the balance between union and national law.

At first sight, regulations seem to be the most intrusive legal instrument, as directives may leave member states more leeway and flexibility to adjust to national circumstances. Directives are usually used for harmonization (also called approximation), in principle leaving discretion as to how to achieve the goals of the directive.[45] Regulations, in contrast, are used to create uniformity, leaving no discretion to the member states. However, a regulation may be used for very narrow issues, while a directive may be either very detailed in its content (thus occupying a field) or used for minimum harmonization only, thus setting nothing but a floor of regulation. Instrument choice is subject to the principle of subsidiarity and proportionality: if a directive suffices, a regulation may not be used.

With respect to nonexclusive competences, supremacy and preemption arrangements depend crucially on the legal basis in primary law for any given act of EU legislation. The legal basis determines not only what legislative procedure must be used but also in some cases the instruments to be used and, even more important, which powers are reserved to the member states. Different legal bases thus mean different levels of intrusion into a member state's sovereignty.

It is settled case law that the choice of the legal basis for a measure must rest on objective factors that are amenable to judicial review. The only relevant factors are the aims and the content of the measure, that is, the wording of the act in question. The questions are essentially the following. First, under what circumstances may a measure rest on more than one legal basis? Second, may community legislators, in regulating several matters that cannot be brought under one single legal basis, incorporate those different matters in a single measure? Third, are the procedures and restrictions laid down in the different legal bases compatible?

As a rule, a measure should be based on a single legal basis in order to prevent a disruption of the institutional balance. By way of exception, if a measure simultaneously pursues several objectives that are inseparably linked without one being secondary and indirect in relation to the other, the measure may be founded on the corresponding, multiple legal bases.[46] Thus, the case law confers the necessary competence on the community legislature to base legislation on more than one article of the EC, provided that use of a legal basis is genuine.

Crucially, however, a cumulation of legal bases is barred when the adoption procedures set out for both legal bases are incompatible and may circumvent restrictions of one legal basis. In its seminal 2000 *Tobacco Advertising Judgment*, the ECJ for the first time struck down a European directive for lacking a legal basis.[47] The directive, which member states had to implement by July 30, 2001, banned all direct and indirect advertising of tobacco products and sponsorship of events. The proffered legal basis was primarily Art. 95 EC, which authorizes harmonizing legislation to promote the establishment and functioning of the internal market.[48] Germany alleged that the directive was not an attempt to remove obstacles to the free movement of goods, persons, services, and capital but rather public health legislation, which cannot be based on Art. 95 EC and is an area of regulation belonging to member states. In addition, because Art. 152 (4) EC expressly prohibits harmonization of public health laws, Germany argued that neither the EU Parliament nor the council had the authority to adopt the directive. The ECJ, which had theretofore actively expanded the power of the community legislature in areas where its competences were relatively weak, substantially agreed with Germany's arguments and annulled the directive.

Nevertheless, the ECJ left the door open for a new directive, should barriers to cross-border trade arise from tobacco advertising in periodicals and at sponsorship events. Not surprisingly, a few months after the ECJ's judgment, the commission drafted a new directive 2003/33/EC banning tobacco advertising for all printed publications, internet services, radio broadcasting, and sponsorship events with cross-border effects, explaining that "differences in national legislation" would probably pose unwanted "barriers to the free movement" of products and services. In some instances, the directive stated, such barriers had "already been noted." After Germany again filed a complaint for partial annulment of the new directive, Advocate General Philippe Léger found that press, radio, and other media are used ever more internationally and therefore Art. 95 EC can be used as a legal basis after all.[49] That was confirmed by the ECJ on December 12, 2006.

Some European legal scholars have argued that the tobacco advertising judgment signals an important shift in European federalism and has altered the balance of competences between the European Union and its member states.[50] That view gains support from another recent case in which the ECJ found that Art. 95 EC was not an appropriate legal basis for decisions by the commission as well as the council on the transfer of passenger flight data to the United States. That arrangement, the ECJ determined, was mainly concerned with public security and the activities of the state in areas of criminal law, thus falling outside the scope of Art. 95 EC.[51] In any case, the control of an appropriate legal basis has unquestionably proved a more effective tool to safeguard the member states' competences than the subsidiarity principle.

Preemption

As noted, primary law largely determines how far secondary legislation may preempt national law. The ECJ confirmed in *Simmenthal* (1978)[52] the supremacy of community legislation by holding that a judge of a member state cannot apply state law which conflicts with directly effective community law. The Court added that national legislatures are likewise precluded from enacting contrary law. In elaborating the general principles, the ECJ has developed an extensive jurisprudence on preemption. As in the United States, preemption analysis in Europe is more than a matter of simple statutory analysis; it is also a question of determining the purposes of the EU and national legislation and the level at which the national law can be deemed to frustrate EU purposes. While the doctrines are not always entirely clear, scholars have attempted to clarify the underlying principles. I here draw on that literature.[53]

Express Preemption. The easiest cases are to be found when there is a primary exclusive competence of the union: no preemption problems arise, as the EU competences explicitly and *ex ante* preclude member states from legislating. Express *saving* occurs when either the primary law prohibits harmonization of laws or when secondary legislation allows member states to preserve a specific national law or provides them with room for their own legislation. Sometimes directives leave specific options for the member states to implement EU objectives in different ways. As long as the member state stays within the given options of the directive, there is no case for preemption. In such (rare) cases of "optional harmonization," the directive provides that it shall be "without prejudice" to national law or that it does "not affect the rights of the Member States to lay down requirements." Thus, certain community legislation allows member states to derogate from community requirements, leaving room for flexibility. For example, a 2005 directive on the recognition of professional qualifications permits several derogations.[54] In the case of minimum harmonization, member states are allowed to deviate from the floor of community legislation.

Implied Preemption. In the field of nonexclusive competences, express preemption may expressly forbid certain member states' legislation or expressly state that the EU measure is exclusive or exhaustive. Generally, though, secondary legislation is not very direct on this issue and contains only provisions relating to the intended effect on member state law, which are framed in terms of affirmative obligations of the member states ("Member States shall ensure. . . ."). This kind of nonexpress or implied preemption is the most difficult field.

The ECJ implies *field preemption* when secondary legislation creates a comprehensive and exhaustive system of law that leaves no room for enacting national law.[55] Secondary legislation may address a field or a sector so exhaustively that the community has left no room for member states to legislate, regardless of whether those measures are contrary to or obstruct the objectives of the community legislation. (Such field preemption may occur in the field of concurrent competences but not in the field of parallel or complementary competences.) "[O]nce the Community has . . . legislated for the establishment of the common organization of the market in a given sector, member states are under an obligation to refrain from taking any measure which might undermine or create exceptions to it."[56] Agricultural policy is a prominent area of field occupation. Here, the court held that "it is one of the fundamental characteristics of a common organization of the market that in the sectors concerned the Member States can no longer take action through national provisions adopted unilaterally. Their legislative competence can only be residual; it is limited to situations which are not governed by the community rules and to cases where those rules expressly give them power to act."[57] Whether or not a member state may exercise its residual legislative competence depends on whether the common organization of the market is intended to establish an exhaustive scheme of regulation.

Still more difficult is the question of *obstacle preemption*. Often, the ECJ examines first whether or not EU legislation covers the same ground as the member states' law. But even if national law addresses a different subject-matter from the secondary legislation, other legal factors, especially aims and effects, may still trigger preemption. The ECJ initially compares the aim of the secondary legislation with the aim of national law. If the national legislation has a different and directly conflicting aim, the national legislation cannot be upheld. Indirect interference with community legislation raises yet more difficult questions, especially where the treaty prescribes a domain for future community action. The subsidiarity test can assist in this determination by providing a presumptive rule which identifies the boundaries of possible member state interference.

Despite Art. 5 (1) EC, the court has stated on numerous occasions that certain areas, although in principle within the exclusive power of the member states, may still be preempted if a competence of the union is affected, especially in the realm of the internal market.[58] Here, the ECJ determines whether the operation or effects of national law obstructs union objectives, irrespective of whether the matter has been dealt with exhaustively or not.[59] Direct conflicts usually do not arise because member states do not enact directly conflicting rules, preferring to try to circumvent community legislation by adding limiting conditions to harmonizing directives.[60] That could be the case, for example, in product safety harmonization, when member states add in their transformational law certain product requirements. If the harmonizing directive is sufficiently clear on what product requirements are sufficient, the conflict is clearly solved in favor of the directive. In other words, the European legislation is viewed as an optimum rather than as a minimum.[61] The case law suggests that the prohibition on adopting prejudicial or conflicting measures also covers measures outside the scope of the rules on market organization. The reason for extending the scope of the prohibition is to preserve the effectiveness of community law. Thus, the community's concurrent powers preclude the member states from adopting measures which infringe the latent exclusive competence of the community even if the national measures do not relate directly to the EU policy.[62]

Conclusion

In the European Union (as in the United States) the courts—foremost, the ECJ—have played a significant role in the construction of an integrated internal market. Primary law and especially the four freedoms of the internal market have a deregulating effect on the member states and hinder national interest groups from rent-seeking. In seizing upon these provisions and giving direct—and often preemptive—effect to primary and secondary law, the ECJ has often fostered a market preserving federalism.[63] In contrast, treaty amendments that assigned more competences to the EC (by consent of all member states), as well as harmonizing measures by EU legislators, may seem to have had largely stultifying, centralizing effects. But this libertarian dichotomy is far too simplistic.

For one thing, the centralizing tendencies have been nuanced, differentiated, and at times ambivalent. Environmental policy, for example, started off in 1972 on the basis of Art. 308 EC which, though based on unanimity voting, contained no express savings for the member states. Now, the policy is based on Art. 174 EC et seq., which explicitly allow an "opt-up" of the member states and which place a constitutional limit on the possibility of field preemption. Similarly, when the Single European Act enhanced European competences, express language of nonpreemption was introduced into the treaty for the first time. And while the Maastricht Treaty did not introduce similar preemption limits or a general presumption against pre-emption, it did establish the generalized (though not very effective) princi-ple of subsidiarity as a safeguard against union usurpation of powers.

Moreover, in the EU as in the United States, the construction of a com-mon market has demanded a removal not only of outright tariffs but also of nontariff barriers to trade. There is more than one way to skin that cat. National treatment—that is, nondiscrimination, the basic principle of the dormant Commerce Clause—is one means. Mutual recognition—the ECJ's *Cassis de Dijon* principle—is another, stronger means of market integration. But mutual recognition often presupposes a great deal of trust in the stan-dards and legal systems of the other member states. In the area of financial services, for example, a heavily regulated area of economic activity, this became very clear in the debate over the EC's so-called Financial Services Action Plan (2001) of the European community. That plan set out the frame-work for the construction of the still largely divided market of financial serv-ices. A prerequisite for the so-called single license (European passport), which allows a financial services provider to operate in the whole market through a single license issued in one member state, was the minimum harmonization of supervisory standards. Similar legislation was required concerning the mutual recognition requirements of professionals. The European arrest war-rant provides a third example: the German Federal Constitutional Court invalidated the national law transforming the council's framework decision—*inter alia*, on the grounds that the German legislature had failed to ensure ade-quate correspondence between Germany's rule-of-law principles and the standards of member states that would issue the arrest warrant.[64] In sensitive policy areas, mutual recognition without some safeguards in the form of min-imum harmonization is not easily feasible.

Preemption is a two-edged sword. It is difficult to draw a clear line between protectionist harmonization and harmonization that attempts to remove hindrances to the internal market, and clearly, the EU is not free from protectionist harmonization and superfluous centralization—no more so than the United States. But the European member states continue to be separated not only by high language barriers and maybe cultural barriers, but also by national laws. Market integration cannot be the work of the ECJ alone, and EU legislation has done quite a bit to facilitate the process.

Notes

*Thanks to Michael Greve and Jürgen Bast for very helpful comments.

1. Eugene Daniel Cross, *Preemption of Member State Law in the European Economic Community: A Framework for Analysis*, 29 Common Market L. Rev. 447 (1992), has applied the U.S. doctrine most systematically to European law.

2. "The transfer by states from their domestic legal systems to the Community legal system of rights and obligations arising under the Treaty carries with it a permanent limitation of their sovereign rights, against which a subsequent unilateral act incompatible with the concept of the Community cannot prevail." *Case 6/64, Costa v. ENEL*, [1964] E.C.R. 585. See also Case 11/70, *Internationale Handelsgesellschaft mbH v. Einfuhrund Vorratsstelle für Getreide und Futtermittel* [1970] E.C.R. 1125. For a critical view, see Paul Kirchhof, *The Balance of Powers Between National and European Institutions*, 5 Eur. L. J. 225 (1999).

3. Case 26/62, Algemene Transport-en Expedetie Onderneming van Gend en Loos NV [1963] E.C.R. 1, at para. 13: "Art. 12 must be interpreted as producing direct effects. . . ."

4. The direct effect plays vertically between citizen and state, but only to the benefit of the citizen. (Case 80/86 Kolpinghuis Nijmegen [1987] E.C.R. 3969; Case 374/85 Oscar Traen and Others [1987] E.C.R. 2141). The horizontal effect between citizens is disputed. The ECJ denied horizontal effect, see Case 152/84 Marshall [1986] E.C.R. 723, at para. 48, concerning a directive on gender equality. See also Case C-91/92, Faccini Dori [1994] E.C.R. I 3325, at para. 24. For a discussion on horizontal effects, see Takis Tridimas, *Horizontal Effect of Directives: A Missed Opportunity?* 19 Eur. L. Rev. 621 (1994). For a discussion on "incidental effect" of unimplemented directives against private parties, see Michael Dougan, *The "Disguised" Vertical Direct Effect of Directives?* 59 Cambridge L. J. 586 (2000).

5. For a discussion, see Ingolf Pernice, *The Framework Revisited: Constitutional, Federal and Subsidiarity Issues*, 2 Col. J. of Eur. L. 403 (1996).

6. See Art. 48 EU. Only rarely do the treaties allow for autonomous amendment (see, for example, Art. 213 (1) (2) EC concerning the numbers of the members of the commission). The CT, Art. IV-444, allows a transition from the unanimity requirement in the council for secondary legislation in Part III CT to a qualified majority voting, if the council so decides unanimously. Art. IV-445 (3) CT allows for a simplified treaty amendment procedure of Part III, provided that it does not increase the union's vertical competences vis-à-vis member states.

7. See Philipp Dann, Parlamente im Exekutivföderalismus (Berlin, Springer, 2004).

8. For an extensive comparative discussion, see Kalypso Nicolaidis and Robert Howse, eds., *The Federal Vision: Legitimacy and Levels of Governance in the United States and the European Union* (Oxford, Oxford University Press, 2001).

See also George A. Bermann, *Taking Subsidiarity Seriously: Federalism in the European Community and the United States*, 94 Col. L. Rev. 331 (1994); Pernice, *The Framework Revisited*, *supra* note 5; Armin von Bogdandy and Jürgen Bast, "The Vertical Order of Competences," in *Principles of European Constitutional Law*, eds. Armin von Bogdandy and Jürgen Bast (2006) 344; Franz C. Mayer, *Die drei Dimensionen der Europäischen Kompetenzdebatte*, 61 ZaöRV 577, 587 et seq. (2001). Justice Stephen Breyer has rightly emphasized the administrative dimension of European federalism. See *Printz v. United States*, 521 U.S. 898, 976 (1997) (Breyer, J., diss.).

9. The only sanctioning device is Art. 228 EC, which can impose fines on non-complying member states. The ECJ used that device as a penalty in case of future noncompliance for the first time only recently in Case C 304/02 *Commission v. France* [2005] E.C.R. I 6263, where the ECJ found a continuing breach of obligations and noncompliance with EU law and imposed not only a lump sum payment but also a penalty for future noncompliance with the common fisheries policies.

10. Franz C. Mayer, "Competences—Reloaded? The Vertical Division of Powers in the EU after the New European Constitution," in *Altneuland: The EU Constitution in a Contextual Perspective*, eds. Joseph H.H. Weiler and Christopher L. Eisgruber (Jean Monnet Working Paper 5/04, NYU School of Law, 2004), 498 http://www.jeanmon netprogram.org/papers/04/040501-16.html (accessed 1 March 2007).

11. The treaties contain no express definition or catalogue of powers either in the EC or formed by the ECJ; instead the powers are found scattered over the treaties.

12. Bogdandy & Bast, "The Vertical Order," *supra* note 8 at 344.

13. See Case 9/56 *Meroni v. High Authority*, [1957/8] E.C.R. 133 et seq. and 157 et seq. For a discussion, see Giandomenico Majone, *The Commission Debates the Delegation Problem*, 4 Cahiers Européens de Science Po (2001), available at http://www.portedeurope.org/publications/cahiers/cahier_4_2001.pdf; Alexander Somek, *On Delegation*, 23 Oxford J. of L. Studies 703 (2003). It is often assumed this doctrine is to be viewed as a nondelegation doctrine and is thus the main legal obstacle to the delegation of rulemaking powers to European agencies.

14. Hans D. Jarass, *Die Kompetenzverteilung zwischen der Europäischen Gemeinschaft und den Mitgliedstaaten*, 121 Archiv des öffentlichen Rechts 173, 180 (1996). In contrast, Ingolf Pernice, *Kompetenzabgrenzung im europäischen Verfassungsverbund*, 55 Juristenzeitung 866, 872 (2000), views the finality structure as competence-limiting in comparison with the list of area fields. Christiane Trüe, *Das System der EU-Kompetenzen vor und nach dem Entwurf eines Europäischen Verfassungsvertrags*, 54 Zeitschrift für ausländisches öffentliches Recht und Völkerrecht 391, 398 (2004) clarifies that objectives may limit area fields (such as concerning common trade policy) but may also extend competences, as the objectives in Art. 2 EC potentially cover all fields. Bogdandy & Bast, "The Vertical Order," *supra* note 8 at 342 find that "the derivation of competences from general goals . . . does not respect the principle of conferral."

15. For a critical view of the competences "mess," see Peter Orebech, *The EU Competency Confusion: Limits, "Extension Mechanism," Split Power, Subsidiarity, and "Institutional Clashes."* 13 J. of Transn'l L. & Pol. 99 (2003).

16. Mayer, "Die drei Dimensionen der Europäischen Kompetenzdebatte," *supra* note 8 at 588 et seq.; Bogdandy & Bast, "The Vertical Order," *supra* note 8 at 346.

17. For a list, see Mayer, "Die drei Dimensionen der Europäischen Kompetenzdebatte," *supra* note 8, who understands negative competences broadly. He also cites the respect for identities of the member states (Art. 6 (3) EU).

18. Art. I-13 CT lists as exclusive competences (1) customs union; (2) the establishing of the competition rules necessary for the functioning of the internal market; (3) monetary policy for the member states whose currency is the euro; (4) the conservation of marine biological resources under the common fisheries policy; (5) common commercial policy. The union shall also have exclusive competence for the conclusion of an international agreement when its conclusion is provided for in a legislative act of the union or is necessary to enable the union to exercise its internal competence or insofar as its conclusion may affect common rules or alter their scope. This provision substantially mirrors the status quo.

19. Case 120/78, *Rewe-Zentrale AG v. Bundesmonopolverwaltung für Branntwein* [1979] E.C.R. 649 (Cassis de Dijon). This decision modified the stricter formula of Case 8/74, *Procureur du Roi v. Dassonville* [1974] E.C.R. 837, 852, where the ECJ held that "[a]ll trading rules enacted by Member States which are capable of hindering, directly or indirectly, actually or potentially, intra-Community trade are to be considered as measures having an effect equivalent to quantitative restrictions."

20. Joined Cases C-266 and 267/91, Criminal proceedings against Bernard Keck and Daniel Mithouard [1993] ECR I-6097.

21. See Case C-350/97 *Wilfried Monsees v. Unabhängiger Verwaltungssenat für Kärnten* [1999] E.C.R. I-02921; Case C-5/94 *The Queen v. MAFF ex parte Hedley Lomas* [1996] E.C.R. I-2553, at para. 18.

22. Case C-285/98 *Tanja Kreil v. Germany* [2000] E.C.R. I-69; Council Directive 76/207/EEC.

23. For a discussion, see Robert Schütze, *Co-operative Federalism Constitutionalised: The Emergence of Complementary Competences in the EC Legal Order*, 31 Eur. L. Rev. 167, 174 et seq. (2006).

24. See Mayer, "Competences—Reloaded," *supra* note 10 at 7; Mayer, "Die drei Dimensionen der Europäischen Kompetenzdebatte," *supra* note 8 at 586.

25. See Opinion 1/75 [1975] E.C.R. 1355 (Local Cost Standard).

26. Opinion 1/94, WTO-Agreement [1994] E.C.R. I-5267. For details, see Piet Eeckhout, *External Relations of the European Union* (Oxford: Oxford University Press, 2004), 9–100.

27. Case 22/70 *Commission v. Council* [1971] E.C.R. 263 (ERTA; sometimes named as AETR).

28. For details, see Eeckhout, *External Relations*, *supra* note 26 at 58 et seq. The Nice Treaty gave the competence to the EC to negotiate and conclude agreements insofar as these were not already covered by 133 EC but included a sectoral carve-out for sensitive issues as cultural and audiovisual services, educational services, and social and human health services. In other areas individual member states may enter into international agreements that are not already covered by community legislation or the subject of community action.

29. Case 22/70, *supra* note 27 at paras. 16–18, 22.

30. See Case C-466/98 *Commission v. United Kingdom* [2002] ECR I-9427 (and the other cases concerning the "Open Sky") and especially the Advocate General Opinion, at para. 67: "I concur with the commission that the ERTA judgment is not confined to precluding the Member States from undertaking international obligations that are in conflict with common rules, especially as such conduct would in itself constitute a separate breach of Community law, which could be held unlawful even without regard to ERTA. What the ERTA judgment requires of Member States, and in clear terms, is not to assume obligations which may even merely affect the common rules."

31. See The Principle of Subsidiarity, Communication of the Commission to the Council and the EP, Parl. Eur. Annex Doc. SEC (92) 10. The Treaty of Amsterdam has as annex the protocol on the application of the principles of subsidiarity and proportionality, which gives guidance to the institutions on how they have to apply the principles. There is extensive literature on that principle, see, *e.g.*, Bermann, *Taking Subsidiarity Seriously*, *supra* note 8; Koen Lenaerts, *Subsidiarity and Community Competence in the Field of Education*, 1 Col. J. of Eur. L. 1 (1995); Pernice, *The Framework Revisited*, *supra* note 5; Christian Kirchner, *Competence Catalogues and the Principle of Subsidiarity in a European Constitution*, 8 Const. Political Econ. 71 (1997); Reimer von Borries & Malte Hauschild, *Implementing the Subsidiarity Principle*, 5 Col. J. of Eur. L. 369 (1999); Christoph Henkel, *The Allocation of Powers in the European Union: A Closer Look at the Principle of Subsidiarity*, 20 Berk. J. of Int'l L. 359 (2002); Antonio Estella, *The EU Principle of Subsidiarity and Its Critique* (Oxford: Oxford University Press, 2003); Orebech, *The EU Competency Confusion*, *supra* note 15.

32. Cross, *Preemption of Member State Law*, *supra* note 1 at 470. Henkel, *The Allocation of Powers*, *supra* note 31 at 368; Manfred Zuleeg, "Justiziabilität des Subsidiaritätsprinzips," in *Subsidiarität: Idee und Wirklichkeit: Zur Reichweite eines Prinzips in Deutschland und Europa*, eds. Knut Wolfgang Nörr and Thomas Oppermann (Tübingen: Siebeck/Mohr, 1997), 185–204.

33. Case 84/94, *United Kingdom of Great Britain and Northern Ireland v. Council* [1996] E.C.R. I-5755, at para. 23.

34. Case C-233/94, *Germany v. EP and Council* [1997] E.C.R. I-2405 (action under Art. 230 EC).

35. Henkel, *The Allocation of Powers*, *supra* note 31 at 374, compares the proportionality principle with the rational basis test developed in accordance with equal protection and the Fourteenth Amendment in the case law of the U.S. Supreme Court. See also

Rudolf Streinz, *Europarecht* (Heidelberg, C.F. Müller, 2003), 65. See Bermann, *Taking Subsidiarity Seriously*, supra note 8 at 386 et seq. for a slighty different understanding.

36. Case 40/72 *I. Schroeder KG v. Germany* [1973] E.C.R. 125, 142. See also Case 256/90 *Mignini SpA v. Azienda di Stato per gli Interventinel Mercato Agricolo* (AIMA) [1992] E.C.R. I-2651; Case 265/87 *Schräder HS Kraftfutter GmbH & Co. KG v. Hauptzollamt Gronau* [1989] E.C.R. 2237; Joined Cases 279, 280, 285, and 286/84 *Walter Rau Lebensmittelwerke and Others v. Commission* [1987] E.C.R. 1069.

37. See Case C-55/94 *Reinhard Gebhard v. Consiglio dell'Ordine degli Avvocati e Procuratori di Milano* [1995] E.C.R. I-4165.

38. Here again, the court showed its deference to the legislators, see Case 280/93, *Germany v. Council* [1994] E.C.R. I-4973. Judicial review of the exercise of discretion is "thereby limited to the examination of whether it has been vitiated by manifest error or misuse of powers, or whether the institution concerned has manifestly exceeded the limits of its discretion." See also Henkel, *The Allocation of Powers*, supra note 31 at 376.

39. Bermann, *Taking Subsidiarity Seriously*, supra note 8 at 378; Henkel, *The Allocation of Powers*, supra note 31 at 369 ("[T]he adverb "sufficiently" illustrates the emphasis on effectiveness. However, it is highly questionable whether the determination of effectiveness in this context is justiciable. Instead, the determination of effectiveness is a political question to be answered by the legislature.") If ever enacted, the CT would introduce a major innovation by suggesting that the national parliaments should be directly involved in monitoring the proper application of the subsidiarity principle, thereby taking a procedural way of guarding subsidiarity (early warning system). Before the European legislative procedure per se is initiated, every national parliament would have six weeks in which to give a reasoned opinion as to whether the proposed legislation is in accordance with the principle of subsidiarity. A challenge by a third of the national parliaments (in matters of home affairs or justice, only a quarter) would require the commission to review its proposal and to provide reasons if it decides to maintain the proposal. According to the protocol on the application of the principles of subsidiarity and proportionality, the ECJ would have jurisdiction to hear actions by member states on behalf of their national parliaments, claiming infringement of the principle of subsidiarity by a legislative act, brought in accordance with the rules laid down in Art. III-365 CT (now Art. 230 EC). The Committee of the Regions would also have standing in such matters. These new provisions would allow national parliaments to establish political control and to ensure that the commission does not take initiatives for which it is not competent while taking care not to prejudice the commission's right of initiative or to slow down the legislative process. Nevertheless, it is problematic that the ECJ is still the ultimate judge on the principle of subsidiarity, given the court's deference to the legislator. A more effective solution would have been to give a certain number of national parliaments a veto.

40. Of the legal instruments listed in Art. 249 EC, 21.4 percent are regulations, 8.8 percent are directives, 33.8 percent are decisions, 3.8 percent are recommendations, and 1.4 percent are opinions. For statistics and case law, see Armin von Bogdandy,

Jürgen Bast, & Felix Arndt, *Handlungsformen im Unionsrecht. Empirische Analysen und dogmatische Strukturen in einem vermeindlichen Dschungel*, 62 Zeitschrift für ausländisches öffentliches Recht und Völkerrecht 77 (2002). The remainder consists of instruments (so-called acts *sui generis*) that are not listed in Art. 249 EC, such as the addressee-less decision (*Beschluss*) or communications from the commission. For an overview, see Jürgen Bast, "On the Grammar of EU Law: Legal Instruments" (Jean Monnet Working Paper No. 9/03, NYU School of Law, 2003), http://www.jeanmon netprogram.org/papers/03/030901-05.html (accessed 1 March 2007); Jürgen Bast, *Grundbegriffe der Handlungsformen der EU* (Berlin: Springer, 2006). On the development of the use of "soft law" in the community, see David M. Trubek, Patrick Cottrell, and Mark Nance, "'Soft Law,' 'Hard Law,' and European Integration: Toward a Theory of Hybridity," in (Jean Monnet Working Paper No. 2/05, NYU School of Law, 2005), http://www.jeanmonnetprogram.org/papers/05/050201.html (accessed 1 March 2007).

41. Case C-106/89, *Marleasing SA v. La Comercial Internacional de Alimentación SA*, [1990] E.C.R. I-4135, at para. 8. See also Paul P. Craig, *Directives: Direct Effect, Indirect Effect and the Construction of National Legislation*, 22 Eur. L. Rev. 519 (1997).

42. See Joined Cases C-397/01 to C-403/01 *Pfeiffer and Others* [2004] E.C.R. I-8835, at para. 113, and the case law cited.

43. See Case 41/74 Van Duyn [1974] E.C.R. 1337.

44. Joined Cases C-6/90 and C-9/90, Francovich [1991] E.C.R. I-5357, at para. 39; Case C-91/92 Paola Faccini Dori [1994] E.C.R. I-3325, at para. 27.

45. National measures that alter the scope or supplement a regulation's provisions are not permissible. See Bast, "Legal Instruments," *supra* note 40 at 379 with further references.

46. Case 165/87 *Commission v. Council* [1988] E.C.R. 5545.

47. Case C-376/98 *Germany v. EP and Council* [2000] E.C.R. I-8419, followed by Case C 491/01 (BAT), at para. 94. This marks also the growing assertiveness of the ECJ vis-à-vis the council; see Bogdandy & Bast, *The Vertical Order, supra* note 8 at 345.

48. Art. 95 (1) EC: "The Council shall . . . adopt the measures for the approximation of the provisions laid down by law, regulation or administrative action in Member States which have as their object the establishment and functioning of the internal market."

49. Opinion of Advocate General Léger delivered on June 13, 2006, Case C-380/03 *Germany v. EP and Council*. At this writing, the case is awaiting decision. The ECJ typically follows the advocate's opinions.

50. See, *e.g.*, Werner Schroeder, *Vom Brüsseler Kampf gegen den Tabakrauch - 2. Teil*, 16 Europäische Zeitschrift für Wirtschaftsrecht, 489 (2001); Tamara K.Hervey, *Community and National Competence in Health after Tobacco Advertising*, 38 Common Market L. Rev. 1421 (2001). For an extensive discussion, see Fernanda Nicola & Fabio Marchetti, *Constitutionalizing Tobacco: The Ambivalence of European Federalism*, 46 Harv. Int'l L. J. 507 (2005).

51. Joined Cases C-317/04 and C-318/04, *EP v. Council* and *EP v. Commission* [2006] ECR I 0000.

52. Case 106/77, *Administrazione delle Finanze dello Stato v. Simmenthal S.p.A.* [1978] E.C.R. 629.

53. See especially M. Waelbroeck, "The Emergent Doctrine of Community Pre-emption: Consent and Re-delegation," in *Courts and Free Markets: Perspectives from the United States and Europe*, eds. Terrance Sandalow and Eric Stein (1982), 548–80; Cross, *Preemption of Member State Law, supra* note 1; Martin Hession & Richard Macrory, *The Legal Framework of European Community Participation in International Environmental Agreements*, 2 New Eur. L. Rev. 59 (1994); Andreas Furrer, "The Principle of Pre-emption in European Union Law," in *Sources and Categories of European Union Law*, ed. Gerd Winter (Baden-Baden: Nomos, 1996), 521; Trüe, *Das System der EU-Kompetenzen vor und nach dem Entwurf eines Europäischen Verfassungsvertrags, supra* note 15.

54. Directive 2005/36/EC of the EP and of the council of September 7, 2005. For an additional example, see Regulation (EC) No 336/2006 of the EP and of the council of February 15, 2006, on the implementation of the International Safety Management Code within the Community, at preamble consideration 10: "If a Member State con-siders it difficult in practice for companies to comply with specific provisions of Part A of the ISM Code for certain ships or categories of ships exclusively engaged on domestic voyages in that Member State, it may derogate wholly or partly from those provisions by imposing measures ensuring equivalent achievement of the objectives of the Code. It may, for such ships and companies, establish alternative certification and verification procedures."

55. Case 264/86 *France v. Commission* [1988] E.C.R. 973.

56. Case 83/78 Redmond [1978] E.C.R. 2347, at para, 56. See also Case 51/74 Van der Hulst [1975] E.C.R. 79. See also Case 215/87 Schumacher [1989] E.C.R. 617, at para. 15; Case C-369/88 Delattre [1991] E.C.R. I-1487, at para. 48; Case C-347/89 Eurim-Pharm [1991] E.C.R. I-1747, at para. 26; Case C-62/90 *Commission v. Germany* [1992] E.C.R. I-2575, at para. 10; Case C-317/92 *Commission v. Germany* [1994] E.C.R. I-2039, at para. 14; Case C-320/93 Ortscheit [1994] E.C.R. I-5243, at para. 14. See also Case 247/84 Motte [1985] E.C.R. 3887, at para. 16; Case C-42/90 Bellon [1990] E.C.R. I-4863, at para. 10.

57. Case 48/85 *Commission v. Germany* [1986] E.C.R. 2549, at para. 12. See also Case 154/77 *Procureur du Roi v. Dechmann* [1978] E.C.R. 1573.

58. See, *e.g.*, concerning criminal law and criminal procedure law, Case C-274/96 Bickel and Others [1998] E.C.R. I-7637, at para. 17. Concerning the organization of the educational system and educational policy, see Case 9/74 Casagrande [1974] E.C.R. 773; Case 293/83 Gravier [1985] E.C.R. 593. Concerning the structure of social security systems, see Case C-229/89 *Commission v. Belgium* [1991] E.C.R. I-2205; Case C-317/93 Nolte [1995] E.C.R. I-4625; Case C-120/95 Decker [1998] E.C.R. I-1831. Concerning direct taxes, see Case C-107/94 Asscher [1996] E.C.R. I-3089. Concerning membership of religious or philosophical associations, see Case 196/87 Steymann [1988] E.C.R. 6159. Concerning rules of administrative and judicial proce-dure, see Case 33/76 REWE Zentralfinanz [1976] E.C.R. 1989; Case C-312/93

Peterbroeck and Others [1995] E.C.R. I-4599; Joined Cases C-430/93 and C-431/93 Van Schijndel and van Veen [1995] E.C.R. I-4705.

59. Case 218/85 *Cerafel v. Le Campion* [1986] E.C.R. 3513, at para. 13. See also judgments in Case C-27/96 *Danisco Sugar v. Allmänna Ombudet* [1997] E.C.R. I-6653, at para. 24; Case C-1/96 Compassion in World Farming [1998] E.C.R. I-1251, at para. 41; Case C-507/99 Denkavit [2002] E.C.R. I-169, at para. 32; Case C-332/00 *Belgium v. Commission* [2002] E.C.R. I-3609, at para. 29.

60. Cross, *Preemption of Member State Law*, *supra* note 1 at 464.

61. See, *e.g.*, Case 60/86 *Commission v. United Kingdom* [1988] E.C.R. 3921, where the United Kingdom prohibited cars driving without the so-called Dim-Dip Car Lights for security reasons even though the Council Directive 76/756/EEC on lighting and light-signaling devices on motor vehicles did not contain this requirement.

62. See, *e.g.*, Case 31/74 Galli [1975] E.C.R. 47; Case 51/74 *Van der Hulst's v. Prodshap voor Siergewassen* [1975] E.C.R. 79; Case 65/75 Tasca [1976] E.C.R. 291; Joined Cases 88/75 to 90/75 SADAM [1976] E.C.R. 323; Case 154/77 Dechmann [1978] E.C.R. 1573; Case 137/00 Milk Marque and National Farmers' Union [2004] E.C.R. 410.

63. Barry R.Weingast, *The Economic Role of Political Institutions: Market-Preserving Federalism and Economic Growth*, 11 J. of L., Econ. & Org. 1 (1995).

64. Judgment of July 18, 2005, 2 BvR 2236/04.

Conclusion:
Preemption Doctrine and Its Limits

Richard A. Epstein and Michael S. Greve

Our introduction to this volume stressed the historical and constitutional issues that governed the troubled interaction between federal and state law. The key feature of the earlier constitutional system was its commitment to a division between federal and state activities, which, while not airtight, was nonetheless quite suspicious of the exercise of concurrent powers over any particular issue. The inexorable expansion of the commerce power during the New Deal period brought that formative era to a close. The "dual" system of parallel powers gave way to a system of concurrent jurisdiction, where the federal government may decide whether to rule the roost alone or to share power with the states. So long as Congress makes its intentions clear, it can displace the states, either in whole or part, for any reason, except in some marginal cases.[1]

Modern preemption doctrine—the preemption doctrine of the New Deal—is a self-conscious attempt to counter the centralizing effects of a boundless Commerce Clause with a "presumption against preemption." In Madison's universe, the union's powers were federal in scope—meaning limited and enumerated—but national in their operation. When the New Deal rendered the central government's powers effectively national in scope, the Court responded with what legal theorists now call a "translation" or a "compensating adjustment": it made those powers less than fully national in their operation.[2] The stated purpose of this maneuver—the presumption against preemption, especially in areas of "historic" state powers—was to maintain federalism's "balance." Many scholars—prominently Ernest A. Young, in this volume and elsewhere—have cast the preemption debate in this light.

Similarly, the Rehnquist Court has deployed the presumption against pre-emption extensively (though not universally, and never consistently) to the same end. In closely related legal contexts, the Court has described the Supremacy Clause as an "extraordinary" and slightly uncouth power.[3]

Any overarching notion of a federalism balance strikes us as problematic. After all, the Constitution mandates no balance. Instead it allocates specified powers to the national government (and often imposes corresponding state disabilities), which is a very different approach. For example, while the Constitution may leave some room for "gubernatorial foreign policy," not even the most ardent states' rights advocate would propose to restore some mythical federalism balance by entrusting the 82nd Airborne to a state attorney general.[4] But for purposes of this conclusion, we put that problem aside. Rather, our concern has to do with the constitutional "compensating adjustment" at issue. It is *possible* that the optimal legal response to one bad move (unlimited federal powers) is another bad move (weak preemption of state laws), but courts are not particularly good at identifying the best moves in a second-best world.[5] Moreover, even an optimal readjustment—assuming that it can be obtained—will rarely return the law to the original position in most relevant respects. Weak federal preemption bears little resemblance to the constitutional world and in its own way offers a powerful object lesson about the dangers of fine-tuning.

Under the earlier constitutional arrangements, the principle of state autonomy imposed a certain discipline by forcing states to compete in the areas that were then thought to be beyond federal control, from labor conditions to land-use law. The compensating presumption against preemption creates precisely the opposite institutional dynamic. When Congress legislates in areas once reserved to the states, the new federal "floor" puts an end to state competition. Yet simultaneously, the presumption against preemption facilitates additional state regulation on top of that floor. So conceived, concurrent powers cut in only one direction—stricter regulation. That problem is rendered more acute both by the increased scale and scope of modern production and by the conjunction of New Deal preemption rules with the expansive reach of personal jurisdiction and malleable rules governing choice of law. Under those conditions, individual states can often rival the federal government's capability to regulate on a global basis. Regulated firms must then comply with each of fifty-one different regulatory regimes, which again implies that the strictest regulator will dominate. Thus, while the *ancien régime* achieved some rough balance between regulatory incentives and political discipline at the state level, the modern regime creates a strong proregulatory bias.

Even and especially from the vantage of state autonomy, moreover, the preemptive effect of a federal statute must not be viewed in isolation from the regulatory "floor" established in the same statute. A federal statute that targets primarily *in-state* conduct effectively liberates states from having to compete with each other to attract businesses—which is the "autonomy" most states crave, most of the time. That outcome may be good or bad in any given case, but respect for state autonomy does *not* point to preemption rules that encourage state regulation above the floor. (Look at it this way: less-regulation-minded states lost when the federal floor was established. Why should proregulation states, having already won once, get yet another bite at the apple?) When a federal statute primarily curbs *interstate* externalities and spillovers, the case for antipreemptive presumptions is still harder to discern, especially in light of the enormous expansion of extraterritorial state power that accompanied the creation of the modern preemption regime. Given the ever present threat of retaliation, in what sense is the states' "right" to inflict costs on each other a net gain in state autonomy? Viewed in this light, giving full preemptive force to federal statutes is best understood as seeking a regulatory optimum (to borrow Gasaway and Parrish's term) and not as an assault on federalism, let alone a preference for libertarian policy positions. Rather, it mimics—"translates," if you must—the original constitutional logic.

This somewhat abstract disquisition illustrates our broader agenda. We do not in this discussion propose a return to the original constitutional arrangements. We merely suggest that the presumption against preemption is not the only alternative to an old, "exiled" Constitution, nor even the most plausible one. The implausibility of either option warrants an exploration of a third approach—an implied preemption framework that traces and approximates, however imperfectly, our earlier constitutional arrangements.

We start with the proposition that either federal *or* state government, but not both, should handle any given matter. That one stroke should minimize the coordination problems, administrative confusion, and political intrigue that typically characterize a regime of concurrent jurisdiction. One problem, one sovereign. Our lodestar in determining *which* sovereign rests on generally shared federalism assumptions. Very roughly, in the context of network regulation, from interstate airline transport to communications, we are inclined to support exclusive national regulation. Conversely, we favor exclusive state or local regulation where the effects are purely local and where active state competition seems possible.[6] But in the preemption context (as opposed to pure federalism theory) the assignments are less important than the terms of government-to-government interaction, both "vertically" between the states and the nation and "horizontally" among the several states. Vertically, we favor exclusivity, regardless of where the line of separation may fall under any given statute. With respect to what Issacharoff and Sharkey call "horizontal federalism," we think that preemption should track the dormant Commerce Clause, or more precisely the constitutional precepts that it embodies.[7] Instead of aiming for some unattainable federal-state balance, preemption doctrines should reduce the federalism risks that lie at the heart of the dormant Commerce Clause: state protectionism, balkanization, and what *The Federalist* called state "aggression"—in modern terms, cost externalization.

Implied Preemption and the Anti-Circumvention Principle

Before applying this framework to a post–New Deal world, we must address a general objection: by rejecting the presumption against preemption, do we not load the dice in the opposite direction by accepting a broad notion of implied preemption? The "notwithstanding" language of the Supremacy Clause, Stephen Gardbaum and others have argued, goes to conflicts, not "obstacles" to, or "frustration" of, artfully constructed congressional purposes.[8] Preemption, under that logic, is either express or a straightforward conflict. Otherwise it is nonexistent, for it can never be implied. In our view, this argument is inconsistent with more basic principles of statutory interpretation, which can only function by resort to bounded doctrines of implication.

In dealing with matters of text, structure, and purpose, the first cut is to give the statutory terms their ordinary, common meaning. By and large, preemption doctrine must take federal statutes as it finds them. Once Congress has divvied up power between federal and state governments in specific ways, its decisions should not be undone by the dark art of statutory interpretation. But that principle cannot preserve statutory integrity unless it is backed up by an additional principle that guards against circumvention. Statutes are directed against (more or less well) defined abuses. Once the direct route is blocked by the statute, the regulated parties—states as well as individuals—will search out byways to achieve their illicit objectives without running afoul of the literal statutory language. The hard interpretive question is how far to extend the statutory reach to block the evasions without cutting off legitimate conduct that the statute never meant to forbid. That two-sided inquiry should determine the scope of implied preemption.

An anti-circumvention principle, it bears emphasis, is anything but a hand-crafted adjustment to the realities of the administrative state or, perhaps, the lack of congressional capacity to adjust convoluted statutes, time and again, to unforeseen circumstances and ever-more creative evasions. Those real concerns only reinforce the need for a general principle that operates in just about all statutory settings. The principle appeared in English law when British courts began to treat acts of Parliament as authoritative law (roughly, the mid-sixteenth century). Sometimes called the "mischief rule," it admonished all judges "always to make such [statutory] construction as shall suppress the mischief, and advance the remedy, and to suppress subtle inventions and evasions for continuance of the mischief . . . and to add force and life to the cure and remedy, according to the true intent of the makers of the act."[9] Anti-circumvention and its limitation—"the true intent of the makers"—go hand in hand. Long before even that canon of construction, the Roman Lex Aquila made it unlawful to kill (*occidere*) the slave or work animal of another person.[10] That prohibition easily covers forcing poison down a victim's throat. But what about setting a drink laced with poison before an innocent suspect, or setting a trap into which another person falls? Neither case is covered by the literal terms of the statute, because both require some act of the victim to complete the causal chain. No matter: by an early application of the anti-circumvention principle, the Romans created an adjacent category of wrongs—to furnish a cause of death (*causam mortis praestare*) to cover these situations. The "action in the case" in English law, as an extension of the law of trespass, covers much the same ground. But neither the Roman statute nor the English common law was ever read to impose liability where a person committed suicide by concocting his own poison out of ingredients supplied by some other person or by jumping off a cliff. Killing was covered, suicide was not.

The same logic governs modern legal doctrines far removed from pre-emption. For example, patent law protects from infringement particular inventions or devices as described in great detail in the patent application. But suppose someone creates some new invention by altering the specifications for the patented device in some trivial way that pulls the new invention out of the original literal patent description. Infringement is no longer literal but is covered by the doctrine of equivalents.[11] The effort to stop free-riding on prior work has not, however, gone so far beyond literal infringement as to stifle competition from rival inventions. The doctrine of equivalents, for example, never blocks a different device that served the same end as the patented invention. Copyright law has developed similar principles to deal with derivative forms of infringement that do not copy the original work word for word.

As we suggested in our Introduction, the United States Constitution reflects the same logic. At one end, a Constitution of limited, enumerated powers reinforces the general observation that an anti-circumvention principle must have a limit. At the other end, federal powers, constitutionally specified state disabilities, and federal statutes enacted pursuant to the Supremacy Clause cannot escape the Madisonian logic: they all "suppose the disposition which will evade them."[12] Even the most detailed and explicit federal pre-emption statute still needs an anti-circumvention principle.

A distinction between "conflicts" within the reach of the Supremacy Clause and implied preemption supposedly outside that reach, we conclude, puts an impossible weight on the notion of "conflict" and, in the process, defeats the constitutional logic. Viet Dinh's essay shows that the justices of the nineteenth century struggled mightily, and in the end unsuccessfully, to delineate a realm of "conflicts" in contradistinction to—what? Harmonious coexistence? Arguably, there was no genuine "conflict" even in *Gibbons v. Ogden*: one could have read the federal statute as operating on top of whatever licensing requirements states might choose to impose with respect to their own ports. True, *Gibbons* speaks the language of conflicts. But unless it is read as a case of what we now call implied preemption, it was either wrong or else should have been decided on the grounds of Justice Johnson's concurrence: federal statute or not, New York must not disrupt commerce.[13] The same structural issue is presented, albeit in a constitutional rather than a statutory setting, in *Brown v. Maryland*: when the state evades the Import-Export Clause through the clever device of imposing a tax on importers rather than imports, John Marshall declared, the law must be struck down under the anti-circumvention principle. The dissent in *Brown* criticized Marshall's formulation of the principle in that case as internally incoherent, overbroad, and poorly circumscribed.[14] But these questions go to the reach and content of the anti-circumvention principle, not its underlying validity. They are the right questions to ask, and the ones we mean to address. Our effort to understand the principle in continuity with the constitutional logic of exclusivity and Commerce Clause risks, we believe, would yield better results—doctrinally and pragmatically—than the reigning orthodoxy. In support of that proposition, we start with the *fons et origo* of modern preemption doctrine—*Rice v. Santa Fe Elevator*.

Rice Reexamined

Rice v. Santa Fe Elevator by all accounts offers the canonical statement of modern preemption doctrine. Yet it has met the fate of many a New Deal case: enthralled with the purported "principle" of the case, scholars have rarely paused to examine what it was actually about.[15] In a nutshell, the statute at issue, the 1931 Warehouse Act, entrusted the U.S. secretary of agriculture with exclusive "power, jurisdiction, and authority" over warehouse operators that chose to operate under a federal license.[16] Rice, a grain dealer and customer of the Santa Fe warehousing operation, brought suit under the Illinois Public Utility Act claiming that Santa Fe had discriminated against it, and in favor of the federal government, in setting and maintaining its storage rates. Among other remedies, the case sought to have the Illinois Public Utilities Commission set appropriate rates for Santa Fe's operation.

The federal preemption (if that is what one chooses to call it) was express, unequivocal, and unadulterated by any savings clause in favor of state law. But *Rice* was not a true preemption case at all: it was a case about *exclusive jurisdiction*. The Warehouse Act preempted nothing whatever. For warehouses that continued to operate under a state license, the 1931 statute established neither a floor nor a ceiling; states remained free to regulate to their hearts' content. By design the federal regulation of warehouse operators kicked in only *at the operators' own choice.* The perceived blow to state authority had nothing to do, then, with the Supremacy Clause. It had everything to do with the federal government's decision to offer a regulatory option at variance and in competition with those of the states.

Against this backdrop, the now-canonical statements about "implied preemption" look like dicta. *Rice* did not have to struggle with statutory ambiguity over implied preemption. Rather, it gave Justice Douglas an opportunity to transform a crystal-clear statute, informed by pre–New Deal intuitions, into a post–New Deal concurrent powers construct. By starting with the presumption against preemption, Douglas was able to recast the inquiry and to ask whether there was some real conflict between the federal statute and the state regime. Rice had claimed, for example, that no conflict existed with respect to setting rates: while Illinois had that power, the secretary of agriculture was authorized only to disallow rates that were adjudged exorbitant. Instead of rejecting that claim out of hand—a conclusion that should follow from the "exclusive" language and structure of the act—Douglas looked closely at the legislative history to determine whether Congress had desired a single system of regulation, so that the state would have to yield. Examining the statutory provisions on a retail-only basis, he concluded that the state scheme survived in areas where no conflict was evident (for example, in obtaining prior approvals for such matters as construction, engineering, leasing, and insurance—matters that were regulated under Illinois law but not under the federal statute). The bias in favor of concurrent regulation was sufficient to sustain the state's authority over these matters.

Justice Frankfurter's neglected dissent lurched even more sharply in favor of concurrent jurisdiction. In Frankfurter's view, preemption turned on the demonstration of an actual conflict between state regulation and the actions of the secretary, given the historical presumption that the state had the power to regulate warehouses in all aspects of their business. No such conflicts, he thought, could be shown. For one thing, the statute imposed on the secretary the duty to cooperate with state officials. Further, the federal statute by design had failed to "establish a compulsory, uniform, nationwide system for the regulation of grain warehouses." Notably, the secretary of agriculture—unlike state regulators—lacked the authority to fix rates. Finally, Frankfurter argued, congressional appropriations under the statute failed to increase after the 1931 enactment, again belying the notion that the statute was intended as a serious regulatory scheme. "As a result of today's decision," Frankfurter lamented in conclusion, "the gates of escape from deeply rooted State requirements will be open."[17] Plainly, Frankfurter's concern was not a diminution of the states' police powers: contrary to his intimations, the Warehouse Act imposed no legal control or restraint whatever on state regulators. His concern was the chasm between the competitive regime of the Warehouse Act and the New Deal's preferred equilibrium: concurrent powers everywhere, cartels at every level.[18]

Viet Dinh has denounced the presumption against preemption as inviting courts to enact statutes that Congress never wrote.[19] Whatever one may think of that charge in the abstract, it manifestly applies to the origin of that presumption in *Rice*. And certainly, the determination to press resistant pre–New Deal statutes into a concurrent powers framework has driven the judicial administration of other regulatory arenas—foremost, antitrust law. Pre–New Deal cases often observed that federal antitrust laws were meant to supplement, not supplant, complementary state laws (many of them enacted prior to the Sherman Act). What the courts meant was that the Sherman Act would apply to the subject-matter that it specifies—conspiracies "in restraint of trade or commerce *among the several states, or with foreign nations.*"[20] As the verbatim use of the constitutional language illustrates, the Sherman Act was enacted against the backdrop of the "old" understanding: it would operate on interstate conspiracies that were then thought beyond the states' authority, while leaving state law to operate on internal commerce. Nothing in the statute, and nothing in the real world, compelled the New Deal reinterpretation, under which the Sherman Act—in the teeth of its language— applies to purely local events and effects, and where "supplemental" means that states may circumvent, pile onto, or piggyback on federal antitrust authority and enforcement against national and global corporations.[21] We would be far better off today with the actual Sherman Act.

Too much water may have flowed under the antitrust bridge to revisit this particular misfortune judicially or even legislatively.[22] But the baseline choice—exclusive regulation, or the intense preference for concurrent powers that comes with the presumption against preemption—still has potency in many regulatory arenas. Mercifully, the modern Supreme Court has sometimes given force to presumptions of exclusivity rather than concurrent powers. With respect to federal electricity regulation, for example, the Court has declared repeatedly that the authority of the Federal Energy Regulatory Commission is fully exclusive, so far as it extends. (As European lawyers would say, the question is the breadth of federal authority, not the "intensity" of the intrusion into state powers.)[23] Another example is the regulation of banks and other financial institutions, discussed in Hal Scott's essay. Supreme Court decisions over the past two-plus decades have consistently recognized the exclusivity logic that sustains our "dual" banking system. State attorneys general and consumer advocacy organizations have waged a relentless assault on that regime, on precisely the grounds of Justice Frankfurter's *Rice* opinion: an optional federal charter for banks and lending institutions—and perhaps for insurers, a legislative reform urged by Scott and by many companies in that sector—would open "the gates of escape from deeply rooted State requirements." In our judgment, courts should continue to resist efforts to *Rice*-ify sensible statutory schemes that protect enclaves of regulatory competition.

The Dormant Prong of Dormant Commerce

We have started with the easy cases, where exclusivity presumptions work in tandem with the statutory schemes and the presumption against preemption against those schemes. But our analysis applies with equal force in more ambiguous statutory settings, where implied preemption should be understood as an extension of the logic of the dormant Commerce Clause.

The "old" Commerce Clause defined the states' disabilities in terms of subject-matter. The New Deal's dormant Commerce Clause, in contrast, turns on specified federalism risks: state discrimination, balkanization, and cost externalization. The watershed decision, by all accounts, is *South Carolina Highway Department v. Barnwell Brothers* (1938), which defined the scope of the Clause as follows:

> The commerce clause, by its own force, prohibits discrimination against interstate commerce, whatever its form or method, and the decisions by this Court have recognized that there is scope

> for its like operation when state legislation nominally of local concern is in point of fact aimed at interstate commerce, *or by its necessary operation is a means of gaining a local benefit by throwing the attendant burdens on those without the state. . . .*[24]

This formulation seems as sensible as one can reasonably expect in this uncertain terrain. In proposing to set preemption presumptions in accordance with the *Barnwell* regime, we are, as it were, die-hard New Dealers[25]—in part because in *this* dimension, New Deal federalism used the "old" account of the police power: close judicial monitoring of the states' police-power justifications prevented them from spiraling out of control. Harlan F. Stone eloquently articulated that position before he became a member of the Court,[26] and he held to it throughout his tenure. In *Barnwell*, he found—probably correctly—that South Carolina had offered a *bona fide* police power justification *for requiring shorter trucks on curvy roads.* In *Southern Pacific v. Arizona* (1945), in contrast but consistently, Chief Justice Stone held that Arizona could *not* require shorter trains within its state when grade conditions for track were constant across the nation and the state's proffered safety rationales proved implausible.[27] States, the post–New Deal Court insisted in an oft-quoted formulation originally coined by Justice Holmes, may not defeat the Commerce Clause "by simply invoking the convenient apologetics of the police power"—among them, the "convenience" of segregating passengers on interstate motor carriers.[28]

Our focus on federalism risks rather than "balance" implies the demise of the antipreemption presumption's close cousin, the undifferentiated notion of "historic" state powers. We hope and trust that this step will meet with cries of "good riddance" on all sides. The supposed test is infinitely malleable—for example, by manipulating the level of specificity. Generic descriptions such as "health and safety regulation," "torts," or "fraud prevention" create broad protective umbrellas for state authority. More specific descriptions—for example, "state court litigation of class actions involving nationally traded securities," make the "historic" analysis cut the other way even when administered by Justice Stevens, a determined foe of federal preemption.[29] The *Barnwell* framework rightly reorients the inquiry from balance and history to identifiable and, as it were, constant and constitutional federalism risks. Protectionism, balkanization, and cost externalization may now and then generate gains for an individual state, but such stratagems cannot generate *collective* gains, either in economic terms or in terms of state autonomy. What one state gains, the others lose, and the risk of retaliation makes the game doubly unattractive. Guarding against the ongoing prisoner's dilemma is, in a nutshell, the constitutional logic behind the dormant Commerce Clause.[30] When Congress legislates, it should be presumed to have legislated in accordance with that logic, absent evidence to the contrary.

At times, the Supreme Court has clearly recognized this continuity. For example, in cases of "reverse" preemption, where Congress authorizes states to enact laws that would otherwise violate the antidiscrimination prong of the dormant Commerce Clause, Congress must speak clearly before the Court will infer a legislative intent to that effect.[31] Similarly, the Supreme Court has often read preemption statutes in accordance with an anti-balkanization preemption. One easy application is *United States v. Locke* (2000), which unanimously upheld a challenge under the federal Ports and Waterways Safety Act (PWSA) against local Washington rules that imposed extensive regulation on the ships and crews that entered Washington state waters, in response to major oil spills such as that of the Exxon Valdez. The PWSA gave the U.S. Coast Guard general authority to "regulate the design, construction, alteration, repair, maintenance, operation, equipping, personnel qualification, and manning of tankers."[32] The act (as amended) also contained two savings clauses that preserved state statutory and common law authority to regulate oil discharges in state waters. The prophylactic state regulations at issue in *Locke*, however, imposed detailed regulations on the operation of the ship, requiring (among other things) a comprehensive management and training program for crews, English proficiency requirements, special watch rules, and rigorous reporting requirements for actual and near accidents. The sensible accommodation in *Locke* was to allow the savings clause to preserve the common law of nuisance, while barring the state from creating its own alternative administrative apparatus to avoid discharges and spills before they occur. In that latter respect, the case would be close even without the PWSA: under our understanding of *Barnwell* and its legacy, state police power justifications that conflict with the free flow of goods and services across state lines typically encounter considerable judicial skepticism.[33]

The cost externalization test—the third, italicized portion of the *Barnwell* quote above—has followed a more erratic course. Although it exerts strong influence in dealing with direct forms of state regulation, it vanishes in other context. For example, only five years after *Barnwell*, in the notorious *Parker v. Brown* (1943) decision, the Court unanimously sustained a state-created raisin cartel (California's) against challenges on antitrust grounds, preemption grounds, and under the dormant Commerce Clause. California at the time supplied upward of 90 percent of the domestic raisin market. There was no doubt, nor even a serious dispute, that the cartel was calculated for precisely the purpose condemned in *Barnwell*—to tax the nation for California's benefit. The situation is doubly troublesome because the state enforcement of the cartel increases the danger by preventing its erosion through the inveterate and honorable practice of cheating on cartels. Another six years later, though, in *H.P. Hood & Sons v. DuMond* (1949), a divided Court found a dormant Commerce Clause violation when New York denied Hood a license to build a new receiving facility in New York state in order to ship its raw milk for processing in the Boston, Massachusetts market. Instructively, the ground on which the New York commissioner denied the license was chiefly his authority to prevent, under state law and in good New Deal style, "destructive competition in a market already adequately served." In invalidating the license denial, Justice Jackson's majority opinion relied principally on the distinction, "deeply rooted in our history and our law," between economic protectionism and legitimate police power regulations.[34] The dissenters—Justice Hugo Black, joined by Justice Frank Murphy, and Justice Frankfurter, joined by Justice Wiley Blount Rutledge—argued primarily that the states were well within their powers to enact laws against destructive competition, and that this power to control "local" matters followed from the Court's earlier decision in *Cooley v. Board of Wardens* and, of course, *Parker v. Brown*. In fairness, the dissenters had a point: there was no evidence that the out-of-state destination of the dairy-applicant's products played any role in New York's license denial. By ordinary standards of intent or effect, the license denial in *H.P. Hood* had less negative impact on interstate commerce than the raisin cartel that survived in *Parker*.

Both *Parker* and *H.P. Hood* have continued their uneasy coexistence for the past half-plus-century, as the Court continues to look with too much favor on implied state immunities from the antitrust law—regardless of federalism risks[35]—while clamping down more effectively on direct state regulation. While there may be no fully satisfactory way of harmonizing these two lines of cases, one plausible perspective focuses on the influence of Robert Jackson, whose central Commerce Clause value was economic unity, or anti-balkanization. His majority opinion in *Hood* is known principally for its paean to an integrated market and the nation as a single "economic unit." Here as elsewhere, Jackson fought the hard-core New Dealers' determination to "let Commerce struggle for Congressional action to make it free."[36] Economic unity is manifestly endangered by state laws that operate as *de facto* import barriers, which the Court has come, rightly in our view, to condemn as "protectionism." It is likewise imperiled by export barriers (as arguably in *H.P. Hood*) and by inconsistent, even if nondiscriminatory, state regulations of integrated networks, such as highways or railroads. In contrast, exploitation schemes of the *Parker* variety, which "only" remove the antitrust safeguards against state-managed cartels, are neither discriminatory nor balkanizing. This difference may explain why Jackson, otherwise no friend of passivity vis-à-vis the states, did not dissent in *Parker*.

Whatever the late Justice Jackson may have had in mind, though, his legacy lingers. The modern Supreme Court's dormant Commerce Clause case law is quite sensitive to the risk of state discrimination in the sense of exclusion or protectionism. (Perhaps for that reason, it is hard to find preemption cases that deal with that risk: interferences that are monitored, blocked, and redressed under the Constitution need not be arrested by Congress.) The Court has likewise proven sensitive to the risk of balkanization. In contrast, it is virtually oblivious to the risk of mutual state aggressions. The only prohibited form of cost externalization is the direct state regulation of transactions in other states.[37] The likely reason, to our minds, is that cost externalization, unlike discrimination, does not easily lend itself to a manageable judicial test. Once one gets beyond brazen schemes à la *Parker*, the question becomes how much of a regulatory externality is too much. The answer will hang not on the form of the imposition but on its incidence, which is not easily amenable to judicial inquiry. All the more reason, though, to take the risk seriously in the preemption context.

And in precisely this field the preemption battle has been fought with particular intensity. Issacharoff and Sharkey are entirely right in identifying the preemption of state liability rules relating to product labeling and design defects as the central "horizontal federalism" issue. They are also right in suggesting that the principal difficulty in this area is not balkanization *per se* but rather cost externalization.[38] The strong industry push for federal preemption under various regulatory schemes is driven not by the desire for uniformity but by the need for some safe harbor on design or warning questions *before* the product is marketed, in order to foster innovation and lower costs. Issacharoff and Sharkey argue that the Rehnquist Court has by and large accommodated that insistent demand and the logic on which it rests. We wish we could endorse their sunny assessment, but we have our doubts. *Geier v. American Honda Motor Co., Inc.* (2000), Issacharoff and Sharkey's principal piece of evidence and for them, as for many other contributors, a central case, was an extremely close, 5–4 decision, and subsequent cases raise serious questions about its reach. Preemption doctrine in this area would benefit from a clearer-headed appreciation of cost externalization as a distinct constitutional risk.

Warnings, Labels, and Design

Product liability law seeks to impose liability for defective warnings or design on parties or trading partners, not on strangers. In principle, these cases could be governed by contractual provisions that meet the joint satisfaction of the parties, but the widespread rejection of contractual solutions has led to extensive regulation of both warnings and design. For mass-marketed products and services, dissemination of reliable information about product use and safety is critical to users and consumers. How then is that information best generated?

One option is a generalized duty-to-warn action at common law, which the aggrieved user can bring against the product manufacturer or other parties in the chain of distribution. This instrument, however, is not particularly attractive. Juries must decide what warnings are adequate and what impact a different warning would have had on consumer behavior and personal injury. These questions require extensive expert evidence, with little carryover between cases on the causation and damage issues. Case outcomes supply no useful feedback to manufacturers, due to the major time

lags (and rapid innovation) between the adoption of a practice and its ultimate judicial evaluation. Worse yet, inconsistent verdicts across states and
across juries within states offer little concrete guidance but are very expensive. Parallel considerations arise in design defect cases.

A second approach for dealing with information flows rejects *ex post* litigation and instead mandates warnings and labels that seek to present the
best available information. Get the warnings and labels right; insulate the
manufacturer from tort liability suit based on allegedly incorrect or incomplete information; and revise warnings in response to difficulties reported
from the field. Blocking parallel tort actions in this context reduces price
and increases availability. It also spurs third parties to provide independent
information to complement warnings required by statute. Again, parallel
rules apply to design cases.

States could adopt this approach unilaterally, by providing that all
warnings and designs that comply with federal standards are immune from
state law liability. Such statutes, however, are surprisingly hard to coordinate with federal regulatory regimes, especially when they fall (as they have)
into the hands of judges who are fiercely determined to shield expansive
tort doctrines against both federal preemption *and* a state legislature's unilateral decision to restrict liability.[39] More fundamentally, states have little
incentive to protect mostly out-of-state defendants against their own citizens' liability claims, in their own courts. And so state law theories prolif-
erate: express warranty; implied warranty; fraud; concealment; negligence;
product design defect. These multiple exposures then drive defendants to
use federal theories of preemption to create the safe harbors denied under
state law.

The fit, admittedly, is often awkward. Most statutes in this field were
drafted before the explosion of product liability law in the 1970s and generally content themselves with providing that states may not impose
"requirements in addition to or different from" those mandated under federal law. The "requirements" and "standards" language clearly covers state
interventions by legislation or administrative action. But does it also preclude state common law actions for damages caused by products made in
compliance with all applicable federal standards? The question is made
more difficult yet because many of those ancient statutes contain savings
clauses for then-extant state common law.

One possibility is to view such statutes as incomplete regulatory regimes: they govern deterrence (*ex ante* standards substitute for *ex post* litigation) but not the compensation of injured victims. On that view, occasionally intimated by the Supreme Court,[40] federal standards and state tort law, express preemption provisions and savings clauses, may live together in perfect harmony—and, by some accounts, did so coexist until quite recently. We disagree. We would quarrel with the peaceful coexistence view on empirical grounds, and we share the legal profession's generally dim view of tort law as an efficient compensation mechanism.[41] In any event, the great majority of legal scholars have come to view state tort law as a kind of regulatory system, running parallel to federal statutory regimes. The Supreme Court's preemption law reflects that recognition: in principle at least, state liability rules qualify as the type of state "requirement" or "standard" that is subject to preemption. And on that score, our position is roughly the one urged by Robert Gasaway and Ashley Parrish. The federal statutes at issue unambiguously preempt state legislative or administrative standards that are backed by fines for noncompliance, but those sanctions are child's play compared to an onslaught of private law damage actions. Unlike fines, moreover, which depend usually on clear rules, common-law actions rest on principles of adequacy that are never known or articulated in advance. Federal law preempts the state fines and directives because firms would be foolhardy to enter the market when they are exposed to legal sanction no matter what they do. *A fortiori*, federal law should be read to preempt common-law actions that function as close—and more draconian—substitutes for preempted statutory or administrative prohibitions.

There is every reason to view state products-liability law, as well as generalized antifraud and failure-to-disclose obligations, as evasive maneuvers that ought to be caught by the anti-circumvention principle. At times, the connection is manifest. When the federal government deregulated airline rates, routes, and services, states responded by regulating the *advertising* of airline pricing. The Supreme Court held—in a rather angry opinion—that this backdoor attempt to reregulate airlines under a different label was preempted by the federal deregulatory statute.[42] Rightly so: the anti-circumvention principle should guard against the Madisonian risk that proregulation interests, having been defeated at the national level, will seek to reverse their loss at the state level. The same dynamic, it bears note, has played out in practically every industry that experienced (partial) federal deregulation: in banking, energy, health care, telecommunications, and other sectors, state attorneys general and regulators, often aided by the trial bar, substituted "consumer protections" and common law actions for the preempted regulation of rates and conditions. As Thomas Hazlett rightly points out in his instructive essay on mobile phone regulation, such stratagems pose a systemic risk that state regulators will consistently undervalue the external costs of their impositions.

Products liability is a longer-playing variation on the same theme. As noted, federal preemption statutes often date back a long time. Prior to their enactment—the reference point of the "historic" police powers claim that is so often mobilized to defeat preemption claims—*no* case imposed duties to warn on manufacturers, or crashworthiness requirements in automobile cases. Proximate cause and privity limitations blocked any effort to impose large liabilities on drug or auto manufacturers, except in rare cases of deliberate mislabeling or deliberate concealment of known defects.[43] The demise of those limitations sparked efforts by individual producers to limit liability by contract, but that maneuver was decisively rejected in the early 1960s in both medical malpractice and products liability cases.[44] Next, defendants sought to persuade state courts to treat compliance with federal standards as conclusive evidence of "no defect" under state law, but the federal standards typically were treated as mere minimums that juries could disregard in deciding design defect cases. Finally, state courts uniformly rejected the view that the FDA intended its warnings to block common law actions on the same subject.[45] Preemption is the only tool left to accomplish what has been the purpose of federal regulation all along—the creation of a predictable market environment for nationally distributed products.

The "damned-if-you-do, damned-if-you-don't" dilemma lies behind the Supreme Court's decision in *Cipollone v. Liggett Group, Inc.* (1992) which held that the Delphic term "requirement" did, after all, embrace certain common law actions. But the Court has been less than sure-footed in grounding this principle and in ascertaining its scope. *Geier* illustrates the problem. The National Traffic and Motor Vehicle Safety Act of 1966 (NTMVS) contains a preemption clause that blocks any state from imposing "any safety standard applicable to the same aspect of performance of such vehicle or item of equipment which is not identical to the Federal standard." But the act also contains an explicit savings clause to the effect that compliance with a federal safety standard "does not exempt any person from any liability under common law."[46] This forked-tongue statute was passed just at the cusp of the products liability revolution but before any state had adopted the general crashworthiness cause of action that *Larsen v. General Motors* ushered in some two years later.[47] Against that backdrop, it appears the Safety Act's savings clause was originally targeted, largely and perhaps even exclusively, at preserving rights of actions in cases where cars were affirmatively unsafe as measured against a manufacturer's own expectations—as when a car exploded when the ignition key was turned. Once the common law expanded to include crashworthiness cases, (unintended) conflicts arose at every juncture. Among them was the issue in *Geier*—the conflict between a common-law challenge predicated on the want of an airbag in a particular car and the Motor Vehicle Safety Board's decision, after exhaustive deliberation, to introduce an airbags mandate in stages over a period of time. Justice Breyer refused to find express preemption under a statute that set "standards" (and did not prohibit state "requirements"), but he still held that the private action was preempted by implication. The comprehensive administrative action made it clear that the regulation meant to set an optimal path for regulation, not a minimum one. State common law actions would distort or undermine the carefully crafted administrative compromise.

In light of the messy statutory language, it is understandable that Justice Breyer relied heavily on the agency's expertise, careful consideration of risk-risk trade-offs, and reasoned judgment, as well as on the solicitor general's litigation position.[48] Subsequent decisions, however, reveal the fragile nature of that approach. In *Sprietsma v. Mercury Marine* (2002), the Court held that the Federal Boat Safety Act of 1971 (FBSA) did not preempt a state tort action brought on behalf of a decedent who was fatally struck by an unguarded propeller after she fell overboard. The FBSA authorized the secretary of transportation to establish safety standards for boats and prohibited states from imposing "a law or regulation" that is not identical to the federal standard. The statute also preserved common law rights of action.[49] After an exhaustive study, the agency had declined to require propeller guards on the ground that the devices might pose risks equal to or greater than those posed by unguarded propellers (for example, because the boxes might injure people whom a propeller missed). And yet, a unanimous Supreme Court let the design defect case go forward. In an opinion by Justice Stevens (author of the firm *Geier* dissent), the Court first rejected the defendant's claim of express preemption—on the authority of *Geier*, and, moreover, the fact that the FBSA's preemption provision barred states from establishing "a law or regulation," thus implying "a discreteness . . . that is not present in the common law."[50] Turning to implied preemption, the Court held that "the Coast Guard's decision not to require propeller guards was undoubtedly intentional and carefully considered,"[51] but nonetheless not authoritative. In *Geier*, Justice Stevens explained, the Court had relied heavily on the agency's own position and on that of the solicitor general— who, in *Sprietsma* (unlike in *Geier*), disavowed any preemptive intent. Administering his *coup de grâce*, Justice Stevens again deferred to the government's litigation position in rejecting a claim of field preemption. The act's principal goal of fostering uniformity in manufacturing regulations, Justice Stevens concluded, was not "unyielding," as demonstrated by the government's own position.

The result, fully understood but nonetheless endorsed by the Court, is a regime of design-defect actions both against boats that do have propeller guards and against those that do not—in other words, a series of inconsistent legal commands under, alas, a fairly uniform set of state products liability rules, all of them with cost-exporting purpose and effect. Push us and we will insist that those types of actions should be blocked in the absence of *any* federal enactment, but we need not go there. Even under the most restrictive notions of federal preemption, preemption must be implied when a regulated party cannot simultaneously comply with the federal and state law—when one forbids what the other commands. We take it, moreover, that this principle cannot be thwarted by tenth-hour lobbying of, and an eleventh-hour submission by, the solicitor general. Objective impossibility should operate horizontally as well as vertically, at least where manufacturers cannot tailor their products to varying and conflicting state regulations.

One might argue that post-*Sprietsma*, federal agencies, the solicitor general, and Congress will know how to make regulations preemption-proof, and surely the Court will pay heed to those judgments, at least so long as they are sufficiently reasoned. But the very next Supreme Court case in this vein, *Bates v. Dow Agrosciences, L.L.C.* (2005), casts serious doubt on that cheerful view. The Federal Insecticide, Fungicide, and Rodenticide Act (FIFRA) authorizes the EPA to license pesticides for use after inspections and labeling and provides that states "shall not impose or continue in effect any requirements for labeling or packaging in addition to or different from those required" under the act. Dow had marketed its Strongarm weedkiller with the approved labels and represented to its customers that it was fit for peanut crops in all areas. In fact, the product failed in soils where the pH levels exceeded 7.2, producing extensive losses in some areas. When Dow discovered the risk, it issued, with EPA approval, a new label with the following warning: "Do not apply Strongarm to soils with a pH of 7.2 or greater." The question in *Bates* was whether the preemption clause insulated Dow from suits for crop damage caused by Strongarm.

As a common-law matter, this duty-to-warn case looks a lot easier on the causation issues than many of this sort. After all, the revised warning conceded the truth of the basic allegations. On a decidedly positive note, the administrative process actually worked on the problem at hand, with a prompt change of the warning (but not the product composition). The Fifth Circuit treated all the state causes of action as pretexts for a mislabeling claim, which makes preemption the correct result. Justice Stevens brushed all this aside. He first acknowledged the *Cipollone* rule that common-law suits are preempted as state law "requirements," but then reversed course:

> A requirement is a rule of law that must be obeyed; an event, such as a jury verdict, that merely motives an optional decision is not a requirement. The proper inquiry calls for an examination of the elements of the common-law duty at issue, not for speculation as to whether a jury verdict will prompt the manufacturer to change its label.[52]

Sorry—no. The first sentence only raises the exploded error that the payment of lots of money by doing X does not require one to not do X. (On that theory, there goes *New York Times Co. v. Sullivan*: large jury verdicts in defamation cases do not "require" parties to avoid potentially defamatory publications.) Justice Stevens then backs off his exotic proposition by saying that not all common-law causes of action should be treated alike, but that qualification hardly dampens the fatal blow already inflicted. Express warranty, defective design, and inadequate testing charges, Justice Stevens writes, are *not* preempted because they do not relate to the transmission of information. He proceeds to entertain the possibility, to be sorted out on remand, that "claims based on fraud and failure-to-warn are not pre-empted because these common-law duties are equivalent to FIFRA's requirements that a pesticide label not contain 'false or misleading' state-ments, or inadequate instructions or warnings."[53] But this generalized duty allows circumvention of the preemption provision in *all* cases, because the explicit warnings are sure to omit some hazards. The same litany of com-plaints could be raised for the revised Strongarm label on the ground that it too is incomplete in some critical respect.

Ironically, at the end of the day, the warning question is *all* that was involved in *Bates* anyhow. The complete cure to each and every plaintiff's claim was contained in the additional warning, for it is not a credible argu-ment in this commercial relationship that the plaintiff could recover on any of the aforementioned theories by using the Strongarm pesticide in cir-cumstances counterindicated by the warning. There can be no express war-ranty for risks that are expressly disclaimed; and there can be no design defect claim that requires Dow to make a new product that works in high pH soil solely because its previous try failed. The corrective process here worked well. As between merchants, we see no reason to whittle away pre-emptive provisions to allow a proliferation of private causes of action. Only manufacturing defects (which rarely present common mode failures) should survive.

Formalism? Functionalism? Expertise?

Our constitutionally inspired preemption formalism has its limits—both because generalized presumptions carry only so far in a messy statutory universe and because the adjacent fields of (constitutional) law may also lie in ruins. Thomas Merrill's intriguing discussion of *California v. FERC* (1990) provides an illustration. The statute at issue authorized the FERC to regu-late hydroelectric power projects (among other things), but it also con-tained this proviso: "Nothing contained in this chapter shall be construed as affecting or intending to affect or in any way to interfere with the laws of the respective States relating to the control, appropriation, use, or distribution of water used in irrigation or for municipal or other uses, or any vested right acquired therein."[54] The FERC had set the amount of water for powering a hydroelectric plant and the minimum amounts that would bypass it. The lower the amount in the bypass, the more power that comes from the dam, and the more disruptive the dam is to local in-stream uses. Quite naturally, the FERC set a lower minimum for bypass than the California State Water Resources Board, as each regulator was responsive to its own constituency. Merrill notes this conflict and brands California's opposition as indefensible NIMBY politics, and he may be right. But we think the case is more complex, owing to the sad state of United States water law. The paramount navigation servitude essentially displaces all local interests that rise to the level of property interests in water, including the use of flows and access.[55] This federal interest starts from Chief Justice Marshall's sound pronouncements that the commerce power reaches all navigation into the interior of the state. But the extrapolation to the navigation *servitude* conflates federal power with a federal ownership claim that sweeps all traditional state law water claims to one side.[56] It thus plays havoc with a preemption statute that protects any "vested right acquired" under state law. The consistent rejection of takings claims against federal government actions in violation of state water law allows the federal government to set policy while ignoring the costs imposed on both local political *and* property interests. Let the nation prosper and the state suffer, but how do we compare the relative gains and losses from choosing different bypass levels? The right solution would let the FERC impose whatever standard it chooses, but only if compensation is paid to cover the diminution of traditional water uses that state law does (or at least should) protect against a taking without just compensation. It is well-nigh impossible, however, to mimic that solution within the existing regulatory system. The weak system of constitutionally protected property rights in water makes it hard to get any sound reading of what hydroelectric plants should be constructed and where. No preemption doctrine can compensate, even imperfectly, for that problem.

Our attempt to tie preemption analysis to a narrower set of constitutional considerations—the federalism risks that are recognized under the dormant Commerce Clause—strikes us as more promising, both because the dormant Commerce Clause is in better shape than takings law and because it connects more directly and straightforwardly to preemption. Even here, difficult questions arise. The two of us agree, for example, on the appropriate set of presumptions with respect to the preemption of state law claims among contracting parties, as in products liability: the rule against cost externalization unambiguously cuts in favor of preemption. But what about liability among strangers, as in environmental pollution cases that arise in a field of comprehensive federal regulation? Plainly, our analysis forbids a regime that would give preference to an individual state's law. But what is the appropriate default rule—federal common law of the pre-*Erie* variety, as Epstein would say? Wholesale preemption of state *and* federal common law claims, as Greve would advocate? Questions of this sort would require a fuller discussion. But we believe that our general precepts—anti-circumvention, exclusivity, protection against dormant Commerce Clause risks—push the inquiry in the right direction and limit the range of plausible answers.

Gasaway and Parrish arrive at this destination by a different route.[57] Their project, as ours, is to cabin an anti-circumvention principle and to render it internally coherent. In the Gasaway-Parrish world, the enterprise boils down to two propositions: a plea to merge conflict and obstacle preemption (a useful proposal that is wholly consistent with our anti-circumvention principle), and a distinction between preemptive "golden mean" statutes and nonpreemptive, preclusive (but not prescriptive) federal statutes. Their approach is not wholly unproblematic. In any given case, lawyers will have to persuade the justices that an ambiguous federal statute, or, more likely, an agency acting under an ambiguous statute, is in fact shooting for an optimum rather than a floor. Moreover, the authors' focus on health and safety regulation, where the optimum-versus-floor distinction is central, does not easily capture regulatory schemes where state-federal separation is still the rule and the preferable norm. In banking regulation, for example, the question is not whether federal regulators are statutorily bound to ensure an optimum or a floor. The question is whether a dual banking system with competing regulators, as opposed to a single federal norm, should be viewed as a stab at an optimum. That said, the authors' formalism strikes us as preferable to the alternatives.

Consider in this context Thomas Merrill's ingenious approach, which turns on functional default rules. We have no quarrel with his aspiration to rid preemption law of its empty formalism, but we worry about questions of application. Consider Merrill's discussion of *Engine Manufacturers Association v. South Coast Air Quality Management District* (2004), involving a preemption provision in the Clean Air Act: "No state or any political subdivision thereof shall adopt or attempt to enforce any standard relating to the control of emissions from new motor vehicles or new motor vehicle engines subject to this part."[58] The Court had to decide whether this provision preempted a California law that required fleet operators within the state to purchase only those vehicles that met emissions standards more stringent than those that the federal government had set. Justice Scalia held that it did. To analyze the case, Merrill invokes an anti-balkanization criterion, which supports preemption when individual state standards lead to sharp divisions in an otherwise national market but would let such standards in place when they do not force the artificial creation of submarkets (in this case, for automobiles). Merrill's functional analysis leads to what looks like a full-scale antitrust inquiry into how this one provision works with countless product lines in different state markets. A change in sales volume between years could tip the preemption balance first one way, then the other. In large states fleet sales of some types of vehicles (cars, trucks, vans) are covered, but in others not. This unwieldy approach comes out second best to formalism, or at least a formalism that remains alert to the circumvention risk. Seizing control over fleet purchases is clearly an indirect effort to reach back to the manufacture of those same vehicles, a maneuver that should be caught by the anti-circumvention principle. That principle generates a uniform answer in all cases, regardless of the probable market impact, and avoids an expensive, time-consuming, and inconclusive factual inquiry. It yields quickly and easily the across-the-board results that the words, "No state or subdivision," require.

Similar but stronger concerns apply to Daniel Troy's defense of preemption in the field of federal drug regulation. At one time, the FDA took an antipreemption position that boosted private suits. Alarmed at jury verdicts that contradicted its own extensive scientific deliberations, the FDA, under Troy's leadership, changed course and has come to argue, both in *amicus* briefs in individual court cases and by issuing a general "preamble," that its determinations should be regarded as conclusive on the adequacy of warnings and labels in all civil litigation.[59] We are loath to look a gift horse in the mouth—least of all when the animal, as in this case, was hardly a gift but rather brought home at considerable cost, over the trial bar's and its congressional patrons' formidable obstacle course. Still, the technique and its intimate connection to judicial (*Chevron*) deference trouble us. Troy's insistence on agency expertise, as Justice Breyer's insistence in *Geier*, cuts both ways: let the expert agency, or for that matter an inexpert and opportunistic solicitor general, disclaim preemptive intent, and preemption vanishes into the mists, as it did in *Sprietsma*. Our real worry, however, is more fundamental. Like the trial bar, we lack confidence in the FDA's expertise. Unlike the trial bar, however, we believe—not as an article of faith, but for good and sufficient reasons—that the errors will cut both ways.[60] If anything, excessive caution is a far more serious risk than agency "capture." Adverse experiences with FDA-approved drugs, no matter how rare and isolated, will push the agency into a "better safe than sorry" posture long before expensive tort verdicts hit the industry. The central flaw with common-law liability is not that juries lack expertise or suffer from hindsight bias, although those failures are all too common. The central *institutional* flaw is that the supposed error-correction mechanism works only one way. There is no common law cause of action for the people who died while the FDA dawdled. *Sans* preemption, there *will* be a cause of action for the people who suffered after the most painstaking (and often counterproductive) FDA examination. In some venues, there will even be a cause of action for the people who did *not* suffer but affirmatively benefited from an approved drug.[61] Needless to say, plaintiffs' lawyers will find the venues most favorable to the plaintiffs, so that generous verdicts and settlements will follow.

So long as preemption analysis continues to be driven by the metaphysics of the *Chevron* doctrine, the FDA's propreemption position should qualify for judicial deference, or at least respect.[62] Most emphatically, the courts should discard the presumption against preemption in this context. As suggested earlier, the notion that federal drug law collides with a "historic" state power is simply a conceptual artifact: define the subject-matter not as "health and safety" (as the Supreme Court did in *Medtronic v. Lohr*)[63] but as "the marketing and sale of drugs and medical devices in interstate commerce," and the spurious conflict dissolves. The preemptive effect of the Food, Drug, and Cosmetic Act follows fairly from the structural features of the law, its comprehensive system of direct regulation, and the very nature of the regulatory process in this arena. Were the FDA to revert to its older position that its elaborate risk-risk trade-offs are only minimums, a court should disregard that position—not because the FDA's decisions are always "optimal" in any substantive sense, but because the agency is authorized and in fact called upon to pursue any regulatory objectives that even a well-functioning liability system could serve. Most likely, FDA disclaimers of preemption reflect not any optimization efforts but rather the bureaucratic incentive to interpose manufacturer-defendants between the agency and the adverse events that inevitably attend even the most scrupulous risk-risk trade-off.[64] Deference to governmental avoidance, let alone a presumption against preemption, would only compound the errors.

The Limits of Doctrine

At one end, our proposal to understand preemption in light of constitutional precepts may seem strangely diffident. If the idea is to salvage federalism's original logic, why not go back to the constitutional original? At the other end, our project has a whiff of underhandedness. The point of the New Deal project was to reject the earlier constitutional baseline. What warrant is there for resurrecting that baseline in preemption drag? We recognize these difficulties. But at the end of the day, it seems to us, preemption doctrine must make the best of a lousy hand.

Constitutional rules carry only so far. A federal Constitution can command states, as ours commands them, to give "Full Faith and Credit" to sister-states' public acts. But it cannot specify what exactly that will require in an endless, ever-changing array of contexts and conflicts. (In recognition of that fact, the clause provides for congressional as well as judicial enforcement.) A federal constitution can forbid, as ours forbids, discrimination and mutual aggression among states, but it cannot specify what is to count as an externality in the ever-larger arena of economic warfare. While the general principles can be expounded by courts, federalism's countless coordination and assignment problems will require extensive and varied federal legislation supplemented by ongoing regulation.

At that point, courts must not simply draw boundaries around the permissible laws; they must also understand and interpret those laws on their own terms but consistently with constitutional precepts. Unlike other scholars, we look to the original precepts (or what is left of them), rather than an arguable translation. And unlike many other contemporary scholars, we do not believe that statutory preemption questions raise occult issues of expertise that only the intelligent hand of the administrative or executive agencies can resolve.[65] None of the cases arrayed in this conclusion, nor any other preemption case that we can think of, raises hard questions of science, technology, and policy to which courts cannot respond by making their best efforts to make sense of the underlying statute. (We note, wistfully, that our view tracks the ostensible naïveté of the Administrative Procedure Act, with its declaration that the "reviewing court shall decide all relevant questions of law, [as well as] interpret statutory provisions.") The constant but erratic appeal to *Chevron* deference seems to us unsound not only for the exalted position that it confers on administrative expertise, but also for the massive political forces—think again of *Sprietsma*—that it unleashes at the highest levels inside the executive branch and administrative agencies.

Yes, the statutory universe is messy and unruly. By inadvertence or design, statutes rarely exit the Congressional foundry in mint condition. But when all is said and done, most preemption problems seem manageable. Tellingly, Supreme Court preemption decisions feature a much greater degree of judicial unanimity than does the Court's docket at large—quite probably, because the justices know how to read a statute. The unanimity breaks down only in cases dealing with tort claims under state statutory or common law.[66] Among the reasons, we think, is this: when it comes to the risk of cost externalization, all other protections—constitutional and infraconstitutional— have collapsed. If contractual defenses were still operative; if federal common law were still available as a protection against the doctrinal bias of state law; if the Full Faith and Credit Clause constrained plaintiffs' and state courts' choices of the most pro-plaintiff state law; if the Constitution were still read to control today's "minimum contacts" rule that exposes defendants to remote and hostile jurisdictions; if the dormant Commerce Clause treated cost externalization with the same suspicion that it accords to discrimination; if removal and abstention doctrines did not so severely limit defendants' access to federal courts: would corporations insist so vehemently on federal preemption? Would the constitutional arguments that now drive the preemption debate have ever disturbed this once esoteric field? We doubt it.

As it is, preemption law must compensate for a lot of defunct doctrines. We have tried to sketch a doctrine conducive to that end. But we agree with Gasaway and Parrish and, we think, Issacharoff and Sharkey: the true preemption problem probably transcends preemption *per se*. Speaking for ourselves, we find two culprits. One is legal realism, which encouraged judges to abandon the traditional tools of statutory interpretation, on the grounds that their use cannot remedy the technical shortfalls. (Call it Tinkerbell's legal theory: if you say it often enough, it becomes true.) The other is the naïve belief that government is immune to the law of diminishing returns. The proposition that more regulation is always better regulation reflects the New Deal view that there are no principled reasons to prefer competition over monopoly—nay, that the presumption runs the other way. These attitudes presage the rise of the administrative state, the fondness for judicial deference, the expansion of tort liability, the rejection of contractual defenses, and the weakening of private property protections at a constitutional level, where the rational basis test does what the *Chevron* doctrine does to administrative law.

While legal realism and New Deal commitments have lost much of their once-unquestioned appeal, they continue to exert a powerful gravitational pull in the form of default assumptions, when more natural canons and intuitions are put to the test. In one way or the other, the forceful contributions to this volume all revolve around the question of whether and to what extent those default assumptions should govern preemption law. Our conclusion has sketched a different set of default rules, which harkens back to what we take to be the constitutional presumptions. We would cheerfully defend that modest plea for constitutionally inspired coherence against fundamentalist attacks from either side. Failing that, we hope that this volume will contribute to a better understanding of an arcane but central theme of American law.

Notes

1. For recent discussion of the half-a-loaf (at best) resurgence of the Commerce Clause, see Richard A. Epstein, *The Federalism Decisions of Justices Rehnquist and O'Connor: Is Half a Loaf Enough?* 58 Stan. L. Rev. 1793 (2006). For praise of the new system of federalism as empowerment, see Erwin Chemerinsky, *The Assumptions of Federalism*, 58 Stan. L. Rev. 1763 (2006).

2. Lawrence Lessig, *Federalism in Translation*, 71 Tex. L. Rev. 1165 (1993); and Ernest A. Young, *Making Federalism Doctrine: Fidelity, Institutional Competence, and Compensating Adjustments*, 46 Wm. & Mary L. Rev. 1753 (2005).

3. See, *e.g.*, *Gregory v. Ashcroft*, 501 U.S. 452, 460 (1991) (describing the Supremacy Clause as an "extraordinary power in a federal system"). See also Edward L. Rubin & Malcolm Feeley, *Federalism: Some Notes on a National Neurosis*, 41 UCLA L. Rev. 903, 904 (1994) (observing that the Rehnquist Court has tended to view the Supremacy Clause as suspect).

4. See Julian Ku, *Gubernatorial Foreign Policy*, 115 Yale L. J. 2380 (2006).

5. Adrian Vermeule, *Hume's Second Best Constitutionalism*, 70 U. Chi. L. Rev. 421, 435–37 (2003).

6. For a similar approach, developed in the context of antitrust law, see Frank Easterbrook, *Antitrust and the Economics of Federalism*, 26 Journal of Law & Econ. 23 (1983).

7. Viet D. Dinh, *Reassessing the Law of Preemption*, 88 Geo. L. J. 2085, 2098 (2000), likewise emphasizes the continuity between the dormant Commerce Clause and preemption. Arguably, the Import-Export Clause and Privileges and Immunities Clause cover the same ground, so long as they apply to interstate as well as foreign commerce and corporations count as citizens. However, that question is beyond the scope of our inquiry here.

8. Stephen Gardbaum, *The Nature of Preemption*, 79 Cornell L. Rev. 767 (1994); Caleb Nelson, *Preemption*, 86 Va. L. Rev. 225 (2000).

9. *Heydon's* Case, 3 C. Rep. 7a, 7b (Ex. Exch. 1584).

10. For detailed discussion, see Richard A. Epstein, *A Common Lawyer Looks at Constitutional Interpretation*, 72 Boston U. L. Rev. 699 (1992).

11. See, *e.g.*, *Festo Corp. v. Shokeetsu Kinzoku Kogyo Kabushiki Co.* 535 U.S. 722 (2002). For a general discussion, see Richard A. Epstein, "Intellectual Property in a Technological Age" NAM (2006) http://www.nam.org/s_nam/bin.asp?CID= 202515&DID=236749&DOC=FILE.PDF, 19-22.

12. See our introduction to this volume. Illustrations come readily to mind. For example, when Congress decided to block securities class actions—so-called "strike suits"—in federal courts, those actions migrated to state courts (where they had been virtually unknown). Congress promptly responded by barring state as well as federal class actions alleging public companies' noncompliance with certain disclosure obligations "relating to the sale or purchase of a covered security." In turn, state courts

invented a new cause of action that permits identical claims so long as plaintiffs allege that the failure to disclose prompted them to *hold*, rather than purchase or sell, the security. The Supreme Court unanimously rejected that maneuver—though not without noting that individual plaintiffs and state treasurers remained free to bring those actions. *Merrill Lynch v. Dabit*, 126 S.Ct. 1503 (2006).

13. *Gibbons v. Ogden*, 22 U.S. 1 (1824). Nelson, *Preemption, supra* note 8 at 272, argues that "*Gibbons* plainly involved a contradiction between the challenged state law and a federal statute (*as interpreted by the Court*)." (emphasis added). The parenthesis simply shifts the central problem—what counts as a "conflict"?—into the statutory interpretation part of the analysis.

14. The dissenting Justice Thompson clearly, and correctly, understood the majority opinion to establish an anti-circumvention principle. He questioned the coherence of that principle because it barred state duties only on the first in-state wholesale transaction, by wholesalers. By its logic, Thompson argued, the purported principle should forbid state-imposed duties on imported goods at *any* stage of sale and distribution—an obviously untenable proposition. Similarly, the majority left untouched state duties on *retailers* who imported goods—an economic distortion that the Maryland statute, which arguably did no more than to put all sellers on a par, would have avoided. *Brown v. Maryland*, 25 U.S. 419, 449 (1827) (Thompson, J. diss.).

15. Other New Deal chestnuts also benefit from retelling. See Geoffrey Miller, *The True Story of Carolene Products*, 1987 Sup. Ct. Rev. 397 (1987).

16. Section 29 of the act provided that "the power, jurisdiction, and authority conferred upon the Secretary of Agriculture under this Act shall be exclusive with respect to all persons securing a license hereunder so long as said license remains in effect." 7 USC § 242.

17. *Rice v. Santa Fe Elevator Corp.*, 331 U.S. 218, at 247 (1947).

18. See Epstein, *How Progressives Rewrote the Constitution* (Washington D.C.: Cato 2006).

19. Dinh, *Reassessing the Law of Preemption, supra* note 7 at 2087–88.

20. Sherman Act, 15 U.S.C. § 1.

21. See *Summit Health v. Pinhas*, 500 U.S. 322 (1991 (extending the reach of the Sherman Act to purely local transactions with exclusively local price effects); *California v. ARC America Corp.*, 490 U.S. 93 (permitting, under state antitrust law, "indirect purchaser" actions that are not permitted under federal law). See D. Bruce Johnsen and Moin A. Young, "A Geographic Market Power Test for Sherman Act Jurisdiction" in Richard A. Epstein & Michael S. Greve, *Competition Laws in Conflict: Antitrust Jurisdiction in the Global Economy* (Washington, D.C.: American Enterprise Institute, 2004).

22. A congressionally sponsored operating Antitrust Modernization Commission appears determined to ignore the preemption elephant in its quarters. See Antitrust Modernization Commission, memorandum on state antitrust enforcement (November 10, 2006) www.amc.gov/pdf/meetings/061114_EnfInstStateDisc2dSuppOutline.pdf (accessed February 13, 2007).

23. See Anne van Aaken's essay in this volume. On jurisdiction rather than preemption as the principle of federal power regulation, see *Missisippi v. Power & Light v. Mississippi ex rel. Moore*, 487 U.S. 354 (1988); *New York v. FERC*, 535 U.S. 1 (2002). We are not particularly fond of the Court's disposition in *New York*, which attempts to separate the regulation of (federal) wholesale regulation from (local) retail regulation. The attempt to segregate regulatory authority within a single network often produces bizarre price effects and thus vexing regulatory difficulties. On those as well as statutory grounds, Justice Thomas, whose partial dissent in *New York* read FERC's authority to extend over both sets of transactions, may have had the better of the argument. Either solution, however, is much preferable to concurrent state and federal powers.

24. 303 U.S. 177 at 185–86 (citation omitted) (italics added).

25. Shocking perhaps, but not new. We have voiced our support for an antidiscrimination principle, as distinct from and opposed to a territorial conception, on an earlier occasion. Richard A. Epstein and Michael S. Greve, "Introduction: The Intractable Problem of Antitrust Jurisdiction," in *Competition Laws in Conflict: Antitrust Jurisdiction in the Global Economy*, eds. Epstein and Greve (Washington: AEI Press, 2004).

26. Harlan F. Stone, "Fifty Year's Work of the United States Supreme Court," *American Bar Association Journal* 14 (1928): 430.

27. 325 U.S. 761 (1945).

28. *Morgan v. Virginia*, 328 U.S. 373, 380 (1946) (quoting Justice Holmes's opinion in *Kansas City Southern R. Co. v. Kaw Valley Drainage Dist.*, 233 U.S. 75, 79 (1911)), invalidated a Virginia state law requiring racial segregation of interstate passengers as a violation of the dormant Commerce Clause. The pithy Holmes formulation is also quoted in *Southern Pacific*, 325 U.S. at 780.

29. Compare in this context Justice Stevens' account of "historic" police powers in *Medtronic v. Lohr*, 518 U.S. 470, at 475 (1996) with his account in *Merrill Lynch v. Dabit*, 126 S.Ct. 1503, 1511 (2006).

30. See Maxwell Stearns, *A Beautiful Mend: A Game Theoretical Analysis of the Dormant Commerce Clause Doctrine*, 45 Wm. & Mary L. Rev. 1 (2003).

31. *Prudential v. Benjamin*, 328 U.S. 408 (1946); *Western & Southern Life Ins. v. State Bd. of Equalization of Calif.*, 451 U.S. 648 (1981).

32. 529 U.S. 89, 91 (2000).

33. See, *e.g.*, *Southern Pacific*, 325 U.S. 761; and *Kassel v. Consolidated Freight Corp.*, 450 U.S. 662 (1981). For a "split the baby" disposition similar to *Locke*, and also correct to our minds, see *CSX v. Easterwood* 507 U.S. 658 (1993) (federal law preempts state law tort claims with regard to train speed but not railroad warning signs).

34. 336 U.S. 525, 553 (1949).

35. See Easterbrook, *Antitrust and the Economics of Federalism*, supra note 6.

36. *Duckworth v. Arkansas*, 314 U.S. 390, 401 (1941) (J. Jackson, concurring).

37. *Healy v. Beer Inst.*, 491 U.S. 324 (1989).

38. To see why substance matters more than uniformity, compare two legal regimes. Regime one adopts a uniform federal standard that follows the Restatement (Third)

Torts. Regime two has fifty different sets of prescribed state warnings, each of which is conclusive against liability in that state, even if in no other. Which regime would the regulated firms prefer? The uniform federal standard harmonizes on the worst possible outcome, which helps explain why most industries shy away from a federal legislative process that they might influence but never control. Fifty different warning labels are a logistical headache that raises the cost of product distribution for no visible benefit. But that small-time management problem will in time be eased by cooperation among states. "Balkanization" per se is not the issue. The forces that push corporate defendants to favor preemption all have to do with cost externalization from state to state.

39. A Michigan statute (Mich. Stat. Ann. § 600.2946 (5)) purports to insulate drug manufacturers from duty-to-warn suits when drug warnings meet FDA standards but, like comparable statutes, lifts the statutory protection when and if the drug maker obtained approval by committing fraud on the FDA. The exception is intended to render the statute consistent with the Supreme Court's decision in *Buckman v. Plaintiffs' Legal Committee*, 531 U.S. 341 (2001), which held that federal law preempts "fraud on the agency" claims. The Sixth Circuit Court of Appeals sustained that accommodation: *Garcia v. Wyeth-Ayerst Labs*, 385 F.3d 961 (6th Cir. 2004). In contrast, the Second Circuit (per Judge Calabresi) has held that lawsuits under Michigan law that *combine* open-ended common law claims and fraud-on-the-FDA claims—which, standing alone, would be barred under the Michigan statute and *Buckman*, respectively—could still proceed: *Desanio v. Warner-Lambert Co.*, 467 F.3d 85 (2d Cir. 2006).

40. See, *e.g.*, *Sprietsma v. Mercury Marine*, 537 U.S. 51 (2002) at 527.

41. Moreover, we believe that our approach to preemption has merit even if it cuts out *ex post* compensation in individual cases. The real gain comes from the increased incentives to invest and market drugs which on balance have high positive rates of return that all can share. For a fuller discussion of the issues covered in this section, see Richard A. Nagareda, *FDA Preemption: When Tort Law Meets the Administrative State*, 1 Tort Law article 4 (2006); and Richard A. Epstein, *A Response to Nagareda*, 1 Tort Law article 5 (2006) (available at www.bepress. com/jtl).

42. *Morales v. TWA*, 504 U.S. 374 (1992).

43. See, *e.g.*, *Huset v. J. I. Case Threshing Machine Co.*, 120 F. 865, 867–71 (8th Cir. 1903); *Kuelling v. Roderick Lean Mfg. Co.*, 75 N.E. 1098, 1101 (N.Y. 1905).

44. See *Henningsen v. Bloomfield Motors, Inc.*, 161 A.2d 69 (N.J. 1960); *Greenman v. Yuba Power Products*, Inc., 377 P.2d 897, 900–1 (Cal. 1963); *Tunkl v. Regents of Univ. of Calif.*, 383 P.2d 441, 445–46 (Cal. 1963).

45. See *MacDonald v. Ortho Pharmaceutical Corp.*, 394 Mass. 131, 139 (Mass. 1985) ("The regulatory history of the FDA requirements belies any objective to cloak them with preemptive effect. In response to concerns raised by drug manufacturers that warnings required and drafted by the FDA might be deemed inadequate by juries, the FDA commissioner specifically noted that the boundaries of civil tort liability for failure to warn are controlled by applicable State law.").

46. 15 U.S.C. § 1392(d); 15 U.S.C. § 1397(k).

47. *Larsen v. General Motors Corp.*, 391 F.2d 495 (8th Cir. 1968). The earlier decision in *Evans v. General Motors Corp.*, 359 F.2d 822 (7th Cir. 1966) had rejected such causes of action.

48. *Geier v. American Honda Motor Co.*, 529 U.S. 861 at 861 (2000) (agency consideration and justification); at 883–85 (solicitor general's position).

49. 46 U.S.C. § 4306, 4311(g).

50. *Sprietsma*, 537 U.S. at 63 (italics added).

51. Ibid. at 67.

52. 544 U.S. 431, at 445.

53. Ibid. at 447.

54. 16 U.S.C. § 821.

55. See *United States v. Chandler-Dunbar Water Power Co.*, 229 U.S. 53 (1913); *United States v. Willow River Power Co.*, 324 U.S. 499 (1945); *United States v. Rands*, 389 U.S. 121 (1967) (denying property right status to port access).

56. Eva Morreale, "Federal Power in Western Waters: The Navigation Power and the Rule of No Compensation," *Natural Resources* 3 (1963): 1.

57. We are gratified to learn that our views are consistent with those of Aquinas, Kant, and Hegel, but we shall not rely on their support.

58. 42 U.S.C.A. § 7543.

59. Other agencies, such as the Consumer Product Safety Commission and the National Highway Traffic Safety Administration, have taken similar positions. For discussion, see Catherine Sharkey, *Preemption by Preamble: Federal Agencies and the Federalization of Tort Law*, 56 DePaul L. Rev. (forthcoming 2007).

60. For fuller discussions and references, see Epstein, *Response to Nagareda*, *supra* note 41; and Epstein, *Regulatory Paternalism in the Market for Drugs: Lessons from Vioxx and Celebrex*, 5 Yale J. Health Policy, Law & Ethics 741 (2005).

61. One such venue is the Second Circuit Court of Appeals. See *Desiano v. Warner-Lambert Co.*, 326 F.3d 339 (2nd Cir. 2003).

62. *Skidmore v. Swift & Co.*, 323 U.S. 134 (1944) (calling for "respect" for agency determinations).

63. *Medtronic v. Lohr*, 518 U.S. 470 (1996).

64. Lars Noah, *Rewarding Regulatory Compliance: The Pursuit of Symmetry in Products Liability*, in *Symposium: Regulatory Compliance as a Defense to Products Liability*, 88 Geo. L.J. 2147 (2000); Peter Huber, *Safety and the Second Best: The Hazards of Public Risk Management in the Courts*, 85 Colum. L. Rev. 277, 334 (1985).

65. For that position, see Adrian Vermeule, *Judging Under Uncertainty* (Cambridge: Harvard University Press, 2006), 230–33. The origin of this view dates back to James Bradley Thayer, *The Origin and Scope of the American Doctrine of Judicial Review*, 7 Harv. L. Rev. 129 (1893).

66. For data, see Michael S. Greve & Jonathan Klick, *Preemption in the Rehnquist Court: A Preliminary Empirical Analysis*, 14 Sup.Ct.Econ.Rev. 43, 55–57 (2006).

About the Authors

Kenneth W. Starr is Duane and Kelly Roberts Dean and professor of law at Pepperdine University School of Law and counsel to the law firm of Kirkland & Ellis, P.C., specializing in appellate work, antitrust, federal courts, federal jurisdiction, and constitutional law. As Solicitor General of the United States from 1989 to January 1993, Judge Starr argued twenty-five cases before the Supreme Court and represented the U.S. government on legal issues involving regulatory and constitutional statutes. He served as United States circuit judge for the District of Columbia circuit from 1983 to 1989, as counselor to U.S. Attorney General William French Smith from 1981 to 1983, and as law clerk to Chief Justice Warren E. Burger from 1975 to 1977 and Fifth Circuit judge David W. Dyer from 1973 to 1974. Judge Starr was appointed to serve as independent counsel for five investigations, including Whitewater, from August 1994 to October 1999.

Richard A. Epstein is the James Parker Hall Distinguished Service Professor of Law at the University of Chicago, where he has taught since 1972. He has also been the Peter and Kirstin Bedford senior fellow at the Hoover Institution since 2000. He has been a member of the American Academy of Arts and Sciences since 1985 and a senior fellow at the Center for Clinical Medical Ethics at the University of Chicago Medical School since 1983. He served as editor of *The Journal of Legal Studies* from 1981 to 1991, and of *The Journal of Law and Economics* from 1991 to 2001. At present he is a director of the John M. Olin Program in Law and Economics at the University of Chicago Law School. His books include *Overdose: How Excessive Regulation Stifles Pharmaceutical Innovation* (Yale University Press, 2006), *Skepticism and Freedom: A Modern Case for Classical Liberalism* (University of Chicago Press, 2004), *Torts* (Aspen Publishers, 1999), *Principles for a Free Society: Reconciling Individual*

Liberty with the Common Good (Basic Books, 1998), and *Takings: Private Property and the Power of Eminent Domain* (Harvard University Press, 1985).

Michael S. Greve is the John G. Searle Scholar at AEI, where he directs the Federalism Project and the Liability Project. His research and writing cover American federalism and its legal, political, and economic dimensions. Mr. Greve co-founded and, from 1989 to 2000, directed the Center for Individual Rights, a public interest law firm that served as counsel in many precedent-setting constitutional cases, including *United States v. Morrison* and *Rosenberger v. University of Virginia.* He has written widely on constitutional and administrative law, federalism, environmental policy, and civil rights.

Viet D. Dinh is a professor of law as well as co-director of the Asian Law and Policy Studies Program at Georgetown University Law Center. Professor Dinh was Assistant Attorney General for Legal Policy at the U.S. Department of Justice from 2001 to 2003. As the official responsible for federal legal policy, he conducted a comprehensive review of Department of Justice priorities, policies, and practices after the September 11 terrorist attacks, and played a key role in developing the USA Patriot Act and revising the Attorney General's Guidelines.

Stephen Gardbaum is a professor of law at UCLA, where he teaches courses in constitutional law, comparative constitutional law, European Union law, comparative law, and international human rights. He is a graduate of Oxford, London, Columbia, and Yale universities, and a solicitor of the Supreme Court of England and Wales. His scholarship focuses on federalism and comparative constitutional law, and he has written extensively on preemption. His articles on constitutional law have appeared in, among other publications, the *Harvard Law Review*, *Stanford Law Review*, *Michigan Law Review*, *University of Chicago Law Review*, and the *American Journal of Comparative Law*. They have also been cited by both the U.S. and Canadian Supreme Courts.

Daniel E. Troy, a partner in Sidley Austin LLP's life sciences practice as well as its appellate litigation group, is the former chief counsel of the Food and Drug Administration (FDA). Mr. Troy practices administrative and constitutional law and litigation, with a focus on the medical products, food, cosmetic, and media industries. He played a principal role in the FDA's generally successful assertion of preemption in selected product liability cases. He has published broadly and currently heads the American Bar Association's Section of Administrative Law and Regulatory Practice. He was an associate scholar at AEI from 1996 through 2000.

Thomas W. Hazlett is professor of law and economics at George Mason University, where he also serves as director of the Information Economy Project. Professor Hazlett, who has previously held faculty appointments at the University of California at Davis, Columbia University, and the Wharton School, writes extensively on economic and public policy issues in both academic journals and the popular press (including the *Financial Times*, where he is a columnist in the New Technology Policy Forum). Professor Hazlett's special expertise is in the government regulation of telecommunications markets and the information sector. His book, *Public Policy Toward Cable Television*, was co-authored with Matthew L. Spitzer (MIT Press, 1997). In 1991–92, he served as chief economist of the Federal Communications Commission.

Hal S. Scott is the Nomura Professor and director of the Program on International Financial Systems at Harvard Law School. His recent books include *International Finance: Transactions, Policy and Regulation* (Foundation Press, 2006) and *International Finance: Law and Regulation* (Sweet & Maxwell, 2004), and he edited *Capital Adequacy Beyond Basel: Banking, Securities, and Insurance* (Oxford University Press, 2005). He is also the director of the Committee on Capital Markets Regulation and an independent board member of Lazard, Ltd. He is past president of the International Academy of Consumer and Commercial Law and a former member of the board of governors of the American Stock Exchange.

Thomas W. Merrill is the Charles Keller Beekman Professor of Law at Columbia Law School. Formerly, he taught at Northwestern University School of Law from 1981 to 2003. From 1987 to 1990, Professor Merrill served as deputy solicitor general in the Department of Justice, where he represented the United States before the U.S. Supreme Court. He has published numerous articles in important journals. His teaching and research interests include administrative law, property, and environmental law.

Samuel Issacharoff recently joined the New York University faculty as the Reiss Professor of Constitutional Law. Over seventy of his articles have been published in every leading law review, as well as in leading journals in other fields. He is one of the pioneers in the law of the political process, for which his *Law of Democracy* casebook, co-authored with Stanford's Pam Karlan and NYU's Rick Pildes (Foundation Press, 2006), and dozens of articles have helped create a vibrant new area of constitutional law. He is also a leading figure in the field of procedure, both in the academy and outside. In addition to ongoing involvement in some of the front-burner cases in this area, he now serves as the reporter for the newly created Project on Aggregate Litigation of the American Law Institute.

Catherine M. Sharkey is professor of law at Columbia Law School. She teaches and writes scholarly articles in the areas of torts, products liability, punitive damages, class actions, remedies, and empirical legal studies. Professor Sharkey is an adviser to the American Law Institute's *Restatement Third of Torts: Liability for Economic Loss* and a senior editor of the peer-reviewed *Journal of Tort Law*. After graduating from Yale Law School, where she was executive editor of the *Yale Law Journal*, she served as law clerk to the Hon. Guido Calabresi of the U.S. Court of Appeals for the Second Circuit and to the Hon. David H. Souter of the U.S. Supreme Court.

Robert R. Gasaway is a partner at Kirkland & Ellis LLP in Washington, D.C. He focuses his practice on appellate litigation, with a specialty in representing clients in the preparation of integrated, multi-forum trial and appellate strategies in related sets of cases. In addition to high-profile commercial disputes, Mr. Gasaway has worked on high-stakes administrative, environmental, antitrust, criminal, and class-action litigation, as well as constitutional law and related issues arising in the context of federal bankruptcy proceedings. He is a recognized expert on legal reform and constitutional law issues, and is a frequent law review contributor and panelist at legal conferences.

Ashley C. Parrish is a partner at Kirkland & Ellis LLP in Washington, D.C. He focuses his practice on appellate litigation and on high-stakes administrative and class-action litigation. In addition to working on high-profile appellate matters, Mr. Parrish has substantial experience handling critical motions and strategic issues in federal and state trial courts. He also frequently advises clients on federal administrative law and practice.

Ernest A. Young holds the Charles Alan Wright Chair in Federal Courts at the University of Texas School of Law. Professor Young joined the University of Texas faculty in 1999 after practicing law with Cohan, Simpson, Cowlishaw & Wulff in Dallas and Covington & Burling in Washington, D.C. He served as a law clerk to the Honorable Michael Boudin of the U.S. Court of Appeals for the First Circuit and the Honorable David Souter of the U.S. Supreme Court. Professor Young has been a visiting professor at Harvard Law School, Dartmouth College, and the Villanova School of Law, and an adjunct professor at Georgetown University Law Center.

Anne van Aaken is the Max Schmidheiny Foundation Tenure-Track-Professor for Law and Economics, Public, International and European Law at the Law School of the University of St. Gallen, Switzerland. From 2003 to 2006 she was a senior research fellow at the Max Planck Institute for Comparative Public Law and International Law in Heidelberg as well as at the Max Planck Institute for Research on Collective Goods in Bonn, Germany. She has written and edited several books and more than twenty scholarly articles. Her research interests include public international law (especially international economic law), investment law, human rights, regulation of financial markets, theories of regulation, administrative law, and regulatory impact assessment.

Index

Research Staff

Gerard Alexander
Visiting Scholar

Joseph Antos
Wilson H. Taylor Scholar in Health
Care and Retirement Policy

Leon Aron
Resident Scholar

Claude Barfield
Resident Scholar

Roger Bate
Resident Fellow

Walter Berns
Resident Scholar

Douglas J. Besharov
Joseph J. and Violet Jacobs
Scholar in Social Welfare Studies

Edward Blum
Visiting Fellow

Dan Blumenthal
Resident Fellow

John R. Bolton
Senior Fellow

Karlyn Bowman
Senior Fellow

John E. Calfee
Resident Scholar

Charles W. Calomiris
Visiting Scholar

Lynne V. Cheney
Senior Fellow

Steven J. Davis
Visiting Scholar

Mauro De Lorenzo
Resident Fellow

Thomas Donnelly
Resident Fellow

Nicholas Eberstadt
Henry Wendt Scholar in Political
Economy

Mark Falcoff
Resident Scholar Emeritus

John C. Fortier
Research Fellow

Ted Frank
Resident Fellow; Director,
AEI Liability Project

David Frum
Resident Fellow

David Gelernter
National Fellow

Reuel Marc Gerecht
Resident Fellow

Newt Gingrich
Senior Fellow

James K. Glassman
Senior Fellow; Editor-in-Chief,
The American magazine

Jack L. Goldsmith
Visiting Scholar

Robert A. Goldwin
Resident Scholar Emeritus

Scott Gottlieb, M.D.
Resident Fellow

Kenneth P. Green
Resident Scholar

Michael S. Greve
John G. Searle Scholar

Christopher Griffin
Research Fellow

Robert W. Hahn
Resident Scholar; Executive
Director, AEI-Brookings Joint
Center for Regulatory Studies

Kevin A. Hassett
Senior Fellow; Director,
Economic Policy Studies

Steven F. Hayward
F. K. Weyerhaeuser Fellow

Robert B. Helms
Resident Scholar

Frederick M. Hess
Resident Scholar; Director,
Education Policy Studies

Ayaan Hirsi Ali
Resident Fellow

R. Glenn Hubbard
Visiting Scholar

Frederick W. Kagan
Resident Scholar

Leon R. Kass, M.D.
Hertog Fellow

Herbert G. Klein
National Fellow

Marvin H. Kosters
Resident Scholar Emeritus

Irving Kristol
Senior Fellow Emeritus

Desmond Lachman
Resident Fellow

Michael A. Ledeen
Freedom Scholar

Adam Lerrick
Visiting Scholar

Philip I. Levy
Resident Scholar

James R. Lilley
Senior Fellow

Lawrence B. Lindsey
Visiting Scholar

John H. Makin
Visiting Scholar

N. Gregory Mankiw
Visiting Scholar

Aparna Mathur
Research Fellow

Mark B. McClellan, M.D.
Visiting Senior Fellow, Health Policy
Studies and AEI-Brookings Joint
Center for Regulatory Studies

Allan H. Meltzer
Visiting Scholar

Thomas P. Miller
Resident Fellow

Joshua Muravchik
Resident Scholar

Charles Murray
W. H. Brady Scholar

Roger F. Noriega
Visiting Fellow

Michael Novak
George Frederick Jewett Scholar
in Religion, Philosophy, and
Public Policy

Norman J. Ornstein
Resident Scholar

Richard Perle
Resident Fellow

Alex J. Pollock
Resident Fellow

Sarath Rajapatirana
Visiting Fellow

Michael Rubin
Resident Scholar

Sally Satel, M.D.
Resident Scholar

Gary J. Schmitt
Resident Scholar; Director,
AEI's Program on Advanced
Strategic Studies

Joel Schwartz
Visiting Fellow

Daniel Shaviro
Visiting Scholar

Kent Smetters
Visiting Scholar

Christina Hoff Sommers
Resident Scholar

Samuel Thernstrom
Managing Editor, AEI Press;
Director, W. H. Brady Program

Bill Thomas
Visiting Fellow

Fred Thompson
Visiting Fellow

Richard Vedder
Visiting Scholar

Alan D. Viard
Resident Scholar

Peter J. Wallison
Senior Fellow

Ben J. Wattenberg
Senior Fellow

John Yoo
Visiting Scholar

www.ingramcontent.com/pod-product-compliance
Lightning Source LLC
Jackson TN
JSHW011931131224
75386JS00041B/1325